Trade with Japan

A National Bureau
of Economic Research
Project Report

Trade with Japan
Has the Door Opened Wider?

Edited by   Paul Krugman

The University of Chicago Press

Chicago and London

PAUL KRUGMAN is a professor of economics at the Massachusetts Institute of Technology and a research associate of the National Bureau of Economic Research.

The University of Chicago Press, Chicago 60637
The University of Chicago Press, Ltd., London
© 1991 by the National Bureau of Economic Research
All rights reserved. Published 1991
Printed in the United States of America
00 99 98 97 96 95 94 93 92 91   5 4 3 2 1

ISBN 0–226–45458–4

Library of Congress Cataloging-in-Publication Data

Trade with Japan : has the door opened wider? / edited by Paul Krugman.
        p.   cm. — (A National Bureau of Economic Research project
    report)
    Includes bibliographical references and index.
    1. Japan—Commercial policy.   2. Industry and state—Japan.
    3. United States—Commerce—Japan.   4. Japan—Commerce—
    United States.   I. Krugman, Paul R.   II. Series.
    HF1601.T734   1991
    382'.0952073—dc20   91-29616
                                                                 CIP

Relation of the Directors to the
Work and Publications of the
National Bureau of Economic Research

1. The object of the National Bureau of Economic Research is to ascertain and to present to the public important economic facts and their interpretation in a scientific and impartial manner. The Board of Directors is charged with the responsibility of ensuring that the work of the National Bureau is carried on in strict conformity with this object.

2. The President of the National Bureau shall submit to the Board of Directors, or to its Executive Committee, for their formal adoption all specific proposals for research to be instituted.

3. No research report shall be published by the National Bureau until the President has sent each member of the Board a notice that a manuscript is recommended for publication and that in the President's opinion it is suitable for publication in accordance with the principles of the National Bureau. Such notification will include an abstract or summary of the manuscript's content and a response form for use by those Directors who desire a copy of the manuscript for review. Each manuscript shall contain a summary drawing attention to the nature and treatment of the problem studied, the character of the data and their utilization in the report, and the main conclusions reached.

4. For each manuscript so submitted, a special committee of the Directors (including Directors Emeriti) shall be appointed by majority agreement of the President and Vice Presidents (or by the Executive Committee in case of inability to decide on the part of the President and Vice Presidents), consisting of three Directors selected as nearly as may be one from each general division of the Board. The names of the special manuscript committee shall be stated to each Director when notice of the proposed publication is submitted to him. It shall be the duty of each member of the special committee to read the manuscript. If each member of the manuscript committee signifies his approval within thirty days of the transmittal of the manuscript, the report may be published. If at the end of that period any member of the manuscript committee withholds his approval, the President shall then notify each member of the Board, requesting approval or disapproval of publication, and thirty days additional shall be granted for this purpose. The manuscript shall then not be published unless at least a majority of the entire Board who shall have voted on the proposal within the time fixed for the receipt of votes shall have approved.

5. No manuscript may be published, though approved by each member of the special manuscript committee, until forty-five days have elapsed from the transmittal of the report in manuscript form. The interval is allowed for the receipt of any memorandum of dissent or reservation, together with a brief statement of his reasons, that any member may wish to express; and such memorandum of dissent or reservation shall be published with the manuscript if he so desires. Publication does not, however, imply that each member of the Board has read the manuscript, or that either members of the Board in general/or the special committee have passed on its validity in every detail.

6. Publications of the National Bureau issued for informational purposes concerning the work of the Bureau and its staff, or issued to inform the public of activities of Bureau staff, and volumes issued as a result of various conferences involving the National Bureau shall contain a specific disclaimer noting that such publication has not passed through the normal review procedures required in this resolution. The Executive Committee of the Board is charged with review of all such publications from time to time to ensure that they do not take on the character of formal research reports of the National Bureau, requiring formal Board approval.

7. Unless otherwise determined by the Board or exempted by the terms of paragraph 6, a copy of this resolution shall be printed in each National Bureau publication.

(Resolution adopted October 25, 1926, as revised through September 30, 1974)

Contents

Acknowledgments

The papers and comments contained in this volume were presented at a National Bureau of Economic Research conference held in Cambridge, Massachusetts, on October 18–20, 1989. Financial support for the research was generously provided by The Ford Foundation. I would like to thank Kirsten Foss Davis, Ilana Hardesty, and Mark Fitz-Patrick of the NBER staff for their assistance with both the conference and publication.

Paul Krugman

Introduction

Paul Krugman

To someone who looked only at the aggregate numbers, it would be hard to explain the U.S. preoccupation with Japan. Only about one-fifth of U.S. imports come from Japan, and little more than one-tenth of our exports are sent there; Japanese firms account for only about 20 percent of the stock of foreign direct investment in the United States, and still employ only a relative handful of U.S. workers. Japan is an important trade and investment partner, but European trade and investment are more important to the United States by any measure and by most measures even Canada bulks larger. Yet for most Americans—not just the general public, but policymakers and academics as well—Japanese trade and investment are *the* central international economic issue.

No doubt much of the focus on Japan represents a mixture of fascination and envy. Fascination, because of Japan's remarkable rise from relative backwardness and crushing military defeat to an extraordinary position of financial and increasingly technological leadership. Envy, because this rise stands in sharp contrast to the gradual decline of U.S. preeminence, which has been accompanied by stagnation or even decline in the living standards of large numbers of American residents. To an important extent Japan stands out because it is a symbol of America's shortcomings, of the disappointing failure of our economy to deliver what we hoped it would.

But there is more to the "Japan issue" than American sourness over a second-place showing. There is also a widespread sense that as Japan has moved from the periphery to the center of the world economy, it has continued to play the game by somewhat different rules than other advanced nations. Rightly or wrongly, more and more opinion leaders in the United States have come to the view that Japan's economy simply functions differently from

Paul Krugman is a professor of economics at the Massachusetts Institute of Technology and a research associate of the National Bureau of Economic Research.

those of other industrial countries—and that as a result the traditional tools
and stance of U.S. international economic policy, which worked well enough
in a world in which Japan was a minor player, are now no longer good enough.
Only some of those who emphasize the Japanese challenge are "bashers," urging the United States to get tough; others are simply admirers, who want the
United States to emulate what they perceive to be the Japanese system.

The problem is that, while the debate over U.S.-Japanese trade and investment relations has generated a remarkable amount of heat, facts and serious
analysis are still in short supply. Preoccupied with the latest wave of Japanese
exports or investments, the debate has done little to resolve the basic questions: In what way does the Japanese economic system differ from those of
other industrial countries? What are the effects of these differences? Do they
pose problems for amicable economic relations? What can be done to resolve ·
the tensions?

In the fall of 1989 a group of Japanese and U.S. participants held a conference at the National Bureau of Economic Research in Cambridge, Massachusetts, to discuss a number of the key issues in the economic relationship between the United States and Japan. This volume is the result. In introducing
the volume, I want to begin with some background to the debate, then review
the main issues that arose in the conference.

Defining the Japan Issue

To Japanese government officials and to a considerable number of economists and other observers, the U.S. preoccupation with Japanese differences
seems unwarranted. In terms of the conventional measures of international
economic policy, Japan is not too exceptional. Agriculture is highly protected,
by most measures more so than in any other industrial country; but because
Japan remains an agricultural importer, its food protectionism creates less
strain on the trading system than the massive export subsidies of Europe's
Common Agricultural Policy. Meanwhile, Japan's tariff rates on manufactured
goods, like those of other advanced countries, are quite low. And Japan has
hardly any of the voluntary export restraint agreements that limit shipment of
many manufactured goods into both the United States and Europe. Looking
only at the de jure structure of trade policy, one would not be surprised to find
Japanese officials claiming, as they often do, that Japan has freer trade than
the United States.

Few people in the U.S. policy community, however, accept this benign interpretation. A few still hold to the view of a monolithic "Japan, Inc." More
common, however, is a conventional wisdom that runs something like this:
despite its relative absence of legal barriers to trade, the Japanese market is de
facto protected because it is not competitive in the same way as those of other
countries. Collusive behavior involving both firms and a highly cartelized distribution sector effectively shut out many foreign products, even when the

imports would be cheaper and/or of higher quality than the Japanese version. Foreign direct investment is similarly choked off by an inability to get local business cooperation, and the inability to establish local subsidiaries inhibits exports to Japan. And this more or less conspiratorial system tends particularly to close ranks when a key new technology is at stake, assuring Japanese firms of a chance to capture new markets even when foreign firms have an initial lead.

What is the basis for this conventional wisdom about Japan? Much of the public case rests on anecdotal evidence—on the stories of businessmen who claim that they could not sell demonstrably superior goods in Japan. Influential commentators on Japanese society, like Karel van Wolferen, have reinforced the anecdotes by offering a portrait of a society very much unlike the freewheeling individualism of the United States or even Western Europe. To economists, however, this is not enough. Anecdotes are useful, but not conclusive—especially when the tellers of the anecdotes are by no means disinterested. Sociology is important, but economists tend to be skeptical of suggestions that social factors lead to a systematic disregard for profit opportunities. In other words, to be persuaded by the conventional wisdom economists would need to be convinced, first, that the anecdotes are borne out by harder, preferably quantitative, evidence and, second, that the supposed preference of Japanese buyers for more expensive domestic products makes some kind of economic sense.

For much of the 1980s, economic controversy over Japanese performance concentrated on a rather crude question: Does Japan import abnormally few manufactures? In terms of raw numbers, Japan looks clearly different from other advanced countries, with 1988 imports of manufactures of only about 2 percent of GNP, versus 7 percent for the United States and 14 percent for the average European Community (EC) nation. On the face of it this comparison seems to confirm the anecdotal evidence of a closed domestic market. But as many economists—perhaps most notably Bergsten and Cline—have pointed out, this raw comparison is unfair.[1] The United States is a resource-rich nation, able to pay for its oil imports by exporting agricultural products; Japan must pay for its raw materials by running a trade surplus in manufactures, presumably in part by importing less. European countries do more than half their manufactures trade with each other; Japan has no neighboring advanced nations.

A number of economists have tried to ask whether, taking these factors into account, Japan still looks like an outlier. The models used to answer this question are themselves the subject of dispute; Srinivasan and Hamada have argued that the whole process of testing for abnormalities in trade is flawed.[2]

1. C. F. Bergsten and W. Cline, *The United States-Japan Economic Problem* (Washington, D.C.: Institute for International Economics, 1987).

2. T. Srinivasan and K. Hamada, "The U.S.-Japan Trade Problem" (Yale University, 1990, mimeographed).

Nonetheless, it seems fair to argue that, in the general debate, the view that Japan does import less than one might have expected wins on points. Particularly influential was a paper by Lawrence that suggested that, after taking resources and location into account, Japan still imports only a little more than half as much manufactures as one would otherwise expect.[3]

Another piece of loose supportive evidence for the conventional view of Japan as a closed economy comes from looking at foreign direct investment. In the United States, foreign-owned firms now produce about 4 percent of GNP and more than 10 percent of manufacturing value added; in European nations the percentages are substantially higher, while in Japan the role of foreign production is negligible.

On the whole, then, the conventional wisdom survives crude empirical testing more or less intact. But this only raises further questions. *Why* does an economy that is de jure open appear to remain relatively closed? Is there an economic rationale for Japanese behavior? Or, alternatively, will Japan in future begin to look more like other industrial nations?

Japanese Trade Patterns

Three of the papers presented at the conference and included in this volume represent, in effect, a continuation of the debate over the openness of the Japanese economy.

Robert Z. Lawrence offers some new kinds of evidence on the ways in which Japan's economy interacts with the rest of the world. Instead of fiddling further with data on the volume of imports, he brings several other kinds of data to bear. One is price data: he shows that prices of many manufactured goods within the Japanese market are much higher than they are abroad, seemingly confirming the supposition that the Japanese market is de facto protected in spite of the absence of conventional barriers. A second piece of evidence is the role of intrafirm trade. Lawrence points out that if the mechanism that blocks imports relies essentially on collusion among firms, then products of Japanese subsidiaries abroad should find it easier to enter the Japanese market—and he finds that indeed Japanese imports are marked by an unusually high volume of intrafirm trade.

Lawrence also draws attention to a new development: the surge of manufactures imports into Japan since the rise of the yen in 1985–87. That surge, starting from such a low base, still leaves import penetration in Japan well below U.S. or European levels. But it shows that access to the Japanese market is not completely insensitive to incentives—that the implicit barriers to imports are more like tariffs than quotas.

Peter A. Petri focuses more specifically on the developments in Japanese

3. R. Lawrence, "Imports in Japan: Closed Markets or Minds?" *Brookings Papers on Economic Activity,* no. 2 (1987).

trade since the onset of the strong yen. He finds that import growth in manufactures has proceeded more rapidly than estimates from the pre-1985 period
would have predicted. To some extent the unexpected surge in imports has
been concentrated in imports from East Asian NICs, but Petri finds that this
trend is too modest to justify talk of an emerging yen bloc.

Petri follows a different approach from Lawrence in trying to understand
the sources of traditional low imports into Japan; that is, he asks whether
cross-sectional variation in import penetration corresponds to industrial organization in the way that the conventional wisdom predicts. Broadly speaking,
he finds that it does. While the principal determinant of Japanese trade patterns in manufactured goods seems to be technology intensity, imports do tend
to be lower when collusive insider relationships are most plausible, that is,
when the government is the customer, when goods are sold to other businesses, or when high distribution margins suggest a noncompetitive distribution sector.

Yung Chul Park and Won-Am Park pursue further the recent increase in
Japanese imports of manufactured goods from East Asian nations. Like Petri,
they find clear evidence of a structural shift toward more Japanese imports
from Western Pacific developing countries. As Lawrence's analysis would
have suggested, however, they find that Japanese foreign direct investment
plays a key role in this shift: NIC and NIE exports seem to get into Japan
largely because they originate in Japanese-controlled firms. Park and Park
also find that the changes in East Asian trade patterns remain far too limited
to envision the emergence of a yen trading bloc anytime soon.

Market Structure and Trade

The next three papers focus on the question of market structure in Japan,
and how it may affect international trade.

Richard C. Marston uses data on pricing behavior of firms as a clue to the
functioning of markets. He shows that Japanese firms engage in strong "pricing to market": cutting the yen prices of exports, but not of the same goods
delivered to domestic markets, when the yen rises. This pricing to market
reveals two important facts about Japanese manufacturing firms. First, the
firms behave strategically, not at all like the atomistic competitors assumed in
much of the empirical testing of hypotheses about trade. Second, the firms
evidently are able to segment markets, charging very different prices at home
and abroad.

Marston also shows that structural change has proceeded at a rapid rate
within the Japanese manufacturing sector, with sharp trends in relative prices
associated with differential rates of productivity growth. This observation
helps explain why there appears to be a secular upward trend in the equilibrium real yen—a theme that comes back later in Jeffrey Frankel's paper.

Japan's distribution system has attracted much foreign attention. With its proliferation of small stores and many layers of wholesaling, the system appears inefficient to outsiders; it is also accused of fostering vertical relationships that effectively close the Japanese market to foreigners. Two of the papers presented here, by Takatoshi Ito and Masayoshi Maruyama and by Motoshige Itoh, examine this distribution system.

Ito and Maruyama focus on the question of efficiency. Somewhat surprisingly, they do not find much evidence of striking inefficiency: although there are many shops and many layers, the overall level of employment per unit of final sales is not out of line with other industrial countries. Nor is the retailing and distribution markup exceptionally high. In essence, Ito and Maruyama suggest that Japan's distribution system uses a different ownership structure to do pretty much the same things that are done elsewhere.

Itoh focuses instead on the question of market structure. He documents the substantial extent to which Japanese distribution does in fact engage in practices that appear noncompetitive to U.S. eyes. But he points out that many of these practices can be rationalized as responses to problems of imperfect information, especially in the context of a legal system that makes formal contracts less feasible, and long-term relationships correspondingly more important, than in the United States.

Financial Markets

In the last few years, Japan has emerged as a spectacular financial powerhouse: the world's largest investor, with a stock market that rivals or surpasses America's in value, and—very lately—a scene of wild fluctuation in asset values that belie any image of a tightly controlled society where everything is under central direction.

Two of the papers in the conference, by David M. Meerschwam and Jeffrey A. Frankel, focus on Japanese financial markets: Meerschwam on institutional structure and Frankel on prices.

Meerschwam highlights the special role, via the *keiretsu*, of Japan's banks in industrial structure. He points out that there is an important distinction between the forces that gave rise to the special role of large banks and the function that these banks play. It was to an important extent the controlled economy of early postwar Japan that pushed banks into a key role: controlled interest rates meant that access to credit became crucial to business success, leading to the predominance of industry groups clustered around banks. Yet this institutional arrangement turned out to have other benefits: because banks were uniquely situated to monitor their firms and resolve problems of information, Japanese industry was allowed to adopt a long-run view rather than to appease stockholders by focusing on the bottom line.

Meerschwam points out, however, that the traditional structure of Japanese financial markets is under strain and may indeed be on its way out. Deregulation and the opening of Japan's financial system to the outside world have undermined the automatic special role of banks, and a more Anglo-Saxon style system may be emerging. Interestingly, Meerschwam suggests that this increase in competition may not be a desirable thing, that even though firms may voluntarily move away from the old style of finance they may collectively lose as a result.

Frankel addresses instead the question of asset prices. In particular, why did Japanese land and stock prices move to such high levels in the 1980s?

Frankel first argues that the high ratio of prices to earnings in Japan can be explained to a significant degree, though not entirely, by two factors: low real interest rates and high growth prospects. He makes the important point that real interest rates internationally are not necessarily equalized by arbitrage: if a country is expected to show persistent real appreciation, then it will have a low real interest rate even in an integrated world capital market. Since this appears to be true of Japan, for reasons touched upon by Marston's paper, high asset prices should be expected.

If this is true, however, why did the boom come in the 1980s and not before? Here Frankel appeals to the institutional changes that Meerschwam identified. Under the traditional financial system, savings were channeled into business investment and were not available to bid up prices of financial assets. With the erosion of that system, the underlying reasons for high asset prices have been able to assert themselves.

Industrial and Trade Policy

The final two papers of this volume, by Masahiro Okuno-Fujiwara and Amelia Porges, treat the role of government in Japan's trade relations.

Okuno-Fujiwara traces the history of Japan's industrial policy. Echoing the discussion of financial markets, he points to the gradual evolution of that policy away from dirigisme. At one time, control over the allocation of rationed credit and foreign exchange gave the idea of "Japan, Inc." some reality. Since the early 1970s, however, the role of government guidance has shifted to something more modest and subtle. In part, government acts in ways perfectly acceptable to a neoclassical economist, attempting through such activities as technology promotion to overcome problems of external economies with their resulting divergence between private and social returns. He also emphasizes the role of government policy in helping the private sector form consistent expectations—in effect, arguing that the Japanese government is now engaged to an important extent in noncoercive indicative planning.

In the final paper of the conference, Porges takes us from the world of analytics to that of actual trade policy, with a blow-by-blow account of the trade negotiations between the United States and Japan. Her paper reminds us of the difficulty of converting academic assessments into operational demands and of the importance of interest group politics in both countries. For an American her paper is, in particular, a useful reminder that Japan is not only a major economic power but also a real country, with real politics, no more able to deliver sweeping change on demand than we are ourselves.

Lessons of the Conference

This conference was not intended to deliver immediate policy advice. Instead, it aimed to provide new evidence on the truth about Japan and its economic relationship with the United States. What did we learn? I would stress three main themes.

First, Japan *is* different. That part of the conventional wisdom that emphasizes sharp institutional differences between Japanese and U.S. markets is clearly borne out by many of the papers, in everything from the pricing behavior of exporters to the financial role of banks.

Second, in some ways Japanese difference does contribute to trade tension (which is not the same thing as saying that it is in any sense "unfair"). Japan does appear to be marked by a style of relationships between firms that makes it difficult for outsiders, including foreigners, to break in.

Third, this Japanese difference in many cases appears to make sense—that is, there are real efficiency advantages to the Japanese style of business, arising from the virtues of long-term relationships in a world of incomplete information. Even where it is commonly supposed that Japan is very inefficient, this conference showed some surprising performance. We must therefore be cautious about lecturing Japan about noncompetitive practices: they may know what they are doing.

Fourth, Japan itself is changing. Imports of manufactured goods are increasing; financial markets are becoming less distinctive. We should beware of applying stereotypes from a decade ago to the very different Japan that is now emerging.

1   How Open is Japan?

Robert Z. Lawrence

Few issues in international economics are more contentious than the allegedly closed nature of the Japanese market. In the early 1980s, the issue so vexed the European Community that it sought redress through the General Agreement on Terms of Trade (GATT). Similarly, over the years the United States has conducted an extensive set of bilateral negotiations to open the Japanese market for its firms and products ranging from beef to baseball bats.

Generally, the U.S. focus has been on ensuring equal treatment for foreign firms and products through changes in rules and procedures. In 1985, for example, negotiations focused on Market-Opening, Sector-Specific (MOSS) talks in four sectors—telecommunications, electronics, forest products, and medical equipment and pharmaceuticals. In medical equipment, for example, the major issues were related to improvements in administrative procedures for granting new product approvals and manufacturing licenses and for setting reimbursement prices under Japan's national health insurance program (see U.S. International Trade Commission 1986). Currently the United States is delving even deeper into the structure of the Japanese economy in the so-called Structural Impediments Initiative.

Official U.S. policy has generally sought to avoid setting quantitative import targets for Japan.[1] It continues to try to change the rules of the game so that foreigners can compete equally in Japan. But increasingly, there are calls for the United States to shift its demands from equal opportunity to affirmative action. Some argue that Japan will never play by Western rules. Indeed, given the outstanding performance of the Japanese economy, the outside world has

Robert Z. Lawrence is the Albert L. Williams Professor of International Trade and Investment at the John F. Kennedy School of Government, Harvard University.

1. The sideletter to the 1986 U.S.-Japan semiconductor agreement was a noteworthy exception. It called for semiconductors produced by foreign-owned firms to increase their Japanese market share to 20 percent by 1991.

no right to demand that Japan change the practices that have served it so well. Instead of trying to change Japan, the outside world should simply negotiate quantitative import targets and allow the Japanese government, which best understands its economic system, to ensure these are attained. The new slogan is therefore "results rather than rules."

In a recent paper, for example, Rudiger Dornbusch (1990) advocated setting quotas for aggregate Japanese imports of manufactured goods from the United States. Dornbusch believes the United States should demand that U.S. manufactured goods exports to Japan maintain an annual growth rate of 10 percent for the next decade. Absent such a response, Dornbusch advocates the imposition of a tariff on Japanese exports to the United States. Others advocate a more detailed sectoral approach to setting import levels. A report issued by the Advisory Committee for Trade Policy and Negotiations (ACTPN), a private-sector advisory group to U.S. Trade Representative Carla Hills, has suggested that the United States should require that the Japanese set quantitative import targets for specific commodities.

These new proposals are being advanced because it is felt that past U.S. policies simply have not worked. The Japanese economy is closed to foreign products and firms and fails to respond to market incentives as do other countries. Advocates of a results-oriented approach to Japanese trade generally agree that a managed trade system is not ideal. They also generally agree that the United States in particular is not well equipped to deal with a system that requires the detailed management of the international economy. But they suggest it is an appropriate second-best approach given the lack of effective alternatives.

But before policy shifts to such an approach, several questions need to be answered. What precisely is an "open" market? Are managed-trade policy approaches likely to achieve it? Is the Japanese market closed? Is it closed and unresponsive to price changes and negotiations over rules? In this paper I will try to answer these questions.

One important distinction is between markets that are open to products and markets that are open to firms. In a world in which multinational corporations dominate trade, it is clearly inappropriate to think only of national production by national firms. Particularly when embarking on a policy that manages *results*, it is important to be clear on precisely what kinds of results are being sought.

Many of the intangible barriers in the Japanese market may inhibit the sale of *products made by foreign firms*, but they need not preclude the sale of products manufactured by foreign subsidiaries of domestic firms. Ford and General Motors may not know how to make and sell an automobile that Japanese consumers will buy, but Toyota and Honda surely do. Japanese firms already have an established reputation with their Japanese customers. They understand how to deal with unusual aspects of Japanese institutions and customs.

Policy initiatives that stress achieving a Japanese market that allows a given quantity of imports equate openness with increased imports. But higher Japanese import volumes need not entail increased participation by foreign firms in the Japanese economy. Dornbusch, for example, emphasizes that what is important, from a U.S. perspective, is "good jobs and good wages" (1990, p. 125). He argues that it is irrelevant whether the employer producing the exports for the Japanese market is American or Japanese.

But, from some perspectives, it is surely not irrelevant. An increased demand by Japan for imports raises the demand for foreign labor. However, if the bulk of the imports are brought in by Japanese firms, the official and private practices that limit the degree to which newcomers can contest the Japanese market could continue. While the Japanese market might have more imported products, these could still be priced to maximize the profits of Japanese firms with monopoly power. Japanese consumers would not necessarily enjoy the full benefits of access to cheaper imported products.

While a results-oriented approach might raise the volume of Japanese trade, it could actually lead to a market with *more* rather than less government and corporate control. In fact, such an approach gives up on the idea that the Japanese economy will ever be genuinely open. It settles for making sure that at least Japan buys a certain amount of imports as a quid pro quo for its exports. By insisting Japan implement such a system, the United States would severely limit Japan's ability to become a genuinely liberal economy. Sector-by-sector targets can only be enforced if the MITI (Ministry of Trade and Industry) is powerful enough to guide Japanese firm behavior in great detail. The MITI would be forced to organize and monitor numerous buying cartels. Firms would be forced to collude on how imported products are to be handled. Instead of encouraging Japan in the liberal direction urged in its own official Maekawa report, the policies would be driving it back toward precisely the system the world finds so difficult in the first place.[2] Japanese firms would enhance their profits by buying cheaper foreign inputs and producing some products abroad, but they could continue to exercise their power over domestic pricing and marketing practices.

Between 1985 and the first quarter of 1989, according to the Japanese Economic Planning Agency (Government of Japan 1989), the volume of manufactured goods imports by Japan has doubled. In the light of this discussion, it might be important to examine the corporate identity of these imports: Is Japan being opened by Japanese or foreign-owned firms? That is a question I will try to answer below.

On the other hand, barriers at the border against products made in other

2. The discussion presumes such a policy could actually be achieved. But in many sectors, given the nature of the barriers, it would be virtually impossible for the Japanese government in good faith to enforce such an agreement. In consumer goods or goods sold in markets with many firms the proposal is impractical. You can put goods on the shelves but you cannot make people buy them.

countries do not necessarily hinder products made by foreign firms in Japan. It is sometimes assumed that there is a positive relationship between imports and the establishment of foreign firms in Japan. But of course, there is no *necessary* linkage. If foreign-owned firms gain entry in Japan, particularly if import barriers remain, they may decide to produce *more* locally. Thus imports may actually decline rather than increase. A more "open" Japanese market for foreign firms need not lower the Japanese trade surplus or provide the benefits for foreign workers, foreign terms of trade, and spillovers in foreign economies that many seem to expect.

While increased access of foreign firms may bring some benefits to Japanese consumers, these could be limited given the structure of the market. Recently, the Japanese Fair Trade Commission (FTC) contended that a joint venture of Apple (USA) and Canon unfairly maintains higher prices of Apple computers in the Japanese market by various restrictive trade practices. As this example reminds us, once established in Japan, foreign firms may find it in their interest to bolster rather than remove entry barriers.

The U.S.-Japan Semiconductor Trade Agreement is an example of a results-oriented trade policy in which the results that have been negotiated for and the results claimed by advocates of the approach do not necessarily correspond. Laura Tyson (1990), an advocate of managed trade in high-tech industries defends this agreement. She argues that without such managed trade agreements the structure of the U.S. economy will deteriorate.

She argues that in some industries knowledge does not flow easily across national borders. Such knowledge accumulates in firms in the form of skilled workers, proprietary technology, and difficult-to-copy know-how (Tyson 1990, p. 160). "The goal of intervention, therefore, is not simply to improve the trade balance or to address external barriers abroad, but *to secure a share of world production and employment* in such industries with the local knowledge, skills and spillover benefits which they generate" (Tyson 1990, pp. 167–68). That may be the goal of some advocates of managed trade. But it is striking that the sideletter to the Semiconductor Trade Agreement (STA) negotiated between the United States and Japan called for the products of *foreign-owned* companies to achieve 20 percent of the domestic sales by 1991. The semiconductors Texas Instruments produces in Japan or Korea, with Japanese or Korean labor and spillovers, qualify for this quota, but the semiconductors NEC or Fujitsu produce in the United States with U.S. labor and spillovers do not. As it has been implemented, this initiative is certainly not framed in terms of its direct impact on the U.S. structure of production.

A second major recent U.S. initiative also emphasizes corporate participation rather than the U.S. trade deficit or production structure. Robert Reich (1989) has noted that the major U.S. initiative to open the Tokyo market for cellular telephone sales by Motorola will increase the sales of telephones designed and manufactured in Malaysia. Of course, policies may legitimately reflect a variety of objectives. But, particularly when results are being managed, clearly the devil lies in the details. Unless there is a clear rationale for the policy, the specifics could make the results disappointing. For some purposes, for example, enhancing the welfare of U.S. workers, it may suffice to emphasize greater import volumes; for other purposes, for example, enhancing the profits of U.S. firms, it may suffice to seek increased participation by U.S. firms in Japan. But these approaches should not be confused with policies that aim at maximizing global welfare by achieving a market that is open in the most fundamental sense, that is, a market that can be readily contested by new firms, both foreign and domestic, who choose to supply products made at home and abroad.

Finally, it should be stressed that although they are often justified in terms of their impact on the aggregate trade balance, there is no necessary relationship between the size of a nation's trade balance and the openness of its markets. West Germany, for example, has one of the world's most open markets, but it often has a trade surplus that is a higher share of its GNP than Japan's. In general, a nation's trade balance in goods and services is a macroeconomic relationship that reflects in aggregate saving and investment behavior. While there are some channels by which changes in trade barriers may alter saving and investment behavior, the linkages are subtle and unlikely to be robust. After surveying some of these arguments, Richard Clarida has recently concluded "the macroeconomic implications of opening foreign markets with Super 301 are likely to be negligible" (1989, p. 28).

In the rest of this paper, I turn to the evidence. In particular I will examine several facets of the question, "How open is Japan?" Given the importance of the distinctions made in this introductory section, I will, in the first section of this paper, examine the corporate role in Japanese trade using primarily 1986 data. I will present evidence of the unusually strong role played by the intra-firm shipments of Japanese companies in Japanese trade. Japanese trade is distinctive because foreign exports to Japan have, until recently, generally been shipped by the foreign affiliates of Japanese firms. I will argue that this behavior results from unusual market imperfections in Japan that have induced Japanese firms to move *upstream* through international backward vertical integration. I will also argue that these same imperfections led to the unusually low share of intraindustry Japanese trade or, more precisely, to the low share of imports and exports of different varieties of similar products.

In the second section of this paper I consider price behavior in Japan. Several empirical studies have tried to answer the question, "Does Japan import too little?" To explore the issue they have been forced to overcome complex methodological obstacles that make it difficult to provide conclusive answers. Some studies have concluded Japanese import levels can be explained by the fundamental attributes of the Japanese economy. Other studies have concluded they cannot. But it has been difficult to pin down precisely the role played by import barriers. I will argue, however, that too little attention has been focused on the more important evidence of barriers: the large and persistent price differences between Japan and other industrial economies. I will show that these differences persist at the manufacturing level when distribution margins are removed. There is also strong evidence that imported products in Japan are subject to unusually high markups. It appears, therefore, that potential arbitrage opportunities between Japan and the rest of the world are not fully exploited.

The third section examines the adjustment of imports in Japan to the strong yen. It suggests that many of barriers to the Japanese market operate like tariffs rather than quotas. They keep imported products expensive in Japan, but they do not prevent marginal responses to price and cost incentives. I will show that, at the margin, manufactured import flows into Japan are quite normal in their responses to changes in relative costs. The result has been a dramatic increase in the volume of manufactured goods imports into Japan between 1985 and 1989—an increase that actually exceeds what might have been expected on the basis of historical relationships between import volumes, domestic activity, and the real exchange rate. While only preliminary data are available, it appears that intrafirm shipments by Japanese firms continue to account for a substantial imports share. Nonetheless the data also show that the share is declining and the intrafirm shipments of U.S. firms is rising. There is also some evidence that the sectoral approach to opening the Japanese market has worked. In the light of this evidence the Japanese market does appear closed, but there is also considerable evidence it is responding to price changes and sectoral negotiations.

1.1 Intrafirm Trade Patterns

Much of the theory of international trade ignores the role of corporations in the conduct of trade. Trade is presumed to take place in arms-length transactions between buyers located in the importing country and sellers located in the exporting country. Yet, a remarkably high proportion of international trade occurs through intrafirm shipments. This institutional reality underscores the complementarity that frequently exists between foreign trade and direct foreign investment. There appear to be major benefits from international vertical integration.

If the markets for goods or factors were perfect, there would be no multinational companies (MNCs). Market transactions would dominate intrafirm transactions. But where imperfections do exist, they can be internalized when a firm engages in direct foreign investment (see Rugman 1980). As Hymer (1976) first pointed out, when the firm has a specific advantage developed in response to a market imperfection, it will benefit from exploiting its advantage in other national markets. These advantages include acquiring factor inputs at a lower cost than its rivals; better distribution and marketing facilities; and monopoly advantage in information, research, knowledge, or some other aspect of the production process.

These explanations for direct foreign investment suggest that, if market imperfections differ across countries, the degree and nature of international investment could differ as well. Indeed the patterns of international investment could provide clues about differences in market imperfections.

Japan has an unusually small amount of intra-industry trade. Lawrence (1987) estimated, for example, that in 1980 an index of intra-industry trade for Japanese manufactured goods trade measured 30 compared with an average of 70 in other major industrial countries. But what is perhaps less well appreciated about Japanese trade, however, is the large amount of intrafirm trade. Using Department of Commerce Surveys on the trade flows associated with U.S. MNCs and those with the foreign affiliates located in the United States, we can put together the following picture: as reported in table 1.1, in 1986 intrafirm trade accounted for 48.5 percent of U.S. exports to Europe and 42.0 percent of U.S. imports from Europe. But intrafirm shipments accounted for 75.0 percent of U.S. imports from Japan and 72 percent of U.S. exports to Japan.

A striking feature of these numbers is the unusual degree to which *Japanese* MNCs dominate Japanese imports. In U.S. and European exports to each other, the *exporting* country firms dominate the intrafirm sales. In 1986, intrafirm shipments of U.S. exporters accounted for 36.9 percent of U.S. exports to Europe, while intrafirm shipments by European exporters account for 29.8 percent of EC exports to the United States. Similarly, Japanese exports to the United States were dominated by the intrafirm shipments of Japanese exporting firms—their share was 66.1 percent of all U.S. imports from Japan. This suggests typically the international vertical integration process moves *downstream* internationally from producers to their markets. Usually firms that develop a differentiated product in their home market discover they can exploit that advantage by selling it abroad.

The literature suggests several reasons why firms find it preferable to exploit their advantage by an internal rather than an arms-length transaction. Explanations for international integration include preserving firm-specific knowledge in the face of appropriability problems or preserving oligopoly power. Explanations for downstream vertical integration more generally include the advantages conferred in (i) providing information and knowledge to the seller about complex products; (ii) obtaining feedback from customers; (iii) overcoming the risks associated with investment by retailers and wholesalers in highly specific assets; and (iv) internalizing the externalities associated from quality debasement. (Independent distributors may not take account of the full adverse impacts of improper installation and service on reputation).

But the structure of Japanese *imports* is unusual because movements have typically been *upstream*. Intrafirm shipments from Japanese subsidiaries abroad to their parent companies dominate Japanese imports. In 1986, Japanese affiliates in the United States shipped 58.4 percent of all U.S. exports to

Table 1.1   Intrafirm Trade in 1986 (%)

	Europe				Japan			
	Total	Foreign Affiliates to/from Foreign Parent	U.S. Affiliates to/from U.S. Parent	Of Which Majority-owned Affiliate	Total	Foreign Affiliates to/from Foreign Parent	U.S. Affiliates to/from U.S. Parent	Of Which Majority-owned Affiliate
U.S. exports	48.5	11.6	36.9	32.8	72.0	58.4	13.6	9.7
U.S. imports	42.0	29.8	12.2	10.5	75.0	66.1	8.9	1.8

Source: Survey of Current Business (U.S. Department of Commerce 1989).

Japan back to their Japanese parents. By contrast, U.S. affiliates in Japan imported from their parent companies only 13.6 percent of all Japanese imports from the United States (see table 1.1).

One potential explanation for this unusual corporate involvement could be an unusual commodity composition of Japanese imports. The United States could export commodities in which direct shipments by U.S. firms *typically* play a relatively small role. But this does not explain the small direct U.S. company role. In their 1986 sales to other countries, U.S. companies shipped directly to their affiliates 27.6 percent of the manufactured goods exports that have the same mix as those imported by Japan from the United States. By contrast, they shipped only 9.4 percent of U.S. manufactured exports to Japan. As reported in table 1.2, intrafirm shipments by U.S. companies in their trade with Japan are an unusually small share of U.S. exports to Japan in every major export category. Similarly, the kinds of imports Japan buys from the United States are not typically imported by parent firms in the importing country.

Firms with established positions in the Japanese market find it profitable to invest in production or purchasing entities abroad. Apparently the structure of the Japanese economy provides unusually strong incentives for upstream movement and results in Japan's international trade being conducted by *Japanese* distributors.

These patterns of corporate involvement are actually complementary to the observation that Japan has an unusually small degree of intra-industry trade. Krugman and others have explained *intra-industry* trade as resulting from preferences for variety and economies of scale in production. Krugman (1983) has also shown that, where the fixed cost that yields scale economies is not in production research but in research and development (R&D), firms may prefer to carry out some of the production abroad. When intrafirm shipments of imports are dominated by foreign firms, as they generally are, they are likely to reflect the importation of new product varieties. But intrafirm imports by *do-*

Table 1.2   **Percentage of Total U.S. Exports Shipped by U.S. Multinationals to Their Foreign Affiliates, by Commodity, in 1986**

	EC (12)	Japan	World
Total	34.1	13.6	32.8
Petroleum	38.3	4.6	52.2
Total, Manufactures	25.4	9.4	28.4
Food and kindred	13.7	0.2	6.3
Chemicals excluding electric	36.3	13.9	25.0
Machinery	22.4	19.0	14.4
Electric machinery	40.6	24.9	52.3
Transportation	10.0	4.0	69.3
Other	45.3	12.2	30.6

Source: U.S. Department of Commerce (1989).

mestic firms are more likely to reflect domestic market imperfections. They are likely to involve shipments of inputs that are cheaper abroad or imports of varieties produced by the domestic firm that can be manufactured more cheaply abroad. Domestic firms are less likely to import directly products that compete directly with those they (or their associates) manufacture at home. Intrafirm shipments by domestic firms are thus less likely to result in the importation of *new varieties* produced abroad.

1.1.1 Trading Companies

The majority of intrafirm import shipments in Japan appear to be undertaken by general trading companies. As indicated in table 1.3, the Japanese affiliates reporting extensive shipments of U.S. exports to Japan are concentrated in, but not confined to, wholesale trade—particularly in farm products and metals and minerals. While trading companies are not unknown elsewhere, in no other country have they grown to the extent and size that they have in Japan. It is difficult to obtain data on some of the large foreign companies that are not publicly held, but according to Young (1979), for example, in 1976 only three of the 12 large multiproduct trading companies that existed in other countries had sales above $1 billion, whereas each of Japan's big 10

Table 1.3   U.S. Exports to All Countries Shipped by Japanese Affiliates in 1986 and 1987

	1986		1987	
	Exports in Millions of $U.S.	% of Total Exports	Exports in Millions of $U.S.	% of Total Exports
All industries	22,693		20,838	
Manufacturing	906	4.0	1,048	5.0
Primary & fabricated metal	15	0.1	29	0.1
Machinery	276	1.2	307	1.5
Excluding electric	188	0.8	243	1.2
Electric	88	0.4	64	0.3
Other manufacturing	292	1.3	356	1.7
Wholesale trade	21,629	95.3	19,673	94.4
Motor vehicles	. . .	. . .	. . .	. . .
Metals & minerals	9,697	42.7	10,922	52.4
Other durables	828	3.6	. . .	. . .
Farm product raw materials	7872	34.7	4,066	19.5
Electrical goods	N.A.	N.A.	483	2.3
Machinery & equipment	N.A.	N.A.	368	1.8
Groceries	N.A.	N.A.	623	3.0

Source: U.S. Department of Commerce (1989).

had sales between $5 billion and $33 billion. Total annual sales of the largest non-Japanese trading company (Kooperativa Foroundel of Sweden) were $2.95 billion—which made it as large as the seventh largest Japanese company.

It is an error to view the trading companies only as purveyors of raw materials imports. They play a major role both as exporters and importers of a wide variety of manufactured goods. They have acted as agents for imports of nuclear plants from Westinghouse and General Electric and aircraft from Boeing and Lockheed. In its business profile, the Nissho Iwai Trading Company notes, for example, that it serves as "the exclusive agent for the Boeing Aircraft Company for sales to airlines, McDonnell Douglas for military aircraft to Japan's self defense forces and DeHaviland for commuter aircraft" (Nissho Iwai Business Profile).

It is also an error to view these companies simply as brokers or traders. They provide their customers with an extensive set of services, including information and intelligence, medium-term finance, shipping, warehousing, and distribution. Their international and domestic equity relationships extend backward into mining, agriculture, and manufacturing and forward to retailers and shopping centers. The trading companies are firmly rooted in the domestic distribution system, and they have complemented this position with extensive import distribution systems. These include huge complexes—*kombinatos*—for the unloading, warehousing, and distribution of imported products such as food, chemicals, and steel products (for a description, see Kojïma and Ozawa 1984). These centers allow the efficient allocation of imports to downstream affiliates and independent customers.

From a transactions cost perspective, these companies' role in imports derives from some unique attributes of the Japanese economy, in particular, its distance both physically and culturally from the rest of the world. It is costly for Japanese buyers to purchase products directly from abroad. The trading companies are a conduit between Japan and the world, and they provide specialized intermediation services that are obviously subject to economies of scale and scope. Firms buying imports can obtain these services more cheaply from specialized agents than they could obtain them for themselves. On the other hand, as Yamamura (1976) has suggested, "because of linguistic and cultural similarities and geographical proximity among the Western trading partners . . . the absolute costs of information, of negotiation, and of enforcement of contracts . . . were significantly lower than they were for Japan."

But government policies and other practices also account for the trading companies role. As Kojima and Ozawa (1984, p. 62) have written:

> Japan's major trading companies enjoy monopsonistic positions in securing vital industrial resources and foodstuffs from overseas, partly as a result of the commercial tradition dating back to the Meiji period. The trading companies operate very closely—if not exclusively—with the member companies of their respective industrial groups. These unique features of Japanese

industry enable them to create *"shoken"* or the commercial right to inter-mediate in trade. Indeed trading companies monopolize the import and dis-tribution channels for iron ore, coking coal and other mineral resources, as well as grains—albeit in a climate of fierce rivalry.

In the nineteenth century, Japan was dependent on foreign merchant trading companies for the conduct of its trade (for historical accounts, see Kojima and Ozawa 1984; Yamamura 1976; and Young 1979). Partly because of conscious government policy, control was handed over to domestic trading companies. Indeed, the role of the trading companies in Japanese trade appears to be a case in which the Japanese comparative advantage was nurtured by policy. Government policies actually granted the trading companies monopolies to trade or *shoken* in commodities such as iron ore and coking coal.

Government nurturing of the trading companies was particularly important when imports and foreign exchange were tightly controlled. During the 1950s and 1960s when foreign exchange was rationed, the trading firms that gener-ated the largest amounts for export revenues were granted lucrative import quotas. According to Tsurumi (1980), "Import licences for such lucrative con-sumer goods as bananas, whiskey and crude sugar were given to the trading firms which had already met the export targets for ships, rolling-stock and machine tools. The export of ships was particularly subsidized through this linking process. Lasting well into the 1950s, the linking policy naturally pre-cipitated the diversification of goods and services handled by one firm" (p. 21).

The trading companies served as key agents in the Japanese policy of im-port substitution in the 1950s and 1960s. But government policies were rein-forced by the practices of industrial groups. In particular the connections that exist between the companies and the large *keiretsu* groups—themselves de-scendents of the *zaibatsu*. Today's large trading companies such as Mitsui Busan and Mitsubishi Shoji expanded as commercial wings of their *zaibatsu* groups with secure sources of income derived from their rights to intermediate group transactions.

Today, the connections between the companies and their groups are not ex-clusive. Trading companies do not limit their dealings to group firms and affil-iates, but group manufacturing firms do provide them with assured, if not captive, customers. Long-term relationships between buyers and sellers are of course pervasive in the Japanese economy. While these relationships do not always entail formal internalization in the form of vertical integration, they frequently entail a complex set of associations through membership in the same industrial group, *keiretsu,* the exchange of equity, and the adoption of deliberate techniques that require a large measure of mutual trust between buyers and sellers. The pervasiveness of these relationships suggest that, par-ticularly within Japan, these organizational relationships offer distinct trans-actional advantages.

Many of these practices may well be economically rational. Indeed, they may be more effective than the arm's length practices elsewhere—particularly in a society in which adversarial and litigious responses to contract breeches are deemed particularly costly.

It is noteworthy, for example, that having learned about Japanese methods for relationships with suppliers by observing and participating in joint ventures with Japanese automobile companies who have located assembly operations in the United States, the big three U.S. producers have changed their own supplier relationships. As Schnapp (1988, p. E-4) concluded in his review of the U.S. auto parts industry, "The U.S. components supply structure is evolving into one similar to the Japanese model . . . [which] will involve greatly intensified interdependence between automakers and their first tier suppliers and between those first tier suppliers and their own vendor networks. . . . For original equipment parts makers, it's conform to the Japanese model or die."

But while they may enhance efficiency in some respects, these relationships also increase market power. As Perry has pointed out, vertical integration can be particularly useful for a monopsonist. Vertical integration permits a monopsonist to capture the rents that are enjoyed by intramarginal sellers when the price is driven up by purchases.[3] It is an interesting confirmation of the Perry thesis that Japanese trading companies became more active in direct foreign investment when Japan became a significant purchaser of raw materials. Once their purchases had grown large enough to affect the prices they paid, it paid trading companies to internalize these purchases. But if the system of bringing raw materials inputs into Japan had been competitive, firms in the Japanese distribution system would have been content to buy inputs from a variety of international distributors.

The major role played by Japanese firms abroad in exports to Japan is consistent with the evidence, adduced by Kreinen, that Japanese purchasing behavior in general differs from that of other countries, even where the purchases are made abroad. In particular, Kreinin (1988) finds that Japanese firms abroad have an unusually strong preference to buy from Japanese rather than other foreign suppliers.

In sum, the Japanese economy provides trading companies with major advantages as procurers for Japan. They are extremely efficient providers of intermediation services, which are required by Japanese firms who engage in trade because of the cultural and geographic distance of Japan from its markets. In addition, however, their positions have been bolstered by policy and other practices. In particular, the companies have functioned as the buying and selling arms of industrial groups. The existence of the large array of entry barriers to selling in Japan implies that companies who have already sunk the costs in overcoming them have an inherent advantage as buyers of attractive foreign products.

---

3. See the discussion of this case in Krugman (1983).

1.1.2 Implications

Given the importance of the trading companies in Japanese imports, a key issue is their willingness to import products that compete directly with domestic firms with whom they have close relationships. Gerlach (1989), for example, suggests they do not do this freely. "Whatever price reductions might be passed along to the Japanese buyer of foreign products are at least partially 'absorbed' by the vertical channels through which these products must flow. Japanese firms are as interested in protecting their relationship with domestic suppliers as they are in passing along cost savings to others."

On the other hand, the trading companies do appear willing, indeed eager, to encourage imports in cases where these are in the interests of domestic manufacturing firms. They have not only played a crucial role in providing raw materials for the economy but, according to Kojima and Ozawa (1984), "they have also been instrumental in persuading firms to locate abroad to serve the Japanese market when it appears production is no longer competitive. Kojima and Ozawa describe how the trading companies responded to the decline in Japanese competitiveness in labor-intensive low-skill products in the early 1960s by encouraging Japanese manufacturers to establish overseas manufacturing ventures. Typically they organized ventures with consortiums of companies within their affiliated *keiretsu* (Kojima and Ozawa 1984, p. 83).

As Japanese *manufacturing* firms increase their direct foreign investment abroad, they will become less reliant on the trading companies for their supplies of foreign inputs. But if the trading companies' role in trade diminishes, an alternative source of intra-Japanese-firm shipments of Japanese imports is likely to increase.

1.1.3 Foreign Affiliates in Japan

While the intrafirm shipments to Japanese parents from their overseas affiliates are an unusually high share of Japanese imports, the shipments from foreign parents to Japanese affiliates are an unusually small share of foreign exports to Japan. In 1986, U.S. companies shipped 13.6 percent of all U.S. exports to Japan to their Japanese affiliates and just 9.7 percent of these exports to majority-owned affiliates. In manufactured goods the U.S. company role is even smaller. In 1986, U.S. firms shipped just $947 million to their majority-owned manufacturing affiliates in Japan (and $1.6 billion to all affiliates). *Japanese* intrafirm trade in U.S. manufactured exports to Japan is as important as U.S. intrafirm trade.

Kenichi Ohmae (as quoted in Bergsten and Cline 1985, pp. 107–8) has made much of the large sales by U.S. owned and affiliated companies in Japan, but in fact these sales are extremely small for a country with an economy the size of Japan. In 1987, for example, sales by nonbank affiliates of U.S. companies in Japan were $114.7 billion, of which $23.3 billion were by petroleum companies and $70 billion by manufacturing companies. However, a sizable share of the manufacturing sales is by companies, such as Mazda, Mitsubishi Motors, Isuzu, and Suzuki Motors, in which U.S. firms have minority holdings but are not generally regarded as American. Sales by majority-owned U.S. affiliates were $42.416 billion of which just $17.6 billion were by manufacturing companies. This is not much larger than the $14.6 billion sales recorded by U.S. majority-owned manufacturing affiliates in Australia, New Zealand, and South Africa. By contrast, sales by majority-owned U.S. affiliates in European manufacturing were $228.8 billion.

The total value of owners' equity in U.S. majority-owned affiliates in Japan amounted to $11.5 billion in 1987, of which just $6.4 billion was in manufacturing. Thus while there are U.S. companies that have successfully penetrated the Japanese market, they remain the exception rather than the rule. Despite the lifting of formal restrictions on inward direct foreign investment, foreign entry into Japan remains low compared with investment in other major industrial nations.

The result, therefore, is that U.S. exporters to Japan remain highly dependent on Japanese distributors for the sale of their products in Japan. This suggests that the argument that the Japanese market is closed to imports needs to be modified. If foreign goods are directly competitive with domestic products they will have difficulty entering. If imports are complementary with the interests of domestic companies they will not. However, in most cases, corporate control over the trade rests in Japanese hands.

The role of Japanese companies in Japanese trade also has significant political implications. It is striking, for example, that while Japanese and West German manufactured goods exports are of similar magnitudes, Japan encounters obstacles to its exports regularly, while Germany rarely does. Part of the explanation may lie in the speed with which Japanese exports have grown—they represent a new entrant whose presence is disruptive to existing relationships. But I have argued elsewhere (Lawrence 1987) that another reason is Japan's low share of intra-industry trade. The high level of West German exports of a wide variety of products means that when domestic firms complain about German export competition, there are other *domestic* firms that have an important stake in the German market and will tend to counteract them. But since Japanese imports are low, there are rarely such offsetting forces when there are complaints about Japanese exports. The evidence in this section reinforces this explanation: not only are Japanese imports of manufactured goods low, but U.S. firms play an unusually small role in selling the American products Japan does import. Since U.S. firms are generally more politically influential than foreign subsidiaries, Japanese influence in offsetting protectionist actions is even weaker than the low level of its imports would suggest.

1.2   Prices

In 1985, according to the OECD, imports accounted for 5.8 percent of Japanese expenditures on manufactured products. By contrast, they were 12.9 percent of U.S. expenditures. While it is clear that Japanese-manufactured imports are low, the explanation for this level remains controversial. There is an extensive set of anecdotes on Japanese import barriers in specific sectors. But economists mistrust anecdotal evidence because it may be selectively biased (only the losers complain) and not subject to quantitative appraisals. They have, therefore, sought firmer evidence that barriers have had a significant impact on Japan's trade structure.

The problem is that factors other than trade barriers could, in principle, account for Japan's trade structure. Thus some basis is required for determining what import level would be expected if no barriers existed (or if Japanese barriers were no different from those in other countries). While Japan may well have unusually extensive barriers to manufactured goods imports, its low level of imports is undoubtedly also influenced by its distance from its trading partners (physically and culturally) and its relatively poor endowments of natural resources.

Back-of-the-envelope calculations indicate the quantity of Japanese manufactured goods imports are unusually low. Krugman (1987), for example, suggests Japan might be expected to have an import share of manufactured goods at least as large as the extra-EC imports of the European Community. While it has fewer natural resource endowments, which would lead to lower manufactured goods imports, Japan is smaller than Europe, which should lead it to import more. In fact, in 1984, Japanese-manufactured imports of 2.9 percent were less half the 6.5 percent share of GNP accounted for by extra-EC manufactured goods imports. Similarly Krugman has compared German and Japanese imports of U.S. manufactured goods exports to reach a similar conclusion. Srinivasan and Hamada apply parameters to some analytic models of trade under imperfect competition and conclude that the total Japanese import penetration ratio would be expected to be between 30 and 60 percent higher than that in the United States, while the expected import penetration ratio in manufacturing would be 24 percent higher than in the United States.

More extensive studies of Japan's trade structure have reached different conclusions. Saxonhouse (1988) (with the exception of several agricultural sectors), Leamer (1987), Bergsten and Cline (1985), Noland (1987), and Balassa and Noland (1988) have run tests that conclude that Japanese import levels are "normal" given the other attributes of its economy. Lawrence (1987) and Balassa and Noland (1988), on the other hand, find evidence that Japanese—manufactured imports are unusually low.

Srinivasan and Hamada (1989) have appraised these studies and (with the exception of Leamer) found methodological weaknesses in all of them. The empirical tests of the models do not appear to be precise specifications of the theories on which they are based. Saxonhouse is criticized for using a theory that requires assuming the same number of products as factors, using the inappropriate forecast interval for his test, and running a test in which the coefficients may also be subject to simultaneity bias (because protection may systematically affect factor prices). In fact, as Saxonhouse has pointed out (although not noted by Srinivasan and Hamada) Leamer's tests are subject to the same simultaneity problem.[4] My own work (Lawrence 1987) is criticized for misspecification of my estimation equation due to the use of an additive distance variable, independent variables that are not exogenous, and expressing the variables in logarithms rather than levels. Balassa and Noland (1988) fall short for not using a model that is clearly derived from theory.

It appears, therefore, that these empirical tests do not settle the issue. The problem with all these tests is that they do not explicitly test for the presence of trade barriers. They are tests for determining if Japanese imports are unusually low. But even if Japanese imports are unusually low, other facts that do not appear in the model, such as unusual preferences or technology, rather than trade barriers, might be the reason. To provide a flawless test, it appears the barriers must be explicitly modeled. But this is rather difficult when, by their very nature, they are "intangible" or even invisible.

1.2.1   Prices

But perhaps all the tests discussed above are not asking the most relevant question. They focus too much attention on the question of quantities or trade structure and not enough on the question of prices. Perhaps the important question is not "Does Japan import too little?" but "Are imports too expensive in Japan?" Before we descend into the knotty issues of national differences in taste and factor endowments, it seems necessary to clear up the earlier question of whether consumers in Japan are given the same choices. The direct observation of price behavior may be a more accurate measure of openness than tests of quantities that test on elaborate statistical models.

Actual trade flows may be low for fundamental economic reasons such as factor endowments and the competitiveness of Japanese products, but if the Japanese market is contestable, we should see the potential for entry keeping Japanese prices in line with those in other markets. If the same product sells for different prices in different locations over long periods of time, however, it seems reasonable to infer the existence of barriers to arbitrage.

It is, of course difficult empirically to isolate precisely equivalent products. A one-pound bag of Colombian coffee sold by a grocer in Tokyo is not the same product as a one-pound bag of Colombian coffee sold by a grocer in New York. The products differ in the cost required for transportation and distribution to different locations. In addition, they may be associated with a different degree of service by the store that is selling them. Nonetheless if there are no (or equivalent) barriers in both markets we would expect them to sell for the same price or for their prices to differ by no more than the costs of arbitrage between them.

There is considerable evidence that the prices of goods are much higher in Japan than in most other countries. Table 1.4 compares the dollar prices of

4. See the Saxonhouse comment on this paper below.

major expenditure categories in Japan with those in the United States and the EC as estimated on a purchasing-power-parity basis by the OECD. A summary measure of goods prices in general is the purchasing-power-parity estimates used for deflating measures of inventories (of both consumer and producer goods). In 1985, by this indicator, goods prices in Japan were 25 percent higher than they were in the United States and 42 percent higher than those in the European Community (OECD 1987).

Table 1.4 reports the results of calculations updating this estimate using 1987 exchange rates and inflation rates in the United States and Japan. Given the decline of the dollar from 200.5 yen in 1985 to an average of 123 yen in 1987, this implies, measured in U.S. dollars, goods prices (as represented in inventories) in Japan were 75 percent higher than in the United States.

In 1987, these calculations indicate that, compared with the United States, the cost of food, clothing, and fixed capital formation was 85, 62, and 76 percent higher in Japan. As reported in table 1.4, purchasing-power estimates for all goods and services shows that in 1985, a year in which the dollar was strong, the overall Japanese price level for all goods and services was 7 percent lower than in the United States. But even in 1985, the Japanese price level was 26 percent higher than in the European Community. In 1988, the OECD estimates the prices of goods and services in Japan are 60 percent higher than in the United States.

But these comparisons at the *retail* level are plagued with problems, partic-

Table 1.4   **Comparative Dollar Price Levels of Final Expenditure on GDP, United States = 100**

	1985		1987
	EC	Japan	Japan[a]
Private final consumption expenditure	77	91	141
Food, beverages, & tobacco	76	123	185
Clothing and footwear	83	100	162
Gross rent, fuel, and power	57	66	103
Household equipment & operations	87	103	158
Medical and health care	52	45	70
Transport & communication	113	117	188
Education, recreation, & culture	96	122	194
Miscellaneous goods and services	87	106	161
Net purchases abroad	59	91	81
Government final consumption expenditure	61	72	113
Gross fixed capital formation	81	115	176
Increase in stocks	88	125	175
Gross domestic product	74	93	147

Source: OECD (1987), pp. 52–53.

[a]Author's calculations are based on data from OECD National Accounts, vol. 2, 1987 series.

Table 1.5   **Wholesale and Retail Trade Margins**

	Japan, 1985		United States, 1983	
	Value (in Trillions of Yen)	Share	Value (in Billions of U.S.$)	Share
Intermediate inputs	20.122	.33	194.347	.34
Real estate	2.815	.046	27.609	.048
Value added	41.024	.67	378.355	.66
Total output	61.146		572.702	
Final sales of good (C + I + G + X)	160.052		1,667	
Whole and retail margin	.256		.227	
Distribution margin	.38		.34	

Sources: For United States: *Survey of Current Business* (February 1989), Input-output table 1; Department of Commerce, U.S. National Income Accounts. For Japan: *Economic Statistics Annual* (March 1989), Input-output table; Economic Planning Agency Annual Report on National Accounts (1989), p. 174.

ularly because distribution margins could, in principle, differ across countries. Assume, for example, that the Japanese distribution sector is extremely inefficient.[5] The market could be completely open, but both foreign and domestic products could be subject to the same, extremely high costs of distribution. It could also be the case that the distribution system for these markets is highly competitive and markups *have* to be more expensive in Japan because of higher real estate costs; Japanese retail prices could be higher, but this would simply reflect the underlying economic costs of distribution. Moreover, in this case, making the distribution system more "efficient"—through large stores and other changes in rules—might improve Japanese living standards tremendously but do little to raise the level of imports.

I have therefore analyzed distribution margins using input-output tables in Japan and the United States. As reported in table 1.5, the payments by the retail and wholesale trade for indirect inputs in both countries are remarkably similar—around one-third of total output of these sectors. The payments by these sectors to the real estate sector are also remarkably similar shares of their output. Overall, as a share of total goods sales (domestic absorption plus merchandise exports), value added in wholesale and retail trade is 25.6 percent in Japan in 1985 and 22.7 percent in the United States in 1983. In 1987 the ratios for Japan and the United States were 26 and 24 percent respectively (Government of Japan 1989; U.S. Department of Commerce 1989). The more extensive analysis undertaken for this conference by Ito and Maruyama (in this volume) comes to similar conclusions about Japanese margins in the distribution sector.

---

5. Ahearn (1989) has argued, e.g., that the multitiered distribution system in Japan raises markups on goods.

The similarity in distribution margins should not be taken as evidence of similarities in efficiency. If distribution margins are the same in Japan and the United States, but final goods are much higher in Japan, this implies higher prices are being paid *both* for manufacturing services and for distribution services. Indeed, using purchasing power estimates, according to the OECD (1988), output per worker in Japanese distribution was 72 percent of the U.S. level. The inefficiency in the Japanese distribution system is thus partly to blame for higher Japanese retail prices. But it is not the full story. Japanese manufacturers appear (on average) to charge prices in Japan that are higher than those in world markets. This confirms, in aggregate, the anecdotal evidence, discovered by many Japanese tourists, of what James Fallows has called the 47th Street photo phenomenon: some Japanese goods cost less in other countries than they do in Japan. A survey of the prices of the same products in Japan and the United States was conducted jointly by the U.S. Department of Commerce and the Japanese Ministry of Trade and Industry in 1989. Of the Japanese products studied, 21 of 50 were cheaper in the United States than in Japan (by contrast, only four of 35 U.S. products studied were cheaper in Japan than in the United States; see table 1.6).[6]

The comparative data on profit rates in manufacturing, as calculated by the OECD, lend further support to the notion that Japanese manufacturers have considerable market power. According to Chan-Lee and Sutch (1985), rates of return in Japanese manufacturing have typically been twice as high as those in the United States and other industrial countries.[7] Similarly, the share of profits in value added in Japanese manufacturing (48.7 percent) in 1987 was much higher than in the United States (28.8 percent). See table 1.7.

But while distribution margins on products in Japan in general appear similar to those in the United States, this does not hold for margins on imported products. As reported in a survey conducted by the Ministry of Trade and Industry, the prices of *imported* brand name goods in Japan are 30–60 percent higher than those in the USA and Europe. The study, conducted in November 1988, compared prices of products in 11 categories such as perfume, handbags, fountain pens, and golf clubs in five overseas cities and 41 Japanese cities. The survey showed that prices in New York, Paris, and Dusseldorf were 38, 29, and 27 percent lower than those in Tokyo.

Similarly, Ahearn (1989) cites a study by the Economic Planning Agency that found that unregulated consumer goods (goods not subject to any restrictions in Japan) were 36 percent more expensive in Japan in 1987 than in New York. Consumer goods that were subject to restrictions in Japan (e.g., food, liquor, and energy) were 92 percent more expensive.

---

6. In his comments on this paper, Gary Saxonhouse interprets the evidence from this survey as indicating that Japanese goods are typically not sold for higher prices in Japan. This ignores the more pervasive evidence in the purchasing-power-parity studies.

7. Contrary to the assertion in Saxonhouse's comment on this paper (see below), the OECD *does* adjust its measures of profits to take account of the self-employed. See, e.g., OECD (1990).

Table 1.6   **U.S.-Japan Product Price Comparison**

Product	Lower/Japan	Lower/United States	Total	% Lower in United States
Capital goods	7	15	22	68.18
Food	1	22	23	95.65
Miscellaneous	5	19	24	79.17
Auto parts	2	9	11	81.82
Autos	2	5	7	71.43
Electronics	21	14	35	40.00
Total	38	84	122	68.85

Source: Joint Survey of U.S. Department of Commerce and Ministry of International Trade and Industry (MITI).

Table 1.7   **Profit Share and Rates of Return in Manufacturing (%)**

	1960s Average		1970s Average		1980/ 1984	1986	1987
	Profit Share	Rate of Return	Profit Share	Rate of Return	Profit Share	Profit Share	Profit Share
Japan	58.3	36.5[a]	50.8	26.4	48.4	47.9	48.7
United States	31.1	22.2	27.8	16.8	25.7	39.1	28.8
Germany	45.8	20.9	36.9	15.7	32.9	36.6	36.9
France	41.6	15.6	31.9	16.0	37.4	32.1	32.1

Sources: "Underlying Data for Indexes of Output per Hour, Hourly Compensation, and Unit Labor Costs in Manufacturing Twelve Industrial Countries, 1950–1988," U.S. Department of Labor, Bureau of Labor Statistics, Office of Productivity and Technology, June 1989. Also, Chan-Lee and Sutch 1985.

Note: Profit share = gross operating surplus as a percentage of value added. Calculated from data from Department of Labor. Rate of return = gross operating surplus as a ratio of the gross capital stock. From Chan-Lee and Sutch.

[a]1965–69.

In its survey, the OECD (1988, p. 81) found car prices (net of sales taxes) of German autos to be significantly more expensive in Japan than in the United States or France. The OECD suggests part of the explanation is the toleration of sole-agent contracts that allow the importer and/or the producer to restrict supply and earn monopoly profits. Finally, as reported in table 1.5 above, the joint survey by MITI and the U.S. Department of Commerce in 1989, which examined 122 products found 84 priced higher in Japan than the United States. Accordingly, it appears that many *imported* products in Japan *are* subject to higher markups than other Japanese products. According to Christelow (1985–86), "A [1985 Japanese] Government survey of distribution markups for domestic and imported products found that for whiskeys, candies, edible oils, men's overcoats and footwear, markups on imports were double those on domestic products."

It is hard to understand, in the face of this evidence, how Japan could exhibit "normal" import behavior when the evidence on differential pricing is so strong. In principle, in an open market, over long periods of time, there should be major opportunities for arbitrage.

1.2.2   Prices Responses

Price levels can differ, but since it is difficult to isolate these, useful information can be obtained from the responses of prices to shocks. That is, if the marginal costs of producing a product change, in open markets, one would expect similar price responses. If markets are fragmented and producers capable of pricing to market, one might see very different responses. As Marston (in this volume) and others have shown, Japanese export prices are characterized by this type of behavior.

In his comments on this paper, Gary Saxonhouse argues that these higher prices on imports reflect the marketing strategies of *foreign* oligopolistic firms. However, as I have demonstrated above, foreign goods in Japan are overwhelmingly marketed not by foreign firms but by Japanese distributors. This is why, contrary to his assertions, it is significant that Japanese importers take title to their goods in the United States. If they are bringing in the goods, they are earning the rents from the higher markups, and the Japanese distribution system operates like a privately administered set of tariffs.

1.3   Adjustment

Some of the barriers that allegedly inhibit the entry of imported products in Japan will function like quotas. In particular, administrative guidance or buying cartels may not be responsive to price changes. Other barriers may lead to high domestic products (as do tariffs) but may nonetheless be compatible with adjustments to price changes. Indeed, if an imported product is sold by an agent with a monopoly over its distribution, the agent will generally apply a higher markup on that product than if distribution was competitive. Nonetheless, if the agent's costs declined (in the face of a constant elasticity of demand), we would expect a proportional decline in the price charged to consumers. Similarly, as Becker (1971) has noted in his theory of discrimination, if consumers have a preference for buying domestic products, ceteris paribus, they will not necessarily be less responsive at the margin to changes in relative price of imported products.

A major reason given for the adoption of dramatically new U.S. policies toward Japan is the assertion that the Japanese economy fails to respond to relative price changes. Support for this view is derived from the apparent lack of adjustment in the U.S.–Japan bilateral trade deficit—measured in U.S. dollars. But it should be stressed that since the devaluation of the dollar has taken place from a position of substantial initial imbalance, the failure of the trade deficit to decline in dollars is not necessarily indicative of a lack of adjustment in Japan. If the U.S. import demand elasticity is close to unity, as it appears to be, measured in dollars, imports from Japan will not be affected by changes in the exchange rate. This means that *all* of the decline in the Japanese surplus has to come from a rise in the value of U.S. exports to Japan. Since, in 1985, when U.S. exports to Japan (of $22.6 billion) were 31.3 percent of U.S. imports from Japan ($72.4 billion), exports have to grow over three times as fast as imports, simply to stay even. The fact that the nominal trade deficit has remained fairly constant actually indicates a dramatic increase in the value of U.S. exports to Japan.

Indeed, between 1985 and 1988, according to the U.S. Department of Commerce (1989), U.S. exports to Japan increased from $22.6 billion to $37.7 billion. Similarly, U.S. manufactured goods imports increased from $12.3 billion to $22 billion—a rise of 79 percent in a period of relative price stability. Over this same period, according to the Economic Planning Agency of Japan, the volume of Japanese imports increased by 39.4 percent and the overall volume of Japanese imports of manufactured goods increased by 78.3 percent.

In 1987 I wrote a paper that suggested that Japanese imports of manufactured goods were "unusually" low by about 40 percent *in 1980*. This number has now been subject to considerable abuse. Since the volume of Japanese manufactured imports has increased by over this amount since 1985, some have used this result to suggest that the levels of Japanese manufactured goods are now "normal" (see, e.g., Japan–U.S. Business Council 1989). But an application of the methodology I used in that paper would not endorse this conclusion. Since the study was cross-sectional it used nominal data measured in *domestic currencies*. In 1980, as measured by the OECD, imports accounted for 5.8 percent of Japanese expenditures on manufactured products. In 1985 they accounted for 5.3 percent. Using Japanese National Income Accounts data (Government of Japan 1989), I estimate, on a similar basis, that the share in 1987 was actually 7.5 percent lower than in 1985. Measured on the OECD basis this would entail a share of roughly 4.9 percent. The reason is that, for purposes of this calculation, the yen value of manufactured imports is relevant.

Nonetheless, as the Japanese trade data indicate, it would be inappropriate to argue that there has been no response in manufactured imports into Japan. In fact, measured in 1980 prices, data from the National Income Accounts suggest that the share of imported manufactured goods products spending in Japan increased by 36 percent from 6.0 to 8.2 percent of domestic absorption.

In my 1987 paper, I also observed that imports into Japan were as responsive to relative price changes as imports in other industrial countries. Table 1.8 reports a set of regressions that indicate that the response in Japanese manufactured goods to the rise in the yen and the rapid expansion in domestic

Table 1.8   Japanese Manufactured Import Equations (Volume), Annual Data (*t*-statistics in parentheses)

	Constant	LIP	LDD	LREX	LRPM	D86	D87	D88	R^2	SE	D-W	ρ
1970/85, Eq. 1	1.77	2.02		1.004		.14	.07	.11	.994	.0507	1.4	.58
	(1.5)	(16.5)		(4.2)		(2.4)	(.94)	(1.3)				
1971/85, Eq. 2	4.3	1.54			1.02	.07	.05	.16	.993	.053	1.7	.46
	(6.4)	(8.2)			(4.1)	(1.1)	(.8)	(1.9)				
1970/85, Eq. 3	−14.6		2.08	.89		.06	.001	.09	.977	.097	1.9	.31
	(5.1)		(10.9)	(2.1)		(.5)	(.06)	(.6)				
1970/85, Eq. 4	−9.5		1.76		.71	.02	.05	.17	.973	.101	1.9	.21
	(2.9)		(4.4)		(1.4)	(.14)	(.41)	(1.2)				
1970/85, Eq. 5	.2	1.86	.18	1.004		.13	.06	.1	.994	.053	1.44	.52
	(.05)	(5.2)	(.48)	(4.0)		(2.0)	(.69)	(1.1)				
1971/85, Eq. 6	11.3	2.1	−.88		1.34	.097	.07	.18	.995	.046	1.7	.53
	(3.1)	(6.4)	(−2.03)		(5.04)	(1.6)	(1.1)	(2.3)				
1970/88, Eq. 7	−2.4	1.72	.42	1.08					.991	.056	1.8	.46
	(4.7)	(4.7)	(1.1)	(4.7)								

Sources: OECD Economic Outlook Database and JP Morgan (real exchange rate).

Note: IP = industrial production; DD = final domestic demand (C + I + G); REX = real exchange rate; RPM = ratio of wholesale prices to manufactured import prices; D86 = dummy variable for 1986; D87 = dummy variable for 1987; D88 = dummy variable for 1988; L = logarithms.

demand between 1985 and 1988 was actually somewhat faster than might have been expected on the basis of the historic relationship (a similar conclusion is reached by Corker 1989). The regressions, specified in logarithms so the coefficients may be interpreted as elasticities, explain the volume of Japanese manufactured goods imports as a function of an activity and relative price/cost variable. Because of endogeneity problems, there are well-known problems associated with providing structural interpretations to such regressions, but they are nonetheless interesting as statistical summaries of the historic relationships between the variables. I have experimented using two proxies for activity: industrial production and domestic final demand. The former will capture the role of imports as inputs into industrial production, the latter as components of domestic absorption. Generally, the industrial production variable provided a better fit (compare, e.g., eqq. [1] and [3]). When both variables are inserted in the equation, the coefficient on final demand is not significant (eq. [5]). However, when estimated with the period 1986–88, the coefficient on domestic demand increases from .18 to .42 although it is still not significant.

The real exchange-rate variable (the ratio of Japanese to foreign manufactured goods prices in yen) estimated with a current and one year lag has coefficients that sum to about unity (see eqq. [1], [3], and [5]). This cost formulation is less subject to simultaneity bias than the price variable and also provides a slightly more robust coefficient and a smaller standard error. But the specifications are all interesting in showing not only that Japanese manufactured imports are responsive to changes in relative prices and real exchange rates but also that the recent rise in manufactured imports is higher than might have been expected, given this historic relationship. An out-of-sample forecast of the volume of manufactured imports given the actual behavior of domestic activity and relative prices underpredicts the volume of manufactured imports in 1988 by between 9 and 18 percent (see the coefficients on the dummy variables for 1988).

1.3.1 Corporate Role

Judged by the volume of products being sold, the Japanese economy is becoming more open. But what about the corporate role? There is considerable anecdotal evidence that Japanese investment in foreign beef stockyards in the United States and Australia has increased in response to the anticipated opening of the beef market. Similarly, that Japanese investment in citrus orchards has increased in response to the potential in that market. But what does the aggregate data indicate?

Unfortunately, the data that are available are limited. *But they do suggest that the Japanese corporate role in Japanese imports is declining.* As reported in table 1.9, in 1985 almost 70 percent of U.S. exports to Japan was shipped by a Japanese affiliate in the United States to its Japanese parent. In 1986 the share of Japanese affiliates was 58.4 percent and in 1987 the share was 39.6

Table 1.9   Percentage of U.S. Exports and Imports with Affiliates of Foreign
                   Multinational Corporations, by Area of Affiliates, for 1983–87

	Exports			Imports		
	EC	Japan	World	EC	Japan	World
1981	11.9	75.1	11.5	37.7	69.4	20.0
1982	16.1	65.5	11.8	37.1	71.4	21.3
1983	12.2	63.9	11.3	35.4	68.8	21.2
1984	15.0	66.9	12.4	30.8	67.7	21.6
1985	13.7	69.7	12.2	29.5	69.6	23.7
1986	11.6	58.4	11.6	29.8	66.1	25.4
1987	7.5	39.6	7.7	31.5	67.3	26.2

Source: Survey of Current Business, Department of Commerce, various issues.

percent. Between 1986 and 1987, U.S. exports to Japan increased from $26.9 billion to $28.2 billion. The decline in the share of U.S. exports shipped by Japanese foreign affiliates indicates that the dollar value of their sales actually declined quite considerably. The hold of the general trading companies appears to be slipping. And, indeed, there are reports of them seeking a variety of new business opportunities (see Choy 1988).

The trading companies' role is particularly conspicuous, for Japanese data show and U.S. data suggest that, while the overall share of intrafirm shipments by Japanese firms in Japanese imports has declined, the share shipped by the foreign affiliates of Japanese manufacturing companies—so-called reverse imports—is growing. According to a survey conducted by MITI (1989) of the overseas activities of Japanese businesses, reverse imports accounted for 5.3 percent of all Japanese imports and 11.5 percent of all manufactured goods imports in fiscal year 1987. While this share was relatively low, it has been rising rapidly. The 1987 total of ¥ 1.18 trillion was a 45 percent increase over the total for fiscal year 1986, when reverse imports accounted for 9.2 percent of all Japanese manufactured imports.

On the other hand, as reported in table 1.10, the intrafirm trade from parents in the U.S. to their affiliates located in Japan has increased steadily, from 11.0 percent in 1983 to 14.8 percent in 1985 and 17.3 percent in 1987.[8]

Finally, it is noteworthy that U.S. exports have surged in sectors in which negotiations to change the rules have been concluded. According to the ACTPN (1989) report, after 10 years of pressure, it concludes that virtually all barriers to the importation of tobacco into Japan have fallen. The four sectors that were singled out for negotiation under the maligned Market-Opening, Sector-Specific (MOSS) talks in the mid-1980s have shown impres-

8. The major rise in U.S. exports to Japan actually came between 1987 and 1988. During this period, U.S. manufacturing exports to Japan increased from $16.3 to $21.96 billion while the total value of exports increased from $28.2 to $37.7 billion. Unfortunately, data on the corporate involvement in trade was not available when this paper was compiled.

Table 1.10   **Percentage of U.S. Exports and Imports with Affiliates of U.S. Multinational Corporations, by Area of Affiliates, for 1983–87**

	Exports			Imports		
	EC (12)	Japan	World	EC (12)	Japan	World
1983	39.5	11.0	28.7	15.1	9.4	20.6
1984	38.2	12.3	30.4	13.7	7.2	19.2
1985	39.7	14.8	32.7	14.7	9.2	19.7
1986	36.9	13.6	32.8	12.2	8.9	17.7
1987	36.3	17.3	31.0	14.5	10.9	18.6

Source: Survey of Current Business, Department of Commerce, various issues.

sive growth in Japanese imports. According to the report, from 1985 to 1987, U.S. exports to Japan in the four product categories, combined, increased by 46.5 percent, well above the 24. 8 percent increase in total U.S. exports to Japan over the same period. The report dismisses this performance because the total increase in exports of the products (of $1.3 billion) was small relative to the entire bilateral trade imbalance. But no one expected negotiations in a few sectors to turn the entire imbalance around. The problem may not be the approach, that is, emphasizing rules, but the limited resources and narrow focus of the number of sectors brought into consideration. We need not only tough, persistent negotiations but enough patience to let the results begin to build.

1.3.2   Concluding Remarks

Traditionally, U.S. policy has sought a more open Japanese market for foreign firms and products by negotiating rules that would remove barriers. But demands are growing for the United States to seek managed trade agreements that ensure results. Some results-oriented approaches might open the Japanese market in the sense of increasing the demand for U.S. products; others might increase the profits of U.S. firms. But they are unlikely to open the market in the crucial sense of making Japanese markets genuinely contestable by foreigners. Indeed, a results-oriented approach is likely to lead to a market with more rather than less Japanese government and corporate control.

How open is Japan? Several noteworthy features have emerged from the data, and three point to the role still left to play by the removal of barriers: (1) Imports continue to account for an unusually small share of Japanese expenditures on manufactured products. (2) Barriers continue to inhibit the international arbitrage of prices differences between Japan and other markets. And (3) the intrafirm shipments of Japanese firms continue to account for an unusually high share of Japanese imports.

But there are also signs that, since 1985, the Japanese economy has made major adjustments. (1) the Japanese economy has undergone a major adjustment in response to the strengthening of the yen. According to the Japanese Economic Planning Agency, in the first quarter of 1989, Japan imported twice the volume of manufactured goods it imported in 1985. (2) Japanese manufacturing firms are playing an increasing role in "reverse imports." (3) U.S. affiliates based in Japan are raising their share of U.S. exports. And (4) the intrafirm shipments of Japanese trading companies has declined conspicuously. Those who claim exchange rates do not change Japanese buying patterns have simply not examined the data.

In the light of this evidence, it is not surprising that the trade disputes between Japan and the United States about the closed nature of the Japanese market continue. But it *is* surprising, given the major shifts in Japanese behavior that have taken place over the past few years, that some Americans feel so exasperated that they are driven to advocate an entirely new approach that emphasizes results rather than rules.

References

Advisory Committee for Trade Policy and Negotiations (ACTPN). 1989. Analysis of U.S.-Japan Trade Problem. Report to Carla Hills. Washington, D.C., February.
Ahearn, Raymond J. 1989. Japan: Prospects for greater openness. Library of Congress, Congressional Research Service.
Balassa, B., and Marcus Noland. 1988. *Japan in the world economy.* Washington, D.C.: Institute for International Economics.
Becker, Gary. 1971. *The economics of discrimination.* Chicago: University of Chicago Press.
Bergsten, C. F., and W. Cline. 1985. *The U.S.-Japan economic problem.* Washington, D.C.: Institute for International Economics.
Chan-Lee, James, and Helen Sutch. 1985. Profits and rate of return in OECD countries. OECD Working Paper no. 20. May.
Choy, John. 1988. Japan's sogo sosha: Back to the future? *Japan Economic Institute* 34(a) (September).
Christelow, Dorothy. 1985–86. Japan's intangible barriers to trade in manufactures. *Federal Reserve Bank of New York Quarterly Review* 10 (Winter):11–18.
Clarida, Richard H. 1989. On the U.S. trade deficit, protectionism and policy coordination. Paper presented at Columbia University conference on U.S. trade policy. New York, September 8.
Corker, Robert. 1989. External adjustment of the strong yen. *IMF Staff Papers* 35, no. 2 (June):464–93.
Dornbusch, Rudiger W. (1990). Policy Options for Freer Trade: The Case for Bilateralism. In *An American Trade Strategy: Options for the 1990s,* ed. Robert Z. Lawrence and Charles L. Schultze. Washington, D.C.: Brookings.
Gerlach, Michael. 1989. Keiretsu organization in the Japanese economy: Analysis and trade implications. In *Politics and productivity: How Japan's development strategy works,* ed. Chalmers Johnson, Laura D'Andrea Tyson, and John Zysman, pp. 141–76. Cambridge: Ballinger.
Government of Japan. 1989. Source for Japan national income accounts: Supply and disposition of commodities. Tokyo: Economic Planning Agency.

Hymer, Stephen H. 1976. *The international operations of national firms: A study of direct foreign investment.* MIT Monographs in Economics, no. 14. Cambridge, Mass.: MIT Press.

Japan-U.S. Business Council. 1989. Can a "results-oriented" trade strategy work? Critical comments on the ACTPN report, August 25.

Kojima, Kiyoshi, and Terutomo Ozawa. 1984. *Japan's general trading companies: Merchants of economic development.* Paris: Organization for Economic Cooperation and Development.

Kreinin, Mordechai E. 1988. How closed is Japan's market? Additional evidence. *World Economy* (December):529–42.

Krugman, Paul R. 1983. The "new theories" of international trade and the multinational enterprise. In *The multinational corporation in the 1980s,* ed. Charles P. Kindleberger and David B. Audretsch, pp. 57–73. Cambridge, Mass.: MIT Press.

Lawrence, R. 1987. Imports in Japan: Closed markets or minds? *Brookings Papers on Economic Activity,* no. 2.

Leamer, Edward E. 1987. Measures of openness. Paper presented at National Bureau of Economic Research Conference on Trade Policy Issues and Empirical Analysis. Cambridge, Mass., February 13–14.

Ministry of Trade and Industry (MITI). 1989. The 18th survey on Japanese business activity abroad, April 27. Tokyo.

Noland, Marcus, 1987. An econometric investigation of international protection. Institute for International Economics, Washington, D.C., June.

Organization for Economic Cooperation and Development (OECD). 1987. *Purchasing power parities and real expenditures, 1985.* Paris: OECD Department of Economics and Statistics.

——. 1990. *OECD Economic Outlook* (June):176.

Perry, M. 1978. Vertical integration: The monopsony case. *American Economic Review* 68:561–70.

Reich, Robert B. 1989. Members only. *New Republic* (June 26): pp. 14–18.

Rugman, Alan M. 1980. Internalization as a general theory of foreign direct investment: A reappraisal of the literature. *Weltwirtschaftliches Archiv* 116, no. 2:365–79.

Saxonhouse, Gary R. 1988. Differentiated products, economies of scale and access to the Japanese market. Seminar Discussion Paper no. 225. University of Michigan, Economics Department.

Schnapp, John. 1988. Struggle for tier one status. *Automotive News* (July 18), p. E-4.

Srinivasan, T. N., and Koichi Hamada. 1989. The U.S.-Japan trade problem. Yale University, mimeographed.

Tsurumi, Yoshi, with Rebecca R. Tsurumi. 1980. *Sogoshosha engines of export-based growth.* Montreal: Institute for Research on Public Policy.

Tyson, Laura D'Andrea. 1990. Managed trade: Making the best of second best. In *An American trade strategy: Options for the 1990s,* ed. Robert Z. Lawrence and Charles L. Schultze. Washington, D.C.: Brookings.

U.S. Department of Commerce. 1989. *Survey of Current Business* 68, no. 7 (July).

U.S. International Trade Commission. 1986. Operation of the Trade Agreements Program, 37th Report 1985. Publication no. 1871.

Yamamura, Kozo. 1976. General trading companies in Japan: Their origins and growth. In *Japanese industrialization and its social consequences,* ed. Hugh Patrick. Berkeley: University of California Press.

Young, Alexander K. 1979. *The sogo shosa: Japan's multinational trading companies.* Boulder, Colo.: Westview Press.

Comment   Gary R. Saxonhouse

Robert Lawrence reviews once again an issue that has been much debated throughout the 1980s. He asks whether Japan, either by government action or by the private exercise of market power, interferes with the access of foreign products and/or foreign firms to its domestic markets.

Lawrence makes a special effort to emphasize the distinction between access to the Japanese market for foreign products and access for foreign firms. Foreign firms may have access to the Japanese market, but they might exploit this access by marketing goods produced largely in Japan. Alternatively, foreign goods may gain access to Japan as the by-product of intrafirm transactions between Japan and its overseas affiliates without foreign firms necessarily having access at all. Lawrence argues persuasively that the type of access foreigners have to the Japanese market has important implications for the economic welfare and income distribution of both Japan and its trading partners.

Japanese trade is distinctive, Lawrence finds, because foreign exports to Japan have generally been shipped by foreign affiliates of Japanese firms. Whereas international vertical integration generally proceeds forward from producers to markets, in Japan it appears to proceed backward from control of markets to sources of supply.

Lawrence thinks that this distinctive pattern of backward vertical integration in turn may be responsible for Japan's distinctively meager participation in intra-industry trade. When intrafirm imports are dominated by foreign firms, new varieties of products presently produced domestically will be imported. If intrafirm imports are dominated by domestic firms, such imports, Lawrence argues, will consist primarily of inputs that are found to be cheaper abroad or imports of varieties produced by the domestic firms that can be manufactured more cheaply abroad. Intrafirm shipments by domestic firms are much less likely to result in the importation of new varieties produced abroad, which compete directly with domestic production.

While in Japan vertical integration moves distinctively backward from sales in domestic market to foreign suppliers, it also proceeds forward from domestic producer to overseas market. Like Japanese imports, Lawrence finds that Japanese exports are also heavily dominated by intrafirm transactions. Such evidence, Lawrence notes, is consistent with well-known survey evidence by Mordechai Kreinin, which finds that Japanese purchasing behavior, in general, differs from that of other countries even where the purchases are made abroad. Kreinin finds that Japanese firms abroad have an unusually strong preference to buy from other Japanese rather than from foreign suppliers.

Lawrence believes that not only do foreign firms play a distinctively small role in Japan's international trade, he also believes that foreign products have a distinctively low share of Japan's domestic market. Citing a paper by T. N. Srinivasan and Koichi Hamada, Lawrence finds the econometric evidence to

Gary R. Saxonhouse is professor of economics at the University of Michigan.

be inconclusive on whether, after allowance is made for Japan's distinctive national endowments, particularly its lack of natural resources, there is really anything distinctive about Japan's trade structure.

Lawrence prefers to look directly at cross-national price differences to uncover whether or not foreign products' access to the Japanese market is restricted. While it is often difficult to assemble comparable price data across countries, Lawrence feels enough evidence is available to conclude that there are large and persistent price differences between Japan and other countries that cannot be accounted for by higher distribution margins or real estate costs. He concludes that Japanese manufacturers charge higher prices for the goods they sell in Japan than for the goods they sell in the rest of the world. In consequence, Lawrence notes that it is not surprising that the profits of Japanese manufacturers as a proportion of value added are unduly large by international standards. Potential arbitrage opportunities between the Japanese market and the rest of the world are not being fully exploited.

While Lawrence finds considerable evidence that leads him to conclude that Japanese markets are not genuinely contestable by foreign products or foreign markets, he appears to be impressed by the capacity for change within the Japanese economy. He finds that many of the barriers to the Japanese market operate like tariffs rather than quotas. They keep imported products expensive in Japan, but they do not prevent marginal responses to price and costs incentives. The exchange rate changes in the mid-1980s have resulted in a dramatic increase in the total volume of manufactured goods imported into Japan over the past four years. At a sectoral level, where tangible barriers have been removed as a result of negotiations, significant increases in imports have resulted. Given the major shifts in Japanese behavior that have taken place over the past few years, Lawrence finds it surprising that some Americans feel so exasperated as to advocate an entirely new approach to dealing with U.S.-Japan economic relations.

Intrafirm Transactions

While Lawrence's analysis is full of good insight and is highly plausible, it is possible also to disagree with some of the inferences he draws from the evidence he has assembled and, indeed, with some of the evidence itself. While an unusually large share of Japanese imports are the result of intrafirm transactions, it is not at all clear that these transactions represent backward vertical integration in the way that term is normally understood. These intrafirm transactions, by and large, are neither the purchases of Japanese manufacturing firms, nor of Japan retailers, nor the sale of goods produced by their overseas subsidiaries and affiliates. While this may change in the 1990s, by comparison with firms in other major industrialized countries, firms with established positions in the Japanese market have only rarely found it profitable to integrate backward into production entities abroad. In 1987 only 5.3% of Japanese imports were intrafirm transactions of goods produced by Japanese entities abroad. By contrast, for the United States in 1987, no less than 18.4% of all imports were the result of intrafirm transactions of goods produced abroad by American subsidiaries and affiliates.[1]

Intrafirm transactions dominate Japanese imports only because Japanese importers are taking title to their goods abroad rather than when they reach Japanese ports. That Japanese importers happen to take title to their goods via separately incorporated subsidiaries in Los Angeles rather than directly in Yokohama is by itself, not very significant at all. While issues may remain about the volume and composition of Japanese imports, a distinctively high proportion of the imports that do reach the Japanese market are produced by foreign-owned firms.

Japanese *keiretsu*

Intrafirm transactions play such a large role in Japan's foreign trade because of Japan's giant general trading companies. In 1986, Japan's nine largest trading companies handled 66% of all Japanese imports. Is it possible that Japanese trading companies restrict what they import, not so much to protect their own domestic production, of which they do little, but rather to protect the interests of other firms to which they are tied through their *keiretsu* affiliation? In considering this possibility, it is important to keep some perspective on the strength of *keiretsu* ties. Japan has many *keiretsu* of one type or another, but currently the six best known are Mitsui, Mitsubishi, Sumitomo, Fuyo, Dai-Ichi Kangyo, and Sanwa. Mitsui, Mitsubishi, and Sumitomo are directly descended from the prewar *zaibatsu,* which SCAP (Supreme Command of the Allied Powers) tried to break up during the American Occupation of Japan. By contrast, the Fuyo, Dai-Ichi Kangyo, and Sanwa *keiretsu,* were formed largely in the years after 1945. Members of all six *keiretsu* are much less closely tied than is generally realized. The member firms in *keiretsu* with strong prewar roots purchase only 14.8% of their procurement from fellow *keiretsu* members. For the more recently organized *keiretsu,* procurement from fellow *keiretsu* members is still less important. Only 8.9% of procurement is purchased from affiliated firms.[2]

While reciprocal purchasing seems to be too weak to tie *keiretsu* together, it is often suggested that cross-shareholding among member firms does allow the *keiretsu* as a whole effective control over any individual-member firm. In fact, cross-shareholding is not nearly as pervasive or so exclusive among *keiretsu* members as is commonly believed. Among the six best-known *keiretsu,*

---

1. Gary R. Saxonhouse, "Kawase reeto, kozo chosei to Taiheiyo chiiki ni okeru sankaku boeki" (Exchange rates, structural change and triangular trade in the Pacific region), *Keizai shakei seisaku* (Economy, society and policy) no. 205 (May 1989).
2. Kosei torihiki iinkai (Fair Trade Commission), *Kigyo shudan no jittai ni tsuite* (The structure of enterprise groups) (Tokyo: Kosei torihiki kyokai, 1983), pp. 39–42.

the average of a member firm's equity held by all other members of its *keiretsu* is 17.9%.[3] While this may be a relatively small amount of cross-shareholding, if ownership of the firm's remaining equity is widely dispersed, this may be sufficient to give the *keiretsu* control of the member firm. In fact, for the typical member firm, the main holders of equity outside of the *keiretsu* are characteristically members of other *keiretsu*.[4] These holdings, if exercised in concert, are sufficient to block *keiretsu* control of member firms.

Keiretsu ties have substance where member firms are dependent on the *keiretsu* main bank for their finance. Dependence on these main banks has declined dramatically over the past fifteen years. Between 1972 and 1983, over one-quarter of the companies listed on the first section of the Tokyo Stock Exchange changed their main bank.[5] This weakening of *keiretsu* ties goes hand in hand with the declining dependence of large Japanese firms on *keiretsu* banks. In 1974, Japanese firms, capitalized at more than one billion yen, relied on banks for 46.7% of their new financing. Just 10 years later no more than 2.6% of new investment by these large Japanese firms was financed by bank borrowing.[6]

If *keiretsu* ties are relatively weak, if such ties have been made still weaker by financial deregulation, and if reciprocal purchasing by *keiretsu* member firms is a relatively minor matter, it is hard to believe that Japan's distinctive trade structure can be explained by Japan's trading companies exercising what market power they have to protect their fellow *keiretsu* members by discriminating in their purchases against competitive imports. As noted, Lawrence does cite Mordechai Kreinin's case study of foreign investment in Australia as persuasive evidence in support of discriminatory purchasing of goods and services by Japanese companies. Unfortunately, not only does Kreinin's study not square with what is known about *keiretsu* behavior in the 1980s, it does not square with Lawrence's own study of Japanese foreign investment in the U.S. In this study, Lawrence notes

> Although it is widely perceived that Japanese-affiliated automakers depend overwhelmingly on parts bought from Japanese-affiliated suppliers, a detailed GAO survey calls this perception into question. It found, for example, that of the 119 U.S.-based suppliers used by Honda, only 28 had Japanese affiliations. Similarly 15 of Nissan's 121 suppliers were Japanese-affiliated and 8 of the 60 suppliers used by Toyota were Japanese affiliated.[7]

---

3. Toyo keizai (Oriental Economist), *Kigyo keiretsu soran* (Handbook of industrial groups) (Tokyo, 1989).

4. Ken-ichi Imai, "Kigyo gurupu" (Enterprise groups), in *Nihon no kigyo* (The Japanese firm), ed. Ken-ichi Imai and Ryutaro Komiya (Tokyo: Tokyo daigaku shuppankai, 1989).

5. *Kigyo keiretsu soran.*

6. Nihon ginko (Bank of Japan) "Shuyo kigyo keiei bunseki" (Analysis of the performance of major companies), *Keizai tokei nenkan* (Economic statistics yearbook) (Tokyo, 1989).

7. Robert Z. Lawrence, "Japanese Affiliated Automakers in the United States: An Appraisal" (October 1989).

Not only does Lawrence find, contrary to Kreinin, that Japanese firms do not rely primarily on Japanese suppliers, he also finds, again contrary to Kreinin, that (1) value added by Japanese firms in the United States is high; (2) Japanese firms do considerable research and development and design work in the United States, and (3) Japanese firms rely heavily on American managers.

In general, findings such as Kreinin's can be explained on grounds that have little to do with discriminatory or restrictive practices by Japanese firms and groups. Most Japanese manufacturing investments in Australia are of quite recent origin and are designed to produce substitutes for products that were recently exported (and indeed continue to be exported) to Australia from Japan. Japan continues to retain (or until recently retained) a comparative advantage in most of what it is producing in Australia. Japanese manufacturing in Australia is an effort to put more value added into the Australian economy. By contrast, much of the European and American direct investments in Australia with which Kreinin compares Japanese practices were made a decade or more (in some instances six or seven decades) ago. While originally substitutes for exports, many of these investments are in product lines where the home country of the firm making the investment has long since lost much of its comparative advantage. It is hardly surprising that, unlike the Australian subsidiaries of Japanese firms, the Australian subsidiaries of European and American firms should have to source broadly in order to retain their local market share.

Kreinin's findings for Australia are entirely consistent with the traditional histories of multinational corporations and overseas direct investment and do not suggest truly distinctive Japanese practices.[8] The early history of Ford and General Motors, among other American enterprises in Japan, is hardly different from the Japanese experience. More generally, this issue comes up so often in the experience of so many firms and host countries that it is hardly surprising that there are hundreds of local content laws on national statute books throughout the world.

Econometric Studies on Japanese Trade Volume and Trade Structure

If *keiretsu* ties are weaker and Japanese firm procurement behavior appear to be far less discriminatory than is generally supposed, it may not be so surprising to find that there are now quite a few econometric studies (including a number by me) that show, after allowance is made for Japan's distinctive national endowments, particularly its lack of natural resources, that there is relatively little that is really distinctive about Japan's trade structure. While it is certainly true that there are studies (including one in 1987 by Lawrence himself) that come up with contrary findings, it is not entirely fair to argue that since some econometric issues can be raised about all of these studies, they

---

8. Mira Wilkins, *The Maturing of Multinational Enterprise: American Business Abroad, 1914–1970* (Cambridge, Mass.: Harvard University Press, 1975).

should all be discounted. Some econometric issues are more important than others. The Srinivasan and Hamada survey, which Lawrence cites, certainly does not view all these studies as equally flawed. After noting that "except for the study by Leamer [which like my study is dubious about the extent of Japanese underimporting] and arguably by Saxonhouse, the others are subject to a number of estimation biases," They conclude that "the empirical support in favor or against the hypothesis that Japanese are underimporting is subject to criticisms which are most damaging particularly to studies in favor of the hypothesis."[9]

Lawrence may find this conclusion surprising, but only because he may be misinterpreting the Srinivasan and Hamada comments on my work. While Srinivasan and Hamada are uneasy about my cavalierly assuming away the consequences of leaving out, because of the unavailability of data, those factor endowments that would allow my Heckscher-Ohlin specification to have the same number of goods as factors (Leamer also assumes away this problem), they reserve most of their attention to my use of forecast intervals. It is clear I should be using tolerance intervals rather than forecast intervals when conducting my tests on the distinctiveness of Japanese trade behavior. Given my findings, however, my failure to use tolerance intervals should make no difference at all. Except for the case when the sample size is infinite, for any given probability, the forecast interval will always be smaller than the tolerance interval.[10] Since I find Japan to fall within the forecast interval, it will also fall within the tolerance interval. In neither case will Japan be the outlier.

Price Differentials

While weak *keiretsu* ties make studies that find little evidence of Japanese underimporting all the more plausible, Lawrence is entirely correct to argue that if there are persistent price differentials between Japan and other countries for comparable products the credibility of such studies is weakened. It has long been appreciated that cross-national price differentials are a good way to measure the impact of nontariff barriers.[11] Unhappily, the absence of strictly comparable cross-national price data has made it difficult to use this approach.

For example, during the past year, much has been made of the so-called "Forty-Seventh Street Photo phenomenon," which claims that Japanese products, in general, and cameras, in particular, are sold abroad at lower prices than at home.[12] Many Japanese government officials have vehemently rejected

9. T. N. Srinivasan and Koichi Hamada, "The U.S.-Japan Trade Problem" (Yale University, mimeograph), pp. 3, 36.

10. Carl Christ, *Econometric Models and Methods* (New York: Wiley), pp. 549–65.

11. Alan V. Deardorff and Robert N. Stern, "Methods of Measurement of Non-Tariff Barriers," University of Michigan Institute of Public Policy Studies Discussion Paper no. 203 (June 1984); Gary R. Saxonhouse, "What's Wrong with Japanese Trade Structure?" *Pacific Economic Papers* (July 1986):1–36.

12. James M. Fallows, "Containing Japan," *Atlantic Monthly* (May 1989).

this claim, arguing that the products being priced cross-nationally are simply not comparable. For example, they argue that Forty-Seventh Street Photo charges low prices only because it is selling older models of cameras no longer desired by the Japanese consumer. This controversy bubbled over in the U.S.-Japan Structural Impediments Initiative discussions in the fall of 1989. As an outcome of this controversy, the U.S. Department of Commerce and Japan's Ministry of International Trade and Industry (MITI) agreed to undertake a detailed joint price survey that would take special pains to price comparable products in the United States and Japan.

The survey actually conducted appears to have been scrupulous in its efforts to obtain comparable retail price data. Considerable effort has been extended to insure that comparable products are being priced in comparable retail locations. Price observations have been segregated according to whether they have been taken in speciality shops, discount houses, or department stores. Unfortunately, the products included in this survey are in no sense a random sample of the universe of comparable products available in the U.S. and Japanese markets. Rather they are the outcome of weeks of acrimonious negotiation between the Department of Commerce and MITI. Indeed, the final list could not be agreed upon until the day before the survey started.

The actual survey results contain some surprises. While there are certainly many instances of Japanese goods having lower prices in the United States than in Japan, the Forty-Seventh Street Photo phenomenon is not pervasive even at Forty-Seventh Street Photo. Of 14 Japanese-produced cameras and video-camera-related products, six are cheaper in the United States. Overall, 26 of 57 Japanese products have been found to be cheaper in the United States than in Japan. By striking contrast, only four of 35 U.S. products and only two of 21 European products are cheaper in Japan than in the United States.[13]

Simply counting up observations of what, in any event, is not a randomly drawn sample may yield a misleading impression. William R. Cline of the Institute for International Economics has analyzed the determinants of the U.S. and Japanese price differences found in this sample.[14] Cline rejects the Forty-Seventh Street Photo phenomenon and finds that there is no statistically significant difference between U.S. and Japanese retail prices for goods produced in Japan. By contrast, the hypothesis that there are no statistically significant differences between U.S. and Japanese retail prices for goods produced in the United States and Europe cannot be accepted.

Cline's results present a problem for those who would argue that the Japanese market for manufactured products is highly protected. If the Japanese market is highly protected, both Japanese and foreign products should have much higher prices in Japan than abroad. That only foreign products have high

---

13. U.S. Department of Commerce and Japan Ministry of International Trade and Industry, *Joint Survey on United States and Japanese Retail Prices* (Washington, D.C., November 1989).

14. William R. Cline, "Japan's Trade Policies" (paper delivered to Ministry of International Trade and Industry Research Institute, Tokyo, May 1990).

prices in Japan suggests a different interpretation. The high prices for U.S. and European products in Japan may reflect the marketing strategies of oligopolistic firms. As Cline notes, U.S. and European firms appear to have concluded that they can maximize profits in the Japanese market through low-volume, high-price sales.

It is not at all surprising that, in the absence of trade barriers, U.S. and European firms can successfully maintain price differentials in excess of transport costs. For example, if it is assumed that demand for many of these products is relatively price inelastic, and if it is further assumed that there are fixed costs (perhaps because of economies of scale in transportation) in the arbitrage of the kinds of differentiated final products examined in the Department of Commerce/MITI price survey, such price differentials are not at all implausible.

The absence of statistically significantly different prices in U.S. and Japanese markets for Japanese products is largely consistent with Lawrence's finding that both distribution margins and the cost of distribution as a proportion of final goods prices are more or less the same in both Japan and the United States. It may not be consistent, however, with Lawrence's findings on the very high rates of return for capital invested and the very high share in value added of profit for Japanese manufacturing. The relatively high profit rates compared to other major industrialized countries, which Lawrence cites, however, may be a statistical mirage. Relative to all other major industrialized countries, save possibly Italy, Japan's manufacturing sector includes disproportionate numbers of self-employed. The profit numbers Lawrence cites include self-employment income as part of operating surplus and therefore overstates the Japanese (and the Italian) rates of return. Japanese profit rates are likely to be high relative to most other countries not because Japanese market power allegedly keeps prices high and goods out, but because the rates include a substantial chunk of labor income.

The Japanese Adjustment Mechanism and the Structural Impediments Initiative

While I may disagree with some of the details of Lawrence's analysis, I certainly share his conclusion that there is little in the character of the Japanese market for manufactured goods that prevents marginal responses to price and cost incentives. The dramatic increase in the total volume of manufactured goods entering Japan during the past four years, largely in response to exchange rate changes, persuades Lawrence that there is little necessity for an entirely new approach to trade relations with Japan. Lawrence intends his conclusion as a rejection of the "managed trade" approach advocated by many critics of Japan's economic practices. Though he does not develop the theme, his conclusions are also an interesting commentary on the U.S.-Japan Structural Impediments Initiative (SII) discussions.

The SII talks link current account adjustment with access to the Japanese market.[15] This linkage reflects long-standing thinking in the OECD and in some quarters of the U.S. Treasury (the U.S. government agency that took the initiative in the spring of 1989 in proposing the SII talks) that structural factors in many of the major industrialized economies (but particularly Japan) prevent the exchange rate mechanism from playing its traditional role in the international adjustment process. The SII is very useful in reassuring both the American and Japanese electorate about the terms of foreign access to the Japanese market. Lawrence's work reminds us, however, that the empirical underpinnings of the conventional OECD and Treasury analysis remain, at best, an open issue.

Comment   Marcus Noland

Robert Lawrence has written a very good paper. Its strength lies in going beyond the now-sterile exercise of running regressions on cross-national data to determine if Japan imports enough, to analyzing the institutions and incentives that condition Japanese importing behavior.

The argument of the beginning of the paper questioning the links between goals and measures is quite useful in delineating these issues. The most important part of the paper is its exploration of the role of intrafirm trade and, more specifically, the trading houses. Japan's uniqueness lies in the importance of domestic firms in importation, and given the degree of concentration in the Japanese economy (and the trading sector in particular), there is the obvious potential for the exercise of market power by firms or the facilitation of administrative guidance by the government. Thus the existing institutional framework provides both the incentives and the mechanisms for impeding the penetration of directly competing imports.

Such behavior has in fact been described by employees of major trading companies and is consistent with the observation that Japan engages in little intra-industry trade. A note of caution may be warranted though. Lawrence's interpretation of intrafirm trade may or may not be consistent with evidence on Japan's trade with the NICs presented in the Park and Park paper (in this volume). Moreover, as Peter Petri observes in his paper (in this volume), European manufactured exports to Japan have grown faster than those of the United States, though one would expect them to encounter similar types of market impediments. So there are still some unanswered questions here. Some attempts to estimate the rent transfers implied by the oligosonistic market structures would be desirable. These firms are not for the most part mon-

15. Interim Report and Assessment of the U.S.-Japan Working Group on the Structural Impediments Initiative (Washington, D.C., 5 April 1990).

Marcus Noland is an assistant professor of economics at the University of Southern California.

opsonists, and what is needed are some very micro-oriented investigations into the sort of noncompetitive behavior Lawrence has intimated.

A second implication of Lawrence's analysis is that manufactured products will find their way into Japan if they are inputs for goods produced by the major firms. Again, this would be consistent with recent increases in manufactured imports from the NICs, which have grown faster manufactured imports overall, although Park and Park appear to suggest that intrafirm trade has not been so important. One theme that Lawrence does not develop is the extent to which this restructuring has been actively supported by government policy, especially foreign aid policy. This is especially important given the rapid growth in Japan's develop assistance programs, which are concentrated on surrounding Asian countries.

To a great extent, current Japanese thinking on development assistance is driven by visions of restructuring and a furthering of the vertical division of labor. Historically, one of the main priorities of economic policy has been the need to assure access to supplies of imported raw materials, much of which have come from surrounding Asian countries. In the 1960s and 1970s development assistance and the trading companies both played roles in this policy. Now, under the high yen, the Japan-as-processing-country analysis has been pushed one step further to Japan-as-high-value-added processor, which means that Japan must secure access to low-cost intermediate inputs. Policy still supports Japan's access to the required inputs, except now these are increasingly manufactures. Two examples may be made that illustrate the point.

The first is a 1988 study by the Economic Planning Agency. It explicitly calls for the coordination, by Tokyo, of the industrial policies of the Asian countries by something called "the Asian brain." (If the geography is any guide, Korea would be the right hand. You can fill in the rest of the body parts yourselves.) The "Asian brain" would coordinate industrial investment and the supporting industrial policies throughout the region, much as MITI did in the Japanese economy of the 1950s and 1960s.

Farfetched as this sounds, this kind of thinking does inform Japanese development assistance. An example is JAIDO (the Japan International Development Corporation), a recently formed organization to promote public- and private-sector joint development projects. To support Japanese strategic interests, JAIDO has made the Philippines the focus of its efforts to date. There, JAIDO is supporting four projects: (1) the development of a copper refining industry (this is the old-style secure-access-to-raw-materials strategy); (2) the development of an industrial park (this is the new-style facilitate-Japanese-FDI-and-secure-access to-low-cost manufactured-inputs strategy); (3) a project to produce and export papayas to Japan (this one is quite interesting since it runs directly counter to agricultural protectionism. When I asked a JAIDO official about this he admitted that, yes, as yet they had been unable to export any of the papayas because of the quarantine, but they were still trying). The fourth project is my favorite: to teach Filipino computer software engineers

Japanese, so that they can write Japanese language computer software, and thus help ease the software shortage in Japan.

The point of this is that the Japanese market may be becoming more open to some manufactured imports, while remaining inhospitable to others. To use the distance metaphor, if you are producing inputs for major producers, Japan may be close, but if you are producing competing products (or even worse, products that the government has targeted for development) Japan may be very far away.

Finally, though I largely agree with Lawrence the economist, I am much less comfortable with Lawrence the political analyst or trade negotiation strategist. Lawrence expresses surprise that increasing numbers of Americans are exasperated with the apparent lack of substantive progress in America's long-running trade negotiations with Japan. I cannot help but believe that this is a tad disingenuous (especially from someone who made *Newsweek's* top 10 Japan-bashers list, a distinction that no other participant in the conference that produced this volume can claim).

Lawrence takes the position that all we need to do is increase the number of sectors under negotiation from four to 40, then wait for the imports to start rolling in. To support his contention, Lawrence cites the examples of cigarettes, and the four original MOSS-talk sectors, as success stories. By his own admission, it took nearly 10 years of pressure to get liberalization of the cigarette market, longer than it took to negotiate SALT I, SALT II, or the INF treaties with the Soviets. As for the MOSS talks, conducted at the undersecretary level, there has been some progress, but at the cost of tremendous expenditures of human and material resources, as made clear by Amelia Porges (in this volume). Moreover, the U.S. Trade Representative's 1989 report on the foreign trade barrier includes many of the sectors previously negotiated—including all four of the MOSS categories. In fact, the three Japanese practices under Super 301 investigation are all issues left unresolved by the MOSS talks.

The question is, have the narrow gains been worth the expenditures of real resources and political capital necessary to bring sufficient pressure to bear on Japan to enter into and abide by market opening agreements? In the case of the United States, where the government is obligated under U.S. trade law to investigate producer-initiated complaints, to ask the question is to answer it: the U.S. government will be under considerable pressure to pursue further market-opening initiatives for the foreseeable future. The question then is, is a fundamentally new strategy needed? Lawrence says no, just do more of the same stuff.

If one believes Lawrence's analysis (which I generally do) that an important part of market access problems stem from noncompetitive markets, not Japanese government policy per se, there is a real policy problem. Probably the only thing that could really address the situation is a comprehensive, proactive policy undertaken across a number of the ministries of the Japanese government. Unfortunately, I suspect that neither Lawrence nor I can offer much advice on how to go about encouraging this. Perhaps the Structural Impediments Initiative (SII) will encourage it; perhaps exchange-rate appreciation will loosen up the system, as some of Lawrence's results suggest. In the meantime, my prognosis is for increasing prominence of "monitored trade"—careful surveillance of practices and outcomes combined with explicit and credible threats of retaliation, as in the cases of cellular telephones and the Schumer amendment on the government bond market. As Masahiro Okuno-Fujiwara (in this volume) indicates, industrial policy in Japan is an insider's game—threats of retaliation, complete with preannounced "hit lists" may be useful in mobilizing domestic insider support in the target country (Japan) to support liberalization in the face of possible loss of exports markets in the United States.

But as Koichi Hamada has pointed out, there is a fine line between beating someone over the head with a stick to encourage liberalization, and beating them over the head with an aluminum baseball bat and provoking a trade war. The only thing I can say with much certainty is that the future looks good for trade lobbyists who will probably earn rates of return higher than those who participated in this U.S.-Japan trade conference.

2 Market Structure, Comparative Advantage, and Japanese Trade under the Strong Yen

Peter A. Petri

2.1 Introduction

Between February 1985 and December 1988 the yen appreciated 33 percent in real and 57 percent in nominal terms against a trade-weighted currency basket, and 93 percent against the U.S. dollar. This round of appreciation—called *endaka,* the rampaging yen—was roughly twice as large as that in 1970–73, when the yen first emerged as a major international currency, and also larger than that in 1975–78, when the yen recovered from the first oil crisis. Visible signs of the economic impact of this change abound in Tokyo's streets, shops, and factories—from BMWs and Benetton clothes to Samsung TVs and Taiwanese electronic components. Real Japanese exports are flat, and Japanese firms are aggressively shifting manufacturing operations nearer to markets and to countries with lower production costs.

Recent popular discussions of these developments—for example, most major business journals have recently featured articles on the internationalization of the Japanese economy—have focused on three theses regarding the impact of *endaka* on Japanese trade. The first is that Japan has begun to undergo structural changes that will eventually make it as open to imports as are other advanced economies. *Fortune,* for example, reported that the "retailing revolution the West has been waiting for is here. . . . That's good news for American goods" (as quoted in Rapoport 1989). In a similar, if less sensational,

Peter A. Petri is professor of economics and Director of the Lemberg Program in International Economics and Finance at Brandeis University.

The author wishes to thank Robert Corker (IMF), Sam Lair (World Bank), Masahiko Shimizu (Keio University), Robert Stern (University of Michigan), Andy Symwick (MIT), and Nobuhiro Torii (Brandeis University) for data; without their help this paper would have contained at best a fraction of the evidence it now presents. The author is also grateful to Anne Carter, Daniel Citrin, Dennis Encarnation, Marcus Noland, Robert Stern, and participants in the Japan Economic Seminar for valuable comments on an earlier draft.

vein the Ministry of International Trade and Industry's new *White Paper on International Trade* (MITI 1989) also argued that Japanese import patterns have shifted and presented evidence that imports in recent years have exceeded expectations based on pre-1985 experience.

A second thesis receiving considerable attention is that currency realignments and other recent changes have accelerated the integration of East and Southeast Asian economies, including especially Japan, South Korea, Taiwan, and some ASEAN countries. *The Economist* speaks of "a swirl of forces—not all emanating from Japan—that is re-shaping East and South-East Asia by bringing their economies closer together" (Rapoport 1989, p. 159). Dornbusch (1988) noted that the "recent strength of the yen, relative to the dollar, has surely helped develop this new division of labor. But it is certain that, once established, it will now develop much further." These changes could be extremely significant, since an integrated "yen bloc," combining large markets, advanced technology, and low-cost labor and raw materials, would be a formidable competitor in the world economy (Maidment 1989).

A third thesis, however, is challenging the view that Japan has become more open with *endaka*. It emphasizes the relatively slow adjustment of the Japanese trade surplus in general and of the Japanese bilateral trade surplus with the United States in particular, notwithstanding sharp improvements in U.S. price competitiveness. The proponents of this view have argued that *endaka* shows that exchange rate adjustments, no matter how large, cannot satisfactorily open Japan. In their view, the "best" Japanese markets continue to be closed by invisible structural impediments such as the domestic bias of the Japanese distribution system and the stable, inward-looking pattern of Japanese business-group relationships.[1]

These theses have been buttressed by bits of economic data, but have not been, for the most part, subject to rigorous analysis. This paper examines the recent evolution of Japanese trade under three headings: aggregate trade, partner composition, and product structure. Under the first two headings, the paper provides a detailed empirical review of ongoing developments. Under the last heading, it presents a model with new evidence on the effects of Japanese market structure on the pattern of Japanese trade. The model shows that variables reflecting product distribution, market concentration, and other potential market barriers, in combination with conventional determinants of comparative advantage, play important roles in explaining the structure of Japanese imports.

2.2 Aggregate Trade

At first glance, aggregate measures of Japanese trade paint a pessimistic picture of the effectiveness of exchange rate changes. The dollar value of Jap-

---

1. These arguments are stressed, for example, by the Advisory Committee for Trade Policy and Negotiations (1989).

anese exports increased 49 percent between 1985 and 1988, from $174 to $260 billion, while the value of imports increased only 40 percent, from $118 to $165 billion. As a result, Japan's overall trade surplus nearly doubled, from $56 to $95 billion, and its bilateral surplus with the United States increased from $50 to $55 billion. To what extent, if at all, did appreciation affect aggregate trade? Was the effect of exchange rate changes consistent with historical experience, or is there evidence of structural change that either retarded or accelerated trade adjustment?

Figures 2.1–2.3 display the evolution of Japanese trade since 1980. Figure 2.1 shows movements in the effective exchange rate of the yen. Figure 2.2 shows movements in the dollar value of Japanese trade. Dollar exports entered a period of sustained growth in 1983, while dollar imports were relatively flat until 1987 when imports also began to grow rapidly. This figure shows modest and delayed response in the dollar value of Japanese trade to the appreciation of the yen since 1985—export value growth was essentially unchanged, while the break in import value growth appeared only six quarters after the yen began to appreciate. Figure 2.3 shows movements in trade volumes, which reacted more rapidly. Export volume growth essentially stopped with the break in the yen and import volume growth accelerated by early 1986. One important difference between the value and volume data is that the collapse in oil prices in 1986 effectively lowered the value of imports by roughly 20 percent.

Corker (1989) has recently simulated Japanese trade in the absence of yen appreciation. He found that by 1987 Japanese real exports would have been 19 percent higher, and real imports 10 percent lower, than actually observed, and the real trade balance would have been 6 percent instead of 4 percent of Japanese GNP. In effect, yen appreciation "corrected" the Japanese surplus by approximately 2 percent of GNP. Although the dollar surplus would have been only slightly higher without appreciation than it now is (due to the much higher value of the dollar in the absence of yen appreciation), the real imbalances left to be corrected by subsequent adjustments would have been much greater.

While the effect of yen appreciation was large, it was so because the appreciation itself was large; Corker's estimated price elasticities are low (see table 2.1). The long-run relative price elasticity of exports is -1 (explaining the smooth growth of exports valued in dollars in fig. 2.2), while the long-run relative price elasticity of imports is only -0.55. Furthermore, Corker found little evidence of change in these elasticities; his one export and four import equations all passed statistical tests for coefficient stability across pre- and post-1985 data. Corker's post-1985 forecasts did somewhat underpredict both exports and imports, but in neither case were the errors large relative to estimating error.

Corker's results suggest that, if there was structural change, it affected Japanese exports and imports in opposite ways—that is, the adjustment of exports was smaller, and that of imports larger, than historical experience would

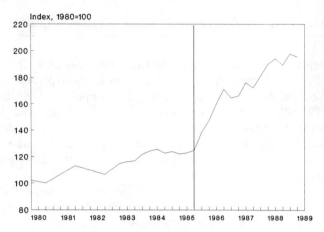

Fig. 2.1   Effective yen exchange rate (IMF Multilateral Model)

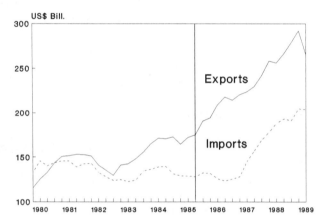

Fig. 2.2   Export and import values ($ U.S.)

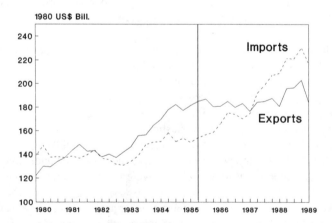

Fig. 2.3   Real exports and imports

Table 2.1   Long-Run Trade Elasticities

Trade Category	Relative Prices	Demand	Production
Exports	− 1.09	2.04	
Imports	− .55	.88	.89
Manufactures	− .91	1.84	.99
Raw Materials	− .27		1.24
Minerals	− .11		1.04
Food and feed	− .55	.45	

Source: Corker (1989).

have suggested. On the export side, there has been much interest in the hypothesis that the pass-through coefficient has declined, or that Japanese export prices have increased less since 1985 than expected given the size of yen appreciation. Several researchers (Baldwin 1988; Marston 1989; Ohno 1988) have found evidence of low pass through, especially with respect to manufactured exports to the United States, but others (Hooper and Mann 1989) have argued that the pass-through relationships have been stable given a proper choice of the input price index. These issues are also addressed by Marston's contribution to this volume.

Has Japanese import behavior changed? One structural reason that suggests such change is the strengthening of distribution channels that aggressively feature imported merchandise (see sec. 2.3 for further details). This transformation in the distribution system is more likely to be evident in recent data than in data from the quarters directly following the break in the yen. In fact, early postappreciation data on Japanese imports suggested less adjustment than implied by historical import relationships (Loopesko and Johnson 1987).[2] Corker's historical equations also suggested that there was too little actual import growth in 1986, but then shifted to increasingly *under*predicting actual imports by late 1987, at the end of Corker's dataset (see fig. 2 in Corker 1989).

We have reestimated equations for Japanese manufactures imports using the several additional data points that have recently become available. The equations used are similar to those estimated by Corker and others.[3] However, the Chow (1960) test now shows considerable evidence *against* stability across the pre- and postappreciation periods (see table 2.2), and experiments with alternative splits indicate that the break occurred in the third or fourth quarter

2. One possible hypothesis cited was that the distribution system absorbed some of the decline in yen import prices in higher profit margins.
3. As in Corker (1989), I found that a very simple specification with current activity and one-quarter price lags performs extremely well and dominates more complex specifications with polynomial lag terms. It should be noted, however, that Noland (1988) has found evidence for longer lags. Although changes in the lag specification do not necessarily affect the size of estimated elasticities and longer-run behavior, they can affect prediction in the immediate neighborhood of a change in the direction of price movements, such as occurred in 1985.

Table 2.2   **Estimated Equations for Real Imports of Manufactures**

	(1) 1975:2 −1989:2	(2) 1975:2 −1985:2	(3) Variable × Dummy	(4) = (2) + (3) 1985:3 −1989:2
Coefficients:				
Constant	−1.310**	−2.109**	−.817	−2.926
	(−4.500)	(−5.904)	(−1.011)	
Lagged imports	.685**	.507**	−.003	.504
	(12.091)	(6.476)	(−.408)	
Industrial production	.581**	.923**	.161	1.085
	(5.196)	(6.2767)	(.959)	
Change in industrial production	1.345**	.482	1.366*	1.848
	(4.649)	(1.399)	(2.407)	
Relative price lagged 1 quarter	−.229**	−.189**	−.229*	−.418
	(−5.705)	(−3.546)	(−2.485)	
Long-run properties:				
Output elasticity	1.846	1.873		2.186
Price elasticity	−.729	−.383		−.843
Statistics:				
Observations	57	57		
R^2	.995	.996		
Adjusted R^2	.995	.996		
F statistic	2568.7	1452.4		
Durbin's H	−.99	−.28		
Durbin-Watson	2.24	2.06		
Standard error	.0306	.0272		
Squared errors	.0488	.0347		
Chow F, eq. (1) vs. eq. (2)		3.75		
5% Significance, $F(5,47)$		2.42		

Note: OLS with all variables in logs. Dependent variable is import volume. Relative price is ratio of manufacturing import price index to domestic GNP deflator. *T*-ratios in parentheses. Col. 3 shows results for variables multiplied by a dummy which is set equal to 1 in the second subperiod.
*$P = .05$.
**$P = .01$.

of 1985. Forecasts based on the preappreciation equation at first overpredict and then substantially underpredict imports starting in 1987 (see fig. 2.4).

The differences between pre- and post-1985 equations are captured in "coefficient change" variables, constructed by multiplying each independent variable with a dummy set to one in the third quarter of 1985 and thereafter (table 2.2, col. 2–4). Column 2 shows the coefficients appropriate to the period prior to appreciation, column 3 presents changes between the periods, and column 4 calculates coefficients appropriate in the postappreciation period. Evidently, the sensitivity of imports increased significantly after 1985 with respect to changes in both industrial production and the relative price of imported goods.[4]

4. The price variable used to represent Japanese domestic costs in these equations was the GDP deflator. Since the import price/GDP deflator ratio is somewhat more sensitive to exchange rate

Index, 1980=100

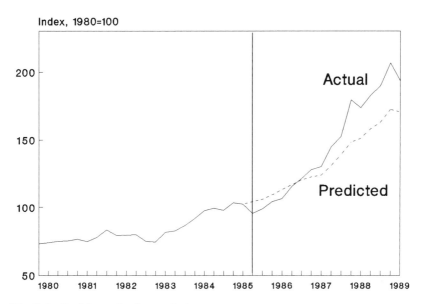

Fig. 2.4   **Real imports of manufactures**

2.3   The Partner Composition of Trade

There has been a dramatic expansion in Japanese trade with East Asian newly industrialized countries (NICs) and developed countries other than the United States. These two groups of countries together accounted for a smaller share of Japanese exports than the United States in 1985,[5] but each accounted for a larger share of the increase in exports between 1985 and 1988 than did the United States (see fig. 2.5). In Japanese imports (see fig. 2.6), the combined share of the East Asian NICs and other industrial countries in the increase between 1985 and 1988 was nearly three times as large as that of the United States.

The rapidity of change is illustrated in figures 2.7 and 2.8. Figure 2.7 shows that Japanese exports began to shift from U.S. markets to other markets soon after 1985, when global currency realignments resulted in a much larger appreciation against the United States than against other industrial countries. Although the yen initially appreciated sharply also against the East Asian

---

movements than the import price/wholesale price ratio (the denominator in the latter includes a much larger share of tradables), the estimated price elasticities are smaller than those obtained by using the wholesale price index.

5. Group definitions are as follows. "Other industrial countries" includes all industrial countries (see World Bank 1987) except the United States; "East Asian NICs" includes Hong Kong, (South) Korea, Singapore, and Taiwan; "East Asian LDCs" includes China, Indonesia, Malaysia, the Philippines, and Thailand; and "other developing countries" includes all other countries, including oil exporters.

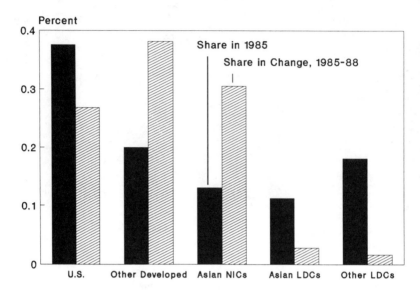

Fig. 2.5   Shares in Japanese exports

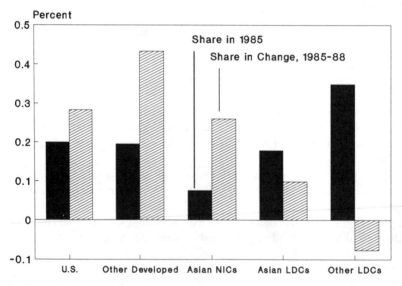

Fig. 2.6   Shares in Japanese imports

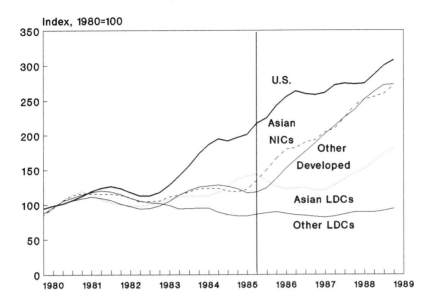

Fig. 2.7   Export values by partner ($ U.S.)

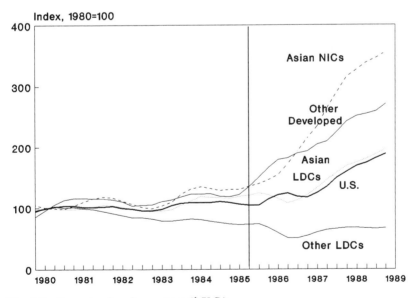

Fig. 2.8   Import values by partner ($ U.S.)

NICs, Japanese exports to these countries nevertheless expanded. A key reason for this was that *endaka* enabled the East Asian NICs to capture markets in the United States and elsewhere in products that required Japanese components and capital goods.[6]

Figure 2.8 shows sharp increases in Japanese imports from the NICs and other developed countries. The remarkable fact behind these statistics is that Japanese consumers have responded very positively to the availability of attractively priced imports. Contrary to conventional wisdom, this response has not been limited to high-quality, luxury goods from Europe, but has included inexpensive clothing, appliances, and consumer electronics from East Asia. To take advantage of these trends, a merchandising boom has developed, complete with the institution of the *bahgen say-ru*. Discount chains such Jusco, Daiei, and I World, feature aggressively priced, imported goods, and have been growing twice as fast as mainline department stores.[7]

These developments are clearly reflected in the changing patterns of Japanese manufactures trade with the NICs and other developed countries (table 2.3). Consumer goods are prominent among the most rapidly expanding manufactures imports, including wearing apparel and consumer electronics from the NICs and automobiles from other developed countries. Exports are dominated by electronic components and machinery to the NICs, and automobiles, consumer electronics, and machinery to other developed countries.

Is this evidence of a "yen bloc" and a new phase in East Asian economic integration? The answer to this question is far from self-evident. Trade links between Japan and its East Asian neighbors have been historically strong, and, given East Asia's high growth relative to the rest of the world, the region's importance to Japan (and every other country) has increased. From the perspective of the East Asian partners, however, the importance of Japanese linkages has declined relative to extraregional trade, especially during the period of the strong dollar and U.S. economic recovery in the mid-1980s. Recent increases in East Asian–Japanese trade have partially retraced this decline (see table 2.4), but only for Malaysia was the share of trade with Japan actually higher in 1988 than in 1975. Thus, the period since 1985 may be alternatively viewed as retracing or slowing the secular *dis*integration of the East Asian economy, which, in turn, is driven by growing worldwide economic integration.

The growth of Japan's trade with the East Asian NICs has recently slowed: exports plus imports grew at a 32 percent annual rate between the second quarter of 1985 and the first quarter of 1988 but only at a 13 percent rate since, as compared to 14 and 13 percent for Japan's overall trade over the two peri-

---

6. The import content of Korean exports, for example, is 43 percent.

7. See, e.g., articles by Meyer, Hoshiai, and Takayama (1987), Darlin (1988), and Rapoport (1989).

Table 2.3   **Shares of Categories in Increase of Trade, 1985–88**

Japanese Imports	%	Japanese Exports	%
TRADE WITH EAST ASIAN NICS:			
Wearing apparel	22.8	Radio, TV, components	24.2
Radio, TV, components	10.5	Basic iron & steel	8.2
Basic iron & steel	9.6	General industrial machinery	8.1
Miscellaneous products	6.0	Special industrial machinery	6.4
Plastic products	3.9	Electrical industrial machinery	6.1
Other metal products	3.2	Motor vehicles	6.0
Office machinery	3.1	Basic industrial chemicals	5.8
Leather footwear	2.9	Office machinery	4.8
Yarn and fabric	2.9	Synthetic resin	3.9
Electrical industrial machinery	2.8	Electronics	3.6
Top 10 categories	67.7	Top 10 categories	77.2
TRADE WITH OTHER DEVELOPING COUNTRIES:			
Motor vehicles	16.0	Motor vehicles	29.1
Basic industrial chemicals	12.6	Radio, TV, components	19.7
Drugs and medicines	6.6	Office machinery	12.5
Pulp	5.5	General industrial machinery	5.0
Lumber and plywood	5.4	Photographic equipment	4.2
Special industrial machinery	5.1	Special industrial machinery	4.2
Yarn and fabric	5.0	Basic industrial chemicals	2.7
Miscellaneous products	4.2	Electrical industrial machinery	2.6
Wearing apparel	3.8	Electronics	2.3
Scientific instruments	3.7	Scientific instruments	2.2
Top 10 categories	67.8	Top 10 categories	84.5

ods. It is possible that some of the rapid increase in East Asian trade during the early months of *endaka* was related to the delayed adjustment of the region's currencies to yen appreciation. Alternatively, the slowdown in recent trade may reflect supply problems in the NICs and thus may be temporary.

Ultimately, however, the outlook for strong economic linkages between Japan and other East Asian economies has to be bright. Japanese demand for foreign consumer goods is coming of age just as East Asian economies are assuming leading positions in the supply of high-quality consumer goods. There is also evidence of increasing direct integration in production. According to Takeuchi's (1989b) data, Japanese direct investment in Asian manufacturing has increased from $642 million per annum in 1980–84 to $1.7 billion in 1987 and $2.4 billion in 1988. More than half of this investment now goes into the machinery industries, where firms often export back into Japan; Asian subsidiaries of Japanese firms exported 16.7 percent of their output to Japan in 1987 as compared to 9.8 percent in 1980. These magnitudes, although not yet large relative to overall Japanese trade, do foreshadow the continued expansion of regional integration and trade.

Table 2.4   **Japanese Trade with East Asia**

	As % of Country's Exports, Imports			As % of Japan's Imports, Exports		
	1975	1985	1988	1975	1985	1988
East Asian NICs:						
Exports to Japan	16.0	12.0	15.3	4.6	7.6	13.3
Imports from Japan	32.6	26.6	31.4	13.0	13.1	18.9
Hong Kong						
Exports to Japan	4.1	2.6	3.3	.4	.6	1.1
Imports from Japan	20.4	22.1	18.3	2.5	3.7	4.4
Korea						
Exports to Japan	25.7	13.7	19.5	2.3	3.2	6.3
Imports from Japan	30.9	23.0	29.8	4.0	4.0	5.8
Singapore						
Exports to Japan	7.4	7.0	5.9	2.3	3.2	6.3
Imports from Japan	18.7	14.8	18.9	4.0	4.0	5.8
Taiwan						
Exports to Japan				1.2	2.6	4.6
Imports from Japan				3.7	3.1	5.5
East Asian LDCs:						
Exports to Japan	32.9	32.0	27.9	13.0	17.9	15.5
Imports from Japan	28.6	25.0	19.8	11.9	11.3	8.5
China						
Exports to Japan	19.9	23.9	20.7	2.6	5.0	5.3
Imports from Japan	28.5	29.6	17.2	4.1	7.1	3.6
Philippines						
Exports to Japan	48.8	27.2	29.1	1.9	1.0	1.1
Imports from Japan	27.3	17.3	20.0	1.8	.5	.7
Thailand						
Exports to Japan	32.8	14.5	31.1	1.3	.8	1.5
Imports from Japan	29.2	22.2	26.4	1.7	1.2	1.9
Malaysia						
Exports to Japan	19.8	28.1	22.5	1.2	3.3	2.5
Imports from Japan	15.9	17.8	18.5	1.0	1.2	1.2
Indonesia						
Exports to Japan	48.3	54.8	49.3	5.9	7.8	5.1
Imports from Japan	38.8	21.4	22.6	3.3	1.2	1.2

2.4   The Product Structure of Trade

2.4.1   Key Trends

In terms of the broadest categories, Japan's imports of manufactures have increased substantially relative to raw materials and now account for nearly one-half of total imports (fig. 2.9). This change is partly due to declining raw materials relative to prices, but, as demonstrated earlier, manufactures have also responded much more vigorously to income growth and appreciation than

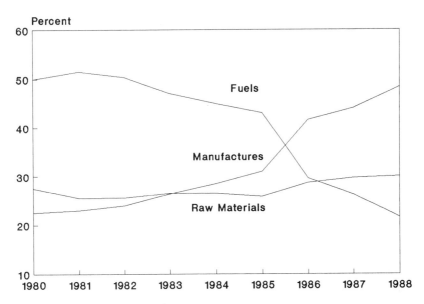

Fig. 2.9   Shares in Japanese imports

other imports. More important, however, the structure of trade in manufactures is also changing rapidly.

Table 2.5 presents trade data for 49 manufacturing sectors grouped into five categories according to their relative requirements for four inputs, raw materials (including energy), labor, capital, and technology. To determine the assignment of a particular sector, I computed its standardized deviation from the manufacturing average in each of the four input dimensions, and then placed it into, say, the labor-intensive category if its deviation was larger in this dimension than in others. Sectors near overall averages in all four dimensions were classified as "mixed." Sectoral assignments are presented in the appendix.

The lead story of table 2.5 is Japan's increasing specialization in technology-intensive products. On the export side, the share of raw-material-intensive, labor-intensive, and capital-intensive exports declined from 44 percent of all manufactures exports in 1970 to just 19 percent in 1988. The share of mixed exports grew between 1970 and 1980 but has been stagnant since. Only technology-intensive exports have shown steady gains in shares. Opposite trends are evident on the import side. Here the shares of labor-intensive, capital-intensive, and mixed imports increased from 36 to 50 percent, while raw-material-intensive imports fluctuated (mostly reflecting relative valuation effects) and the share of technology-intensive imports sharply declined.

A second important feature of Japanese trade patterns is that competitively strong Japanese industries tend to export and not import—intra-industry trade

Table 2.5   **Changing Composition of Manufacturing Trade**

To or From	Japanese Exports				Japanese Imports			
	1970	1980	1985	1988	1970	1980	1985	1988
World:								
Raw-material intensive	6.4	5.4	4.3	4.8	15.9	20.3	21.2	17.2
Labor intensive	17.3	9.0	7.3	6.4	23.7	28.8	24.8	29.0
Capital intensive	20.3	16.5	10.6	8.1	6.7	5.3	6.7	8.9
Technology intensive	40.7	42.3	49.7	53.3	47.8	37.8	40.1	34.3
Mixed	15.2	26.7	28.1	27.5	5.8	7.7	7.2	10.5
United States:								
Raw-material intensive	4.6	3.2	2.6	2.8	14.1	22.5	21.7	19.0
Labor intensive	16.0	6.0	5.1	4.4	14.3	15.9	9.3	12.5
Capital intensive	24.7	14.6	7.5	4.8	2.4	2.5	1.8	2.7
Technology intensive	34.9	34.9	46.0	50.4	62.7	53.2	62.9	59.9
Mixed	19.8	41.4	38.8	37.7	6.5	5.9	4.3	5.8
Other developed countries:								
Raw-material intensive	6.7	5.2	4.2	4.1	20.7	23.9	27.7	23.7
Labor intensive	15.6	9.4	7.5	6.0	21.7	26.5	23.5	23.3
Capital intensive	17.5	10.6	5.3	4.2	4.9	3.9	4.8	4.3
Technology intensive	45.7	48.7	54.9	55.7	46.8	35.9	32.0	30.9
Mixed	14.5	26.2	28.0	30.1	5.9	9.9	11.9	17.8
East Asian NICs:								
Raw-material intensive	8.3	9.7	9.0	8.6	2.0	7.5	7.7	6.4
Labor intensive	29.0	14.9	14.0	10.4	78.1	48.6	43.0	41.2
Capital intensive	13.2	16.5	11.0	10.6	4.6	11.3	16.2	16.4
Technology intensive	40.4	47.7	55.7	60.8	12.0	23.6	25.0	25.1
Mixed	9.1	11.2	10.3	9.6	3.4	8.9	8.2	10.9
East Asian LDCs:								
Raw-material intensive	14.6	9.8	6.1	7.8	20.6	12.9	14.8	11.0
Labor intensive	10.2	6.7	5.2	6.2	73.6	67.5	69.1	66.3
Capital intensive	28.7	24.9	25.1	21.4	.8	4.7	3.6	9.7
Technology intensive	33.5	39.8	47.0	49.3	1.0	8.9	7.0	7.6
Mixed	13.0	18.8	16.5	15.2	4.0	6.1	5.4	5.3
Other developing countries:								
Raw-material intensive	4.7	3.8	3.5	3.8	12.5	24.4	26.9	22.0
Labor intensive	16.6	9.4	8.1	6.9	32.9	33.8	33.7	35.4
Capital intensive	17.9	19.1	13.6	12.5	42.4	15.9	24.0	31.6
Technology intensive	46.5	42.4	49.2	48.0	7.9	20.3	12.1	8.2
Mixed	14.2	25.3	25.5	28.7	4.3	5.6	3.3	2.8

is low (Lawrence 1987; Carliner, as quoted in Takeuchi 1989b). This problem is confirmed in table 2.6, which presents, for broad manufacturing groups, "cross-hauling" ratios—that is, the ratios of overlapping exports and imports in individual sectors to sectoral exports plus imports.[8] This index ranges from

8. Specifically, intra-industry trade index $= 1 - \Sigma_i |E_i - M_i|/[E_i + M_i]$, where E and M are exports and imports, and i ranges over all sectors included in a given sectoral grouping.

Table 2.6   **Intra-industry Trade Index**

	1970	1980	1985	1988
Total:	37.4	29.3	26.1	34.9
Raw-material intensive	76.7	80.9	76.9	81.6
Labor intensive	43.9	50.8	53.4	59.0
Capital intensive	17.2	13.7	22.2	48.0
Technology intensive	40.4	28.1	22.4	28.1
Mixed	19.7	11.0	8.7	17.0

Note: Index $= 100 \times [1 - $ sum of absolute (exports $-$ imports)/(sum of exports $+$ sum of imports)].

zero percent, when a sector only exports or only imports, to 100% when exports are exactly equal to imports. Japan's intra-industry trade has recovered somewhat from its trough in 1985 (when imports were generally low relative to exports) but is still below 1970 levels.

Intra-industry trade appears to be inversely related to competitiveness across Japanese industries; for example, it is high in raw-material-intensive products and low in technology-intensive products. Intra-industry trade also appears to move as a coincident indicator of declining competitiveness; for example, intra-industry trade has risen sharply in capital-intensive sectors at the same time that the share of these sectors in Japanese exports declined. Thus, in Japan intra-industry trade seems to arise largely in industries that have come under general competitive pressure and have abandoned segments of their activities to foreign producers. This mechanism is different from that observed in other countries, where strong industries develop close trade ties with their counterparts in other countries by making different varieties or components of the same or similar products.

2.4.2   Methodology for Econometric Analysis

While the foregoing discussion suggests that Japanese trade may have unusual characteristics, detailed econometric investigation is needed to assess to what extent Japanese trade patterns are governed by comparative advantage as opposed to other determinants. To this end, we now present estimates of the relationship between the structure of Japanese import penetration ratios and export shares (the dependent variables in this analysis) and three types of explanatory factors: comparative advantage, Japanese market structure, and visible barriers. These relationships are examined using observations on 49 Japanese manufacturing sectors (see appendix).

This kind of sector-cross-section analysis of import and export structure—which we shall call the factor "intensity" approach to the study of trade determinants—was pioneered by Baldwin (1971), Harkness (1978), and Baldwin (1979). Most recent studies of Japanese trade, however, have used an alternative factor "endowment" approach, which essentially regresses trade flows on factor endowments in a country-cross-section sample (Saxonhouse 1983; Leamer 1984; Saxonhouse and Stern 1989). It is useful to review the theoretical underpinnings of these alternative approaches.

The theoretical justification of the endowment approach is based on Heckscher-Ohlin assumptions, including factor price equalization (FPE).[9] These assumptions imply that exports and imports, in effect, trade away the differences between each country's relative factor supplies and international relative factor supplies. In Leamer's (1984) notation, trade has to satisfy the relationship:

$$(1) \qquad\qquad At = v - sv_w,$$

where A is the factors-by-products matrix of input coefficients, t is the net trade vector, and $v - sv_w$ is the vector of excess factor endowments—the difference between a country's factor endowments v and its general share s of world factor endoments v_w.

If A is invertible (more on this below), then each product's net trade will be a linear function of the elements of the excess endowment vector:

$$(2) \qquad\qquad t = A^{-1} (v - sv_w).$$

This is the equation estimated in the endowment approach, essentially by using data on factor endowments to estimate the coefficients A^{-1}. A good fit is then taken to confirm the underlying theoretical model.

Leamer and Bowen (1981) also use equation (2) to point out errors in the intensity approach. They argue that, in order to estimate relative factor abundance, it is necessary to estimate the excess factor endowment vector ($v - sv_w$). They then show that to recover this vector, t should be regressed on data that are equivalent to columns of A^{-1}. But A^{-1} is not observed. The usual procedure of regressing t on input intensities A (which are observed) is not a satisfactory alternative, since this regression does not have stable coefficients across sectors and will not yield coefficients that are in any simple way related to ($v - sv_w$).

Looked at this way, the intensity approach is an incorrect substitute for the endowment approach. Yet the failure of the intensity approach rests on the strong assumptions used to derive equation (2). A satisfactory rationale for the intensity approach can be built in the framework of Heckscher-Ohlin theory, provided, however, that the strong assumption of FPE is relaxed.

Suppose factor prices differ at home and abroad. Let product and factor units be normalized so that foreign product and factor prices equal 1. Let the vector of the costs of home products, p, be given by:

---

9. The basic model is developed in detail in Leamer (1984). Lawrence (1987) has sketched a version of the model emphasizing product differentiation; Saxonhouse and Stern (1989) develop a hybrid model which combines a version of the differentiated-products model with the Heckscher-Ohlin framework.

(3) $p = c(w),$

where w is the vector of home factor prices and the vector of cost functions, c, is based on internationally shared technologies. For small deviations of home factor prices from factor prices abroad, dw, home costs will be given by:

(4) $p = 1 + dp = 1 + c_w(w)dw.$

Since the derivative of cost with respect to factor prices is factor demand, $c_w(w) = A'$, and equation (4) becomes:

(5) $p = 1 + A'dw,$

and since, by definition, $A'1 = 1$, equation (5) can be rewritten as:

(5') $p = A'(1 + dw) = A'w.$

The intensity model is completed by adding relationships between p and trade t. Assume that goods are differentiated by country of origin,[10] demand is homothetic, and demand is separable so that the choice among the varieties of one product does not depend on the choice among the varieties of other products.[11] Then the home country will produce some of each product even if its costs are higher than those abroad, with market shares given by the demand relationships s:

(6) $t = \hat{s}[p + b]d,$

where ^ denotes diagonalization, d is the vector of demands for the composite goods that encompass the several varieties of the various products, and b represents trade barriers. Substituting equation (5') into question (6) yields:

(7) $t/d = \hat{s}[A'w + b].$

In other words, home producers' market shares,[12] both in home demand (where the home market share is simply 1 minus the import penetration ratio) and foreign demand (where the home market share is represented as the country's share of world exports) will be a function of the input matrix A multiplied

10. The assumption of "differentiation by country of origin" is used in a stronger sense than by Helpman and Krugman (1985); in their model, if x has lower costs than y in making a particular variety, then x will win that market and become a producer of y-type products. In the present context the stronger Armington assumption is used; y's differentiated products remain permanently associated with y; that is, they possess some technical feature that cannot be duplicated by x.
   11. This demand specification is widely used in computable general equilibrium models, e.g., Petri (1984).
   12. The share functions that apply to different products may reflect differing elasticities of substitution between domestic and foreign varieties, so that a particular cost differential may be associated with different trade effects across the several sectors. In the econometric application, these differences are treated as noise. The effect of this noise on the accuracy of the estimates is mitigated by the fact that it appears in both the import and export equations for a particular sector and can therefore be estimated with Zellner's seemingly unrelated regression method.

by factor prices plus the tariff equivalent of trade barriers relevant to the market. In general, the form of this function is unknown, but in at least one important case it can be shown to be linear.[13]

The intensity approach involves estimation of equation (7). Thus, if factor prices are not fully equalized, then there is a rigorous justification for estimating the intensity model, and, furthermore, the endowment model is incorrect since trade is not a linear function of endowments and the coefficients A^{-1} are not fixed across countries. It would not be surprising, however, if the endowment model produced a good fit in empirical applications, since the excess endowment vector may still be an excellent proxy for international factor price differences.

The fact is that recent results based on the endowment approach are not easily reconciled with Heckscher-Ohlin FPE assumptions. Several studies based on this approach have found that trade performance in *many* industries is accurately predicted with a *small* number of factor endowment variables.[14] Paradoxically, the theory does not predict such "good" results. If the number of products is greater than the number of factors, then the theory predicts *either* that net exports in most product categories will be indeterminate (if transport costs are negligible) *or* that trade will be confined to a small number of goods (if transport costs are significant).[15] Alternatively, should the number of products equal the number of factors, then the theory predicts that a large number of factors will be needed to explain satisfactorily trade in a large number of product categories. *No* version of the theory predicts that a few factors will be sufficient to explain many categories of trade. By contrast, the intensity approach predicts meaningful international rankings of competitiveness for any number of products, regardless of how many factors matter.

2.4.3   Implementation

In this study, the intensity approach (eq. [7]) is used to estimate Japanese trade performance in both domestic markets and world markets. In the domestic market, for the sake of comparability with other similar studies, the depen-

---

13. It is possible to derive a strictly linear version of the relationship between import-penetration ratios (or export market shares) and factor intensities under Cobb-Douglas technologies and market shares. In this case, costs are given by: $\log p = A'$, $\log w$, and $t/d = e(A' \log w + q)$, where e is a substitution elasticity and q is the vector of ad valorem tariff equivalents. In this case, the sector-cross-section regression of t/d on A' and q directly yields the coefficient vector $[e \log (w), e]$.

14. Saxonhouse (1983) and Saxonhouse and Stern (1989), e.g., work with 109 products and only seven factors. In the 74 manufacturing sectors of this sample, only three have R^2 below 0.50, and 17 have R^2 greater than 0.90.

15. Leamer (1984, p. 18) suggests that one way around the dimensionality problem is to assume small transport costs and that trade is determined by a linear program that minimizes transport costs subject to the constraint of eq. (1). It is not clear how agents would know how to trade consistently with the results of such a linear program. In any case, the number of nonzero trading activities will be generally equal to the number of constraints, or, in this case, the number of factors. Most goods would not be traded.

dent variable was defined as *import penetration,* that is, the ratio of imports to total domestic demand. In the world market, the dependent variable was Japan's *share of world exports.* This means, of course, that comparable comparative advantage variables will have opposite signs in the two estimated equations. The estimates were implemented using trade and structural data for 49 manufacturing industries in 1985.

The explanatory variables of the study are collected and defined in three broad groups in table 2.7. The first group of variables focused on *comparative advantage,* and included the input-intensity indexes already mentioned in connection with the classification of industries. The second group described special characteristics of *market structure* that have appeared in the literature as possible "invisible" barriers to trade. Included in this group were measures of the importance of distribution in product marketing, the nature of a product's principal procuror (e.g., the shares of governments, households, and businesses in total procurements of the product), and the seller concentration of the domestic industry with which the import competes. A third group of

Table 2.7   **Variable Definitions for Trade Structure Analysis**

Comparative advantage:
  Raw-material intensity
    Share of mining, refinery products, electricity, and gas in sectoral production costs, derived from 1985 input-output coefficients
  Capital intensity
    Share of operating surplus depreciation in sectoral value added, derived from 1985 input-output coefficients
  Technology intensity
    Share of scientists and engineers in sectoral employment, derived from 1985 data published alongside the input-output table

Market structure:
  Distribution margins
    Wholesale plus retail margins associated with the sale of a product, expressed as fraction of the product's producer price, derived from 1985 input-output coefficients
  Business markets:
    Share of intermediate users plus final investment demand, excluding those sectors classified as government, in purchases of the sector's products, derived from 1985 input coefficients
  Government markets:
    Share of government, government investment, public enterprises and research institutes in purchases of the sector's products, derived from 1985 input coefficients
  Supply concentration:
    Herfindahl index of supply concentration, 1986 (index value for a monopoly = 100)

Visible barriers:
  Protection:
    Tariffs plus tariff equivalent of nontariff barriers, based on 1985 input-output coefficients and Saxonhouse and Stern (1989)
  Transport costs:
    Weight/value ratio, derived from U.S. trade date

variables focused on *visible barriers* such as formal protection, including tariffs and the estimated tariff equivalent of nontariff barriers and transportation costs.

Zellner's "seemingly unrelated equations" technique was used to take advantage of correlation between the residuals of the import and export relationships. This correlation was negative and substantial (-0.37 for the trade structure equations reported in table 2.8, and -0.56 for the trade growth equations reported in table 2.9), presumably reflecting missing factors that affect Japan's competitiveness in both domestic and foreign markets.

The theoretical rationale of the intensity approach, as outlined in the previous section, is consistent with a linear specification of the effects of input-intensity variables, but does not strictly require this functional form. Results are therefore presented both for the simple linear specification and for an equation using log transformations of the dependent variables. In addition, quadratic terms were tried for each independent variable. Except in the case of technology intensity (as discussed below), the quadratic terms had little effect on the results and are not reported here.

2.4.4   Results

The results for import penetration and export shares in 1985 are presented in table 2.8. Most obviously, the results highlight the importance of technology intensity as a determinant of both imports and exports. However, technology intensity does not behave as a simple factor intensity variable; in both the import and export equations, its effects are best captured in quadratic form. A closer look at the quadratic estimates helps to explain why this happens. Typical sample values of the technology-intensity variable imply that the contribution of the quadratic term is generally greatest (most positive in the export equation, most negative in the import equation) for a technology intensity value of approximately 5–6 percent. This is a relatively high value; only one-third of manufacturing sectors have an index value this high or higher—machinery sectors, for example, fall in the 5–7 percent range. With technology values above 6 percent, exports generally decline and imports rise. Evidently, Japan's technology advantage peaks in the second highest quintile of industries and falls off for ultra-technology-intensive products, suggesting perhaps some missing factor (basic research?) that is correlated with very high levels of the technology intensity.

Trade patterns are weakly related to other input intensity measures beside technology. There is a hint that exports are negatively related to raw material intensity and that imports are negatively related to capital intensity, but neither of these coefficients is statistically significant at the 5 percent level. Furthermore, the signs of some of these variables change depending on whether the dependent variables are linearly or logarithmically specified.

The most interesting findings involve the market-structure variables. These variables approximately double the explained proportion of variance in the import equation and also improve the fit of the export equation;[16] the hypothesis that industry structure coefficients are zero is rejected at the 1 percent level for both the import equation and export equations.

Two of the market structure variables, distribution margins and the share of business in the product's market, were introduced both by themselves and in interaction with concentration. The interaction variants reflect the hypothesis that distribution channels and business procurement will have an import-dampening character only when "activated" by a strong domestic supplier. For example, a concentrated domestic supplier should have greater voice in what other products are carried by its distribution channel than a competitive domestic supplier. As the results show, the distribution and business procurement variable indeed have more explanatory power when used in interaction with concentration.

In general, four variables play particularly significant roles:

1. *Distribution margins are negatively related to import penetration.* This finding is significant at a 1 percent level in the linear model, but only at a 12 percent level in the logarithmic variant. In general, the sign of the estimated coefficient is consistent with the hypothesis that the Japanese distribution system acts as a barrier against imports. This hypothesis is discussed, for example, by Christelow (1985–86), the Advisory Committee for Trade Policy and Negotiations (1989), and Japan Economic Institute (1989).

2. *Markets where businesses account for a large share of purchases tend to have relatively low import penetration.* The excluded variable in this case is the share of purchases made by households, which has an implicit coefficient of zero. Goods purchased by businesses appear to have import penetration rates 15 percentage points lower than those purchased by households.

3. *Markets where the government accounts for a large share of purchases tend to have relatively low import penetration.* Goods purchased by the government appear to have import penetration rates 16 percentage points lower than those purchased by households. (The difference between business and government import behavior is not statistically significant.)

4. *Producer concentration is positively related both to import penetration and to exports.* This is an unexpected finding, but consistent with recent industrial organization models of international trade. In models of oligopolistic markets, concentrated industries sell into each other's markets in order to take advantage of high prices and price elasticities abroad. Since industries that are concentrated in Japan are also concentrated abroad

---

16. The improvement of fit in the export equation is expected to be much smaller, since market-structure variables that might have a substantial effect on Japanese exports—variables that capture the effect of foreign market characteristics facing Japanese exporters—are not available for this study.

Table 2.8 **Trade Structure Regressions**

	Import Penetration					World Export Share				
	Percent				Log	Percent				Log
	(1)	(2)	(3)	(4)	(5)	(1)	(2)	(3)	(4)	(5)
Constant	9.32** (3.05)	24.23** (4.03)	9.37 (3.78)	6.05* (2.05)	2.15** (4.20)	.59 (.11)	−.36 (−.07)	−.36 (−.08)	−.04 (−.01)	.92* (2.22)
Comparative advantage:										
Raw-material intensity	−.033 (−.22)	.021 (.17)	.084 (.64)	−.168 (−.90)	.048 (1.75)	−.383 (−1.49)	−.383 (−1.64)	−.383 (−1.64)	−.327 (−.93)	−.008 (−.39)
Capital intensity	−.017 (−.20)	−.078 (−1.07)	−.081 (−1.13)	−.074 (−1.09)	−.032* (−2.13)	.059 (.41)	−.006 (−.05)	.006 (.05)	.005 (.03)	−.009 (−.849)
Technology intensity	−3.28** (−3.20)	−3.67** (−4.05)	−3.20** (−3.78)	−2.78** (−3.24)	−.45* (−2.58)	7.66** (4.38)	6.97** (4.28)	6.97** (4.28)	6.97** (4.28)	.85** (6.03)
Technology squared	.376** (3.69)	.413** (4.79)	.367** (4.51)	.332** (4.04)	.056** (3.35)	−.708** (−4.07)	−.668** (−4.18)	−.667** (−4.18)	−.668** (−4.18)	−.081** (−5.88)
Industry structure:										
Distribution margins		−.163* (−2.52)								
Distribution margins × concentration			−.013** (−3.76)	−.014** (−4.06)	−.001 (−1.47)					

	(1)	(2)	(3)	(4)	(5)	(6)	(7)	(8)	(9)	(10)
Business markets	−.152** (−2.93)									
Business markets × concentration		−.011** (−3.62)	−.011** (−3.60)	−.001* (−2.42)						
Government markets	−.121 (−1.68)	−.177* (−2.47)	−.178* (−2.59)	−.063** (−4.15)						
Supply concentration	.196** (2.73)	1.278** (4.55)	1.325** (4.88)	.172** (2.91)		.26 (1.94)	.26 (1.94)	.26 (1.94)	.25 (1.77)	.02 (1.54)
Protection:										
Tariff and NTB tariff equivalent				.225 (1.45)						
Weight/value					1.486 (1.77)					−.346 (−.21)
Statistics:										
R^2	.276	.458	.504	.547	.450	.337	.386	.386	.386	.491
Adjusted R^2	.207	.344	.400	.421	.334	.273	.311	.294	.276	.415
Standard Error	5.82	4.76	4.61	4.35	.94	9.94	9.04	9.04	9.04	.74
F	3.99	4.44	5.33	5.07	4.29	5.33	5.28	4.41	3.78	6.75

Note: Eq. (1): OLS. Eq. (2)–(5): seemingly unrelated regressions. *T*-ratios are in parentheses.

*P = .05.

**P = .01.

Table 2.9   Trade Growth Regressions

	Import Growth		Export Growth	
	(1)	(2)	(1)	(2)
Constant	1.04**	1.02**	.019	−.025
	(5.03)	(4.99)	(.11)	(−.16)
Comparative advantage:				
Raw-material intensity	−.0033	−.0081	−.0083	−.0085
	(−.30)	(−.71)	(−.91)	(−1.01)
Capital intensity	.0069	.0095	.0054	.0037
	(1.12)	(1.52)	(1.04)	(.76)
Technology intensity	−.0769**	−.0806**	.0418*	.0325*
	(−3.81)	(−3.54)	(2.48)	(1.96)
Industry structure:				
Distribution margins × concentration		.0002		
		(.87)		
Business markets × concentration		.0003		
		(1.17)		
Government markets		.0055		
		(.97)		
Supply concentration		−.4270		.8179
		(−.72)		(1.69)
Statistics:				
R^2	.253	.281	.184	.231
Adjusted R^2	.201	.152	.127	.158
Standard Error	.424	.402	.354	.329
F	4.74	2.34	3.16	3.15

Note: Eq. (1): OLS. Eq. (2): seemingly unrelated equations. *T*-ratios in parentheses. Dependent variable is log[x(1988)/x(1985)], where x is exports or imports.
*P = .05.
**P = .01.

(Caves 1976), it appears that strategic behavior in mutually concentrated industries tends to enhance intra-industry trade.

In interpreting these results, three caveats must be noted. First, since this study addresses only the effects of industrial organization variables in Japan, it cannot determine whether the variables examined have an unusual impact in Japan as compared to other countries. For example, it is possible that high household procurement or low distribution margins are also positively related to import penetration in, say, Germany.[17] We are not aware of other studies

17. Low distribution margins may be associated with high import penetration in general. Assume, for example, some preference bias for domestic goods, implying that foreign products must enjoy a price advantage over similar domestic products in order to be imported. Now consider two different potential imports with the same relative producer's price advantage over their domestic competitors. Of these two, the product with a lower domestic distribution margin will have a greater relative consumer's price advantage (even if the exact same margin is applied to its domestic competitor) and is therefore more likely to be imported.

that have estimated these effects; clearly, it would be useful to know whether they can be found in other economies.

Second, the estimated effects provide information only on relative aspects of the trade performance. Consider a negative coefficient on, say, the distribution margin variable in the import equation. All that the foregoing analysis suggests is that high values of distribution are associated with low value of import penetration and vice versa; the analysis cannot determine whether high values of distribution are associated with too *little* imports, or low values of distribution with too *much* imports.

Third, the analysis cannot determine whether any particular relationship is good or bad from a welfare perspective. For example, even if it is known that close buyer-supplier relationships inhibit international trade, it does not follow that such inhibited trade is "distorted." Indeed, such relationships may play a valuable economic role, say, by facilitating the diffusion of information and technology. Countries without such relationships may in effect import too much—that is, have a distorted trade profile relative to the welfare-maximizing benchmark.

The final group of variables show that explicit barriers, including protection and transportation costs, play a modest role in determining the relative trade performance of different industries. The coefficients of both the protection and transportation variables have incorrect signs and are not significantly different from zero. The likely reason for this is that there is very little formal protection in Japanese manufacturing; average tariff rates are 4.1 percent and the tariff equivalent of NTBs is only 0.9 percent (Deardorff and Stern 1986). Transportation costs are proxied by weight/value ratios; it is possible that transportation costs do not matter, or that more comprehensive measures of transportation and communication costs would produce better results.

To get a better sense of the estimated effects, let us abstract from the caveats and assume that the results reflect the popular hypotheses that distribution and government and business procurement depress Japanese imports. Consider some rough upper limits on the effects of eliminating these biases. Average import penetration rates in Japanese manufacturing in 1985 were approximately 6 percent. Households account for one-third of manufactures demand, and business and government purchasing behavior was estimated to reduce import penetration, on average, by roughly 13.5 percentage points below household rates. Thus, if governments and businesses suddenly behaved like households, then manufactured imports would rise by .135 × .667, or 9 percent of manufactures demand. Similarly, average wholesale and retail margins in manufacturing were approximately 20 percent, and a 1 percent increase in such margins has been estimated to reduce import penetration by .16 percentage points of demand. Thus, if products requiring distribution suddenly achieved import penetration ratios similar to products that are sold directly to purchasers, then imports would increase by − .16 × − .20, or an additional 3.2 percent of demand.

Together, the first-round effects appear to triple manufactures imports to 18 percent of demand. Of course, if imports of the manufactured products constrained by these barriers increased, other imports would likely decline, yielding a substantially smaller net effect—say, a doubling of manufactured imports. This would represent a large change, but the resulting ratio of trade in manufactures relative to GNP (approximately 4 percent) would still amount to less than half that of the next-lowest-ranking industrial country (Takeuchi 1989a).

2.4.5   Recent Compositional Changes

In light of the earlier discussion of structural change since 1985 in the aggregate import and export relationships, it is natural to ask whether these changes are related to changes in the determinants of import and export composition. To this end, additional equations were estimated to see how import and export growth since 1985 have been affected by the explanatory variables used above. The dependent variables for this analysis, for both imports and exports, are the logs of the ratios of 1988 trade to 1985 trade.[18]

The import and export growth equations are presented in table 2.9. Comparative advantage variables carry a substantial part of the explanation of trade growth rates and confirm the earlier finding of increasing specialization in technology-intensive products. Technology intensity is negatively related to import growth and positively related to export growth.[19] In these equations, raw material and capital intensity appear with the same signs in both equations, presumably reflecting general trends in demand growth for these products relative to demand for technology-intensive goods.

Market-structure variables are less helpful in explaining changes in exports and imports than trade composition at a particular time. In the case of import growth, none of the market-structure variables is significant at the 5 percent level. However, the coefficients for distribution margins, business purchases, and government purchases have signs opposite to those estimated in the earlier composition equations. In other words, it appears that import growth during the last three years has been faster in goods that had relatively low penetration ratios in 1985—that is, in goods with larger distribution margins and with markets dominated by business demand. These results, though statistically weak, are tantalizing in light of the earlier finding of structural change in aggregate imports as well as anecdotal evidence on the development of discounted distribution channels.

---

18. The reason for using these dependent variables instead of changes in import penetration ratios and world export shares is that the denominators needed to construct these variables were not available for 1988.

19. In these equations there is no clear statistical preference for a quadratic technology term, and therefore the simpler single-variable specification is used.

2.5 Conclusions

This paper has collected evidence from several data sets regarding trends in Japanese trade behavior since the yen began its steep rise in 1985. On the whole, the evidence suggests that Japanese trade is changing in each of the three dimensions analyzed: in aggregate level, partner structure, and commodity structure.

Aggregate Trade.   In line with historically estimated price elasticities, yen appreciation has only marginally reduced the dollar value of Japan's large trade surplus. But there is some evidence that the "normalcy" of the trade balance hides departures by both imports and exports from historical relationships. Some researchers have concluded that export prices have risen less than suggested by historical pass-through relationships and that export market shares have been held unusually firmly. This paper has presented evidence that imports are now running 10–20 percent ahead of historically estimated import functions and that import functions based on recent data show increased sensitivity to economic determinants.

Partner Trade.   Japan has rapidly expanded its trade linkages with the East Asian NICs and developed countries other than the United States. This trade consists of the exchange of exports of advanced consumer goods and (especially in the case of NICs) capital goods and sophisticated components, for imports of consumer goods (at both ends of the quality spectrum) and industrial supplies. The outlook for regional economic integration is bright, but the increase in intraregional trade so far has no more than retraced the decline in the relative importance of East Asian linkages since 1975. The data do not yet suggest a dramatically new regional economy.

Product Trade.   Japanese trade data have been widely scrutinized for evidence that Japan imports fewer manufactured goods than other similarly endowed countries. This study does not compare Japanese trade to international norms, but it does provide new, related evidence regarding the determinants of Japanese trade. Among the conventional comparative advantage determinants, it appears that Japanese products are competitive in technology-intensive sectors (although not in the most technology intensive sectors).

It also appears that industry-structure variables are important correlates of trade performance:

products with high distribution margins are less likely to be imported than those with low margins, especially when the import-competing Japanese industry is concentrated;

products purchased by business are less likely to be imported than those purchased by households, especially when the import-competing Japanese industry is concentrated;

products purchased by government are also less likely to be imported than those purchased by households;

products with high supplier concentration in Japan are more likely to be both exported and imported than other products.

As discussed in the text, these findings need cautious interpretation since they are consistent with several alternative hypotheses. Nevertheless, they represent the only empirical evidence we are aware of regarding the relationship between widely conjectured "causes" of Japan's low imports of manufactured goods and measures of trade performance. This evidence needs to be further refined, but it suggests that distribution and business and government procurement are indeed negatively correlated with import penetration.

The effect of market-structure variables on recent changes in import penetration are opposite the effects of these variables on levels of penetration. Thus, while the trade structure regressions are consistent with some anti-import bias in the distribution system and in business and government procurement, the trade growth regressions suggest a diminution in this bias.

Overall, the changes reported in this paper raise intriguing questions about the evolution of Japan's external sector. There is evidence of statistically significant breaks with the past, but the economic significance of the changes that can be documented at this time is limited. The key question is whether the changes observed so far represent *shifts* or *trends*. If, say a decade from now, Japan imports a wide range of goods for household, business, and government uses, and engages in substantial intraindustry trade, perhaps with other East Asian countries, then 1985 will be seen as a turning point. But it is also possible that the changes identified so far are once-and-for-all shifts—completed responses to the appreciation of the yen. In this extreme, *endaka* and the changes it wrought have modest long-term significance. It is too soon to tell which scenario lies closer to the truth.

Appendix
Sectoral Classification Scheme

	Commodity	Group	ISIC/Concord	1985 IO/Concord	SITC/Concord
1	Yarn & fabric	Labor	3211	1511,1512,1514	651,652,653,654
2	Knitted fabric	Labor	3213	1513	655
3	Other textiles	Labor	3212,3214,3215,3219	1519,1529	656,657,658,659
4	Wearing apparel	Labor	3220	1521,1522	842,843,844, 845,846,847,848
5	Leather footwear	Mixed	3240	2411	851
6	Other leather products	Mixed	3231,3232,3233	2412	611,612,613
7	Lumber & plywood	Raw	3311	1611	633,634
8	Wood products	Mixed	3312,3319	1619	635
9	Furniture & fixtures	Labor	3320	1711	821
10	Pulp	Raw	3411	1811	641
11	Paper	Raw	3412	1812,1813	641
12	Containers & paper products	Mixed	3419	1821,1829	642
13	Printing, publishing	Labor	3420	1911	892
14	Basic industrial chemicals	Raw	3511	2021,2029,2031, 2032,2033,2039	511,512,513,514, 515,516,522,523,524
15	Fertilizer	Raw	3512	2011	562
16	Synthetic resin	Tech	3513	2041,2051	531
17	Paint, varnish	Tech	3521	2072	532,533
18	Drugs & medicines	Tech	3522	2061	541
19	Soap & cleansers	Capital	3523	2071	551,553,554
20	Other chemical products	Labor	3529	2073,2079	572,582,583,584, 591,592,598
21	Tire & tube	Mixed	3551	2311	625
22	Rubber products	Mixed	3559	2319	621,628
23	Plastic products	Capital	3560	2211	893

(continued)

Sectoral Classification Scheme (*continued*)

	Commodity	Group	ISIC/Concord	1985 IO/Concord	SITC/Concord
24	Pottery china	Raw	3610	2531	666
25	Glass & glass products	Raw	3620	2511,2512,2519	664,665
26	Cement, lime	Raw	3692	2521,2522,2523	661
27	Other nonmetallic minerals	Raw	3691,3699	2599	662,663
28	Basic iron & steel	Capital	3710	2611,2621,2622, 2623,2631	671,672,673,674, 675,676,678,679
29	Structural metal products	Mixed	3813	2811,2812	691
30	Other metal products	Mixed	3811,3812,3819	2891,2899	692,693,694, 695,696,697
31	Engines & turbines	Tech	3821	3011	711,712,713,714, 716,718
32	Machine tools	Tech	3823	3024	736,737
33	Special industrial machinery	Tech	3822,3824	3021,3022,3023, 3029,3112	721,722,723,724, 725,726,727,728
34	General industrial machinery	Tech	3829	3012,3013,3019,3031	741,742,743,744,745,749
35	Office machinery	Tech	3825	3111,3311	751,752,759
36	Electrical industrial machinery	Tech	3831	3411	771,772,773
37	Radio, television	Tech	3832	3211	761,762,763
38	Electronics	Tech	3833,3839	3321,3331,3341,3421,3431	764,774,775,776,778
39	Shipbuilding	Tech	3841	3611	793
40	Railroad equipment	Labor	3842	3621	791
41	Motor vehicles	Mixed	3843	3511,3521,3541	781,782,783,784
42	Motorcycles & bicycles	Capital	3844	3531	785
43	Aircraft	Tech	3845	3622	792
44	Other transport equipment	Labor	3849	3629	786
45	Scientific instruments	Tech	3851	3719	871,872,873,874
46	Photographic equipment	Tech	3852	3711	881,882,883,884
47	Watches & clocks	Labor	3853	3712	885
48	Sporting & athletic goods	Capital	3903	3911	894
49	Miscellaneous	Labor	3901,3902,3909	3919	895,898

References

Advisory Committee for Trade Policy and Negotiations. 1989. Analysis of the U.S.-Japan Trade Problem. Washington, D.C.: U.S. Trade Representative.

Baldwin, Richard E. 1988. Hysteresis in Import Prices: The Beachhead Effect. *American Economic Review* 78:773–85.

Baldwin, Robert E. 1971. Determinants of the Commodity Structure of U.S. Trade. *American Economic Review* 61:126–47.

———. 1979. Determinants of Trade and Foreign Investment: Further Evidence. *Review of Economics and Statistics* 61 (February):40–48.

Caves, Richard, with Masu Uekusa. 1976. Industrial Organization. In *Asia's New Giant: How the Japanese Economy Works,* ed. Hugh Patrick and Henry Rosovsky. Washington, D.C.: Brookings.

Chow, Gregory C. 1960. Tests of Equality between Sets of Coefficients in Two Linear Regressions. *Econometrica* 28 (July): 591–605.

Christelow, Dorothy. 1985–86. Japan's Intangible Barriers to Trade in Manufactures. Federal Reserve Bank of New York *Quarterly Review* 10 (Winter): 11–18.

Corker, Robert. 1989. External Adjustment and the Strong Yen: Recent Japanese Experience. *International Monetary Fund Staff Papers* 36, no. 2: 464–93.

Darlin, Damon. 1988. Japan Is Getting a Dose of What It Gave U.S.: Low-Priced Imports. *Wall Street Journal,* July 20, p. 1.

Deardorff, Alan V., and Robert M. Stern. 1986. *The Michigan Model of World Production and Trade: Theory and Applications.* Cambridge: MIT Press.

Dornbusch, Rudiger. 1988. Comment in *NBER Macroeconomics Annual 1988,* ed. Stanley Fisher, pp. 259–67. Cambridge, Mass.: MIT Press.

Harkness, Jon. 1978. Factor Abundance and Comparative Advantage. *American Economic Review* 68 (December): 784–800.

Helpman, Elhanan, and Paul R. Krugman. 1985. *Market Structure and Foreign Trade: Increasing Returns, Imperfect Competition, and the International Economy.* Cambridge, Mass.: MIT Press.

Hooper, Peter, and Catherine L. Mann. 1987. The U.S. External Trade Deficit: Its Causes and Persistence. International Finance Discussion Papers no. 316. Board of Governors of the Federal Reserve System, Washington, D.C.

———. 1989. Exchange Rate Pass-through in the 1980s: The Case of U.S. Imports of Manufactures. *Brookings Papers on Economic Activity,* no. 1, pp. 297–337.

Japan Economic Institute. 1989. Japan's Distribution System: The Next Major Trade Confrontation? *JEI Report,* no. 11A, March 17.

Lawrence, Robert Z. 1987. Imports in Japan: Closed Markets or Minds. *Brookings Papers on Economic Activity,* no. 2, pp. 517–54.

Leamer, Edward E. 1984. *Sources of International Comparative Advantage.* Cambridge, Mass.: MIT Press.

Leamer, Edward E., and Harry P. Bowen. 1981. Cross-Section Tests of the Heckscher-Ohlin Theorem: Comment. *American Economic Review* 71 (December):1040–43.

Loopesko, Bonnie, E., and Robert A. Johnson. 1987. Realignment of the Yen-Dollar Exchange Rate: Aspects of the Adjustment Process in Japan," International Finance Discussion Papers no. 311. Board of Governors of the Federal Reserve System, Washington, D.C.

Maidment, Paul. 1989. The Yen Bloc: A New Balance in Asia? *The Economist,* v. 71, July 15.

Marston, Richard. 1989. Pricing to Market in Japanese Manufacturing. University of Pennsylvania, Philadelphia.

Meyer, Michael, Yuriko Hoshiai, and Hideko Takayama. 1987. Harnessing the "Yen Monster." *Newsweek,* September 21, p. 60.

Ministry of International Trade and Industry (MITI). 1989. *White Paper on International Trade 1989,* June. Tokyo: MITI.

Noland, Marcus. 1989. Japanese Trade Elasticities and the J-Curve. *Review of Economics and Statistics* 71 (February):175–79.

Ohno, Kenichi. 1988. Export Pricing Behavior of Manufacturing: A U.S.-Japan Comparison. Working Paper no. WP-88–78. International Monetary Fund, Washington, D.C.

Petri, Peter A. 1984. *Modeling Japanese-American Trade: A Study of Asymmetric Interdependence.* Cambridge, Mass.: Harvard University Press.

Rapoport, Carla. 1989. Ready, Set, Sell—Japan Is Buying. *Fortune,* September 11, pp. 159–64.

Saxonhouse, Gary. 1983. The Micro- and Macroeconomics of Foreign Sales to Japan. In *Trade Policy for the 1980s,* ed. William R. Cline. Cambridge, Mass.: MIT Press.

Saxonhouse, Gary, and Robert M. Stern. 1989. An Analytical Survey of Formal and Informal Barriers to International Trade and Investment in the United States, Canada, and Japan. In *Trade and Investment Relations among the United States, Canada, and Japan,* ed. Robert M. Stern. Chicago: University of Chicago Press.

Takeuchi, Kenji. 1989a. Japan's Market Potential for Manufactured Imports from Developing Economies: A Survey of the Literature. Washington, D.C.: World Bank.

———. 1989b. Effects of Japanese Direct Foreign Investment on Japan's Imports of Manufactures from Developing Economies. Washington, D.C.: World Bank.

World Bank. 1987. *Korea: Managing the Industrial Transition.* Washington, D.C.

Comment   Daniel A. Citrin

Peter Petri's paper provides an interesting analysis of recent developments in Japanese trade flows. I focus my comments on the section that deals with structural changes to aggregate Japanese trade, and on that which looks at the product composition of Japanese trade.

On Structural Changes in Aggregate Trade

The first portion of the paper reviews and presents further evidence, based on the predictive abilities of standard trade equations, that suggests structural changes have affected Japanese export and import behavior in recent years.

With regard to exports, updated predictions of Corker's model through 1988 do indeed indicate a continued underprediction of export volume (and value). This underprediction is reflected in a rise in the measured income elasticity and a fall in the relative price elasticity when the export volume equation is estimated through 1988.

Before reaching any conclusions however, I would note the following. First, Japanese exports, especially of capital goods, were pushed up considerably in 1988 by the global investment boom as well as by direct investment

Daniel A. Citrin is a senior economist in the Asian Department of the International Monetary Fund.

overseas by Japanese firms. The activity variable in the export volume equation would not fully capture this investment-oriented demand. Second, some preliminary results of further work on measuring competing prices indicates that Japanese exporters may have lost *less* competitiveness since 1985 than had been previously estimated. This result largely reflects the use of competitor weights that assign a larger weight to non-U.S. third-country suppliers—both European countries and the NICs—against whom the real effective appreciation of the yen has been smaller. In addition, use of a fixed-weight manufacturing export unit value for the United States, rather than nonoil export unit values results in higher competing U.S. export prices. Of course, one would expect the use of such a revised indicator of competitiveness to predict higher Japanese exports over the recent period.

On imports, updated predictions of Corker's model show an increasing underprediction of Japanese import volumes. At the same time, estimation results indicate a significant rise in the relative price elasticity of Japanese imports, particularly of manufactured imports. These results are in line with those contained in the paper and indeed would suggest an increased preference for imported goods on the part of Japanese consumers as well as positive effects of trade liberalization. The results do not seem to reflect the drop in the household saving rate or the strength of investment in Japan, since the measured income elasticity is unchanged. A recent Bank of Japan study also yielded substantial underpredictions using disaggregated equations where the real consumption and capital goods shipments were used as the relevant domestic activity variables.[1]

More generally, however, I think that it is important to remember—and particularly when forecasting future movements in Japanese trade flows—that the increases in measured elasticities are likely picking up the temporary effects of structural transition or adjustments. Once the shift in preferences, or the adjustment to a more liberal trade regime has taken place, it is by no means certain that the elasticities will remain at these higher levels.

On the Product Composition of Trade

The portion of the paper that analyzes the commodity structure of Japanese exports and imports is the most interesting part of the paper and thus naturally the most difficult to comment on. I would like to offer the following remarks.

1. To what extent is the use of 1985 data in the cross-sectional analysis influencing the results of estimation? This was the year that the Japanese economy was subjected to a large exchange rate shock. As a result, real product prices changed substantially, and producers must not have operated on their long-run equilibrium supply curves. In particular, there were substantial

1. Bank of Japan, "Balance of Payments Adjustment in Japan: Recent Developments and Prospects," Research and Statistics Department, Special Paper no. 178 (May 1989).

swings in producers' profit shares, which, inclusive of depreciation, is the measure of capital intensity in the paper. As the exchange rate shock presumably had differential impacts across the spectrum of industries in the sample, one would think that the estimation results would have been affected substantially.

2. The significance of the consumer-markets variable in the import penetration equations could be picking up the influence of comparative advantage. Namely, to the extent that the consumer goods industries are relatively labor-intensive ones in which Japan had already lost comparative advantage by 1985, one would expect that the import-market share would be higher.

3. As I think the paper itself acknowledges, the distribution margin variable is itself an endogenous variable and thus its estimated coefficient is subject to simultaneity bias. In other words, one would expect low rates of import penetration to lead to rents and to higher distribution margins, particularly in a country where close relationships between manufacturers and distributors are common. Moreover, the existence of large margins does not necessarily imply the existence of import restraints. They could just reflect the often-noted observations that the Japanese place a high premium on service and have a high degree of brand loyalty. Thus, I am not convinced that the results can be used to claim that the Japanese distribution system acts as a barrier to imports.

4. In a similar vein, the paper argues that markets where businesses account for a large share of purchases tend to have relatively low rates of import penetration. However, this does not necessarily reflect an anti-import bias amongst Japanese producers. Rather, it could reflect a production structure that is not vertically integrated in a formal sense, but one in which affiliated producers supply goods to other business customers that are tailored to their specific demands.

In sum, it is not at all clear what the market-structure variables are actually capturing. Thus, while the paper presents some interesting correlations, these results should not be taken as new evidence regarding the determinants of Japanese trade.

3

Changing Japanese Trade Patterns and the East Asian NICs

Yung Chul Park and Won-Am Park

3.1 Introduction

The four East Asian NICs (EANICs)—Hong Kong, Singapore, South Korea, and Taiwan—have developed a triangular trade relationship with Japan and the United States. The EANICs depend on the U.S. market for their exports of manufactured products and rely heavily on Japan as a major supply source of capital goods, intermediate inputs, technology, and management know-how. As a group, the four economies have also accumulated a growing trade surplus from their trade with the United States while running a large and persistent deficit with Japan since around the early 1970s. The triangular pattern of trade is often identified as one of the structural rigidities interfering with the adjustment of the trade imbalance between the EANICs and the United States on the one hand and between the EANICs and Japan on the other.

Over the last decade, there have been a number of significant changes in the trade and industrial structure of the Pacific Asian economies. These changes have in turn created powerful economic forces that may lead to closer economic cooperation and integration centering on Japan.[1] From the perspective of this study, one of the most significant changes has been the increase in Japan's capacity to import manufactured products. Much of this increase could be attributed to the real appreciation of the yen, moderately expansionary monetary and fiscal policies since the Plaza Accord, and structural reforms in Japan that include (i) a major improvement in foreigners' access to

Yung Chul Park is a professor of economics at Korea University and Won-Am Park is a fellow at the Korea Development Institute.
1. Regional economic integration in this paper refers to a development in which countries within a particular region depend more on trade with one another than with the rest of the world. See Bradford and Branson (1987, p. 13).

the Japanese market, (ii) investment expansion in housing and social infrastructure, and (iii) restructuring of Japanese enterprise to promote both foreign direct investment and intra-industry division of labor with foreign firms. Due to these structural and policy reforms and the strong growth led by the expansion of internal demand, Japan's imports of manufactures grew more than 30 percent a year during the 1986–88 period. Among Japan's trade partners, the EANICs have been most successful in taking advantage of the growing Japanese market to expand their export market share of manufactured products from less than 14.2 percent in 1985 to almost 20 percent three years later.

The massive real appreciation of the yen combined with protectionist measures directed against Japanese exports has induced Japanese multinationals, as well as small and medium-sized firms in export-oriented industries, to move their production facilities and product development to other Asian countries. As a result, Japan's foreign direct investment (FDI) in the EANICs more than doubled over the five-year period from 1983 to 1988. Much of this investment has been allocated to manufacturing and, in particular, to the machinery sector. Through the expansion of FDI, subcontracting, and outsourcing, Japanese firms have been spearheading the multinationalization of manufacturing in Asia. In the process they are transferring Japanese technology and management know-how to other Asian producers.

The EANICs no longer specialize in exporting labor-intensive and unsophisticated manufactures. With the accumulation of skill and technology, they have moved into many manufacturing sectors requiring skill- and capital-intensive production processes and in so doing have come to compete with Japan in world markets for an increasing number of sophisticated industrial products. The accumulation of trade surpluses and trade conflicts with North America and Europe have also persuaded Taiwan and South Korea to liberalize their trade and financial sectors, redirect their investment resources away from the export-oriented to the home goods industries, and to promote direct investment in other countries of Pacific Asia.

There is widespread belief that the developments described above have contributed to an expansion of intraregional trade and foreign direct investment, which has further promoted growth, industrialization, and economic integration in the Pacific Asian region. Some authors have viewed these structural changes as signs of the establishment of a pattern of development based on product cycles in which Japan serves as the most advanced and innovative country with a large domestic market and the EANICs as the second-tier countries along a ladder of comparative advantage. The upshot of this argument is that the East Asian economies including Japan could rely less than before on the markets of North America and Europe for growth and development, as they are developing a large regional market through an economic integration propelled by market forces. The purpose of this paper is to examine the validity of this argument by analyzing the pattern of trade among the

United States, Japan, and the EANICs and Japan's FDI. Sections 3.2 and 3.3 are devoted to an analysis of changes in respective structures of trade of the United States, Japan, and the EANICs and the trade relations among them. This is followed by a discussion of Japan's FDI in Asia and the possibilities of regional integration through product-cycle development in sections 3.4 and 3.5. Concluding remarks are found in the final section.

3.2   Changes in Patterns of Trade among the EANICs, Japan, and the United States

3.2.1   Overview

In order to analyze changes in the patterns of trade of the United States, Japan, and the EANICs and their implications for future trade relations between the two sides of the Pacific, we have estimated trade flows among these economies since 1970 (table 3.1). We have also classified commodities belonging to SITC 5–8 into raw-material-, unskilled-labor-, human-capital-, and technology-intensive groups following the criteria used by Krause (1987) and the United Nations for Japan, the United States, and the EANICs for the 1975–87 period (tables 3.2–3.4).[2] An examination of changes in the commodity structure of trade will be combined with that of changes in the structure of intra-industry trade among the three partners in section 3.3 to see whether there is any visible trend of integration of the EANICs with Japan and other Asian countries both on the export and import side and also whether the observed changes could facilitate the adjustment of the trade imbalance between North America and East Asia.

According to table 3.1, the share of the United States in world total exports remained virtually unchanged at around 12 percent throughout the 1980s. There has also been no significant change in the commodity structure of U.S. exports, particularly since 1985. Reflecting the loss of export competitiveness—largely to East Asian producers—and the saving-investment imbalance, U.S. imports grew rapidly, from less than 13 percent of total world imports in 1980 to 18 percent in 1985, before dropping to about 16 percent in 1988. About half of the increase in U.S. imports during the 1985–88 period has come from Japan and the EANICs.

Japanese exports grew from 7 percent of total world exports in 1980 to about 10 percent in 1985 and have since remained at that percentage level; meanwhile, Japan's imports have recorded a small decline as a fraction of total world imports. Japan has maintained its competitiveness in the world markets for those manufactures intensive in capital and technology. In particular, it has

2. See the appendix for the commodity classification. Throughout the paper, the unskilled-labor- and human-capital-intensive categories will be referred to as "labor-intensive" and "capital-intensive" for brevity.

Table 3.1   **Triangular Trade Relationships among Japan, the United States, and EANICs**

	Export to:			
Import from:	Japan	United States	EANICs	World
Japan				
1970	. . .	6,015(31.1) (15.5)	2,641(13.7) (29.9)	19,318(6.8)[a]
1975	. . .	11,242(20.2) (12.1)	6,965(12.5) (26.1)	55,728(7.0)
1980	. . .	31,910(24.5) (13.4)	19,459(14.9) (22.3)	130,435(7.0)
1985	. . .	66,684(37.6) (20.4)	22,684(12.8) (23.5)	177,189(9.8)
1987	. . .	85,017(36.8) (21.1)	39,803(17.2) (27.1)	231,332(9.8)
1988	. . .	90,245(34.1) (20.6)	49,819(18.8) (25.7)	264,961(9.8)
United States				
1970	4,652(10.8) (29.9)	. . .	1,810(4.2) (20.5)	43,231(15.3)
1975	9,563(8.9) (19.0)	. . .	5,233(4.9) (19.6)	107,586(13.6)
1980	20,790(9.4) (16.8)	. . .	15,079(6.8) (17.3)	220,781(11.8)
1985	22,631(10.6) (19.8)	. . .	16,918(7.9) (17.5)	213,146(11.8)
1987	28,249(11.2) (21.1)	. . .	23,548(9.3) (16.1)	252,884(10.7)
1988	37,732(11.8) (22.6)	. . .	34,881(10.9) (18.0)	320,385(11.8)
EANICs				
1970	747(11.8) (4.8)	2,031(32.1) (5.2)	500(7.9) (5.7)	6,336(2.2)
1975	2,845(13.1) (5.7)	5,699(26.2) (5.1)	1,966(9.0) (7.4)	21,767(2.8)
1980	7,681(10.1) (6.2)	18,965(24.8) (8.0)	7,009(9.2) (8.0)	76,351(4.1)
1985	11,434(10.0) (10.0)	39,693(34.8) (12.2)	10,165(8.9) (10.5)	114,006(6.3)
1987	20,466(11.5) (15.3)	62,530(35.1) (15.5)	17,001(9.6) (11.6)	177,908(7.6)
1988	27,855(12.4) (16.7)	69,968(31.3) (16.0)	24,091(10.8) (12.4)	223,763(8.3)
World				
1970	15,543(5.5)[b]	38,811(13.7)	8,828(3.1)	282,638
1975	50,310(6.4)	92,925(11.7)	26,661(3.4)	791,391
1980	123,684(6.6)	237,680(12.7)	87,360(4.7)	1,874,800
1985	114,424(6.3)	326,248(18.0)	96,697(5.3)	1,811,500
1987	133,586(5.7)	403,587(17.1)	146,658(6.2)	2,353,300
1988	166,966(6.2)	437,438(16.2)	193,746(7.2)	2,707,500

Table 3.1   (continued)

Sources: IMF, *Direction of Trade Statistics Yearbook,* various issues; and Council for Economic Planning and Development, *Taiwan Statistical Data Book,* various issues.

Note: Amounts shown are in millions of U.S. dollars. In data columns with two sets of figures in parentheses, the first contains the percentage of total exports; the second contains the percentage of total imports.

[a]Percentage of world total exports.
[b]Percentage of world total imports.

Table 3.2   **U.S. Trade Share by Factor Intensity (%)[a]**

	1975		1980		1985		1987	
	Exports to	Imports from	Exports to	Imports from	Exports to	Imports from	Exports to	Imports from
I. Japan								
SITC 0–4	19.0[b]	.6[b]	18.4	.4	20.3	.8	22.8	.9
SITC 5–8	4.5	21.2	6.0	24.4	7.7	27.5	8.5	26.6
Raw material	11.9	7.0	13.0	5.8	14.3	6.7	16.0	4.6
Labor	4.9	10.5	4.7	7.8	6.9	7.2	8.9	5.9
Capital	2.0	29.5	2.9	37.5	3.5	37.6	4.9	36.0
Technology	5.2	18.1	6.6	21.0	8.8	28.5	9.3	30.1
SITC 9	1.3	6.2	1.6	5.4	2.4	8.9	2.2	7.9
Total	8.8	11.8	9.6	13.1	10.5	20.2	11.0	20.9
II. EANICs								
SITC 0–4	6.0	1.0	7.5	.6	10.2	1.5	12.4	1.7
SITC 5–8	4.2	9.4	6.4	13.5	7.2	15.5	8.5	18.2
Raw material	6.0	5.5	7.8	4.6	8.8	5.6	10.8	5.9
Labor	2.9	35.0	3.8	46.9	5.5	44.6	6.4	45.0
Capital	2.4	4.3	3.2	7.4	2.7	7.9	4.1	10.5
Technology	5.0	5.7	7.6	8.7	8.7	12.3	9.9	15.1
SITC 9	1.8	6.6	2.3	8.4	2.9	6.6	2.4	6.4
Total	4.7	5.7	6.6	7.5	7.8	11.7	8.8	14.5
III. World								
SITC 0–4	30.1	43.6	30.1	45.6	24.5	25.7	21.3	20.5
SITC 5–8	66.9	53.8	67.7	52.7	70.8	71.9	71.1	77.0
Raw material	2.5	5.1	3.5	5.5	2.0	4.4	2.1	4.4
Labor	3.9	8.0	4.7	7.9	3.7	12.2	4.0	14.0
Capital	18.5	24.6	15.2	22.3	15.8	30.7	15.6	31.1
Technology	42.0	16.1	44.3	17.0	49.3	24.6	49.4	27.5
SITC 9	3.0	2.6	2.2	1.7	4.7	2.4	7.7	2.6
Total	100.0	100.0	100.0	100.0	100.0	100.0	100.0	100.0

Source: OECD Trade Tape.

[a]Exports are valued in terms of free-on-board prices whereas imports are cost-insurance-freight prices.
[b]Country figures of each category of goods in I and II are the percentages of corresponding world totals in III.

Table 3.3   Japanese Trade Share by Factor Intensity (%)[a]

	1975		1980		1985		1987	
	Exports to	Imports from	Exports to	Imports from	Exports to	Imports from	Exports to	Imports from
I. United States								
SITC 0–4	11.5[b]	16.3[b]	9.4	12.9	16.9	13.1	15.3	16.7
SITC 5–8	20.2	34.9	24.9	34.4	38.0	37.5	37.1	28.4
Raw material	20.9	18.9	22.9	15.7	28.7	11.1	25.6	9.4
Labor	8.1	11.3	13.4	10.1	20.7	10.8	20.5	7.6
Capital	26.9	34.3	30.4	30.6	45.0	26.5	44.5	18.6
Technology	17.4	50.6	20.2	53.4	33.5	58.1	32.7	49.7
SITC 9	38.9	24.3	25.7	16.2	38.4	38.4	40.2	32.8
Total	20.2	20.1	24.4	17.5	37.6	20.3	36.8	21.7
II. EANICs								
SITC 0–4	25.2	2.8	26.2	2.9	28.8	4.7	38.9	7.7
SITC 5–8	12.0	12.3	14.4	13.8	12.4	14.7	16.7	19.8
Raw material	25.0	6.0	31.3	4.9	30.9	5.0	43.7	7.8
Labor	13.0	38.4	16.5	36.7	16.4	38.4	21.8	46.7
Capital	7.7	10.8	9.7	18.9	7.4	21.9	10.0	22.5
Technology	17.1	5.9	19.4	7.3	16.9	7.7	21.7	10.3
SITC 9	18.3	17.9	20.6	17.3	18.2	22.6	20.5	22.1
Total	12.5	4.8	14.8	5.3	12.8	7.7	17.2	12.8
III. World								
SITC 0–4	3.3	79.7	2.9	78.3	1.9	70.6	1.7	58.0
SITC 5–8	95.4	19.9	96.1	21.0	97.1	28.1	97.3	40.7
Raw material	2.5	4.2	2.5	4.4	1.7	4.7	1.4	6.7
Labor	18.8	3.5	10.4	3.9	8.8	5.0	6.5	8.6
Capital	46.0	2.7	50.1	2.8	48.2	3.8	44.1	7.5
Technology	28.1	9.5	33.1	9.9	38.4	14.6	45.3	17.9
SITC 9	1.3	.4	1.0	.6	1.0	1.4	1.0	1.3
Total	100.0	100.0	100.0	100.0	100.0	100.0	100.0	100.0

Source: OECD Trade Tape.
[a]Exports are valued in terms of free-on-board prices whereas imports are cost-insurance-freight prices.
[b]Country figures of each category of goods in I and II are the percentages of corresponding world totals in III.

become one of the largest exporters of technology-intensive products, which, as a proportion of Japanese total exports, rose from less than 30 percent in the middle of the 1970s to over 45 percent in 1987 at the expense of both labor- and capital-intensive products (see table 3.3). On the import side, due to the massive decline in imports of oil and related products, manufactured products as a percentage of total imports almost doubled to 40 percent between 1980 and 1987.

As a group, the EANICs more than doubled their share to 8.3 percent in the world export market over the nine-year period from 1980 to 1988. This rapid

Table 3.4   **EANICs Trade Share by Factor Intensities (%)[a]**

	1975		1980		1985		1987	
	Exports to	Imports from	Exports to	Imports from	Exports to	Imports from	Exports to	Imports from
I. United States								
SITC 0–4	19.6[b]	71.7[b]	11.6	61.6	20.0	53.0	16.1	49.9
SITC 5–8	45.0	23.6	47.5	25.0	63.9	24.1	55.8	20.2
Raw material	42.3	21.1	36.9	22.4	53.8	14.8	41.3	13.8
Labor	41.1	6.7	45.9	10.5	63.6	9.6	54.6	10.3
Capital	54.6	14.3	48.1	10.5	63.8	8.8	55.9	9.3
Technology	50.9	33.0	54.0	35.0	65.6	33.1	59.0	26.3
SITC 9	71.5	24.8	52.9	20.5	47.4	32.7	47.4	36.5
Total	41.3	31.9	42.9	31.2	59.3	29.4	52.5	24.9
II. Japan								
SITC 0–4	59.3	17.5	54.6	12.5	60.0	9.9	69.9	12.1
SITC 5–8	13.0	50.7	10.8	48.6	8.4	48.7	11.1	51.6
Raw material	22.6	45.6	17.7	38.7	18.2	38.3	28.9	35.9
Labor	11.7	75.2	9.9	60.9	8.0	58.0	12.0	53.3
Capital	8.9	61.2	8.6	63.5	7.8	63.9	10.0	60.0
Technology	18.8	39.8	14.8	40.5	8.6	42.7	9.1	49.7
SITC 9	17.5	58.6	23.4	52.2	33.2	36.4	29.5	37.6
Total	20.8	45.1	16.8	42.4	13.9	41.5	16.1	45.5
III. OECD								
SITC 0–4	16.6	17.3	13.1	17.2	9.9	17.9	8.0	14.9
SITC 5–8	81.6	81.2	85.4	81.6	88.4	80.5	90.7	83.7
Raw material	4.9	5.0	3.9	6.0	2.3	4.6	2.3	4.7
Labor	49.7	11.7	46.3	8.1	43.4	8.0	41.9	7.1
Capital	14.0	21.0	19.5	22.1	19.3	18.2	21.2	19.5
Technology	13.1	43.6	15.7	49.9	23.4	49.6	25.4	52.4
SITC 9	1.7	1.5	1.5	1.2	1.7	1.6	1.3	1.4
Total	100.0	100.0	100.0	100.0	100.0	100.0	100.0	100.0

Source: OECD Trade Tape.

[a]Exports are valued in terms of cost-insurance-freight prices whereas imports are free-on-board prices.

[b]Country figures of each category of goods in I and II are the percentages of corresponding world totals in III.

expansion was due in large part to a surge of their exports to the United States, which absorbed more than 35 percent of the EANICs' exports during the 1985–88 period. Unlike Japan, however, their imports have risen gradually to exceed the 7 percent level of total world imports in recent years. More than a quarter of their imports has come from Japan. Since the early 1980s, the EANICs have been steadily losing their export competitiveness of labor-intensive manufactures due to rising labor costs. This loss has been more than offset by a large gain in the exports of technology-intensive products, the share of which jumped from about 16 percent of total exports in 1980 to over

25 percent in 1987 (see table 3.4).[3] On the import side, the EANICs' commodity structure has been relatively stable with a small increase in imports of technology-intensive manufactures.

3.2.2   Bilateral Trade Relations

U.S.-Japan

In the 1970s and the early 1980s, capital-intensive manufactures such as household electrical machinery, road vehicles, and television sets dominated Japan's exports to the United States with a share of more than 60 percent. Reflecting the change in Japan's comparative advantage, these manufactures have been gradually replaced by more technology-intensive products. By 1987 the group of technology-intensive products soared to 40 percent of Japan's total exports to the United States from less than 28 percent in 1980, all at the expense of capital-intensive goods (see table 3.3). Although Japan has become relatively less competitive in exporting capital-intensive manufactures to the world market, it has remained a competitive supplier of these products to the United States. As a result of these developments, Japan's overall share in the U.S. export market climbed to 20 percent in 1987 from about 13 percent in 1980 (see table 3.2). More than 93 percent of these exports to the United States consisted of those capital- and technology-intensive products. The large increase in U.S. import demand for all groups of manufactures has been responsible for much of the increase in Japan's exports to the United States.

In sharp contrast to the dominance of capital- and technology-intensive products in Japan's exports, practically all of Japan's imports from the U.S. are primary products belonging to SITC 0–4 and technology-intensive manufactures and very little in between (table 3.3). During the 1985–87 period, these two categories of products added up to more than 85 percent of Japan's imports from the United States with an approximately equal share for each group. The United States has managed to increase its export market base in Japan in the 1980s by promoting mostly the exports of primary products. In fact, the United States has been losing some of its export market for manufactured products in Japan largely because of the relative decline in U.S. exports of technology-intensive products since 1985.

EANICs-U.S.

Table 3.2 shows that, as a group, the EANICs almost doubled their share in U.S. total imports (from 7.5 percent to 14.5 percent) between 1980 and 1987. Labor-intensive manufactures still dominate their exports to the United States,

---

3. There has been divergent development between Korea and Taiwan with regard to the product composition of exports. Korea has moved into exports of capital-intensive items mostly to the United States whereas Taiwan has been more successful in increasing its market share of technology-intensive products in the OECD region with the United States as the major customer.

but the overall gain has been brought about by their success in marketing capital- and technology-intensive products. In 1987, the United States purchased more than 15 percent of their imports of technology-intensive manufactures from the EANICs, as compared to 30 percent from Japan. Despite the loss of their export competitiveness in the labor-intensive products, the EANICs have managed to hold on to their share in this group since the mid-1980s. As in the case of Japan, the strong U.S. demand for manufactured imports has been responsible for this development.

On the import side, the commodity composition of EANICs' imports from the United States is quite similar to that of Japan (see table 3.4). In the 1980s, more than 85 percent of EANICs' total imports from the United States on average consisted of primary products and technology-intensive manufactures, the proportion of the former group being about 30 percent. From the point of view of U.S. exporters, however, it has not been easy to compete in the markets of the EANICs. In fact, the U.S. has lost its market share in primary products (from 61 percent to 50 percent) as well as in manufactures (from 25 to 20 percent) during the 1980–87 period (see table 3.4).

EANICs-Japan

In the 1980s, the EANICs outperformed all other competitors in the Japanese market, doubling their export market share from less than 6 percent to 13 percent (see table 3.3). The EANICs have done well in exporting all categories of manufactures, but the overall gain has been due especially to a large increase in their exports of labor-intensive products. In 1987, the EANICs supplied more than 46 percent of Japan's total imports belonging to this group of commodities (up from less than 37 percent in 1980), and 22 percent of Japan's capital-intensive imports. Japan now imports more capital-intensive manufactures from the EANICs than from the United States.

On the import side, the EANICs have relied on Japan as their main supplier of capital and intermediate goods. It can be calculated from table 3.4 that almost 80 percent of the EANICs' imports from Japan in the 1980s included capital- and technology-intensive manufactures. This dependence on Japan for capital and technology has increased in recent years. In 1987, the EANICs obtained from Japan almost 50 percent of their total imports of technology-intensive manufactures (up from about 41 percent in 1980) as compared to 26 percent from the United States. Although the EANICs rely less on Japan than before for their supply of capital-intensive manufactures, Japan still accounted for more than 60 percent of their total imports of capital-intensive items in 1987.[4]

While it should be admitted that the level of aggregation in classification of manufactured exports by factor intensity is likely too high for a precise struc-

4. The degree of dependence of Korea and Taiwan on Japan for the supplies of these products has been higher than that of Hong Kong and Singapore.

tural analysis, the preceding discussion nevertheless reveals that a number of significant changes have taken place in the 1980s.

One of the most significant developments has been the rapid growth of trade among the United States, Japan, and the EANICs, in particular the export growth of the EANICs to the United States and Japan. In order to explain this export growth, we have estimated a number of export equations for the EANICs (including only Korea and Taiwan), Japan, and the United States, where real income and current and lagged real exchange rates are included as independent variables. Our results, some of which are given in table 3.5, suggest that the export equations are highly unstable. For what it is worth, it appears that real exports of the EANICs both to Japan and the United States are mostly explained by changes in income and the real exchange rate. Our estimation also suggests that Japan's exports to the EANICs tend to be inelastic with respect to changes in the real exchange rate, whereas their exports to the United States are not. This is because the EANICs do not have any alternative sources other than Japan of imports of capital- and technology-intensive manufactures.

A second development has been the large loss of competitiveness of U.S. manufacturing. In their home markets, U.S. manufactures, in particular those of capital- and technology-intensive products, have seen a continuous erosion of their market shares by Japanese and EANIC exporters. In 1987, for instance, Japan and the EANICs accounted for 47 and 45 percent of the U.S. imports of capital- and technology-intensive products, respectively (see table 3.2). Similar figures for 1980 were 45 and 30 percent.

At the same time, U.S. manufactures have been losing out to other competitors in the export markets of Japan and EANICs. Although the U.S. remains the main exporter of technology-intensive manufactures, it has sustained considerable decline of its East Asian market share in this product category. This has been offset, however, by the expansion of primary exports to Japan, thereby keeping the overall export share of the United States relatively stable.

A third development has been the change in the product composition of the EANICs' exports from one dominated by labor-intensive manufactures to one which includes more capital- and technology-intensive products. The bulk of the EANICs' exports to the United States still consists of labor-intensive manufactures (see table 3.4), but, in line with the change in their export commodity composition, the EANICs have also developed into major suppliers of capital- and technology-intensive products to the United States. As a result, the EANICs' trade relationship with the United States involving manufactures has changed from a complementary to a competitive one in the 1980s.

A fourth trend has been the rapid expansion of trade between Japan and the EANICs. As shown in tables 3.1 and 3.3, the EANICs have succeeded in carving out a large slice of the export market in Japan. Unlike their expansion of exports to the United States, however, the EANICs have increased their Japanese market share by selling mostly labor-intensive manufactures. It ap-

Table 3.5   Trilateral Trade Relationships

	Real Exports[a] to the United States		Real Exports to Japan		Real Exports to the EANICs	
	Japan	EANICs	United States	EANICs	United States	Japan
Constant[b]	−25.41(−10.99)	−19.58(−3.13)	3.18 (1.71)	−23.38(−2.85)	9.58 (5.98)	5.29(18.19)
Y_u	3.62 (18.95)	2.71 (3.95)				
Y_j			.92(12.95)	2.71 (4.33)		
Y_n					.95(21.22)	1.12(15.59)
BRER	.56 (2.11)	.56 (1.54)	.35 (1.51)	.60 (1.16)	1.06 (3.44)	.03 (0.11)
BRER(−1)	.93 (3.45)	1.20 (3.56)	.51 (2.00)	1.34 (2.59)		−.61(−1.97)
R^2	.99	.99	.96	.98	.98	.98
D-W	2.22	2.35	1.70	1.33	1.30	2.00
ρ	.45	.88		.75		.41

Note: Log-linear equations are regressed by using the OLS method (if necessary, the Cochrane-Orcutt method is applied) over the period 1965–88. The numbers in the parentheses are *t*-statistics.

[a]Real exports are defined as nominal exports divided by exporting country's export price.

[b]The letters u, j, n represent the United States, Japan, and the EANICs (including only South Korea and Taiwan), respectively. Y = GNP in terms of domestic currency; BRER = bilateral real exchange rate (WPI of importing country × exchange rate of the exporting country's currency per importing country's currency/export unit value in terms of exporting country's currency).

pears that, in the United States, the EANICs have been moving out of the export markets for labor-intensive goods whereas in Japan they have been moving into those markets.

According to our estimation results in table 3.5, much of the export expansion of the EANICs to Japan during the 1985–88 period has been supported by the real depreciation of the currencies of the EANICs vis-à-vis the yen. In view of the rising labor costs in the EANICs, however, it is difficult to expect that the EANICs could maintain the high rate of growth of exports to Japan for the last few years as they will face stiff competition from low-cost producers in ASEAN (the Association of Southeast Asian Nations) and China. This means that, unless the EANICs succeed in moving into the Japanese markets for capital- and technology-intensive manufactures on a large scale, their exports to Japan are likely to slow down to the pace of their competitors from Europe and North America as already happened in 1989 as their bilateral exchange rates with Japan stabilized.

The expansion of the EANICs' exports has been matched by an almost equal increase in their dependence on Japan for the imports of technology-intensive products. In 1987, for example, 50 percent of EANICs' imports of technology-intensive manufactures were shipped from Japan as compared to 40.5 percent in 1980. Their value was almost twice as large as that from the United States. This deepening dependence has contributed to an increase in complementarity in trade between the EANICs and Japan and, as a result, has not caused very much change in the triangular relationship linking them with the United States.

3.3   Developments in Intra-industry Trade among the United States, Japan, and the EANICs

This section discusses changes in the patterns of intraindustry trade between the EANICs and both Japan and the United States. For this purpose, we have estimated Grubel-Lloyd indices of intra-industry trade (IIT) in manufacturing classified by factor intensity in figures 3.1–3.6.[5]

Figure 3.1 shows a number of significant changes in Japan's intra-industry trade in manufactures with the rest of the world. The level of Japan's intra-industry trade in labor-intensive manufactures has always been high. The steep increase in the index since 1985 has been related to a large drop in Japan's surplus from and hence loss of competitiveness in this category of trade.

A second change is the expansion of Japan's intra-industry trade in capital-

5. The Grubel-Lloyd index of intraindustry trade is defined as

$$IIT_i = [\ 1\ -\ \frac{|\,X_i\ -\ M_i|}{X_i\ +\ M_i}\ ] \cdot 100\%,$$

where X_i and M_i are exports and imports of a product category i, respectively.

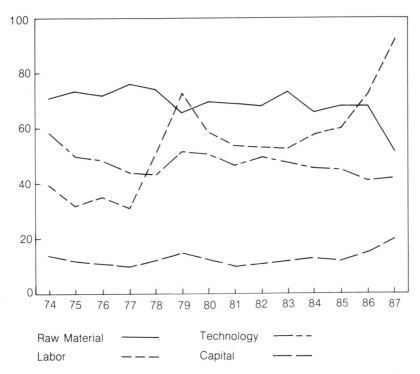

Fig. 3.1   Index of Intra-industry trade by factor intensity (Japanese trade with the world)
Source: OECD Trade Tape

intensive manufactures. Capital-intensive manufactures accounted for more than 45 percent of Japan's total exports and provided the largest source of its trade surpluses in the 1980s. As a result, Japan's intra-industry trade in this category of products had been the least active among the four categories. The rise in the index has largely been brought about by the increase in Japan's imports of these goods from the European Community (EC) and EANICs.

A third change is the large drop in the index for raw-material-intensive manufactures in 1987. It is too early to tell whether this decline indicates a new trend, however. Finally, the index for intraindustry trade in technology-intensive manufactures fell to 40 in 1987 from about 50 seven years earlier. Much of the decline reflects Japan's gain in export competitiveness and its growing surplus from trade in this group of products.

In general, indices for Japan for manufactures excluding labor-intensive products have been stable compared to those of the United States (see fig. 3.2). The high degree of aggregation in our study does not provide many clues as to the causes of the relative stability of Japan's intraindustry trade indices. However, this stability coupled with Japan's strong export performance seems

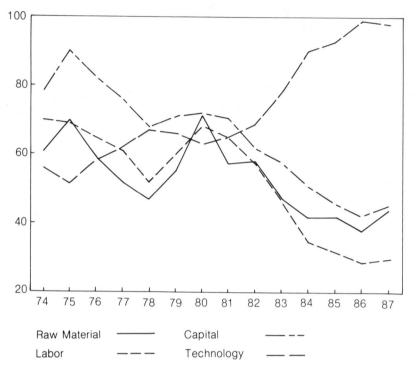

Fig. 3.2 Index of Intra-industry trade by factor intensity (U.S. trade with the world)
Source: OECD Trade Tape

to suggest that Japan's trade in manufactures with the rest of the world should perhaps be explained by comparative advantage and that Japan has been able to maintain its international competitiveness.

Figure 3.3 shows a large increase in intra-industry trade between Japan and the EANICs in the 1980s, much of which has been the result of rapid industrialization in and export growth sustained by the EANICs. As far as exports of manufactured goods are concerned, the level of intra-industry trade between the EANICs and Japan surpassed the level between Japan and the United States and is approaching that between Japan and the EC.

Within manufacturing (fig. 3.4), the index for labor-intensive products had remained well over 90 before dropping to 70 in 1987. This large drop was due to the increase in Japan's deficit in this class of trade, a development that could hardly have been unexpected. Since the surge of exports to Japan started around 1985, for products intensive in raw materials, the IIT index recorded the largest gain, from 50 in 1985 to almost 70 in 1987. This was followed by an equally impressive gain in capital-intensive products. In both cases, the

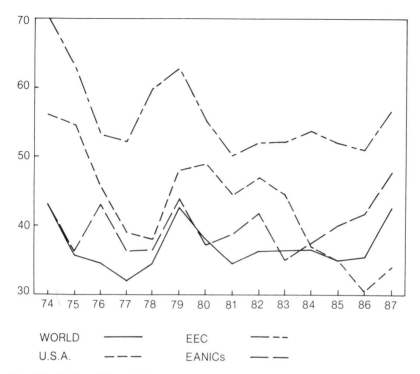

WORLD ————	EEC — — —
U.S.A. — — —	EANICs — —

Fig. 3.3   Index of Intra-industry trade by region (Japanese manufacturing)
Source: OECD Trade Tape

expansion was led by the growth of the EANICs' exports to Japan. In contrast to these changes, the index for technology-intensive products has remained virtually unchanged at the low level of about 20 percent since 1975.

The changes in the IIT indices described above reveal a number of important developments in Japan's trade with both the EANICs and the rest of the world that confirm our analysis in section 3.2. The EANICs have successfully marketed their labor-intensive manufactures in Japan. Since 1986, Japan has been running a deficit with the EANICs in its trade in this product category. Since 1986, Japan has also come to depend on imports from the EANICs to satisfy the bulk of its domestic demand for labor-intensive manufactures. A second development is that the EANICs have been able to make inroads into the Japanese markets for those products intensive in both resources and capital. However, our observations are so limited that it is difficult to judge whether the intra-industry trade expansion in these categories between Japan and the EANICs has been a-once-and-for-all change or is the beginning of a new trend. A third development is that, as noted in the preceding section, the EANICs have become more dependent on Japan for the imports of

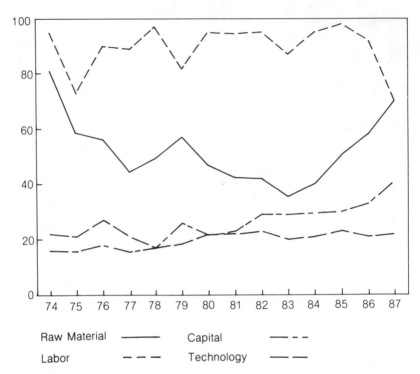

Fig. 3.4   Index of Intra-industry trade by factor intensity (Japanese trade with EANICs)
Source: OECD Trade Tape

technology-intensive items. This dependence explains why the EANICs have not had much success in reducing their deficits with Japan despite the rapid growth of their exports to Japan.

In contrast to the expansion of intra-industry trade in manufactures between the EANICs and Japan, similar trade between the EANICs and the United States, as measured by the IIT index, has declined markedly (see fig. 3.5). By 1987, the index fell below 40 from 75 in 1975. Much of the decrease can be traced to the EANICs' accumulation of large surpluses from their trade in manufactures intensive in labor and capital.[6]

Among manufactures, the index for labor-intensive items has been low throughout the period and has declined further in recent years (see fig. 3.6). However, the contraction of intra-industry trade in capital-intensive manufactures has been most dramatic. Between 1970 and 1987, the index for this group dropped from more than 70 to about 20. This was the result of the

6. The index for the United States with the rest of the world has also recorded a sharp decline in the 1980s.

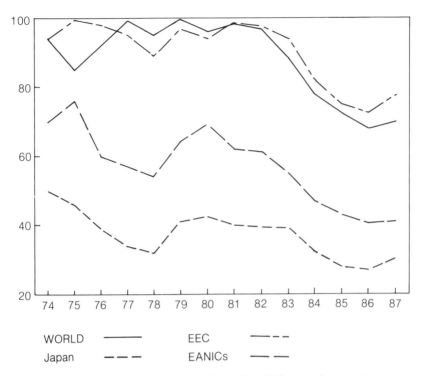

Fig. 3.5   Index of Intra-industry trade by region (U.S. manufacturing)
Source: OECD Trade Tape

EANICs' success in capturing a large share of the U.S. market for these products. Intra-industry trade in technology-intensive manufactures between the
EANICs and the United States has been active, as the high level of the index
indicates. Even in this category, however, the index has declined largely because of the growing trade surplus of the EANICs. Except for those manufactures intensive in raw materials, for which the IIT index has turned upward
since 1985, it appears that the United States has been losing out to the
EANICs in export competitiveness of all manufactures. As is the case with
Japan, it is difficult to explain changes in the patterns of EANICs' trade with
the United States in terms of those factors usually identified as determining
intra-industry trade.

It is generally accepted that intra-industry trade tends to be prevalent between countries with similar factor endowments and skill levels and when
scale economies and product differentiation are significant. That is, intra-
industry trade will expand between economies at similar levels of economic
development. Much of the trade among industrialized countries is characterized by the dominance of intra-industry trade, of which volume is largely
influenced by factors on the demand side. In contrast, intra-industry trade

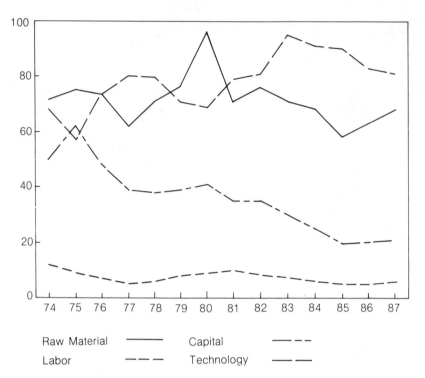

Fig. 3.6   Index of Intra-industry trade by factor intensity (U.S. trade with EANICs)
Source: OECD Trade Tape

between advanced and developing countries includes mostly exchanges of manufactured goods differentiated by different processing stages in the same industry. This type of trade is likely to be determined by comparative advantage based on differences in technology, endowments of research and development (R&D) stock and human capital; that is, factors on the supply side.[7]

The growth of intra-industry trade in capital-intensive manufactures between Japan and the EANICs has been led by two categories of products. The first is made up of products differentiated by quality and price; this is the case in the consumer electronics trade, where Japan exchanges more sophisticated and high-quality products for cheaper, lower-quality electronics from the EANICs. The other category consists of products at different production stages in the same industry. Because of the lack of data and difficulties in disaggregating further product categories, we have not been able to determine the relative importance of the two types, although for the last three years the share of the second group appears to have increased.

7. There is a definitional question of whether the trade of this type should be classified as intra- or interindustry.

In the 1970s it is likely that intra-industry trade in labor-intensive manufactures included a large number of products differentiated by quality and price. That is, Japan exported to the EANICs those labor-intensive items at the high-quality end of the product line while importing from these countries inexpensive, low-quality products to satisfy the diverse tastes of consumers. The EANICs and Japan may also have started exchanging those labor-intensive products with different attributes. In recent years, however, the EANICs' trade with Japan in labor-intensive items has come to consist of inter-industry exchanges and has become increasingly competitive, as suggested by the decline in the IIT index together with Japan's growing deficits. Despite the rapid growth of two-way trade in technology-intensive manufactures between the EANICs and Japan, the IIT index for this group remained virtually unchanged. This is because Japan has been able to maintain a large lead over the EANICs in developing new technologies and hence to increase its surplus from the trade in this category of products with the EANICs.

In summary, our estimates of IIT indices among Japan, the EANICs, and the United States suggest that the EANICs have overtaken and extended their competitive lead over the United States in manufactures trade. With respect to Japan, the EANICs are catching up in the development and export of new manufactures intensive in capital and technology, but they have a long way to go if they are to narrow the gap with Japan in technology, skill and production, and management know-how.

It may take many years for the United States to regain its competitiveness as an industrial power. Japan has maintained its superiority in developing new technology and has demonstrated its ability to adjust to changes in market conditions. The EANICs show no visible signs of slowing down in their race to catch up with Japan. Taken together, these developments suggest a future pattern of trade in which the triangular trade structure among the three partners will become more rigid than before.

3.4   Japan's FDI in Asia and EANICs

A number of recent studies by Japanese economists (Iwata 1989; Kawai 1989; and Urata 1989) suggest that Japan's FDI has served as an important channel for transferring Japan's technology to developing Asian economies and contributing to the expansion of intrafirm trade in Asia, thereby stimulating growth and industrialization throughout Asia. A careful examination of changes in the total amount and sectoral distribution of Japan's FDI and of the behavior of Japanese multinationals suggests that the effects of Japan's FDI on trade patterns between Japan and other Asian countries may have been exaggerated.

At the end of 1988, the cumulative total of Japan's FDI in Asia since 1951 amounted to $31,803 million (in U.S. dollars), which was equivalent to 17 percent of Japan's total FDI, down from the 27 percent three years earlier (see

Table 3.6   Stock of Japanese Direct Investment Abroad (Year-end, in Millions of U.S. Dollars)

Region/Country	Year	Total	Manufacturing Total	Food	Textiles	Paper Pulp	Chemicals	Ferrous, Nonferrous Metals	Machinery[a]	Other Manufacturing
World	1978	26,809 (100.0)	9,174 (100.0)	430	1,457	647	2,074	1,548	2,375	644
	1983	53,131 (100.0)	16,952 (100.0)	806	1,759	899	3,176	3,608	5,409	1,258
	1988	186,356 (100.0)	49,843 (100.0)	1,965	2,669	2,099	6,540	7,671	21,868	7,031
Asia	1978	7,506 (28.0)[b]	3,356 (36.6)[b]	116	831	120	460	669	787	366
	1983	14,346 (27.0)	5,727 (33.8)	166	997	160	986	1,464	1,346	609
	1988	31,803 (17.1)	12,164 (24.4)	506	1,366	385	1,771	2,243	4,532	1,359
EANICs	1978	2,547 (33.9)	1,503 (44.8)	24	304	23	264	94	612	176
	1983	4,999 (34.8)	2,502 (43.7)	51	344	25	604	164	978	336
	1988	15,018 (47.2)	5,544 (45.6)	199	401	42	1,169	354	2,599	779
Other Asia	1978	4,959 (66.1)	1,853 (55.2)	92	527	97	196	575	175	190
	1983	9,347 (65.2)	3,225 (56.3)	115	653	135	382	1,300	368	273
	1988	16,785 (52.8)	6,620 (54.4)	307	965	343	602	1,889	1,933	580

Source: Ministry of Finance, Japan.
[a]Includes general, electrical, and transport machinery.
[b]As percentage of total.

table 3.6). Similar figures for North America and South America at the end of 1988 were 40.2 and 17.0 percent (see table 3.7). The EANICs attracted a total of $15,018 million or 47.2 percent of FDI to Asia since 1951. In 1988 alone, however, the EANICs ran a deficit of $24,810 million in their merchandise trade with Japan. That is, the cumulative total of Japan's FDI in the EANICs between 1951 and 1988 was no more than 60 percent of the EANICs' trade deficit with Japan in a single year.

It is true that Japan's FDI in the EANICs recorded a sixfold increase between 1978 and 1988 and has more than doubled over the past five-year period, but North America and Europe have received a relatively greater share (see table 3.7). Compared to other regions, Asia has been an attractive place for investment in manufacturing (see table 3.8), but less than 40 percent of Japan's FDI in the EANICs was allocated to manufacturing in 1988 as compared to 50 percent in 1985 and 60 percent in 1987. This means that much of Japan's FDI in the EANICs has recently been channeled into nonmanufacturing industries. Within manufacturing, machinery industries have been the most attractive sectors to Japanese investors, followed by chemical industries. At the end of 1988, general electrical machinery and transport equipment made up almost 48 percent of Japan's total FDI in manufacturing. This was followed by 21 percent in chemicals (see table 3.6).

Beginning around 1985, an increasing number of Japanese firms, mostly multinationals but also small and medium-sized firms in export-oriented industries, started to move production and product development offshore on a large scale to remain cost competitive in world markets. The high yen and expectations of its further appreciation together with growing protectionist

Table 3.7   **Japanese Foreign Direct Investment by Destination (in Millions of U.S. Dollars)**

Year	North America	Western Europe	Asia	South America	Oceania	Others	Total
1975	905	333	1,100	372	182	388	3,280
	(27.6)	(10.2)	(33.5)	(11.3)	(5.6)	(11.8)	(100.0)
1980	1,596	578	1,186	588	448	297	4,693
	(34.0)	(12.3)	(25.3)	(12.5)	(9.5)	(6.3)	(100.0)
1985	5,495	1,930	1,435	2,616	525	217	12,218
	(45.0)	(15.8)	(11.7)	(21.4)	(4.3)	(1.8)	(100.0)
1988	22,828	9,116	5,569	6,428	2,669	912	47,022
	(47.5)	(19.4)	(11.8)	(13.7)	(5.7)	(2.0)	(100.0)
Cumulative total	75,091	30,164	32,227	31,617	9,315	7,942	186,356
(1951–88)	(40.3)	(16.2)	(17.3)	(17.0)	(5.0)	(4.3)	(100.0)

Source: Economic Survey of Japan, 1987–88, Economic Planning Agency, Japanese Government, pp. 470–71.

Note: Numbers in parentheses are percentages.

Table 3.8   Japanese Foreign Direct Investment by Industry (in Millions of U.S. Dollars)

Year	Agriculture, Forestry and Fisheries	Mining	Construction	Manufacturing	Commerce	Finance and Insurance	Service	Transportation Service	Real Estate Brokerage	Others	Total
1975	64 (2.0)	707 (21.6)	32 (1.0)	924 (28.0)	668 (20.4)	310 (9.5)	113 (3.4)			462 (14.1)	3,280 (100.0)
1980	73 (1.6)	565 (12.0)	37 (1.0)	1,706 (36.3)	797 (17.0)	380 (8.0)	251 (5.3)			884 (18.8)	4,690 (100.0)
1985	54 (.4)	598 (5.0)	94 (.8)	2,352 (19.3)	1,550 (13.0)	3,805 (31.0)	665 (5.4)	1,240 (10.0)	1,207 (9.8)	652 (5.3)	12,217 (100.0)
1988	206 (.5)	1,013 (2.2)	309 (.7)	13,805 (29.4)	3,204 (6.8)	13,104 (27.9)	3,732 (7.9)	2,372 (5.0)	8,641 (18.4)	587 (1.2)	47,022 (100.0)
Cumulative total (1951–88)	1,686 (.9)	13,949 (7.5)	1,443 (.8)	49,843 (26.7)	20,011 (10.7)	41,878 (22.5)	12,759 (6.8)	12,342 (6.6)	20,599 (11.1)	11,848 (6.3)	186,356 (100.0)

Source: Economic Survey of Japan, 1987–88, Economic Planning Agency, Japanese Government, pp. 470–71.

[a]As percentage of total.

measures directed against Japanese exports provided strong incentives for Japanese multinationals to globalize their operations. The globalization strategy has also been facilitated by advances in communications and transportation technology and liberal policies for FDI in many host countries, both in Asia and elsewhere.

There is little reliable information that can shed light on the behavior of Japanese multinationals, although it is widely believed that they are contributing to the changes in trade patterns and spearheading regionalization in Asia. This section heavily relies on the statistical surveys of Japanese overseas investment published in 1980, 1983, and 1986 by Japan's MITI.[8] According to these surveys, imports by Japanese foreign subsidiaries more than tripled, from less than $30 billion in 1980 to $90 billion in 1986, which was equivalent to 43 percent of Japan's total exports. Meanwhile, their exports to Japan—mostly to their parent companies—declined in absolute value from $36.3 billion in 1980 to $27 billion in 1986, which amounted to 21.4 percent of Japan's total imports in the same year and resulted in an intrafirm trade surplus of $63 billion for Japan.

These surveys show that Japanese multinationals have been major players, accounting for much of the increase in intrafirm trade in Asia that is, in turn, related to the buildup of their network of overseas affiliates and to the expansion of intra-industry trade between Japan and the rest of the world. In so doing, they have assumed a greater role in Japan's external trade in recent years. There is also evidence that a large portion of the exports by Japanese multinational parents have been replaced by the output produced by their overseas affiliates and subsidiaries (Urata 1989).

What are the factors responsible for the rapid growth of intrafirm trade in Japanese multinational firms and the large surplus from such trade? One factor is the large concentration of Japan's FDI in machinery industries (the share was 44 percent in 1988). Unlike other manufacturing sectors, production of general, electrical, and precision machinery requires assembling of a large number of parts and components. This means that the production of machinery can be divided into a number of processes, each of which could in turn be located in different countries through FDI. Then the volume of trade between Japanese multinational parents and their affiliates in products that belong to the same production line but at different processing stages will increase, and much more so than in the case of multinationals producing nonmachinery products. Furthermore, many of Japanese multinationals' overseas subsidiaries were established in recent years, as the data show. During the early stages of operation, these subsidiaries relied heavily on their parent companies for the supplies of parts, components, and other intermediate products. This largely explains Japan's surplus in intrafirm trade.

In Asia, Japan's FDI since the mid-1970s has been mostly allocated to

---

8. The data used in this paper are obtained from Iwata (1989).

export-oriented industries. In fact, Japanese subsidiaries have been established mainly as production and export bases, aiming at expanding sales in
third-country markets (Iwata 1989). That is, the relatively low cost of labor,
together with a high level of technology and production know-how in many
Asian countries (in particular the EANICs), have attracted Japanese firms to
expand and disperse various aspects of their operations—production, R&D,
and sales—throughout Asia by means of FDI. Japanese multinationals have
also made intrafirm agreements and strategic alliances with their counterparts
in other Asian countries as part of their globalization and regionalization
strategy.

These developments point to the important role Japanese multinationals
could play in expanding intra-industry trade and generating market forces for
regional integration in Asia. However, at this stage, the volume of intra-
industry trade created by Japan's FDI in Asia, though growing rapidly, has
been too small to be of any significance in assessing whether Japan's FDI has
contributed in creating or diverting trade in Asia. We have suggested that Japanese overseas affiliates in Asia are concentrated in export-oriented industries
and are more likely to ship their products to third countries than to Japan. The
MITI surveys seem to bear this out, as in 1986 when Japanese subsidiaries in
Asia exported $8.8 billion, or 20 percent of their total output, to Japan and 35
percent to third countries. If this trend continues, it is possible that Japan's
FDI may indeed exacerbate trade imbalances between the United States and
Asia. One reason for this is that Japanese multinationals and firms in export-
oriented industries have expertise and experience in exporting to the United
States and Europe. They are therefore likely to move their production bases to
other Asian countries without changing the destination of their exports.

Another reason that Japanese FDI may worsen U.S.-Asian trade imbalances
is that Japan's FDI and the increase of interfirm agreements and strategic alliances between firms in Japan and other Asian countries will facilitate transfer
of Japanese technology and management know-how throughout Asia. This
process will help EANICs and ASEAN countries to produce and export more
human-capital- and technology-intensive products. Unless Japan is able and
prepared to absorb more of these manufactured exports from other Asian
countries, there is a danger that the EANICs and other Asian economies will
sell the products they learn to produce from Japan to the North American and
European markets.

3.5   Product-Cycle Development in Asia?[9]

In recent years, a number of Japanese economists have claimed that changing patterns of trade and the associated industrialization in Asia could be explained by a variation of the product cycle theory applied in an international
context (Okita 1986; Yamazawa 1988). It has indeed become fashionable to

---

9. This section draws on Park (1989).

describe the pattern of industrialization taking place in Pacific Asia in terms of the product cycle and to compare it to a flock of flying geese. In this metaphor, Japan is the leading goose, or the leading innovative country, that creates a new product and then begins to export it when its supply exceeds domestic demand. After a time lag, the follower countries, having imported the product, learn to produce it for their domestic markets; that is, they engage in import substitution of the product. In the Asian context, the EANICs are the followers flying right behind Japan. When the EANICs saturate their domestic markets for the product, they also begin to export it to countries that are following them—the ASEAN countries, for example, which formerly imported the product from Japan. As the EANICs become more competitive, they first make inroads into Japan's (the innovator's) export markets—ASEAN, for example—and then eventually penetrate the Japanese market itself. In the end, the innovator country becomes a net importer of the product it first invented.

While the second-tier countries—the EANICs—are catching up with Japan, they are also pursued by third-tier countries on the ladder of comparative advantage. The export markets, and eventually the home markets, of the second-tier countries for a particular product will also be penetrated by the pursuers. By this time, however, the second-tier countries—the EANICs— have probably become innovators themselves or begun to produce a new product invented by the leading innovator country. Thus, a development cycle for second-tier countries moves from rising imports to rising exports and then to a new product (see Rapp 1975). As Rapp points out, the flying geese pattern of development focuses on the interaction between countries engaged in trade expected from product cycle development (Vernon 1966) when all industries are taken into consideration. Competition in the flying geese pattern of development is based on changes in comparative advantage.

As discussed in sections 3.2 and 3.3, the EANICs have been able to produce and export more skill- and technology-intensive products to Japan than before. Between the ASEAN and Japan, trade relations have been more complementary or interdependent in that the former exports raw material to and imports manufactures from the latter. As the EANICs have reached a more advanced stage of development with the accumulation of skill and sophisticated technology, exports from the EANICs have displaced those from Japan in the U.S. market, while Japan has moved on to a higher level of technology and sophistication. At the same time, rising labor costs plus a sharp appreciation of their currencies have forced the EANICs out of U.S. markets for unsophisticated labor-intensive products such as textiles. As a result, the ASEAN countries have moved into the markets vacated by the EANICs. While trade patterns, in particular on the import side, among the Pacific countries remain unchanged, Japan has moved on to exporting high-technology products. Meanwhile, the EANICs have increased their exports of consumer electronics, and the ASEAN have become the major suppliers of textiles to the U.S. market (Bradford and Branson 1987, p. 13).

It is often claimed that this pattern of export side integration, centering on the U.S. market, has been slowing down somewhat because of a new trend of Asian-based regional integration with the increased capacity of Japan to absorb more manufactured imports from other Pacific Asian countries. At the same time, the EANICs have begun to play the role of middle-level economies in the trade linkage among the Pacific Asian countries, opening their markets for imports and expanding their direct investment and technology transfer throughout Southeast Asia and China.

Has this regional economic integration taken hold? If it has, how visible is it and could it be sustained in Asia? Beginning in 1986, Japan's trade with the EANICs in labor-intensive manufactures has turned into a deficit. The EANICs have at least established a foothold in the Japanese markets for those manufactures requiring large amounts of raw materials and human capital, while cutting down their deficits with Japan relative to their total trade. At the same time, their imports of manufactured goods from the ASEAN have been growing. These developments are encouraging, for Pacific Asian economies may be able to develop a regional market large enough to absorb the bulk of Asian exports, thereby compensating for the expected shrinking of the U.S. market. In this process, Japan will undoubtedly be playing a leading role.

While some of the market forces leading to regional economic integration are clearly visible, other factors and structural characteristics stand in the way of regional growth and industrialization through the product cycle development. We have examined changes in Japan's balances of trade in several products where the product cycle is most likely to be influential, such as in textile yarn and fabrics, general industrial machinery, electrical machinery, household electrical machinery, and transport machinery.[10] In all five categories, Japan has been running trade surpluses with both the EANICs and the rest of the world. Except for textile yarn and fabrics and household electrical machinery, Japan's trade surpluses in absolute terms have been rising. Another interesting observation is that, in all categories, with the possible exception of household electrical machinery, Japan's surpluses with the EANICs have been increasing. In contrast, however, the U.S. balances of trade in these products with the EANICs and the rest of the world turned into deficits in the early 1980s and have deteriorated sharply since then. We are not able to make any judgment as to whether these phenomena have been the result of Japan's overall accumulation of trade surpluses and the U.S. trade deficits, or whether they have been due to Japan's ability to maintain a large lead in technology development. Regardless, in view of Japan's ability to make structural adjustments, Japan is not likely to lose its export competitiveness in these product categories.

Whether the product cycle development can be sustained will, in the end, depend on the role Japan plays as the leading economy in Asia. If Japan is able to absorb enough imports from the EANICs and ASEAN, so that these

10. Data available on request.

developing economies could supplant the Japanese market in exporting to the United States, while continuously passing on new products and new production processes through foreign direct investment and other channels, then such a pattern of development could speed up the Pacific Asian–based economic integration.

Although Japan is the second largest economy in the world, it is highly doubtful whether it could become a major absorber of other Pacific Asian economies.[11] Only three years after Japan undertook market-opening measures, it is claimed that the EANICs have already saturated Japan's market for labor-intensive manufactures including electronics and machinery (Daiwa Securities Research Institute 1989). One magazine article (*Far Eastern Economic Review* [FEER], 8 June 1989) claims that even Taiwan and South Korea have failed to penetrate Japan's market for consumer goods despite their competitive edge. Apparently, the marked increase in their exports to Japan petered out early in 1989, because the yen depreciated vis-à-vis the U.S. dollar and "Japanese companies were quick to come up with simple, one function products that mimicked the best offering from Taiwan and South Korea" (ibid.). Japanese manufacturers may have weathered the difficult period of adaptation to the high yen and may have regained fully their foreign competitiveness.

There are other factors that also cast serious doubts for the future of regional integration in Pacific Asia. Japan could remain cost competitive in many skill- and technology-intensive products for which Japan is a dominant supplier to world markets. They can produce parts and components and their inputs in foreign countries—mostly in Asia—for factories in Japan through foreign subsidiary and joint venture arrangements. If indeed foreign sourcing produces benefits by saving costs and increasing access to markets without leading to losses in domestic employment, Japan could maintain its competitiveness in skill- and technology-intensive industries for a long time to come since the ratio of domestically sold overseas production to total domestic manufacturing output is only 3.2 percent in Japan, whereas it is 20 percent in the United States (Balassa and Noland 1988, p. 15).

In high-technology industries, Japan is likely to retain informal trade barriers through the use of procurement regulations, administrative guidance, and research and development schemes (Balassa and Noland 1988, p. 183). As they are the sectors that will keep Japanese manufacturing strong and competitive in the coming decades, Japan promotes high-technology industries related to information and communication technology, biotechnology, and material and space science. In all likelihood, Japan will resist trade liberalization in these and protect them as infant industries.

With the rapid increase in per capita income, Japanese consumers' tastes

11. In 1987, the value of manufactured imports per capita for Japan was $540 whereas it was $1,333 for the United States.

are changing to prefer more sophisticated, individualized, and high-quality products. For many products like clothing, consumer electronics, furniture, and automobiles, Japanese consumers are demanding more than ever those products specialized, custom made, and differentiated by their "Japanese attributes" than those standardized and mass produced. Furthermore, if the loss of scale economies from producing small quantities of these differentiated products could be overcome by adopting new production technologies, relatively low labor costs would not be as important an advantage as it was in the past. The EANICs exporters will therefore find it increasingly difficult to compete in the Japanese market.

Despite these difficulties, the EANICs will be able to expand the range of manufactured products in which they will be competitive with Japan in supplying both Asian and third markets. An important question is whether Japan will be able to adjust to this crowding-up problem. Trade relations between the ASEAN and the EANICs will also create a similar tension as the ASEAN moves rapidly up the ladder of industrial and technological development. As a result, the EANICs will find themselves squeezed by Japan at one end and by the ASEAN at the other. Efforts to overtake the countries in the upper tiers will generate strong competitive pressures among the Pacific Asian economies. These pressures will, in turn, induce the EANICs, ASEAN, and China to penetrate the markets of North America and Europe while keeping their markets closed to one another. This pattern of development would then enlarge the trade imbalance and worsen trade conflicts between Pacific Asia and the rest of the world, particularly North America.

One structural characteristic Japan and the EANICs share is poor resource endowment. This requires them to rely almost entirely on imported oil and other raw materials. In order to pay for these imports of primary commodities while keeping their overall trade in balance, they must obtain a surplus in their trade in manufactures with other countries. The ASEAN countries with a rich resource base have traditionally maintained a deficit on their manufactures trade with Japan and the EANICs. Through the promotion of labor-intensive products, however, the ASEAN and China are trying to balance their manufactures trade. This means that, as a whole, the Pacific Asian region will obtain a surplus from outside of the region, if the EANICs and ASEAN continue with their development strategies.

Furthermore, the EANICs, as a group, are likely to run a deficit in their trade with Japan as long as Japan maintains the lead in developing new technology and new products. Despite their market penetration, the EANICs' deficit with Japan was close to 80 percent of their total exports to Japan in 1988. During the process of catching up, which may continue into the next century, the balance of trade between the two parties will remain in Japan's favor. The EANICs' poor resource endowments together with its dependence on Japan mean that, as a group, they will have to run surpluses in their trade with the rest of the world to balance their overall trade accounts. This situation will improve only if Japan opens its market to the EANICs.

3.6 Concluding Remarks

It is undeniable that Japan has been changing in its role as a trade partner of the EANICs since the mid-1980s. Japan has shown its willingness to increase its imports of manufactured products not only from the EANICs but also from other countries. Japan has been active in recycling its trade surpluses in the form of FDI to Asia. These changes have raised expectations for creating a potentially large regional market in Asia, large enough to supplant in part the U.S. market.

As a group, the EANICs have cut down Japan's lead in manufacturing and exporting capital- and technology-intensive products. Equally successful has been their promotion of exports of all categories of manufactures to the U.S. Even a casual observation of raw data shows that the rise of the EANICs to the ranks of semi-industrialized countries has been made possible in part by the huge and growing capacity of the United States to absorb imports from Asia. Without such a market, especially with the relatively closed Japanese market, the EANICs would not have strong incentives for catching up with Japan.

Trade flows in recent years also indicate that the EANICs exporters have made inroads into the Japanese markets even in capital- and technology-intensive products. Does this mean that they would rely less on the U.S. market than before, thereby loosening up the triangular relation involving Japan and the United States? In this regard, our study is not optimistic. If the United States continues to accumulate trade deficits and its market remains open, then there is the danger that the EANICs, ASEAN, and China will all choose the easier path to industrialization and growth. They will continue to depend on U.S. demand for their exports rather than the difficult and uncertain alternative of cultivating the Japanese market.

Appendix

In the text, SITC 5–8 are classified into four groups according to their factor intensities on the basis of Krause (1987). His classification was based in turn on a UN classification scheme using the SITC rev. 1 definition. We have adjusted his classification to be consistent with the SITC rev. 2 definition.

Table 3A.1   Commodity Group by Factor Intensities

SITC Rev. 1	Commodity	SITC Rev. 2	Commodity
	Natural resource intensive:		
61	Leather	61	Leather
63	Wood	63	Wood
661–3	Mineral manufactures	661–3	Mineral manufactures
667	Precious stones	667	Precious stones
671	Pig iron	671	Pig iron
68	Nonferrous metals	68	Nonferrous metals
	Unskilled labor intensive:		
65	Textiles	65	Textiles
664–6	Glass and pottery	664–6	Glass and pottery
735	Ships	793	Ships
81	Sanitary, plumbing, heating and lighting fixtures	81	Sanitary, plumbing, heating and lighting fixtures
82	Furniture	82	Furniture
83	Travel goods	83	Travel goods
84	Apparel	84	Apparel
85	Footwear	85	Footwear
893	Plastic articles	893	Plastic articles
894	Toys	894	Toys
895	Office supplies	895	Office supplies
899	Manufactured articles, n.e.c.	899	Manufactured articles, n.e.c.
	Human capital intensive:		
53	Paints	53	Paints
55	Perfume	55	Perfume
62	Rubber	62	Rubber
64	Paper	64	Paper
672–9	Steel	672–9	Steel
69	Metal manufactures	69	Metal manufactures
7241	Televisions	761	Television receivers
7242	Radios	762	Radios
725	Domestic electrical apparatus	763	Phonographs, recorders
731–3	Railway and road vehicles	775	Household-type electrical machinery
864	Watches	78	Road vehicles
891	Musical instruments, phonograph, recorders	791	Railway vehicles
		885	Watches
		892	Printed matter
892	Printed matter	896–7	Antiques and jewelry
896–7	Antiques and jewelry	898	Musical instruments

Table 3A.1   (continued)

SITC Rev. 1	Commodity	SITC Rev. 2	Commodity
	Technology intensive:		
51	Chemical elements	51	Chemical element
52,57,59	Other chemicals	52,57,59	Other chemicals
54	Medicine	54	Medicine
56	Fertilizer	56	Fertilizer
58	Plastics	58	Plastics
71	Nonelectrical machinery	71–5	Nonelectrical machinery
72	Electrical machinery (other than 7241–2, 725)	764	Telecommunication equipment
		77	Electrical machinery (other than 775)
734	Aircraft		
861–3	Scientific instruments, photographic goods	792	Aircraft
		87	Scientific instruments
		881–4	Photographic goods

References

Balassa, B., and Marcus Noland. 1988. *Japan in the World Economy.* Washington, D.C.: Institute for International Economics.

Bradford, C. I., and W. H. Branson, eds. 1987. *Trade and Structural Change in Pacific Asia.* Chicago: University of Chicago Press.

Daiwa Securities Research Institute. 1989. *Japan's Economic Outlook.* Tokyo, Summer.

Iwata, K. 1989. Changes of Economic and Trade Structure in the Pacific Basin Area. Tokyo: FAIR, June.

Kawai, M. 1989. Change of Trade Structure and Industrial Structure in Asia-Pacific Region. Tokyo: FAIR, June.

Krause, L. 1987. The Structure of Trade in Manufactured Goods in the East and Southeast Asian Region. In *Trade and Structural Change in Pacific Asia,* ed. C. I. Bradford and W. H. Branson. Chicago: University of Chicago Press.

Okita, S. 1986. Pacific Development and Its Implications for the World Economy. In *The Pacific Basin: New Challenges for the United States,* ed. J. W. Morley. New York: Academy of Political Science.

Park, Y. C. 1989. Little Dragons and Structural Change in Pacific Asia. *World Economy* 12, no. 2 (June): 125–61.

Rapp, W. V. 1975. The Many Possible Extensions of Product Cycle Analysis. *Hitotsubashi Journal of Economics* 16, no. 1 (June): 22–29.

Urata, S. 1989. Recent Economic Developments in the Pacific Region and Changing Role of Japan in the Regional Interdependence. Paper presented to FAIR conference, Fukuoka, August.

Vernon, R. 1966. International Investment and International Trade in the Product Cycle. *Quarterly Journal of Economics* 80 (May): 190–207.

Yamazawa, I. 1988. Trade and Industrial Adjustment. *Review on Pacific Cooperation Activities.* Japan National Committee for Pacific Economic Cooperation, Japan Institute of International Affairs, May.

Comment   Alice H. Amsden

The exports of Korea, Taiwan, Hong Kong, and Singapore grew dramatically in the 1970s and 1980s to the point where they caused the United States ulcers. The United States has run a large trade deficit with the East Asian NICs (and Japan) while Japan has run a large trade surplus with the East Asian NICs (and the United States). The question Yung Chul Park and Won-Am Park propose to address in their paper is well chosen. It is whether Japan is likely to absorb more exports from the East Asian NICs (East Asia for short), thereby promoting Pacific trade by relieving pressure on the U.S. trade deficit.

The optimistic presumption has become that Japan's share of East Asian exports will increase as Japanese direct foreign investment and outsourcing in East Asia rise. Japan's direct foreign investment in East Asia more than doubled in the five-year period from 1983–88, leading to expectations that Japan will use East Asia as a base to manufacture and reexport to Japan.

The first part of the paper, which examines changes in trade patterns, is a nightmare for any reader with even a moderately impatient disposition. The "wrong" prices, or prices that deviated from free market equilibria, may have been necessary to stimulate East Asian exports, but what appear to be the authors' wrong or highly confusing data used to describe them do not make understanding trade any easier.

Part of the authors' problem is that table 3.1, which purports to show the grand triangular trade relationships among Japan, the United States, and the East Asian NICs, is difficult to fathom and does not necessarily correspond to tables 3.2, 3.3, and 3.4, which present the same information as table 3.1 but in a simpler form and from the viewpoint of individual traders (Japan, the United States, and all the NICs combined). For example, according to table 3.1, in 1987 the United States exported $28.3 billion worth of goods and services to Japan. This accounted for 11.2% of total U.S. exports and 21.1% of total Japanese imports. These numbers do square with those in tables 3.2 and 3.3, so there is no doubt that the same set of numbers were used in different tables. According to table 3.2, exports from the United States to Japan in 1987 accounted for 11% of U.S. exports while, according to table 3.3, the U.S. accounted for 21.7% of Japan's imports. However, the trade matrix between the East Asian NICs and Japan in table 3.1 does not correspond to entries in tables 3.3 and 3.4. According to table 3.1, in 1987 the value of East Asian exports was $20.5 billion, 11.5% of which went to Japan, accounting for 15.3% of Japan's total imports. According to table 3.3, however, East Asian imports in 1987 accounted for only 12.8% of Japan's total imports, not 15.3%. Moreover, according to table 3.4, East Asian exports in 1987 to Japan

Alice H. Amsden is a professor of economics at the New School for Social Research and a research associate of the Massachusetts Institute of Technology.

accounted for 16.1% of East Asian total exports, not 11.5%. This last discrepancy, although not the previous one, becomes comprehensible from a footnote. The footnote to table 3.4 indicates, in impossibly oblique language, that East Asia's exports to the United States and Japan are not reported as shares of East Asia's total exports, as one would expect from table 3.1, but, inexplicably, as shares of East Asia's exports to the United States, Japan, and the OECD only.

All this is very confusing, *a fortiori* when what is written in the text does not always correspond to what is reported in the tables! In the introductory paragraph on U.S.-Japan bilateral trade, for example, the authors state that "Japan's overall share in U.S. exports climbed to 20% in 1987 from about 13% in 1980 (see table 3.2)." Looking at table 3.2, one observes that, in fact, Japan's overall share in U.S. exports *fell* (rather than climbed) to 11% (not 20%). This discrepancy arises because what the authors were really referring to in the text was not Japan's overall share in U.S. *exports* but its overall share in U.S. *imports*, and so on, and so on.

After snafus like these, understanding Pacific trade patterns seems less important than finding two aspirins, wherever produced or by whom. The authors provide no model to explain trade patterns (probably because none is useful) so their analysis is data driven. In the end we do not know the precise extent to which Japan and East Asia have become better trading partners, which is the major issue in the paper. The bottom line, however, seems to be that Japan's share of the East Asian NICs' exports has remained more or less constant between 1970 and 1988, at around 12%, whereas East Asia has become a more important source of Japan's imports, accounting for about 5% in the 1970s but maybe 12% or 15% (???) by 1987 and possibly 17% by 1988.

Mercifully, the paper gets better and better. The section on intra-industry trade is especially illuminating. The authors estimate Grubel-Lloyd indices of intra-industry trade in manufacturing classified by factor intensity: natural resource, unskilled labor, human capital, and technology. What the authors discover from these estimates is that East Asian–Japanese intra-industry trade has been booming in all categories except technology-intensive products. Overall, such trade surpassed the level between Japan and the United States. By contrast, intra-industry trade registered sharp declines between the East Asian NICs and the United States. The contraction was greatest in capital-intensive manufactures (which were also the mainstay of Japan's intra-industry trade with the rest of the world).

We begin to understand better the source of trade frictions between the United States, Japan, and the East Asian NICs. The trouble is of two types. The first problem is Japan's sluggish import growth. As indicated in table 3.1, Japan's share of world imports remained almost constant between 1970 and 1988 (at about 6%). Therefore, while the East Asian NICs accounted for a larger share of Japan's imports, this translated into Japan's taking a constant rather than rising share of East Asia's rapidly growing exports. The second problem is sluggish U.S. export growth. U.S. exports declined as a share of total world exports from 15% to 12% between 1970 and 1988.

Ignoring the first problem for the moment, declining U.S. competitiveness with the rest of the world (including Asia) appears in all intra-industry trade categories except technology (fig. 3.2). The fact that over the 1980s, one trade category (technology) between the United States and the rest of the world rose while all the others declined, presumably suggests the possibility that there is more to poor American trade performance than merely the macroeconomics of savings and the exchange rate. The authors sound an ominous note for American competitiveness even with respect to the East Asian NICs: "The East Asian NICs have overtaken and extended their competitive lead over the U.S. in manufactures trade" (although not, of course, high tech). Given that "it may take many years for the U.S. to regain its competitiveness as an industrial power," the trade imbalances that bedevil Pacific trade are not likely to vanish soon.

Unlike Japan's share of world imports, which has remained constant, and unlike the United States' share of world exports, which has declined, table 3.1 indicates that East Asia's share of *both* world exports *and* world imports has increased. As shares of world totals between 1970 and 1988, East Asia's exports rose from 2% to 8% while its imports rose from 3% to 7%. Since 1988, the overall trade of the East Asian NICs has probably become even more balanced, if the trade balance of the largest country, South Korea, is any guide. Therefore, a philosophical question arises: Should the United States continue to pressure the East Asian NICs to balance their trade *with the United States,* or is it sufficient for them to qualify as good global citizens if they balance their *overall* trade?

If Park and Park's intra-industry trade estimates are any guide, American trade policy toward East Asia seems to be premised, erroneously, on the idea that if South Korea and Taiwan are persuaded to lower their (considerable) trade barriers, their trade surplus with the United States will fall. The authors' findings and other studies lead one to think that pressures to liberalize merely induce East Asia to import more from Japan, not to increase imports from the United States. This, in fact, is what happened between 1985 and 1987, even though the dollar was depreciating vis-à-vis the yen by over 60%. Therefore, instead of pressuring South Korea and Taiwan to liberalize, a better Pacific trade policy for the United States might be to join forces with both countries to penetrate the Japanese market.

If anybody can penetrate the Japanese market, it is the East Asian NICs. Good luck to them. As Park and Park quite correctly point out, the optimistic view expressed by some Japanese economists, that Japanese direct foreign investment in East Asia will increase Japanese–East Asian trade sufficiently to reduce East Asia's dependence on the American market, is probably exaggerated. The authors note that Japan–East Asian intra-industry trade has been dominated by Japanese multinationals. Such trade has almost certainly tended to be Ricardian in character—engaging countries at different, rather than the same, levels of economic development. Although the NICs have managed to export more skill- and technology-intensive products to Japan, these products are defined to include labor-intensive assembly of nonelectronic and electrical machinery, which are not really at the world technological frontier. Therefore, it is quite possible that the Japanese multinationals will use the NICs as export platforms to enter third markets, including the United States, thereby perpetuating the lopsidedness of Pacific trade.

It should be added that the idea is also exaggerated that Japan's direct foreign investment (DFI) to East Asia diffuses technology and thereby the wherewithal to compete against Japan. The "commanding heights" in East Asia have not been dominated by foreign firms; they are controlled by domestic enterprises, public or private, which have acquired their technology through channels other than DFI. This DFI has largely occurred in export-intensive industries, as just suggested. The technological overspill from export-intensive investments tends not to involve the transfer of leading-edge *product* technology (and the process designs that go with them), which is what the East Asian NICs currently need.

The final part of the paper deals with the product cycle as applied to the division of labor within Asia. As Japan climbs up the ladder of comparative advantage, so the argument runs, it relinquishes more labor-intensive (and then less skill- and technology-intensive) production to countries behind it in industrialization. The authors are appropriately skeptical about whether the law of comparative advantage is well behaved, given that East Asia's deficit with Japan was close to 80% of its total exports to Japan in 1988, despite its penetration of the Japanese market.

The problem seems to be Japan's tenacious competitiveness in mid-tech industries. Japan is not readily relinquishing these to the East Asian NICs, which, in turn, appear unwilling to accede significant market share in many labor-intensive industries to the ASEAN countries—Malaysia, Indonesia, and Thailand. As the authors point out, capital-intensive manufactures accounted for more than 45% of Japan's total exports and provided the largest source of its trade surpluses in the 1980s. Japan has been running trade surpluses with the East Asian NICs and the rest of the world in industrial machinery, electrical machinery, household electrical machinery, transport machinery, and even textile yarns and fabrics.

Part of Japan's trade surplus in mid-tech undoubtedly reflects trade barriers. But another part probably reflects higher productivity than Japan's lower-wage competitors, as well as pockets of low wages within Japan's segmented labor markets, that help Japan retain competitiveness in some labor-intensive goods. Comparative advantage is apparently misbehaving in the Pacific. Key assumptions are being violated: that labor markets are homogeneous and that production functions are identical across countries such that the same product is produced everywhere at the same level of productivity.

To penetrate Japan's mid-tech markets will take a lot of effort by the East Asian NICs. Narrowing the already narrow gap with Japan requires painstaking incremental improvements in productivity and quality. Businesses in Taiwan are showing a lack of enthusiasm for such work by investing overseas. In South Korea, the accumulation of wealth by the big business groups is souring labor relations and eroding the dedication of workers and managers necessary for the task.

General Douglas MacArthur did Japanese productivity and labor relations a big favor when he decapitated the big *zaibatsu* groups after the war. Despite MacArthur's promise of "I shall return," the chances that he will return and cut off the heads of the *chaebol* are about as great as the chances of cutting off the heads of the *chaebol* without him, or of Japan's voluntarily opening its mid-tech markets to East Asia. Therefore, the conclusions of Park and Park, that trade between the East Asian NICs and Japan has come a long way but has too long a way to go to relieve pressure on the American market, rings true.

The wild card is services. The authors say nothing about services although these are the hope of the U.S. balance of payments. It is too soon to say how services will influence Pacific trade, but it is clear that Japan is already emerging as a stiff competitor, especially in financial services.

4 Price Behavior in Japanese and U.S. Manufacturing

Richard C. Marston

In the past 20 years, the manufacturing sectors in Japan and the United States have undergone major transformations. Both countries have experienced technological changes that have shifted production from traditional sectors, such as textiles and steel, to more sophisticated products. At the same time, the relative position of the two countries has changed substantially because Japan's aggregate productivity growth has exceeded U.S. productivity growth by a large margin. Japan has replaced the United States as the leading exporter in one product after another despite the fact that over the period as a whole the yen has appreciated in value. During this period of rapid change, the two countries have been continually buffeted by exchange rate fluctuations that have shifted one country's costs relative to the other's. Although these fluctuations are often soon reversed, in the meantime they disrupt normal trading relationships between two countries. Thus productivity growth and exchange rate fluctuations have combined to produce major changes in the relative competitiveness of the two countries' manufacturing sectors. This study attempts to explain some of these changes.

Most studies of international competitiveness in manufacturing rely on aggregate price comparisons even though there are many changes in relative prices at the sectoral level.[1] Productivity growth varies widely across sectors of manufacturing, with higher productivity growth holding down price in-

Richard C. Marston is professor of finance and economics at the Wharton School of the University of Pennsylvania and a research associate of the National Bureau of Economic Research.

The author would like to thank the discussants, Bonnie Loopesko and Catherine Mann, as well as Robert Feldman, Jeffrey Frankel, Koichi Hamada, Paul Krugman, Robert Lawrence, Masahiro Okuno, and Hugh Patrick for their helpful comments on an earlier draft.

1. Even studies of purchasing power parity that distinguish between traded and nontraded goods, such as Balassa (1964) and Officer (1976), fail to look at individual sectors of manufacturing.

creases in some sectors relative to others. In Japan's electrical manufacturing sector, in fact, productivity growth is so high that Japan's prices in that sector have remained competitive despite the sizable real appreciation of the yen. Many studies of competitiveness, moreover, examine broad trends in relative prices over a decade or more without examining how manufacturing firms cope with short-run changes in exchange rates. Studies of purchasing power parity (PPP) have suggested that exchange rate changes induce large changes in relative prices in the short run.[2] But only recently have economists examined how firms set prices in the short run in response to changes in exchange rates. Such studies emphasize pass-through and pricing-to-market behavior in attempting to understand why price changes occur at different rates depending upon the manufacturing sector.[3]

This paper uses sectoral data for Japanese and U.S. manufacturing to study secular trends in relative prices between the two countries. Because productivity growth varies widely across manufacturing sectors as well as between countries, the prices of U.S. goods relative to Japanese goods change at widely different rates depending upon the sector of manufacturing. The first section of the paper examines these secular changes in prices. Then the paper turns to short-term changes in relative prices induced by fluctuations in exchange rates. Two types of price changes are distinguished depending upon the degree to which the exchange rate fluctuations are sustained. The last section of the paper then examines how manufacturing firms cope with exchange rate fluctuations. Using sectoral data for export and domestic prices, the paper examines pass-through and pricing-to-market behavior. In each country, a period of currency appreciation is studied to determine whether firms in that country follow pricing practices designed to neutralize the effects of appreciation on their relative competitiveness.

4.1   Principal Determinants of Relative Competitiveness

The relative competitiveness of manufacturing in Japan and the United States depends primarily on two factors: secular trends in productivity and changes in relative prices driven by variations in exchange rates. Over periods of a decade or more, trends in productivity can lead to relatively large changes in relative prices within the manufacturing sector as well as between countries. But in the shorter run, changes in exchange rates exert a dominating influence on relative prices between countries. This is true whether relative prices are measured month to month or over periods as long as three to five years. This section of the paper will compare secular trends with these shorter term movements in relative prices.

2. See, e.g., studies of PPP by Kravis and Lipsey (1978) and Frenkel (1981).
3. Recent studies of currency pass-through and pricing to market include Baldwin (1988), Cumby and Huizinga (1989), Feenstra (1987), Froot and Klemperer (1988), Giovannini (1988), Hooper and Mann (1989), Knetter (1989), Mann (1986), Marston (1990), and Ohno (1989).

4.1.1   Secular Trends in Competitiveness

In the past two decades there has been a major shift in production within manufacturing in both countries. These shifts have been accompanied by surprisingly large changes in relative prices, both across industries within each country and between countries in the same industry. Just how large these shifts in production have been can be indicated by a few examples. In 1970, 29.6 percent of Japanese manufacturing output (GDP in manufacturing) was in the machinery and equipment sectors (which include electrical machinery and transport equipment).[4] By 1986 that share had risen to 51.5 percent. In the United States, machinery and equipment already constituted 40.2 percent of output in 1970. But by 1986, that share had grown to 50.2 percent of output. During this same period, Japanese textile production fell from 5.3 percent of manufacturing output to 2.6 percent. In the United States, textile production fell less than in Japan, but basic metal production fell from 10.1 percent to 4.7 percent.

These shifts of production were accompanied by large changes in relative prices. In the period from 1975 to 1987, Japanese producer prices in manufacturing rose by 18.2 percent.[5] But *within* manufacturing, the price changes varied widely from sector to sector. In the metal products sector, prices rose by 22.8 percent, but in the electrical machinery sector, prices *fell* by 15.1 percent. In the United States, the range of variation was also large, though less dramatic. In the U.S. chemical industry, for example, prices rose by 13.8 percent less than in manufacturing as a whole (48.7 percent vs. 62.5 percent).

When relative prices change substantially, measures of competitiveness based on aggregate price indexes can be very misleading. In some industries, a country may experience major changes in the prices of its goods relative to those of other countries even though aggregate real exchange rates between the two countries are stable. The country might gain competitiveness in some industries while losing competitiveness in others.

In the long run at least, changes in relative prices occur primarily because of changes in the cost of producing goods. Although wages can grow at different rates across industries, and some industries can experience greater increases in materials costs than others, the primary reason why costs grow at different rates across industries is that productivity gains vary widely across those industries. In industries producing electrical machinery, for example, productivity growth might be two or three times as fast as in manufacturing as a whole. As a result, the inflation rate for the electrical machinery sector is much lower than in manufacturing as a whole or in most other sectors.

If a country experiences large internal relative price changes, it might be

---

4. The percentage shares are calculated from real GDP data published in the OECD, *National Accounts*.

5. The price changes are calculated from producer price indexes published in the OECD, *Indicators of Industrial Activity*.

able to remain competitive in particular industries even if its currency appreciates in real terms (as measured by broad-based price indexes). In that case the change in competitiveness would be apparent only if real exchange rates were defined for individual industries. To define such sectoral real exchange rates, let R_i be the log of the real exchange rate in sector i for Japan relative to the United States. Then

$$(1) \qquad\qquad R_i = P_i^* + S - P_i,$$

where P_i^* and P_i are the producer price indexes for sector i in the United States and Japan, respectively, and S is the ¥/$ spot exchange rate (all variables being expressed in logs). As defined, a rise in this real exchange rate represents a real appreciation of the dollar and a loss of competitiveness for the United States in that sector or industry.

Figure 4.1 reports percentage changes in sectoral real exchanges between the United States and Japan over the period 1975–87.[6] At the center of the figure is the percentage change for manufacturing as a whole; over this 12-year period, the dollar depreciated a total of -27.7 percent (most of the depreciation occurring at the end of the period). This depreciation, however, was exceeded in four of the industries illustrated, with the largest depreciations over 40 percent in metal products and textiles. At the other extreme, the United States lost competitiveness in one sector, electrical machinery; in that sector, U.S. prices rose by 4.9 percent relative to Japanese prices. The real exchange rate rose for electrical machinery primarily because of high productivity growth in Japan's electrical machinery sector. Japanese firms in that sector were able to lower costs sufficiently to keep prices competitive despite the real appreciation in manufacturing as a whole. In the motor vehicle sector, U.S. prices fell relative to those in Japan, but only by 4.8 percent. As in the electrical machinery sector, the differential growth in productivity kept Japanese prices from rising much in dollar terms. In two other sectors, general machinery and nonferrous metals, the real appreciation of the yen was also smaller than in manufacturing as a whole.[7] Thus trends in productivity introduced considerable variation in real exchange rates across sectors.

7.1.2   Effects of Exchange Rate Variability

The overall trend in real exchange rates for manufacturing as a whole is governed by macroeconomic factors. Productivity performance in a particular

6. The complete titles of the sectors are provided in table 4.1 below. The percentage changes are measured as changes in the logs of the real exchange rates between the years 1975 and 1987. The underlying price data are from the OECD, *Indicators of Industrial Activity* (WEFA data base), and the U.S. Department of Commerce, *Business Conditions Digest* (for the motor vehicle PPI for the United States). The exchange rates are from the International Monetary Fund's *International Financial Statistics* (WEFA data base).

7. The 27.7 percent real depreciation for manufacturing as a whole overstates the actual gain in competitiveness for the United States, since Japanese exports are concentrated in sectors like electrical machinery and motor vehicles where Japan has remained competitive despite the nominal appreciation of the yen.

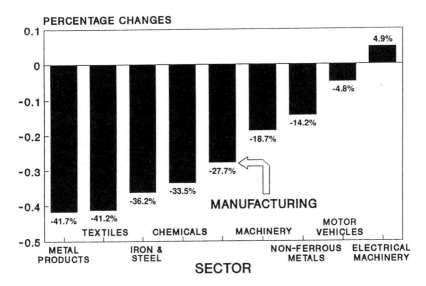

Fig. 4.1   **Sectoral real exchange rates changes in real exchange rates, 1975–87**

sector can *mitigate* the effects of this overall trend in real exchange rates but cannot insulate that sector from exchange rate developments. The relative competitiveness of countries is even more sensitive to exchange rate movements in the short run than in the long run.

Two types of exchange rate movements can be distinguished in the data. The first type is day-to-day or month-to-month *volatility.* Because exchange rates are determined primarily by financial transactions, they exhibit the same variability that is characteristic of prices in financial markets. The second type of exchange rate movement is longer in duration, typically lasting from three to five years. These medium-term swings in nominal exchange rates, referred to as *misalignments,* can lead to changes in real exchange rates by over 40 percent, as they did in the case of the pound sterling in the early 1980s and in the case of the dollar in the mid-1980s. Each type of exchange rate variability is considered in turn.

Volatility

The volatility of exchange rates has been assessed in previous studies by comparing the variances of exchange rates with the variances of goods prices, on the one hand, and financial asset prices, on the other hand. In Marston (1988), for example, the variances of exchange rates for the major industrial countries are shown to be far greater than the variances of goods prices as measured by the wholesale price index and are comparable in magnitude to the variances of asset prices. But such a comparison fails to show clearly enough the extent to which the volatility of exchange rates breaks the link between the prices of identical or similar goods originating in different countries. If exchange rates were stable, the prices of similar goods from different countries would be closely related when expressed in a common currency unless international trade barriers inhibited international competition. But under flexible exchange rates, highly volatile exchange rates are used to convert goods prices into foreign currencies, so the prices of these goods may fluctuate substantially relative to the prices of goods originating in foreign countries.

This study uses prices disaggregated to the sectoral level in manufacturing to examine the following question: Has the randomness of flexible exchange rates so reduced the integration of different national markets in any one sector of manufacturing that internal price adjustment *between* sectors is more complete than external price adjustment in the same sector? In that case prices in sector i in the United States would be more closely linked to those in sector j in the United States than those in sector i in Japan. That is, the random movement in nominal exchange rates would have made the prices of American "apples" more closely linked to those of American "oranges" than to those of Japanese "apples."

To compare internal with external price adjustment, month-to-month variations in producer price indexes are examined over the 1975–87 period. In the case of internal prices, the correlations are between prices in industry i and manufacturing prices as a whole. In the case of external prices, the correlations are between prices in industry i in Japan and those in industry i in the United States. The prices in industry i in Japan are converted into dollars before calculating the correlation coefficients. Table 4.1 reports the correlations by industry for the two countries. For each country, internal price corre-

Table 4.1   Internal and External Price Correlations, 1975–87, Monthly PPI

Sector	$r(i,m)$		$r(i,i^*)$
	United States	Japan	
Textiles, clothing, and leather	.47*	.36*	−.12
Industrial chemicals	.57*	.80*	.06
Iron and steel	.39*	.52*	−.02
Nonferrous metals	.35*	.46*	.55*
Metal products	.44*	.46*	.00
Machinery (except electrical)	.56*	.54*	−.07
Electrical machinery	.59*	.47*	−.06
Motor vehicles	.33*	.02	.02

Sources: OECD, *Indicators of Industrial Activity* (WEFA data base); U.S. Department of Commerce, *Business Conditions Digest* (for the motor vehicle series for the United States).

Note: $r(i,m)$: correlation between (percentage) changes in prices in sector i and in manufacturing as a whole; $r(i,i^*)$: correlation between changes in U.S. prices in sector i and Japanese prices in sector i, where both prices are expressed in dollars.

*Indicates that correlation is significantly greater than zero at the 5 percent level.

lations are reported first. Then external price correlations are reported between prices in Japan (expressed in dollars) and the corresponding sectoral
prices in the United States.

In both countries, correlations between *internal* prices are generally quite
high. In the case of the United States, for example, the correlations between
sectoral prices and prices in manufacturing range from 0.33 to 0.59. In the
case of Japan, the correlations range from 0.36 to 0.80 except in the motor
vehicle sector, where the correlation is only 0.02. Of the 16 internal price
correlations for the two countries, all but one is significantly greater than zero
at the 5 percent level. The correlations are high primarily because there are
common cost factors influencing all sectors of manufacturing in any economy.
Changes in wages, for example, tend to be highly correlated across sectors.
Changes in energy prices and raw materials prices affect all sectors simulta-
neously, although these price changes have greater impact on some sectors
than others. The demand side of the economy may also help to keep the correlations high, although substitutibility between products from different manufacturing sectors should be much smaller than between products of the same
sector produced in different countries.

The *external* correlations are almost invariably smaller than the corresponding internal correlations for the same sector. This should not be surprising
given the well-known variability of nominal exchange rates over periods as
short as one month. In eight of the sectors, the correlations across countries
range from -0.12 in textiles, clothing, and leather to 0.06 in industrial chemicals. In only one sector is the correlation between Japanese and U.S. prices
higher than between that sector's prices and prices in manufacturing as a
whole. In the nonferrous metals sector the external price correlation is surprisingly high at 0.55. Unlike other products, the prices for nonferrous metals
seem to be determined in internationally integrated markets. All other external
price correlations are statistically insignificant at the 5 percent level.

The general conclusion must be that exchange rate volatility imparts so
much variability to the prices of these countries' goods in foreign currency
that it disrupts the links between the prices of similar goods across countries.
Yet if it were the case that changes in relative prices across countries had no
discernible trends, manufacturing firms could learn to cope with this type of
variability, just as they cope with other forms of uncertainty. On the other
hand, if exchange rate movements persist in one direction or another over the
medium term, adjustment by firms is much more difficult. That is the case
with misalignments of exchange rates.

Misalignment

The term "misalignment" refers to medium-term swings in real exchange
rates away from long-run equilibrium. Thus misalignments involve real rather
than nominal exchange rates, and medium-term rather than short-term
changes in exchange rates. Not all swings in real exchange rates are necessar-

ily misalignments, since real disturbances such as supply shocks can lead to changes in equilibrium real exchange rates. For example, the appreciation of sterling in the late 1970s has been attributed, at least in part, to the discovery of oil and gas in the North Sea. But the swings in the dollar relative to the yen (as well as other currencies) have been so large that it is difficult not to regard them as misalignments, especially in the absence of any real disturbances affecting the dollar comparable to the North Sea discovery.[8]

The swings in real exchange rates from one extreme to another are at least as large as the long-run trends previously discussed. Table 4.2 measures the swings in the dollar relative to the yen from the trough of the dollar in 1978 to its peak in 1984 and then to the end of the period in 1987. The figures are based on average exchange rates and prices in these three years. According to the table, the real exchange rate of the dollar rose by 35.7 percent from 1978 to 1984 in manufacturing as a whole. Then the dollar fell sharply by 41.7 percent in the following three years ending in 1987. Similar swings were experienced in each of the sectors of manufacturing, although in the nonferrous metals sector, the swing was only half as large. In the last two sectors, electrical machinery and motor vehicles, the underlying trends in real exchange rates led to a larger real appreciation of the dollar in the earlier period than in manufacturing as a whole and a smaller real depreciation in the later period.

The large swings experienced across manufacturing can hardly be attributed solely to changes in long-run equilibrium exchange rates. Instead, these swings must have involved substantial misalignments of exchange rates. And even to the extent that equilibrium rates changed, manufacturing firms still had to cope with changing relative prices requiring many forms of adjustment.

Defensive Actions by Firms

A firm may have difficulty coping with misalignments because it knows neither the size nor the duration of any swing in real exchange rates. The firm's exports rise and fall with real depreciations and appreciations. And so also do the firm's employment and production at home. In response to a real appreciation, the firm may elect to transfer production abroad. But since the duration of the real appreciation is usually unknown, the firm may find that its transfer of production abroad is accomplished only after the home currency begins depreciating back to normal levels.

An alternative strategy is to follow pricing policies designed to keep the firm competitive in foreign markets despite an appreciation of the home currency. Partial *"pass-through"* refers to the case where the firm increases the *foreign currency* price of its exports less than the appreciation of the home currency. In order for pass-through to be partial, the firm must lower the domestic currency price of its exports. The firm may be able to lower the domestic currency prices of its goods simply because the appreciation lowers the

---

8. For further discussion, see Williamson (1985).

Table 4.2   **Swings in Sectoral Real Exchange Rates between the Dollar and Yen (Based on Average Real Exchange Rates in Years Indicated)**

	% Movement in Dollar	
Sector	Appreciation, 1978–84	Depreciation, 1984–87
Manufacturing	35.7	−41.7
Textiles, clothing, and leather	28.5	−37.8
Industrial chemicals	32.1	−38.9
Iron and steel	36.9	−41.0
Nonferrous metals	18.3	−22.4
Metal products	29.2	−43.2
Machinery (except electrical)	42.1	−42.8
Electrical machinery	52.7	−30.5
Motor vehicles	51.8	−39.6

Sources: See table 4.1.

Note: The percentage changes are measure as changes in the logs of the real exchange rates.

prices of imported materials and fuel. Thus partial pass-through may occur even though the firm charges the same price, in domestic currency, for goods sold to both export and domestic markets.

"*Pricing to market*," in contrast, is an active policy designed to defend the export market of the firm. Pricing to market occurs when the firm lowers the price of its exports in *domestic* currency *relative to* the price of goods for the domestic market.[9] The next section studies both of these pricing phenomena.

4.2   Pass-through and Pricing to Market

With the competitive position of exporting firms shifting so sharply in response to changes in exchange rates, it is not surprising that these firms take defensive actions. As suggested above, one of the primary ways firms defend their market position is by limiting the pass-through of exchange rates into the foreign currency prices of their exports. But by limiting pass-through, these firms may open a gap between the prices of products sold domestically and the prices of their exports expressed in domestic currency.

4.2.1   Different Types of Pricing Behavior by Firms

To be more precise about the behavior involved, it is necessary to distinguish between three prices (for the case of the Japanese good):

9. The terminology is due to Krugman (1987). Recent empirical studies of pricing to market include Froot and Klemperer (1988), Knetter (1989), Giovannini (1988) and Marston (1990).

P_{dit} = the price of product i in the domestic market (in yen);
P_{xit} = the price of product i in the export market, but expressed in *domestic* currency (in yen),
$P_{xit}^\$$ = the price of product i in the export market, but expressed in *foreign* currency (in dollars).

A firm faced with a large appreciation of the domestic currency may decide to charge different prices in the domestic and export markets. If the firm is Japanese, it will lower the yen price of its export (P_{xit}) in order to limit the rise in the dollar price of the export ($P_{xit}^\$$). So the pass-through of the exchange rate change is only partial.

Why should firms vary the price of an export relative to the price of the domestically sold good? This behavior can be rationalized by appealing to simple profit maximization. The appreciation of the domestic currency raises the marginal costs of the export (calculated in foreign currency) proportionally. If the markup of price over marginal cost were constant, the price of the export in foreign currency would also have to rise proportionally to the exchange rate. Under a wide range of demand conditions, however, a rise in the price of a good leads to a fall in the markup of price over marginal cost. So the price in foreign currency increases less than the rise in the marginal cost, and the pass-through is, therefore, only partial. With partial pass-through into the export price in foreign currency, the price of the export in domestic currency must fall relative to the price of the same good sold in the domestic market. So "pricing to market" occurs.

Other rationales have been offered for limited pass-through and pricing to market. Krugman (1987) shows that, in a model of Cournot oligopoly, the price of the export in foreign currency rises less than proportionally to the appreciation even when the demand curve has a constant elasticity. (If the demand curve has a constant elasticity, the markup is constant when there is a monopoly rather than oligopoly in the industry). Froot and Klemperer (1988) specify a dynamic model in which the future demand for a product depends on current market share. In that model, a firm facing an appreciation that it perceives to be temporary may limit increases in the prices of its exports in order to maintain market share for the future. So there are several reasons why firms might modify the degree of currency pass-through by pricing to market.

The degree of pass-through can be measured by the pass-through elasticity, β_i, defined as follows:

$$(2) \qquad \beta_i = \frac{dP_{xit}^\$/P_{xit}^\$}{dS_t/S_t} = \frac{dP_{xit}/P_{xit}}{dS_t/S_t} - 1 < 0.$$

This elasticity measures the percentage rise in the dollar export price in response to a 1 percent fall in the yen price of the dollar. If the pass-through is complete, the coefficient will be equal to minus one. With incomplete pass-through, in contrast, the coefficient will be between zero and minus one.

Pass-through effects are difficult to identify in practice because there are so many other factors that can change the prices of exports. Consider the example of the yen's appreciation beginning in the first quarter of 1985. Suppose that it is found that the appreciation led to increases in the prices of Japanese exports, measured in dollars, which were smaller than the change in exchange rates (measured as an absolute value). The pass-through may be incomplete because Japanese firms are pricing to market, lowering their export prices in yen relative to their domestic prices. But alternatively, the pass-through may be incomplete for reasons having nothing to do with defensive actions taken by Japanese manufacturing firms. It may be the case that Japanese costs of production fell because the prices of imported materials fell when the yen appreciated.[10] (The price index for imported commodities measured in yen fell in half between February 1985 and December 1988.) Or it may be the case that costs fell for reasons totally unrelated to the appreciation. In order to identify pass-through effects, it would be necessary to measure these cost factors for each of the sectors of manufacturing studied. Instead, this paper looks at pricing-to-market behavior where changes in costs are unlikely to be so important.

To determine how firms react to exchange rate changes, it is more useful to examine directly how firms change export prices *relative to* the domestic prices of the same product. Most countries do not report separate price indexes for domestic goods and exports, but Japan and the United States have developed export price indexes to match their producer price indexes for many of their important exports. This makes it possible to calculate pricing-to-market elasticities that directly measure the pricing behavior of these countries' firms.

The pricing-to-market elasticity involves the relative price of exports to domestic goods, or

$$X_{it} = P_{xit}/P_{dit}.$$

This elasticity measures the percentage change in this relative price in response to a 1 percent change in the real exchange rate, R_t:

(3)
$$\alpha_i = \frac{(dX_{it}/X_{it})}{(dR_t/R_t)}.$$

---

10. Consider the following equation relating (percentage changes in) the price of the export in yen to the markup of price over marginal cost, M_{xit}, and to marginal cost, C_{it}:

$$dP_{xit} / P_{xit} = dM_{xit} / M_{xit} + dC_{it} / C_{it}.$$

In response to the appreciation of the yen, the price of exports (in yen) could fall because markups are reduced, as a result of pricing to market, or because marginal costs fall.

The real exchange rate rather than the nominal exchange rate is used because nominal changes matched by offsetting changes in general price levels are unlikely to induce pricing-to-market behavior. If firms vary the relative price of exports to domestic goods, then the pricing-to-market elasticity will lie between zero and one. If firms do not price to market, then of course the coefficient is equal to zero.

The advantage of looking at the ratio of export to domestic prices rather than export prices alone is that changes in marginal costs are likely to have less influence on the former. That is, even though changes in marginal costs normally affect export prices and domestic prices individually, they need not affect the *ratio* of the two prices. As Marston (1990) shows, changes in marginal costs leave this ratio unaffected as long as the markups of prices over marginal costs in the export and domestic markets are equally sensitive to price changes.[11] In such cases, changes in the ratio of export to domestic prices can be attributed to exchange rate changes alone. Even if markups respond differently in the two markets, the price ratio changes only in proportion to the difference in the elasticities of the markups with respect to prices. So cost factors are not a major influence on the price ratio except to the extent that markup elasticities differ substantially in the export and domestic markets.

To illustrate the difference between pass-through effects and pricing to market effects, consider table 4.3, where the effects of a yen appreciation are illustrated for two cases. The first case is one in which the markup of prices over marginal costs is constant, so there is no pricing-to-market behavior. The pass-through of the appreciation of the yen into the dollar price of the export is only partial because marginal costs have fallen as demand for the export falls, thus permitting the yen price of the export to fall. Since there is no pricing-to-market behavior, the yen price of the export remains equal to the yen price charged in the domestic market.

The second case is one in which pricing to market breaks the link between the export price and domestic price. In response to the appreciation, exporting firms reduce the yen price of their exports relative to the domestic price of that same good. So there is again partial pass-through into the dollar price of the export, but this time the partial pass-through is due to changes in markups rather than just changes in marginal costs. It is this second case which is of particular interest.

---

11. If export and domestic prices are tied to the same marginal cost, but are influenced by different markup factors (M_{xit} and M_{dit}, respectively), then changes in X_{it} can be related to these markup factors as follows:

$$dX_{it} / X_{it} = dM_{xit} / M_{xit} - dM_{dit} / M_{dit}.$$

In order for marginal cost to affect X_{it}, it must have a greater impact on one markup than on the other. If the elasticities of these markups with respect to prices are equal, then X_{it} is unaffected by changes in marginal cost.

Table 4.3   **Illustration of Pass-through and Pricing-to-Market Effects in Two Cases**

Case 1: Partial pass-through, but no pricing to market (constant markup of prices over marginal costs; variable marginal costs)

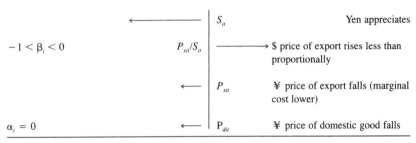

		S_{it}	Yen appreciates
$-1 < \beta_i < 0$	P_{xit}/S_{it}	→	\$ price of export rises less than proportionally
		P_{xit}	¥ price of export falls (marginal cost lower)
$\alpha_i = 0$		P_{dit}	¥ price of domestic good falls

Case 2: Pricing to market (variable markup of prices over marginal costs; variable marginal costs)

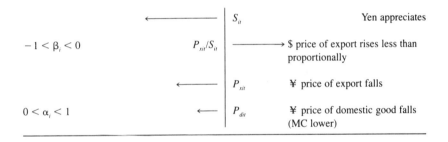

		S_{it}	Yen appreciates
$-1 < \beta_i < 0$	P_{xit}/S_{it}	→	\$ price of export rises less than proportionally
		P_{xit}	¥ price of export falls
$0 < \alpha_i < 1$		P_{dit}	¥ price of domestic good falls (MC lower)

4.2.2   Evidence on Pass-through and Pricing-to-Market Behavior

In this section, Japanese and U.S. pricing behavior is studied in detail. For each country, pricing-to-market elasticities are calculated by comparing changes in the ratio of export to domestic prices with changes in exchange rates. For Japan, pass-through elasticities are also calculated in order to illustrate the difference between pass-through and pricing to market. For each country, a period of currency appreciation is studied because pricing-to-market behavior is more likely to be found when firms are losing competitiveness in export markets.

Japanese Pricing Behavior

For Japan, the period of appreciation begins at the peak of the dollar's rise in February 1985 and ends in December 1988. This period is long enough so that any observed changes in export prices measured in yen can be attributed to pricing decisions by Japanese firms rather than to the translation into yen of export prices set in dollars. (If export prices are set in dollars, then *unanticipated* changes in exchange rates can lead to variations in export prices translated into yen. But since export prices are unlikely to be set more than a few months ahead, observed changes in prices over the period studied must reflect equilibrium pricing decisions rather than translation effects.)

The Bank of Japan provides export and domestic prices for a number of sectors of manufacturing with significant exports. The export prices are free-on-board (FOB) prices for exports expressed in yen, while the domestic prices are those reported at the primary wholesale level for sale in Japan. Nine sectors are studied in this paper, ranging from textiles to precision instruments. The sectors are listed in table 4.4.

Although the United States accounts for a large share of Japanese exports in these sectors, the products are exported to a number of different countries. So the nominal and real exchange rates appearing in expressions (2) and (3) above should be *effective* exchange rates defined over prices and exchange rates for a number of countries that import Japanese products. The United Nations reports export shares by product in its *Commodity Trade Statistics*. Export shares for 1986 are used to form weights for *sector-specific* series for the nominal and real exchange rates. For example, there are nominal and real effective exchange rates for the textile sector based on export shares for textiles.

To form the nominal exchange rate series for each sector, the export shares for that sector are used to weight the corresponding bilateral exchange rates forming a nominal effective exchange rate for that sector (S_{it}). To form the real exchange rate for each sector (R_{it}), wholesale prices are first converted into dollars using monthly average exchange rates. When wholesale prices are not available, consumer prices are used instead. The series for prices and bilateral exchange rates are drawn from the International Monetary Fund, *International Financial Statistics*. [12] The real effective exchange rate is defined as the weighted average of foreign prices converted from dollars into yen and deflated by the Japanese wholesale price index. Twenty-three countries in all are represented in the exchange rate series.

Table 4.4 reports pass-through and pricing-to-market elasticities obtained by calculating the percentage changes in prices and exchange rates over the 34-month period from February 1985 to December 1988. (The percentage changes are calculated as the change in log values between the beginning and ending months).

The upper part of the table reports pass-through elasticities obtained by taking the ratio of the percentage change in the export price to the percentage change in the yen spot rate. [13] Notice first that the changes in nominal effective

12. In the case of Hongkong, export prices from WEFA's Inline Data Base are used in place of wholesale prices. In the case of Taiwan, the prices and exchange rates are drawn from the Taiwanese publication, *Financial Statistics*.

13. Since export prices are reported in yen rather than foreign currency, the table presents the percentage change in the yen price. As eq. (2) indicates, the pass-through elasticity can be obtained by subtracting one from the ratio of the change in the export price in yen to the change in the nominal exchange rate.

Table 4.4   **Pass-through and Pricing-to-Market Behavior in Japan, February 1985 to December 1988**

Pass-through Effects for Japanese Manufacturing

Sector	% Change Export Price (in ¥)	% Change Nominal Effective Exchange Rate	Pass-through Elasticity
Textiles	− 25.8	− 60.0	− .57
Chemicals	− 47.8	− 52.4	− .09
Iron and steel	− 31.5	− 63.0	− .50
Nonferrous metals	− 10.4	− 61.7	− .83
Metal products	− 24.1	− 60.9	− .60
General machinery	− 20.8	− 56.9	− .63
Electrical machinery	− 45.0	− 57.0	− .21
Transport equipment	− 20.4	− 63.3	− .68
Precision instruments	− 15.4	− 53.7	− .71

Pricing-to-Market Effects for Japanese Manufacturing

Sector	% Change Export/Domestic Price	% Change Real Effective Exchange Rate	Pricing-to-Market Elasticity
Textiles	− 14.9	− 37.5	.40
Chemicals	− 34.9	− 32.0	1.09
Iron and steel	− 24.2	− 41.6	.58
Nonferrous metals	− 4.0	− 42.6	.09
Metal products	− 23.5	− 38.6	.61
General machinery	− 18.7	− 34.6	.54
Electrical machinery	− 22.4	− 35.6	.63
Transport equipment	− 16.5	− 40.2	.41
Precision instruments	− 13.2	− 31.7	.41

Sources: See data appendix.

exchange rates are very similar across sectors, ranging from a 52.4 percent appreciation of the yen in the chemicals sector to a 63.3 percent appreciation in the transport equipment sector. Unlike in the case of the United States, all of the sectors studied have fairly similar export patterns. The changes in the export prices, in contrast, range widely from − 10.4 percent in the nonferrous metals sector to − 47.8 percent in the chemicals sector. The pass-through elasticities similarly range widely from one sector to another. In the chemicals sector, the pass-through is only 9 percent, while in the nonferrous metals sector it is 83 percent.

The interpretation of the pass-through elasticities is straightforward. In the case of textiles, for example, the elasticity of − 0.57 means that a 10 percent appreciation of the yen leads to a rise in the export price in foreign currency by 5.7 percent. Since the nominal appreciation was 60.0 percent, the export price rose by 34.2 percent in foreign currency (a partial pass-through made possible by a decline in the export price in yen by 25.8 percent). As noted above, the low degree of pass-through in this and other sectors may reflect a reduction in markups by exporters, but it may also reflect reductions in costs that lower prices in the domestic as well as export markets.

The bottom half of the table reports pricing to market effects. In this case, price changes are compared with changes in real rather than nominal exchange rates. The first column of the table reports percentage changes in the ratio of export to domestic prices. Since both of these prices are expressed in yen, any change in the ratio is evidence of pricing to market. The changes range from only 4.0 percent in nonferrous metals to 34.9 percent in chemicals. To evaluate the size of these changes, it is necessary to form a pricing-to-market elasticity obtained by dividing the relative price change by the change in the real effective exchange rate. Changes in real effective exchange rates range from 31.7 percent in the precision instruments sector to 42.6 percent in the nonferrous metals sector. The pricing-to-market elasticities, in turn, range from 0.09 in nonferrous metals to 1.09 in the chemicals sector.

Consider the case of textiles again. An elasticity of 0.40 means that a 10 percent real appreciation of the yen is followed by a 4 percent fall in the ratio of export to domestic prices. In response to a real appreciation for that sector of 37.5 percent the ratio of export to domestic prices falls by 14.9 percent.[14] The fall in this ratio dampens substantially the increase in the foreign currency price of the exports.

In general, pricing to market plays a major role in Japanese manufacturing. In the three export sectors representing 70 percent of exports, general machinery, electrical machinery, and transport equipment, the pricing-to-market elasticities range from 0.41 to 0.63. So roughly one-half of the yen's real appreciation has been neutralized by changing export prices relative to domestic prices. In a fourth sector, chemicals, the pricing-to-market elasticity is a little over 1.0. In only one sector, nonferrous metals, is the elasticity negligible in size.

American Pricing Behavior

To examine pass-through and pricing to market in U.S. manufacturing, producer price indexes (PPIs) and export price indexes from the Bureau of Labor Statistics were used. These data are disaggregated by sectors like the Japanese data, but not all of the sectors have export prices. Neither textiles nor metal products have export prices for the period studied, and in place of separate

14. The table indicates that the export price for textiles expressed in yen falls by 25.8 percent. To determine how much the domestic price changes, simply subtract the percentage change in the export/domestic price ratio from the percentage change in the export price, since all variables are expressed in logs. Thus, for textiles, the percentage change in the domestic price is −25.8% − (−14.9%) = −10.9%.

Table 4.5   **Pricing-to-Market Behavior in the United States, December 1981 to December 1984 (except as indicated)**

Sector	% Change Export/Domestic Price	Real Effective Exchange Rate	Pricing-to-Market Elasticity
Chemicals (from March 1983)	− 3.0	− 11.3	.26
Primary metals (March 1982)	− 12.5	− 11.1	1.13
General machinery	− 1.5	− 18.9	.08
Electrical machinery	− 3.9	− 16.5	.23
Transport equipment	9.3	− 6.3	− 1.46
Precision instruments	− 1.4	− 21.1	.07

Sources: See data appendix.

series for iron and steel and for nonferrous metals, there is a single series for primary metals. Nonetheless, the most important sectors have export prices available, including chemicals, general machinery, electrical machinery, transport equipment, and precision instruments.[15] As in the case of Japan, series for effective exchange rates were developed based on U.S. export flows.

Because pricing-to-market behavior is more likely to emerge in a period when a currency appreciates rather than depreciates, U.S. behavior was examined over the three-year period prior to rather than following the dollar's peak in February 1985. Some export price series are available for shorter periods only, so the sample period December 1981 to December 1984 applies to only four out of the six sectors studied.[16]

Table 4.5 reports pricing to market elasticities for six manufacturing sectors. The elasticities are quite low with the exception of the one for primary metals. In the chemical sector, for example, the elasticity is 0.26, indicating that an 11.3 percent real appreciation of the dollar leads to a fall in the ratio of export to domestic prices by 3.0 percent. In four other sectors the pricing-to-market elasticities are even lower.

Two sectors have unusual price patterns. The high elasticity in the primary metals sector is probably attributable to the fact that this sector combines iron and steel and nonferrous metals, the latter having a highly volatile price. The negative pricing-to-market elasticity in the transport equipment sector is a reflection of the unusual pattern of auto trade between Canada and the United States. Notice that the 6.3 percent appreciation of the dollar is much smaller than in other sectors because of the relative stability of the Canadian dollar/ U.S. dollar exchange rate. The movement of the export/domestic price ratio

15. There is no PPI for precision instruments, so the domestic inflation rate for electrical machinery had to be used in its place.

16. Export prices are available for the third month of each quarter only, so it was not possible to end the sample period in February 1985, the month that the dollar peaked in value.

in this sector is more a reflection of the particular auto models shipped between the United States and Canada than more general pricing behavior.

If these two sectors are ignored, pricing-to-market behavior appears to be less pronounced than in the case of Japan. In Japan, pricing-to-market coefficients are generally around 0.50, while in the United States, the coefficients are between 0.07 and 0.26.

To investigate U.S. pricing behavior further, more disaggregated (four-digit) data were obtained for three sectors where much of U.S. trade occurs: general machinery, electrical machinery, and precision instruments. In these three sectors, there are 10 four-digit products with both export and domestic PPI data available beginning in December 1982 or earlier. These 10 products are listed in table 4.6 together with the sample period for each product. (No disaggregated data were available for chemicals or primary metals over this period.) The table presents the percentage change in the ratio of export to domestic prices, the percentage change in the real effective exchange rate, and the pricing-to-market elasticity. For each product, the real effective exchange rate is defined for the corresponding two-digit sector.

The table shows that seven of the 10 products have pricing-to-market elasticities smaller than 0.30, three of which are even negative (though close to

Table 4.6   **Pricing-to-Market Behavior in the United States, Products in the General Machinery, Electrical Machinery, and Precision Instrument Sectors**

Products		Period[a]	% Change Export/Domestic Price	% Change Real Effective Exchange Rate	Pricing-to-Market Elasticity
3523	Farm machinery and equipment	D82–D84	1.4	−11.8	−.12
3533	Oil-field and gas-field machinery and equipment	D81–D84	−2.7	−18.8	.14
3537	Industrial trucks and tractors	D81–D84	−1.8	−18.8	.09
3546	Power driven hand tools	D81–D84	−5.1	−18.8	.27
3555	Printing trades machinery	D82–D84	.5	−11.8	−.04
3585	Refrigeration and heating equipment	D82–D84	−4.5	−11.8	.38
3643	Current-carrying wiring devices	D81–D84	−3.4	−16.5	.20
3651	Radio and TVs, phonographs, and related equipment	D81–D84	2.4	−16.5	−.15
3679	Electronic components NEC	J82–D84	−10.5	−10.4	1.02
3841	Surgical and medical instruments and supplies	J82–D84	−4.6	−13.9	.33

Sources: See data appendix.

[a]D = December; 82 = 1982; J = January, etc.

zero). Those products exhibit little if any pricing-to-market behavior. For example, in the case of product 3533, oil-field and gas-field machinery and equipment, the pricing-to-market elasticity is only 0.14; a real appreciation of the dollar by 18.8 percent leads to a fall in the ratio of export to domestic prices of only 2.7 percent. Three other products have larger elasticities, but only one product, miscellaneous electronic components, has an elasticity greater than 0.40 percent. So this table, based on disaggregated data, confirms the earlier evidence that U.S. firms appear to price to market less than Japanese firms.

Why do American firms price to market less than Japanese firms? It may be because pricing to market is more difficult for American firms to carry out without encouraging grey markets for the products. Third parties in the U.S. market may be better able to take advantage of arbitrage opportunities, which are created when different prices are charged for exports and domestic products. Or it may be because American firms have diversified their production facilities enough so that pricing to market is less necessary to preserve export markets. Many large American firms have production facilities in a variety of countries from which they can export, so an appreciation of the dollar may lead to a shift in export production from the United States to a plant or plants abroad. If this is the case, then the recent diversification of production facilities by Japanese firms may lead to less pricing to market there in the future.

4.3 Conclusion

This paper has provided a variety of evidence on pricing behavior in Japanese and U.S. manufacturing. Relative price movements are dominated by real factors such as productivity growth in the longer run, but, in the short-run, changes in exchange rates can disrupt normal relationships between prices.

Since 1975, the yen has appreciated relative to the dollar when measured in real terms using prices in the manufacturing sector as a whole. But the aggregate figures hide considerable variation in the relative performance of individual sectors of manufacturing. Japan has had such high productivity growth in one sector, electrical manufacturing, that the real appreciation has been reversed by the relative decline of Japanese prices in that sector.

These secular trends in relative competitiveness, however, are overshadowed by fluctuations in exchange rates in the short run. The paper has shown that the month-to-month volatility of exchange rates makes prices in the same sector less correlated across countries than prices in different sectors within either economy. Even medium-term movements in exchange rates have major effects on prices, since misalignments are large enough to offset any secular movements in relative prices.

Faced with swings in real exchange rates, firms adopt defensive measures to defend their export markets. The paper presents estimates of pricing-to-market elasticities that suggest that firms lower their export prices relative to their domestic prices in order to limit the effects of currency appreciations. There is evidence that firms in both countries pursue such pricing to market, but Japanese firms appear to change their export prices more than American firms.

Data Appendix
(for pass-through and pricing to market tables)

Japanese export prices and domestic prices: The export prices are FOB prices expressed in yen, while the domestic prices are those reported at the primary wholesale level for sale in Japan. The indexes are calculated using the Laspeyres formula. *Source:* Bank of Japan, *Price Indexes Annual,* various issues.

U.S. export prices and domestic prices: The export prices are from unpublished worksheets compiled by the U.S. Department of Labor, Bureau of Labor Statistics (BLS). The domestic prices are from the BLS's *Producer Price Indexes,* various issues.

Product-specific real effective exchange rates: For Japan, this is the ratio of the weighted average foreign price in yen to the Japanese wholesale price index (WPI). For the United States, it is the ratio of the weighted average foreign price in dollars to the U.S. WPI. The weights used in forming these series are export shares from the United Nations, *Commodity Trade Statistics,* 1986. The countries represented in the series were as follows: United States (in the Japanese series), Japan (in the U.S. series), Canada, Panama, Hong Kong, Korea, Singapore, Taiwan, Belgium, Denmark, France, Germany, Italy, the Netherlands, Norway, Portugal, Spain, Sweden, Switzerland, the United Kingdom, Malaysia, India, Saudi Arabia, and Australia. The underlying price series are WPIs (monthly averages) for most countries, CPIs for France, Panama, Saudi Arabia, Malaysia, and Portugal. The exchange rates are monthly averages. Sources for prices and exchange rates: IMF, *International Financial Statistics,* except for Hong Kong and Taiwan. For Hong Kong, exchange rate and export price series were taken from WEFA's Intline Data Base. For Taiwan, exchange rate and wholesale price index series were taken from its *Financial Statistics.*

Product-specific nominal effective exchange rates (for Japan): These are weighted averages of nominal exchange rates using same weights as the real effective exchange rate series above.

References

Balassa, Bela. 1964. The Purchasing-Power Parity Doctrine: A Reappraisal. *Journal of Political Economy* 72: 584–96.

Baldwin, Richard E. 1988. Hysteresis in Import Prices: the Beachhead Effect. *American Economic Review* 78: 773–85.

Cumby, Robert E., and John Huizinga. 1989. Relative Traded Goods Prices and Imperfect Competition in U.S. Manufacturing Industries. Manuscript. April.

Feenstra, Robert C. 1987. Symmetric Pass-through of Tariffs and Exchange Rates under Imperfect Competition: An Empirical Test. NBER Working Paper no. 2453. Cambridge, Mass., December.

Frenkel, Jacob. 1981. The Collapse of Purchasing Power Parities during the 1970s. *European Economic Review* 16 (May): 145–65.

Froot, Kenneth A., and Paul Klemperer. 1988. Exchange Rate Pass-through when Market Share Matters. NBER Working Paper no. 2542. Cambridge, Mass., March.

Giovannini, Alberto. 1988. Exchange Rates and Traded Goods Prices. *Journal of International Economics* 24 (February): 45–68.

Hooper, Peter, and Catherine L. Mann. 1989. Exchange Rate Pass-through in the 1980s: The Case of U.S. Imports of Manufactures. *Brookings Papers on Economic Activity,* no. 1: 297–337.

Knetter, Michael M. 1989. Price Discrimination by U.S. and German Exporters. *American Economic Review* 79: 198–209.

Kravis, Irving B., and Robert E. Lipsey. 1978. Price Behavior in the Light of Balance of Payments Theories. *Journal of International Economics* 8: 192–245.

Krugman, Paul. 1987. Pricing to Market When the Exchange Rate Changes. In *Real-Financial Linkages among Open Economies,* ed. Sven W. Arndt and J. David Richardson, pp. 49–70. Cambridge: MIT press.

Mann, Catherine L. 1986. Prices, Profit Margins, and Exchange Rates. *Federal Reserve Bulletin,* vol. 72, no. 6 (June): 366–79.

Marston, Richard C. 1988. Exchange Rate Policy Reconsidered. In *International Economic Cooperation,* ed. Martin Feldstein, pp. 79–136. Chicago: University of Chicago Press.

———. 1990. Pricing to Market in Japanese Manufacturing. *Journal of International Economics* 29 (November): 217–36.

Officer, Lawrence H. 1976. The Purchasing-Power-Parity Theory of Exchange Rates: A Review Article. *International Monetary Fund Staff Papers* 23, no. 1 (March): 1–60.

Ohno, Kenichi. 1989. Export Pricing Behavior of Manufacturing: A U.S.-Japan Comparison. *International Monetary Fund Staff Papers* 36(3): 550–79.

Williamson, John. 1985. *The Exchange Rate System.* Policy Analyses in International Economics no. 5. Washington, D.C.: Institute for International Economics.

Comment   Catherine L. Mann

Marston's paper contributes in three ways to the literature on international pricing behavior. The first section of the paper bolsters the argument that issues relating to international competitiveness cannot be discussed without reference to disaggregated data. The second section raises the ante in policy discussions about exchange rate volatility and misalignments by arguing that exchange rate variability and the differential responsiveness of exporters to it is importantly responsible for changes in international competitiveness. The

Catherine L. Mann is an economist at the Federal Reserve Board.

third section gives an initial presentation of the important link between the pass-through (PT) literature and the pricing-to-market (PTM) literature and examines these coefficients for specific industries for both U.S. and Japanese exporters.

I will focus on the last section in my comment, developing the linkage between PT and PTM somewhat further analytically and showing that using both PT and PTM reveals more information about exporters' pricing behavior. The results of other empirical work are reexamined in light of this analysis. My comment concludes with a discussion of how different policy questions can be better answered using one, the other, or both methodologies.

Marston begins with a discussion of international competitiveness. He presents data that shows quite strikingly that aggregate data, even when aggregated only over manufactured goods, masks substantial changes in international competitiveness across different manufacturing sectors. Much discussion in policy circles of international competitiveness revolves around the state of key industries, those that offer "good jobs at good wages." Export-oriented U.S. industries apparently pay a wage premium over that expected based on qualifications alone.[1] Export-oriented industries accounted for less job growth in the United States in 1985 when the dollar was at its peak and increased their contribution to job growth in 1987 after the substantial depreciation. Remember that, in 1985, some policymakers (who measured international competitiveness using exchange-rate adjusted export prices at the industry level) decried the deindustrialization of America, while at the same time, other policymakers (looking at the aggregate dollar exchange rate) lauded the strong value of the dollar as indicative of the international attractiveness of the United States as a location for investment. Clearly, a balance of aggregate and industry-specific data is needed to develop a clear picture of U.S. international competitiveness.

The literatures on "pass-through" and "pricing to market" have existed somewhat separately, perhaps because the pass-through literature has a significantly longer history and one with less of the connotation of "strategic" pricing behavior than that which is associated with pricing to market. The two phenomena are closely related, however, as demonstrated below. Moreover, estimating and using both PT and PTM elasticities reveal more information about the pricing strategies of exporters.

Pass-through is usually defined as the coefficient of proportionality between an exporter's price expressed in destination currency terms (the mirror import price, expressed in home-currency terms) and changes in the nominal exchange rate. Equations (1a) and (1b) below develop the PT concept for exporters, using the variable conventions in Marston (dropping the i subscript).

---

1. See Lawrence F. Katz and Lawrence H. Summers, "Can Inter-industry Wage Differentials Justify Strategic Trade Policy?", *Trade Policies for International Competitiveness*, ed. Robert C. Feenstra (Chicago: University of Chicago Press, 1989), pp. 85–116.

Here, P_x is the exporter's own currency price for good i, C is its marginal cost, and M_x is its markup.

Dividing by the good-specific nominal exchange rate S yields the price of the export in destination-currency terms, $P_x^\$$. Taking the total derivative through yields a pass-through elasticity β, which will lie between 0 and -1.

(1a) $$P_x^\$ = P_x / S = C\, M_x / S,$$

(1b) $$d\ln P_x^\$ / d\ln S = \beta = d\ln P_x / d\ln S - 1.$$

The closer β is to -1, the greater the pass-through of an exchange rate change into the price of the good sold in the destination-market currency, and the less of a change in the export price in domestic currency terms. Little international data are available for bilateral trade flows, so we would not expect, even for individual products, that the elasticity with respect to the export price obtained from the exporter (P_x) to equal that elasticity with respect to the import price $(+1)$ obtained from the importer $(P_x^\$)$; the first incorporates flows to many destinations while the second incorporates flow from many sources. Nevertheless, there is a clear relationship.

However, interpreting this measure of pass-through as an estimate of the strategic change in markups associated with exchange rate movements is incorrect. Early investigations of pass-through, including mine in 1986, implied this, and Marston continues using this method in table 4.4, although he points out its faults. Equation (1c) shows that β is composed to two parts, only one . of which measures "strategic" behavior. The other component measures how costs "naturally" change with exchange rate movements. Thus, β will be closer to zero the more costs change and "naturally" offset exchange rate movements.

(1c) $$\beta = d\ln C / d\ln S + d\ln M_x / d\ln S - 1.$$

Thus the direct calculation of β as the ratio of changes in export prices to nominal exchange rates overemphasizes "strategic" behavior to the extent that costs fall as the exporter's currency appreciates.

An alternative empirical approach can separate these two components. As shown in equation (2), a_2 is the least squares estimate of β when changes in the effect of costs on prices are accounted for (and measured by coefficient a_1).

(2) $$\ln P_{xt}^\$ = a_0 + a_1 \ln C_t + a_2 \ln S_t + \mu_t.$$

Most recent investigations of PT (including Hooper and Mann 1989, Baldwin 1988, and Knetter 1989; see references in Marston) use the least squares approach to estimating pass-through and therefore should not overestimate the effect of strategic effect of exchange rate changes on export prices.

By contrast, Marston defines the PTM elasticity as the coefficient of proportionality between the ratio of domestic and export prices expressed in local currency terms and changes in the real exchange rate.

(3a) $\alpha = d\ln (P_x / P_d) / d\ln R,$

where P_x is the export price in local currency of good i, P_d its price in the domestic market, and R is the product-specific real exchange rate. Expanding (3a) and rearranging as (3b) isolates the components of α for easy comparison to the components of β shown in (1c).

(3b) $\alpha = [(d\ln C_x - d\ln C_d) + (d\ln M_x - d\ln M_d)] / d\ln (S + P^{us} - P^{jp}),$

where the subscript x denotes the export and d denotes the product sold into the domestic market and $P^{us} - P^{jp}$ is the inflation differential used to form the real exchange rate from the spot rate.

Suppose that costs of producing for different markets move the same, then the important information imparted by movements in α is that the markups on domestic and export prices vary given any exchange rate movement. But from a policy standpoint, we really want to know how each markup is moving when the exchange rate changes, not just that there is evidence of price discrimination. Using the least squares estimate of pass-through shown in (3), and assuming that changes in real and spot exchange rates are the same (as has been suggested by aggregate data[2], although not corroborated by Marston's table 4.4), we can separate the two components of α and thus obtain information about exporter's pricing behavior in both home and foreign markets. Equation (4) shows the relationship between α and the components of the least squares estimates of PT.

(4) $\alpha = a_2 + 1 - \sigma,$

where $\sigma = d\ln P / d\ln R$.

Since α and a_2 can be calculated and estimated, σ can be derived. Comparing $(a_2 + 1)$ and σ reveals which price (export or domestic) is changing more with exchange rate movements. Coefficient a_1 estimates the effect on export prices of changes in costs. Assuming the same cost structure yields estimates of the changes in domestic and export margins, given a change in the exchange rate.

The empirical examination of the data in Marston's paper does not give quite enough information to calculate the elasticity of the margins since he presents calculations of β, not estimated coefficients a_1 and a_2. Moreover, real and nominal exchange rates apparently have not moved by the same amount. However, suppose we retain the assumption that the elasticity of a producer's response to real or nominal exchange rate changes is the same. Suppose again that $\beta + 1$ is an adequate measure of $a_2 + 1$. Given these assumptions, σ can be calculated from the information in table 4.4.

---

2. See International Monetary Foundation, "Exchange Rate Volatility and World Trade," IMF Occasional Paper no. 28 (1984).

Sector	α	β + 1	σ
Textiles	.40	.43	.03
Chemicals	1.09	.91	−.18
Iron and steel	.58	.50	−.08
Non-ferrous metals	.09	.17	.08
Metal products	.61	.40	−.21
General machinery	.54	.37	−.17
Electrical machinery	.63	.79	.16
Transport equipment	.41	.32	−.09
Precision instruments	.41	.29	−.12

Given an appreciation of the yen, a positive $\beta + 1$ implies a reduction in the export price in yen terms, while a negative σ implies an increase in the domestic price of the product. These calculations suggest more than simple price discrimination across markets. These data suggest that for all industries except textiles, nonferrous metals, and electrical machinery, domestic price increases cross-subsidized export price declines. Presuming that costs in yen terms fell as the yen appreciated, margins on domestic sales clearly expanded, while those on export sales may have expanded some or contracted. To determine the movement in margins, we would need an estimate of a_1.

Besides relaxing the assumptions already noted above, a more careful examination of PT and PTM would attempt to account for behavioral differences across sectors on account of quantitative restraints and other characteristics of market structure.[3] Although there is insufficient information in Marston to calculate σ for U.S. industries, an important reason for their apparently lower PTM elasticity is that the share of exports in domestic production may be quite small, making separate price lists not worthwhile.[4] Moreover, the issue of currency of contracting has perhaps not been adequately treated here.[5]

The different measures of exporter's pricing behavior each have value depending on the policy issue at hand. To answer the question of how international competitiveness in foreign markets changes with exchange rate changes—for example, what may happen to the price of U.S. exports in foreign markets when the dollar appreciates—the least squares approach provides a more direct answer. For questions with a trade policy focus—for example, are Japanese producers using high domestic prices to subsidize export prices, prima facie evidence of "unfair trade"—the PTM calculation along with the estimate of cost pass-through better quantifies the ability of exporters

3. See Peter Hooper and Catherine L. Mann, "The Emergence and Persistence of the U.S. External Imbalance, 1980–1987," *Princeton Study in International Finance no. 65* (October 1989), pp. 85–91.
4. See discussion in Hooper and Mann, pp. 81–83.
5. See Catherine L. Mann, *Weltwirtschaftliches Archiv* 125, no. 3 (1989): 588–618, and references therein for more on currency of contracting.

to create and exploit a price wedge between locally sold and foreign-sold products.

Comment   Bonnie E. Loopesko

The recent research of Richard Marston, including the paper presented at this conference, has served to substantially clarify the precise meanings of pass through and pricing to market. Marston shows that it is possible to go beyond simple observations about the degree of pass-through of exchange rate changes to export prices in order to determine whether those changes result from pricing-to-market motives.

One important contribution of this line of research is to isolate the pricing-to-market motive from the impact of changes in marginal cost on export prices. In particular, incomplete pass-through may have nothing to do with a strategy to defend market share by cutting profit margins, but instead may result from constant markup pricing over varying marginal costs. Marston shows how these two effects on pass-through may be disentangled empirically, allowing him to test directly for the existence of pricing-to-market behavior.

The earlier empirical work on pass-through, including my own work with Robert Johnson (published in an NBER volume that Marston edited), evaluated the degree of pass-through to Japanese export prices but did not attempt to distinguish empirically between strategic pricing goals and the influences of cost factors in explaining the observed partial pass-through. In our paper, we described some research done at MITI in Japan that showed that the marked decline in costs of imported intermediate goods explained a substantial part of the observed slowness in pass-through to Japanese export prices during the episode of prolonged yen appreciation in the mid-1980s. However, as Marston notes, this approach requires measuring these cost factors for each sector of manufacturing, which is considerably more complicated than the direct test for pricing to market that he proposes.

My comments are organized around three themes. First, I will note one question about some evidence Marston provides on internal and external price adjustment. Second, I will raise some issues regarding the interpretation of the findings on pricing to market behavior. Finally, I will note a few implications of this work for macroeconomic policy.

In the first part of the paper, Marston says his study seeks to answer the following question: "Has the randomness of flexible exchange rates so reduced the integration of different national markets in any one sector of manu-

Bonnie E. Loopesko is a senior international economist in International Capital Markets at the Federal Reserve Bank of New York.

facturing that internal price adjustment *between* sectors is more complete than external price adjustment in the same sector? . . . That is, the random movement in nominal exchange rates would have made the prices of American 'apples' more closely linked to those of American 'oranges' than to those of Japanese 'apples.'" The apples and oranges analogy suggests the reader should be surprised if "internal adjustment" occurs more rapidly than "external adjustment."

Marston's evidence, summarized in table 4.1, shows that internal price correlations across sectors of manufacturing substantially exceed the price correlations for the same goods across countries. Two rather different forces are at work. "External adjustment" requires substantial international arbitrage in the goods market in the short run, which, we know from the extensive empirical literature on PPP, does not occur. In contrast, "internal adjustment" requires a rapid response of pricing in different sectors of manufacturing to changes in common costs. This could result from commonly postulated markup pricing behavior. Thus is appears that Marston sets up something of a straw man that is easily knocked down.

Next, I would like to raise three questions about the interpretation of the findings on pricing-to-market behavior. First, given that Marston establishes the empirical importance of pricing to market behavior, it would be interesting to ask *what* provides the ability to price discriminate. The framework used in this paper is discussed in an earlier paper (NBER Working paper no. 2905, March 1989). In that paper, Marston shows that the pricing-to-market elasticity in equation (3) is a function of the elasticities of domestic and foreign markups with respect to prices. These, in turn, depend on the curvature of the respective demand curves. Thus pricing-to-market behavior appears to derive from factors on the *demand side* and is a form of price discrimination on the part of producers. Of course, in these reduced-form models, the reduced-form coefficients of the demand functions comingle factors from the supply and demand sides.

The ability to price discriminate could derive from a variety of factors relating to market structure and the cost function. It could derive from market power based on the degree of industry concentration and international competition or from the ability of the firm to create individual market power through product differentiation. It could also result from segmentation of markets caused by a combination of high transactions costs and protection. To give one example, differences in the degree of international competition in markets for different categories of manufactured goods may explain some of the differences in markup elasticities across sectors shown in table 4.4. Robert Johnson and I made a related argument in our analysis of pass-through, noting that those sectors that appeared to face increasing competition from the NICs were those that appeared to have the lowest rates of pass-through.

A second question about the interpretation of Marston's results concerns the derivation of the equations used for estimating the pricing-to-market elasticities. The assumption of static, one-period profit-maximizing behavior allows Marston (in his earlier paper) to use the usual first-order conditions to derive the two price markup functions. However, one of the implicit hypotheses of this work is that Japanese firms price to market in order to expand or maintain market share. This would appear to imply a specification that goes beyond short-run profit maximization to incorporate intertemporal effects on profitability of enlarging market share.

Another point relevant to an extension of this work to a dynamic framework is that producers' expectations about the nature of exchange rate changes will influence their pricing behavior. If producers expect an exchange rate change to be permanent, they are more likely to pass through more of that change immediately and to price to market to a lesser degree. If the exchange rate change is large enough, the location of production may be shifted as well. In contrast, if producers expect a rapid reversal of the exchange rate movement, it may be optimal to absorb the exchange rate change in profits. Thus, in a dynamic optimizing framework, expectations about the duration of exchange rate movements would affect the degree of pricing-to-market behavior.

Another possible explanation of the differences in pricing-to-market behavior between sectors of manufacturing, or even across countries, might relate to the level of profit margins. Presumably a firm has more scope to price to market if it currently has large profit margins. It is unclear how this factor fits into Marston's framework.

Finally, I would like to suggest some possible implications of this line of research for the transmission of monetary policy. Consider the case where an easing of U.S. monetary policy leads to dollar depreciation. Pricing-to-market behavior on the part of Japanese exporters would delay the impact of the dollar's decline on U.S. import prices and hence delay demand-switching effects. In this way, pricing to market can affect the *lag* with which monetary policy affects prices and the real economy.

Also, the pricing-to-market behavior of Japanese exporters should imply that monetary-policy-induced exchange rate movements will impart greater variability to Japanese profits, thereby increasing the riskiness of investment in the Japanese tradable goods sector. This should show up in the correlation between the exchange rate and stock prices in Japan. This sort of issue could be explored if pricing-to-market equations were embedded in a broader macroeconomic model.

5   Is the Japanese Distribution System Really Inefficient?

Takatoshi Ito and Masayoshi Maruyama

5.1   Introduction

The Japanese distribution system has been criticized domestically and internationally. It is well known that many Japanese consumer products, such as cameras and VCRs, are sold cheaper in New York than in Tokyo. Korean cars, successful in the United States, are virtually nonexistent in Japan. Famous brand-name goods, such as Louis Vuitton, Hermes, Chivas Regal, and Courvoisier, imported from Europe, are sold in Japan with extraordinary premia. The "price differential between home and abroad" (*Naigai kakaku sa*) has become an important political problem in Japan.

Suspected causes for the price differential are the so-called Japanese characteristics in the distribution system. Many small (family-run) retail stores, which cannot exploit scale economies, have survived thanks to the restriction on the construction and operation (store hours) of large retail (e.g., discount) stores in the neighborhood of small stores. Some of the many layers of wholesale industry seem unnecessary. The (vertically semi-integrated) *keiretsu* stores carry only one (domestic) brand, discriminating against other domestic brands as well as imports. Sole representative agents for imports in many imported goods enjoy its monopolistic rents, reducing the volume (and dollar value) of imports, given that they deal with differentiated products.

The situation described above is often stereotyped as the inefficient distribution system that incurs unnecessary distribution costs and discriminates against imports. Two major questions and issues can be distinguished. First,

Takatoshi Ito is professor of Economics, Hitotsubashi University and the University of Minnesota, and a research associate at the National Bureau of Economic Research. Masayoshi Maruyama is Associate Professor at Department of Business Administration at Kobe University.

The authors wish to thank David Flath and other conference participants for their comments. Comments from Mark Ramseyer, Kiyohiko Nishimura, and Graham Elliott were helpful in revising this paper.

it is important to investigate whether the unique characteristics result in the "inefficiency" of the distribution system in Japan. The distribution system is said to be efficient if the distribution system does not add unnecessary costs in the pipeline from a manufacturer to a consumer.

Second, the distribution system might act as a non-tariff barrier, which limits competition from abroad. This could happen even if the distribution system is "efficient" in terms of the pipeline costs. Suppose that the manufacturer charges a higher domestic price than export price, and/or that importers charge higher domestic wholesale prices than their import costs, then retail prices would be higher. Put differently, if the prices charged upon entry to the pipeline are already high, then the retail prices would be high even under the same distribution margin through the pipeline.

This paper investigates the first question, namely the efficiency of the Japanese distribution system. Most of the discussions on the Japanese distribution system have so far relied on institutional descriptions and anecdotal evidence, failing to substantiate the case, one way or the other, with quantitative measures. The present paper will show that the Japanese and U.S. distribution sectors are about the same in terms of value added and distribution margins. Therefore, it is not true that the distribution sector adds up unnecessary distribution costs or earns monopolistic operating profits.

This paper will not address the second question, namely, whether the distribution system is acting as a non-tariff barrier. Thus, even if the distribution sector in Japan is judged to be "efficient," it leaves open a possibility that the distribution system works as a barrier to potential new entrants from both home and foreign manufacturers. The price differential between home and abroad can be a result of oligopolistic pricing behavior of manufacturers. Japanese manufacturers may set domestic wholesale prices higher than export price. Foreign manufacturers may charge higher export prices on goods bound for Japan than on those for other markets. The price differential may be reinforced by the exclusive *keiretsu* distribution system. If this scenario is the case, the efficiency of the distribution system implies that the monopoly rents are not shared by the distribution sector. This paper does not verify how likely this scenario is.

The rest of the paper consists of four sections. The next section will summarize the conventional wisdom of the Japanese distribution system. Section 5.3 will propose several measures to judge the efficiency of the distribution system. Some preliminary investigations on the U.S.-Japan comparison will be conducted. Section 5.4 is the core of this paper. It will investigate distribution margins of the (comparable) three-digit wholesale and two-digit retail sectors for the United States and Japan. Interpretations of the finding will be offered in the last section.

5.2 Conventional Wisdom

Perceived characteristics of the Japanese distribution system can be summarized as follows.

1. *Many small establishments.* Wholesale and retail stores are of small size both in the number of employees and in sales. They cannot adopt technological advances that take advantage of scale economies. This characteristic also discriminates against imports as well as any new products because financially weak establishments cannot experiment with new products at their own risk.

2. *Many layers.* The distribution system has "many layers and is complex," in that there are relatively many distributors involved in the distribution system that stretches from the makers' warehouses to the consumer. Sometimes there are three different wholesalers involved from the manufacturer to the retailer. This makes the distribution system inefficient; that is, distribution costs in the consumer price is higher than optimal.

3. *Distribution* **keiretsu.** Manufacturers develop their exclusive distribution systems. For example, Panasonic stores, Sony stores, Toshiba stores, and so on carry a set of consumer electronic products, but exclusively their own brands. This vertical semi-integration makes it difficult for new entrants, including imports, to penetrate the market. The new entrant would need to establish its own distributors. The operation would involve a large risk that few foreign firms would like to take.

4. *Unique trading practices* (i.e., returns policy, sales persons on loan, price maintenance, and rebate system). There are a number of so-called unique trading practices that makes the distribution system in Japan "complicated" and "inefficient."

Returns from retail stores to the wholesaler are often allowed even if the retail stores bought the merchandise. In this sense a returns policy of unsold merchandise is said to be "liberal" (from retail to wholesale stores) (*henpin sei*). Many department stores and other large retail stores are staffed with "persons on loan" from manufacturers to retail stores. Although they are on the manufacturer's payroll, they act as sales persons who demonstrate and promote the products in the department store. Retail prices are often "maintained" by implicit agreement between the manufacturers and the retailers via wholesalers. Rebates between retailers and wholesalers are just a means of nonlinear pricing. However, it is alleged that the terms of rebates are often not spelled out beforehand, but left to the discretion of wholesalers and manufacturers.

5. *Dai-ten Ho.* The policy using *Dai-ten Ho* (an acronym of the law and its implementation, concerning the restriction on the construction of and on the operating hours of large-scale retail stores) makes it difficult for large-size retail stores (discount stores, department stores, and supermarkets) to take advantage of scale economies. Since these stores carry more imports than

smaller retail stores (see 2 above), *Dai-ten Ho* works against benefits of foreign makers as well as the Japanese consumers.

6. *Sole representative importer.* Many products are imported to Japan by sole representative importers. If the Japanese consumers have lower price elasticity for brand-name goods, then the sole representative importers of brand-name goods would find it profitable to charge a higher price for the goods in Japan than in the rest of the world. This would be not sustainable if parallel imports were permitted and costless.

7. *Personal relationships and long-term contracts.* It is said that, in order to make business deals, establishing a "personal relationship" is needed in addition to a long-term relationship, marked by a reliable delivery record (even if this implies expensive overtime on the part of makers and wholesale businesses) and by after-sale service.

5.2.1 Many Small Establishments

The characteristic of many small establishments in Japan can be seen in three different statistics in table 5.1.

First, the number of workers (both employees and self-employed) per establishments are compared. The Japanese retail stores are, on average, operated by about four persons. In fact, more than half of the retail stores have only one or two persons running the shop. The number of persons per estab-

Table 5.1   Many Small Establishments, International Comparison

	Japan	United States	Germany
Workers per establishment:			
Wholesale:			
1982	9.3	12.6	10.1
1985	9.4	N.A.	9.6
Retail:			
1982	3.7	8.1	5.9
1985	3.9	N.A.	5.8
Number of establishments per 1,000 residents:			
Wholesale:			
1982	3.3	1.5	2.0
1985	3.1	N.A.	1.9
Retail:			
1982	14.5	8.3	6.7
1985	13.5	N.A.	6.6
Sales floor space:[a]			
Retail:			
1982	55.4	N.A.	167.9
1985	58.0	N.A.	N.A.

Source: Maruyama et al. (1989).

[a]In square meters.

lishment is about a half of that in the United States and two-thirds that in Germany. Workers per wholesale establishment in Japan is about three-fourths of that in the United States; but it is comparable to that in Germany.

Second, the number of establishments per 1,000 residents is much higher in Japan than in the United States or Germany. This is true in both the wholesale and retail sectors. Retailers and wholesalers in Japan are about twice as dense as in the United States or Germany.

Third, the average Japanese retailer has about one-third the floor space of the German counterpart. This could be a result of the high price of land in Japan.

These statistics confirm that the establishments are run by a smaller number of persons in Japan and there are more establishments per capita than the United States and Germany.

Is this Japanese characteristic changing? Table 5.2 shows the time series of the workers per establishment for wholesale and retail sectors. The average number of workers per establishment has in fact declined recently, after peaking in 1972. The wholesale structure shows no evidence that the size of wholesale establishments are increasing at all.

On the retail side, however, workers per retail establishment is steadily increasing. Especially after 1982, the number of individual establishments is declining, while the number of workers continues to grow. This results in an acceleration in this statistic. However, even with the increased pace over the period 1982–88, it would take 20 years to catch up with Germany and 40 years to catch up with the United States in terms of the workers per establishment.

5.2.2   Many Layers within the Wholesale Industry

After the Japanese goods leave a manufacturer's warehouse, they typically go through more than one wholesaler. Japanese wholesalers tend to be more specialized in one type of goods, and sometimes specialize exclusively on one brand. Yet there are many wholesalers involved between the manufacturer and customers. For some goods, there may be a "secondary wholesaler," and even a "tertiary wholesaler" in addition to a "primary wholesaler." Although practice differs from commodity to commodity, and sometimes brand to brand, a stylized notion of "many layers" is true in the sense that even discount stores and large super market chains are often unable to purchase directly from manufacturers.

A primary wholesaler could be a manufacturer's subsidiary. In that case, it deals with their own brands exclusively. (Examples include consumer electronics, cosmetics, detergent, and cameras.) In other cases, a primary wholesaler deals with other brands. A secondary wholesaler is typically a regional distributor, and a tertiary wholesaler is a local distributor. In an extreme, large-scale retailers typically obtain goods from makers via a wholesaler in Japan, but without a wholesaler in the United States.

Table 5.2 Many Small Establishments, Time Series, Japan

	1958	1960	1962	1964	1966	1968	1970	1972	1974
Wholesale									
Number of establishments per residents	193	226	223	229	287	240	256	259	292
Number of workers	1,551	1,928	2,129	2,524	3,042	2,697	2,861	3,008	3,290
Workers per establishment	**8.0**	**8.5**	**9.5**	**11.0**	**10.6**	**11.2**	**11.1**	**11.6**	**11.2**
Retail									
Number of establishments	1,245	1,288	1,272	1,305	1,375	1,432	1,471	1,496	1,548
Number of workers	3,273	3,489	3,550	3,811	4,193	4,646	4,926	5,141	5,303
Workers per establishment	**2.6**	**2.7**	**2.8**	**2.9**	**3.0**	**3.2**	**3.3**	**3.4**	**3.4**

	1976	1979	1982	1985	1988
Wholesale					
Number of establishments	340,249	368,608	428,858	413,016	436,502
Number of workers	3,512,973	3,672,638	4,090,919	3,998,437	4,331,601
Workers per establishment	**10.3**	**10.0**	**9.5**	**9.7**	**9.9**
Retail					
Number of establishments	1,614,067	1,673,667	1,721,465	1,628,644	1,619,599
Number of workers	5,579,800	5,960,432	6,369,426	6,328,614	6,850,478
Workers per establishment	**3.5**	**3.6**	**3.7**	**3.9**	**4.2**

Source: MITI, Census of Commerce.

Note: Boldface type indicates numbers that are useful from the U.S.-Japan comparative perspective.

Table 5.3   **Wholesale/Retail (W/R) Ratio**

	Japan	United States	Germany
W/R in sales			
1982	3.53	1.09	1.67[a]
1985	3.44	.97[b]	1.80[c]
W/R for inventories			
1982	1.60	.82	1.17[d]
1985	1.55	.85[b]	1.17[c]
W/R in number of establishments:			
1982	.225	.176	.290[a]
1985	.229	N.A.	.292[c]

Source: Maruyama et al. (1989).
Note: Wholesale trade data are based on merchant wholesalers.
[a]1978.
[b]1986.
[c]1984.
[d]1981.

As a measure of many layers in the wholesale industry, it is popular to use the wholesale/retail (W/R) sales ratio. We will explain the W/R ratio and then propose an additional measure. The W/R sales ratio in Japan is significantly higher than that in the United States or Germany (see table 5.3, row 1).

The high W/R ratio is interpreted as a reflection of many layers in the wholesale industry because sales of the same commodity are double or triple counted as wholesale sales in the multilayered wholesale industry structure.

However, a high W/R ratio may be a result of another characteristic. Instead of the wholesale level being multilayered, the retail establishments may be especially small in size. If the retail sales per establishment (discussed in the next section) is small due to its small scale of operations (implied by the workers per establishment data given in table 5.1), then a high W/R ratio would be obtained. Therefore, the W/R ratio alone is not conclusive evidence of the multilayered nature.[1]

We can measure the proportion of sales to other wholesalers in total sales, as shown in table 5.4. This table clearly shows that more sales between wholesalers take place in Japan, a piece of evidence for multilayered wholesale industry. Indeed, there are many layers in the wholesale industry.

1. Note that the W/R sales ratio can be decomposed into:

$$\frac{\text{Sales per establishment, wholesale}}{\text{Sales per establishment, retail}} \times \frac{\text{Number of establishments per 1,000 residents}}{\text{Number of establishments per 1,000 residents}}$$

Therefore, if sales per establishment in retail in one country is extremely low, the W/R ratio would be higher, even though other components are comparable with other countries.

Table 5.4   **Proportion of Wholesale Sales by Class of Customers (%)**

Customer class	Japan (1982)	United States (1982)	West Germany (1986)
Other wholesalers	41.9	24.8	16.2
Retailers and repair shops	24.0	28.0	30.0
Export	7.4	9.8	14.9
Household and individual	.6	1.6	2.8
Industrial users, manufacturing and mining	. . .	15.0	26.8
Others	26.1	20.8	9.2

Source: Maruyama et al. (1989). Data source: *Japan,* Census of Commerce, 1982. (These were adjusted by deducting the transactions between companies' headquarters and branches. These data cover manufacturers' and other industrial companies' sales branches and offices, and exclude agents and commission merchants.) *United States,* 1982 Census of Wholesale Trade (WC82-I-4) (only merchange wholesalers). *Germany,* Handel, Gastgewerbe, Reiseverkehr Fachserie 6 (Reihe, 1.3 Warensortiment sowie Bezugs und Absatzwege im Grosshandel 1986) (exports include those to East Germany).

5.2.3   Theoretical Justifications

There are two opposite views on how to understand the existence of many small retail and multilevel wholesale stores in Japan. The first view is that these characteristics are efficient results of Japanese consumer's preference and spatial limitations. (See Flath 1988, 1989a; Maruyama 1988). The second view is that they are largely a result of regulations (see McCraw and O'Brien 1986).

The first view is developed as follows. Many small retail establishments (neighborhood stores) are considered to be a rational result of the consumer's diet and buying habit. Suppose that the Japanese consumer prefers to shop every day in small lots in neighborhood stores. Fresh raw fish must be purchased every day, not once a week. Moreover, a refrigerator is too small to store a whole week's inventories, and automobiles are inefficient to use in congested urban areas. Then, this explains the existence of many small retail stores. In a sense, the large number of shops are a substitute for a household's trip and stock costs. Although establishments that are small seem inefficient, they are usually family-run establishments physically adjacent to the home, with low overhead costs and rents.

The existence of many small retail shops requires extra layers (primary wholesale, secondary wholesale, etc.) of the distribution system if organizational (monitoring) costs approximately fix an optimal number of retailers (or other wholesalers) per one wholesaler. This would explain the multilevel wholesalers in Japan.

The second view is that these Japanese characteristics are indications of some distortions in the market. Even if roads are congested, public transportation is fully developed in Japan, and consumers are quite mobile. There is no reason to suppose that retailers have to be close by. Even if many small retail stores are given, the ratio of wholesalers could be less in Japan, as retailers are located close together geographically. In short, we would expect, in more densely populated Japan, a lower ratio of stores to population. According to this view, the wholesale/retail ratio should be less in Japan than other countries.[2] The stylized facts described above should be a result of some regulations, such as *Dai-ten Ho*.

5.2.4   *Keiretsu* and "Unique" Trading Practices

The conventional wisdom on *keiretsu* can be understood as follows. *Keiretsu* stores in the wholesale and retail level are controlled by the respective manufacturers. In the *keiretsu* stores, manufacturers control decisions, such as which brands to carry, how much discount from the "standard retail price" (or retail price wished by the maker, in the literal translation) can be allowed, and how to deal with unsold inventories. In that sense, the essential part of *keiretsu* in the distribution sector is a package of "vertical restraints" in the sense of Flath (1989b).

Often wholesalers and retailers exclusively deal with one manufacturer. In order to maintain resale prices, the manufacturer has to accept unsold goods as returns. Otherwise, the retail stores face too much risk in their earnings in the presense of uncertain demand. In a sense, the so-called liberal returns policy (*henpin sei*) and the price maintenance system can be understood as a result of a profit maximization of an oligopolist with differentiated products that has a *keiretsu* power to impose vertical restraints and whose retailers face an uncertain demand curve. (This point is forcefully shown in Flath 1989a and Flath and Nariu 1989.) According to this view, there is nothing "unfair" or "inefficient" about "liberal" returns policy in Japan. If there is any problem, it is an institution (or a lack of strict enforcement of fair trade law) that allows oligopolistic vertical restraints by manufacturers with differentiated products.

There is a controversy as to whether *keiretsu* stores are a real cause of *naigai kakaku sa*. Some argue that many *keiretsu* stores deal with more than one brand (Nihon Keizai Shinbunsha 1989, p. 84). However, no estimate of the number of such stores is provided.

Another "unique" business practice in Japan is worth mentioning. Namely, many department stores are staffed by "persons on loan" from manufacturers or wholesalers. The statistics shows that in 12 departments, (sales) persons on loan outnumber own (sales) persons. The Japanese department stores use their basement floors as food and grocery sections. They are usually operated and staffed as branches of small retail stores, and sales persons are usually on loan

2. David Flath drew our attention to the following fact. When the numbers of stores per thousand households are compared for different prefectures in Japan, both Tokyo (most densely populated) and Hokkaido (most sparsely populated) record the lowest. The number of retail stores excluding eating and drinking places for Japan's average is 45.5, while Tokyo is 35.1 and Hokkaido is 34.1. The comparable number for the United States is 23.8.

from respective retail stores. Therefore, the department store with a larger food section, such as Keihin Tokyu, tends to have a higher ratio of sales persons on loan. A new branch of a department store chain also tends to have a higher ratio (see Ito and Maruyama 1989, table 2–5).

The Japanese department stores also have corners for brand-name merchandise, such as cosmetics, jewelry, handbags, and apparel. These sections also have a higher ratio of persons on loan. Manufacturers also send people to retail stores when they think demonstration of new merchandise would help sales.[3] Another reason for manufacturers to send sales persons is to directly gather information on the customer's reaction to the products and to utilize this information in product development.

For department stores, the significant numbers of persons on loan would cause the upward bias for their productivity (sales per person). In fact, when productivities in the retail sectors are examined by size of the establishments, those with more than 500 employees have extremely high productivities (see Maruyama et al. 1989). A significant portion of high productivities are due to the "persons on loan."

5.2.5   Large-Scale Retail Store Law (*Dai-ten Ho*)

In 1956, in order to curb the growth of department stores, the Department Store Law, which required a permit for new construction, was enacted. Then, large supermarkets, discount stores, and other large chain stores, which were not covered by the Department Store Law, became popular. In order to cover these new types of retail stores, the Large-Scale Retail Store Law, or *Dai-ten Ho*, which requires a "reporting" of constructions, replaced the Department Store Law in 1974. It was revised in 1979 to its current form.

The *Dai-ten Ho* covers two types of stores: first, stores with 1,500 square meters or more than 3,000 square meters in large cities (*seirei shitei toshi*); second, stores with 500–1,500 square meters or stores with 500–3,000 square meters that are located in large cities. A construction plan of a large retail store has to be submitted to a governor (of prefecture). Then the *sho cho kyo* (the committee of adjusting retail activities), which is organized under the Chamber of Commerce, "discusses" the plan. For the first type of store, the report from the *dai ten shin* (subcommittee of large retail stores) goes to the Ministry of International Trade and Industry (MITI) minister. For the second type of store, the report goes to the governor. The "adjustment" items include the floor space, the opening day, store hours, and total days closed in a year. On appearance, when a plan is submitted, it should be discussed with neighboring shopping malls and stores and be approved in due time.

However, the law is not the whole story. The MITI issues the ministry guid-

3. Flath (1989a) applies Telser's (1960) argument of resale price maintenance to the vertical restraint behavior (keiretsu) among Japanese firms. However, Telser's argument, which emphasizes the merit of "demonstration," can be applied to the characteristic "persons on loan" in Japan, too.

ance on interpretation and implementation of the law. In fact, in the beginning of the 1980s, the implementation was significantly tightened so that it became not uncommon to take more than two years after a submission of a plan receive final approval. In essense, the law and its implementation can virtually stop the construction of a large retail store if the neighboring stores oppose it.

The time required to build and operate a large-scale retail store, according to the practices of *Dai-ten Ho,* can be anything between two and one-half years to 10 years. First, the management of the prospective store has to "explain" the plan, including the floor space and the days of operation, to local businesses as well as to the Chamber of Commerce and the local government of the prospective store site. Only after the Chamber of Commerce and the local stores "agree" to the plan may the prospective store file an application (Article 3 application) for the building permit. If the local businesses express strong opposition, it may take many years before the application is filed. This is based on the practices imposed by the MITI rather than on the letter of the law.

The governor will send the Article 3 application to the MITI minister. The MITI then asks the local Chamber of Commerce whether the proposed store would affect the existing local businesses. If the answer is no, the prospective store may file an Article 5 application to the governor and it will be approved. However, in many cases the answer is yes. Then the proposed store and the local business must meet in the "pre-council" (*jizen sho cho kyo*). This process takes about eight months. After the pre-council is cleared, the store can file an Article 5 application to the governor. The governor sends the Article 5 application to the MITI minister. Then the formal council (*sho cho kyo*), composed of the local businesses, the Chamber of Commerce, the store, consumers, and some academics, examines (i) when the store will open for business; (ii) floor space; (iii) store hours; and (iv) the number of store holidays in a year. This practice is close to a "hearing" in the U.S. case. The Chamber of Commerce may express its opinion in the council. The Large-Scale Retail Store Commission [*Shingikai*] examines the case, and the local government expresses its opinion. Then, following the *Shingikai*'s discussions, the MITI minister makes recommendations on the conditions for building the store. Finally, the MITI minister will approve the plan. After the Article 5 application is filed, approval has to be given within five months.

A most time-consuming part is, in fact, not a part of the law but merely the "practices" and *gyosei shido* of the MITI. In particular, the "pre-explanation" is not a code or *gyosei shido,* but just a practice. However, some local governments do not accept an Article 3 application without an agreement from the Chamber of Commerce. The local business could simply boycott the "pre-explanation" so that it could take forever before an Article 3 application could filed.

In the case of the Summit Store, *Higashi Nakano,* it took about seven years from the time the plan was made to the time the store actually opened. It really took a long time before the Article 3 application was filed. (The details of the negotiation are documented in *Nikkei Business* [5 June 1989] and reproduced in Ito and Maruyama 1989, p. 21.)

Let us turn to the issue of how the *Dai-ten Ho* affects efficiency. David Flath (1988) investigated how the number of other types of stores change as the number of department stores change in different prefectures. He finds that the number of drug stores is not affected by the number of department stores, while the number of food, liquor, and apparel stores are quite elastic. This partly but not entirely explains how the *Dai-ten Ho* allows many small stores to survive. It should also be pointed out that *Dai-ten Ho* protects the "insiders," that is, the existing department stores, from the "outsiders," that is, the proposed department stores.

5.3 Measures of Efficiency in the Distribution Sector

There have been many studies on productivity and efficiency in the distribution sector. The most popular measure of the productivity and efficiency of the distribution system has been "sales per employee," as in Ingene (1982) and Smith and Hitchens (1985). The latter compared the productivities of the U.S. and European distribution systems. When data are available, "value added per employee" is also used, as in Beckman (1957). As explained in the text, there are some conceptual difficulties in the use of these measures as a criteria for efficiency. Several authors (see Bucklin 1978; Achaval 1984) have also expressed caution against the use of these measures. The Japanese distribution system in the light of international comparison was studied in Tajima and Miyashita (1985), Ryutsu Keizai Kenkyusho (1988), and Maruyama et al. (1989).

This section proposes looking at the gross margin, operating expenses, operating profit, and unit labor cost. We relied on data from the commerce censuses of the United States and those of Japan, such as the Ministry of International Trade and Industry's *White Paper* (1988, p. 73; Nishimura and Tsubouchi 1989 calculated the gross margin from the input-output table).

A contribution of this paper, which we will present in the next section, is that it compares not only gross margins but also operating expenses, operating profits, and unit labor costs at the three-digit wholesale and two-digit retail sectors, using the comparable commerce censuses in the United States and Japan.

Given all facts about the "uniqueness" of the Japanese distribution system, an important question from the economic point of view is whether it is an inefficient system, as is often claimed. We proposed constructing several measures to evaluate the efficiency of the distribution sector.

5.3.1 Sales per worker and Sales per Establishment

"Sales per worker" or "Sales per establishment" has been a popular measure for "performance" and "efficiency." For example, the measure was used in

Takeuchi and Bucklin (1977) and cited by Rangan (1989), and is reproduced in table 5.5. Rangan concluded from this figure that "the performance of the Japanese counterpart was significantly worse." First of all, this data is old, and second, there is a question as to whether this measure really reflects performance and efficiency.

Table 5.6 shows more recent data of the same measure. In this table, Japan does not look inefficient, except for the measure of "retail sales per establish-

Table 5.5   **Productivity Measured by Sales**

	Japan		United States	
	Year	Sales	Year	Sales
Retail sales per establishment	1952	5.8	1948	96.6
	1958	10.6	1958	123.7
	1968	28.0	1967	175.9
Retail sales per worker	1952	2.6	1948	19.0
	1958	3.7	1958	22.8
	1968	8.0	1967	28.2
Number of retail establishments	1952	14.1	1948	11.3
per 1,000 residents	1958	15.7	1958	10.3
	1968	17.8	1967	8.9

Source: Rangan (1989), citing Takeuchi and Bucklin (1977).

Note: In thousands of dollars, 360 yen to the dollar, deflated using the Japanese retail price index, 1968 base year (Japan).

Table 5.6   **Productivity Measured by Sales, 1979–85**

	Japan	United States	Germany
Sales per worker:			
Wholesale:			
1982	390.5	272.4	173.5[a]
1985	448.7	N.A.	299.8
Retail:			
1982	62.3	68.5	51.4[a]
1985	72.4	N.A.	80.3
Sales per establishment:			
Wholesale:			
1982	3614.7	3430.6	1750.8[a]
1985	4219.4	N.A.	2870.8
Retail:			
1982	230.3	554.2	302.9[a]
1985	281.3	N.A.	465.8

Source: Maruyama et al. (1989).

Note: Figures in data cols. represent amounts in $1,000. This is measured in PPP exchange rate of DECD; that is, $1 = DM 2.54 in 1979; $1 = 237 yen in 1982; $1 = 222 yen = DM 2.48 in 1985.

[a]1979.

ment." The wholesale sector look quite comparable to or better than other countries.

There are two caveats. First, productivity in the Japanese wholesale sector could be overestimated, because large scale trading houses (*sogo shosha*) are included in the wholesale sector. Trading houses engage in export, import, and international trade between third countries as well as domestic retail business. Second, the productivities in the retail sectors may be biased upward, because of the "persons on loan" in large scale department stores. (See the argument on persons on loan in sec. 5.2 above). Another contamination is the inclusion of eating and drinking places in retail business.

5.3.2   Value Added

However, the amount of sales is not a good measure of productivity. First, it does not consider any costs of input. Compare a retail store that deals with expensive products (say, diamonds) with high purchase (input) prices (from wholesale level) and a retail store that deals with less expensive products (say, toys) with low purchase (input) prices. Even if the number of workers, their wage rate, and the net profit are the same, the former category would have higher sales per worker. Moreover, double counting in the multilayered wholesale sector may cloud the figure.[4]

Hence, a more accurate measure of productivity is value added. Thus, we examine the value added that is net of input costs. Table 5.7 shows the value added in the distribution sector relative to that in the manufacturing sector. In this measure, the Japanese value added per worker is as high as that of the United States. In this measure, there is no evidence that the Japanese distribution sector is less efficient than that in the United States or Germany.

5.3.3   Gross Profit Margin

If the efficiency of the distribution is measured by how much extra a consumer has to pay on top of the manufacturer's costs, the gross profit margin is an appropriate measure:

(i)   gross profit margin ratio = gross profit margin/sales;
(ii)   gross profit margin = sales − merchandise costs
       merchandise costs = merchandise purchase
                          + beginning-of-period inventories
                          − end-of-period inventories.

---

4. In order to understand why the sales per worker would be an incorrect statistic in the multilayered wholesale system, consider the following example. Suppose that $100 is charged for sales of a product from the single-layered wholesale sector to the retail sector, and that 10 people are working in the (single-layer) wholesale sector. The $10 sales per worker would be recorded as the relevant statistic in this single-layered system. Next, suppose that the same product is sold three times in the multilayered wholesale (recall fig. 5.1): $50 by 5 people in the first wholesale layer, $70 by 7 people in the second layer, and $100 by 10 people in the third layer. Then the sales per capita in each layer is still $10 per person, and is so shown in the Japanese statistic. However, the

Table 5.7   **The Ratio of Value Added per Worker in Different Sectors**

	Japan (1985)	United States (1985)	Germany (1985)
Distribution sector/industry total	.76	.70	.68
Manufacturing sector/industry total	1.19	1.12	.95
Distribution sector/manufacturing sector	.64	.63	.71

Source: Maruyama et al. (1989).

Or,

(iii) gross profit margin = net profits + operating expenses

operating expenses = payroll + rents + advertisement + transportation + depreciation, and so on.

Table 5.8 summarizes this measure. Contrary to popular belief, the Japanese gross profit margin is to be precise, lower than that of the United States and Germany. This shows that operating expenses and net profits are not particularly high in Japan. Apparently small operations in Japan do not suffer from inefficiency.

There are some caveats to this conclusion. First, although the Japanese small retail shops do not keep transportation costs (high physical distribution costs) and purchase costs down (no volume discounts applicable from wholesalers), they do operate on low rent and low payroll. In fact, many small retailers are operated by shop owners themselves whose stores are located in the front of their principal residence. Many of the shop owners are elderly couples who do not require high net profit or payroll.

Second, several U.S. economists have pointed out that an apparent high gross margin among U.S. wholesalers and retailers is a reflection of high incidences of shoplifting, employee theft, and outright burglary in the United States.[5] Unfortunately, we do not have the figures for damages in the distribution sector from such crimes.

Third, it may be possible that the average wholesale and average retail figures may be misleading due to some structural outliers. It is possible, but not examined carefully here, that dominant large-scale wholesalers or retailers pull the average up or that some nondistribution industry subgroup, such as "eating and drinking places," may be distorting the average figures. Calculation of gross margin and other statistics for industry subgroups and for establishment-size subgroups is on the agenda of future research.

"net" or true wholesale sale/worker, i.e., how many people are needed to pass the goods to the retail level, should be $100 / (10 + 7 + 5)$, much less than $10 per person.

5. One of the eye-opening scenes on Japanese sidewalks is rows and rows of vending machines for cigarettes, soft drinks, beer, magazines, telephone cards, etc.

Table 5.8   **Gross Profit Margin Ratio**

Gross Profit Margin	Japan	United States	Germany
Wholesale			
1978	11.9		
1981		N.A.	12.7
1986	11.2	19.4	12.6[a]
Retail			
1978	27.0		
1981		N.A.	34.5
1986	27.1	31.0	34.2[a]

Source: Maruyama et al. (1989)
[a]1985.

Fourth, considering retail and wholesale margins separately may be misleading in light of the fact that the wholesale/retail ratios are quite different between Japan and other countries. The margin of the distribution system as a whole should be constructed to represent the notion of how much a consumer has to pay on top of the manufacturer's cost.

The last concern is taken up in Table 5.9, which describes the margin aggregate for wholesalers and retailers. The aggregate margin/retail sales is defined and decomposed as follows:

$$(MW + MR) / R = (MW/W) \times (W/R) + (MR/R),$$

where MW = gross margin of wholesale, MR = gross margin of retail, R = retail sales, and W = wholesale sales. The figures are calculated and shown in table 5.9.

This table also shows that the Japanese margin is quite comparable to Germany and slightly higher than the United States. In sum, judging from the gross margin figures, we do not detect any inefficiencies in the Japanese distribution system.

5.3.4   Distribution Margin: Input-Output Approach

In the preceding subsection, the gross margin was calculated from the Census of Commerce in Japan and the Census of Wholesale Trade and Census of Retail Trade in the United States. There is another way to calculate the gross margin in the entire distribution sector (the distribution margin, for short).

The MITI (1988) calculated the distribution margin from the input-output table, and Nishimura and Tsubouchi (1989) improved upon the MITI's method. The MITI reported that the U.S. distribution margin is about twice as much as the Japanese counterpart.

Nishimura and Tsubouchi (1989) corrected the MITI figures by reclassifying the repair service and the government-controlled distribution service (in tobacco, rice, etc). Their finding is that the distribution margin for Japan is quite comparable to its U.S. counterpart. The numbers are reported in table 5.10. (For details of the adjustment, please refer to Nishimura and Tsubouchi 1989.) There are two caveats in comparing the Nishimura-Tsubouchi table and our table. First, the Nishimura-Tsubouchi table is only for consumer goods, while our table theoretically includes both consumer and production goods. Second, the survey that our table is based on is an establishment survey, while the input-output table approach does not double count trades within the wholesale industry.

5.3.5 Summary

In this section, various measures of efficiency in the distribution sector were examined. In every measure, Japan seems to be as efficient as the United States. In the next section, the gross margin will be calculated for each subsector.

Table 5.9   **Distribution Margin: Census Approach**

	Japan	United States	Germany
Aggregate margin/ distribution sales:			
1978	15.6		
1981		N.A.	20.3
1986	15.5	25.3	20.0[a]
Aggregate margin/ retail sales			
1978	63.4		
1981		N.A.	58.0
1985	57.6	49.7	58.9[a]

Source: Maruyama et al. (1989)
Note: Wholesale data are based on merchant wholesalers. Aggregate margin is defined in text.
[a]1985.

Table 5.10   **Distribution Margin: I-O Approach**

	Japan		United States, 1977
	1980	1985	
MITI (1988)		29.78	39.44
Official Base	33.4	34.4	35.7
Wholesale	9.9	8.2	N.A.
Retail	23.5	26.2	N.A.
Nishimura (1989)	36.8	38.6	35.7

Source: Nishimura and Tsubouchi (1989)

5.4   Efficiency at Two-Digit and Three-Digit Industry Levels

5.4.1   Gross Margin, Operating Expenses, and Profits

In this section we extend the analysis of the preceding section by two dimensions. First, an analysis of gross margin will be conducted at the three-digit wholesale and two-digit retail industry levels. Since the Standard Industrial Code of Japan (JSIC) is slightly different from that of the United States (SIC), we have devised a matching table of the two SICs for the distribution sector. Second, gross margins will be decomposed into operating expenses and operating profits. To the best of our knowledge, this paper is the first to compare operating expenses and operating profit for the U.S. and Japanese two- and three-digit matching distribution subsectors.

The study of three-digit industry level is necessary in order to account for the following issues in the aggregate data. First, the Japanese wholesale industry include gigantic, general trading houses (*sogo shosha*), to which no institution in the United States is comparable. These Japanese trading houses engage in export, import, and trade between third countries, as well as the domestic distribution system. The same company may deal with importing F-16 fighters as well as exporting cup noodles. These trading houses are known to exploit scale economies, so that the low (operating) profit margin rate suffices for their success. They are quite different entities from those in the domestic distribution system. The effect of general trading houses can be eliminated by suppressing two-digit industry, JSIC 49.

When the retail "aggregate" statistic is constructed, the United States tends to include "eating and drinking places" (SIC 58), while Japan excludes "eating and drinking places" (general JSIC 59 or other JSIC 60). Since restaurants and fast-food outlets have quite different functions and cost characteristics from other retail shops, we would be interested in comparable retail aggregates without eating and drinking places.

First, let us describe how we match the two- and three-digit industries. The wholesale industry is divided into three two-digit industries in Japan and two two-digit industries (nondurables and durables) in the United States. Subdividing into the three-digit wholesale levels, the Japanese SIC tend to include more industries than each U.S. SIC. One exception is that textile and apparel are divided into two SICs in Japan, while those industries are aggregated into one in the United States.

Second, in the two-digit retail level, the Japanese and U.S. SICs are quite comparable. After minor reclassification on the U.S. SIC, such as classifying gasoline stations into miscellaneous instead of motor vehicle (which really is meant to indicate automobile dealers), the two SICs are quite comparable (see Ito and Maruyama 1990, table 4-1, for a summary table of matching the two SICs).

Table 5.11 shows the results of such estimates. The following points summarize the major findings.

1. In the wholesale sector, the gross margin ratio in the United States (17.3% in 1982) is higher than that in Japan (14.0% in 1986), while in the retail sector, the gross margin in the United States (25.9%) is lower than that in Japan (27.0% in 1986). In both sectors, the operating expense ratio is higher in the United States, while the operating profit ratio is higher in Japan.

If the general trading houses (JSIC 49) are included in the Japanese wholesale sector, the operating expenses of the wholesale industry declines by about 1.7%–2.4% points and operating profit by 0.6%–0.9% points. Eating and drinking places are excluded in both countries.

2. Among the three-digit wholesale sectors, operating expense ratios of all but one sector in the United States are higher than the comparable sectors in Japan. In contrast, the operating profit ratios in Japan are higher than those in the United States, except in three subsectors, JSIC 502, 504, and 514.

Among the two-digit retail sectors, similar characteristics hold true. Operating expense ratios of the United States are higher than those of Japan in four out of six sectors, while the operating profit ratios for the United States are lower than those of Japan in all but one sector.

In sum, the following conclusion emerges. The Japanese distribution sectors operate with less operating costs and earn higher operating profit. Casual arguments in the popular press, on the theme of the inefficient Japanese distribution system, are hardly consistent with the evidence presented in this paper.

5.4.2 Labor Costs

In order to investigate the detail of the cost composition, the labor cost component is analyzed. The labor cost ratio is defined as total labor cost divided by the value added. (If the value added was normalized by the respective prices, the ratio would be equivalent to unit labor cost.)

Table 5.12 compares the labor cost ratio. Among the three-digit wholesale sectors, the United States has a higher labor cost ratio in all but one (JSIC 514) sector. Among the two-digit retail sectors, except for one (JSIC 58) sector, the United States has a higher labor cost ratio. Therefore, it is evident that the labor share in value added is higher in the United States than in Japan.

In sum, the share of labor costs in the distribution sector in Japan is no higher than in the United States. Hence, the findings in this section shows that, with respect to many criteria, such as the distribution margin, operating expenses, and the labor cost ratio, the Japanese subsectors in the distribution industry are, in general, as efficient as their U.S. counterparts.

5.5   Concluding Remarks

Let us summarize our findings, our interpretations, and implications as well as some caveats. In this paper, we have explained major characteristics of the

Table 5.11   **Sales, Expenses, and Profits Wholesale: Expense/Sales ratio (E/S) and Profit/Sales ratio (P/S)**

JSIC	Japan, 1979		United States, 1982		Japan, 1986	
	E/S	P/S	E/S	P/S	E/S	P/S
Wholesale:						
49:						
E/S	1.6				1.2	
P/S		1.3				1.8
501:						
E/S	7.5				9.1	
P/S		4.7				4.2
502:						
E/S	8.9		**22.3**		**9.4**	
P/S		3.9		**7.4**		**3.2**
503:						
E/S	6.3		**7.0**		**6.2**	
P/S		3.6		**1.6**		**2.8**
504:						
E/S	11.8		**21.5**		**13.1**	
P/S		6.0		**4.8**		**3.9**
505:						
E/S	11.4		**20.0**		**11.9**	
P/S		7.3		**3.5**		**6.3**
511:						
E/S	14.8				18.1	
P/S		6.1				5.4
512:						
E/S	5.7		**4.8**		**5.5**	
P/S		4.7		**0.2**		**3.1**
513:						
E/S	8.1		**13.5**		**9.8**	
P/S		4.3		**1.9**		**3.9**
514:						
E/S	12.7		**14.8**		**14.6**	
P/S		4.0		**5.4**		**2.2**
515:						
E/S	16.1		**25.4**		**14.9**	
P/S		6.5		**3.9**		**4.6**
519:						
E/S	11.8		**17.5**		**11.4**	
P/S		5.0		**2.3**		**3.9**
Wholesale:						
E/S	7.7				7.8	
Wholesale with general trading companies:						
P/S	4.2				3.3	
Wholesale:						
E/S	9.4		**14.6**		**10.2**	

Table 5.11   (continued)

JSIC	Japan, 1979 E/S	Japan, 1979 P/S	United States, 1982 E/S	United States, 1982 P/S	Japan, 1986 E/S	Japan, 1986 P/S
Wholesale without general trading companies:						
P/S		5.1		**2.7**		**3.8**
Retail:						
53:						
E/S	19.0		**32.2**		**21.6**	
P/S		5.0		**2.5**		**1.6**
54:						
E/S	24.6		**36.7**		**29.5**	
P/S		8.4		**3.4**		**6.7**
55:						
E/S	17.6		**22.0**		**20.4**	
P/S		7.6		**2.3**		**4.9**
56:						
E/S	18.2		**16.1**		**19.3**	
P/S		7.4		**3.5**		**5.4**
57:						
E/S	21.9		**34.5**		**24.1**	
P/S		8.2		**2.8**		**5.3**
58:						
E/S	20.3		**15.9**		**21.9**	
P/S		7.1		**4.3**		**5.3**
Rtl:						
E/S	19.7		**22.9**		**21.9**	
P/S		7.3		**3.0**		**5.1**

Sources: For *Japan,* MITI Small and Medium Enterprise Agency, "Report on 5th Basic Survey of Commercial Structure and Activity"; *United States,* (1) Department of Commerce, Bureau of Census, "1982 Census of Wholesale Trade, Industry Series, Measures of Value Produced, Capital Expenditures, Depreciable Assets, and Operating Expenses" and (2) Department of Commerce, Bureau of Census, "1982 Census of Retail Trade, Industry Series, Measures of Value Produced, Capital Expenditures, Depreciable Assets, and Operating Expenses."

Notes: S = sales; E = operating expenses; P = operating profits. JSIC is the Japanese Standard Industrial Code, with the following changes: General Merchandise (*shosha*) in Japan is excluded; "general eating and drinking places" (JSIC 59), "other eating and drinking places" (JSIC 60), and "eating and drinking places" (US SIC 58) are excluded. The U.S SIC is matched to JSIC as follows: JSIC 502 = SIC 516; JSIC 503 = SIC 505 + 517; JSIC 504 = SIC 508 + 501; JSIC 505 = SIC 503; JSIC 511 = SIC 513; JSIC 512 = SIC 515; JSIC 513 = SIC 514 + 518; JSIC 514 = SIC 512; JSIC 515 = SIC 502; JSIC 519 = SIC 504 + 507 + 509 + 511 + 519. JSIC 53 = SIC 53; JSIC 54 = SIC 56; JSIC 55 = SIC 54 + 5921; JSIC 56 = SIC 55–554; JSIC 57 = SIC 52 + 57; JSIC 58 = SIC 554 + 5912. See Ito and Maruyama (1989, p. 33 and app. 2 for details). Boldface type indicates numbers that are useful from the U.S.-Japan comparative perspective.

Table 5.12   **Labor Cost Ratio**

JSIC	Japan, 1979	United States, 1982	Japan, 1986
Wholesale			
49	35.8		22.0
501	43.3		50.0
502	53.3	55.6	59.2
503	40.4	63.4	47.4
504	47.6	67.6	61.2
505	43.9	72.8	48.6
511	54.9		60.1
512	36.1	89.0	44.5
513	49.2	74.9	53.9
514	62.6	57.5	77.4
515	54.6	74.0	60.9
519	53.3	76.5	57.7
Wsl w/49	46.5		52.6
Wsl w/o 49	47.2	70.3	55.5
Retail			
53	61.6	86.5	82.9
54	59.3	82.8	68.2
55	57.3	82.9	70.0
56	57.0	71.2	65.4
57	59.2	84.0	70.5
58	61.7	63.6	69.0
Rtl	59.2	78.7	69.4

Source: See table 5.11.

Japanese distribution system and presented some quantitative measures on "efficiency" of the distribution system. Although the Japanese distribution system appears to be very different from its U.S. counterpart, its performance, measured by value added, gross margin, operating expenses, and labor costs, is quite comparable with U.S. performance. Hence, we do not have any evidence to conclude that the Japanese characteristics are symptoms of inefficiency.

When our findings are combined with other pieces of evidence, such as the fact that the retail prices are, in general, higher in Japan, and that the behavior of Japanese exporters can be viewed as "pricing to the market" (see Marston, in this volume), the following scenario seems plausible. The *keiretsu*, or whatever structures make possible vertical restraints and resale price maintenance, may segregate the Japanese market from the rest of the world. Then the pricing-to-the-market behavior becomes possible, and the Japanese manufacturers seem to exercise this power. In that sense, the distribution system is guilty of causing the price differential between Japan and abroad.

However, whatever rents accrued from vertical restraints and the pricing-to-the-market behavior, they are not shared by the distribution sector, or the distribution sector itself does not incur extra (operating) expenses that apparently resulted from the Japanese characteristics. The Japanese distribution system is as efficient as its U.S. counterpart once the system receives, as an input to the "pipeline," the goods from manufacturers.

Finally, let us comment on a U.S.-Japanese conflict with regard to the Japanese distribution system. An opinion that considers institutions and business practices in the Japanese distribution system as a significant non-tariff barrier is gaining momentum in the United States and is frequently mentioned in the recent "structural impediments" talks between the United States and Japan. Business leaders and government officials in the United States suspect that the Japanese distribution system discriminates against imports from the United States and other countries. By removing the barriers, it is suggested that the Japanese would import more manufactured goods and the trade imbalances would diminish.

The structural impediments initiative (SII) has recently prompted two types of reactions in Japan. First, "revisionists" in Japan, mainly reacting to attacks from the United States, emphasize that the Japanese characteristics could be a result of "rational behavior and free choices" of the Japanese consumers (see, e.g., Itoh, in this volume, and MITI 1989). Second, "reformers" consider that the Japanese characteristics do represent some sort of market imperfection, by regulations and/or by rent-seeking behavior of oligopolists.

Both domestic reformers and U.S. negotiators would regard some regulations, institutions, and practices as adverse to consumers' welfare and as counterproductive to international efficiency. Reformers may welcome the U.S. demands, because they are politically helpful as a "foreign pressure" (*gaiatsu*) from the United States. However, reformers may be quite different from the U.S. negotiation team in assessing the effects of the structural impediments on trade balances or potential benefits to American firms. Reformers think that removing structural barriers might not reduce by a significant proportion the Japanese trade surplus, especially the bilateral trade imbalance between Japan and United States, but that it would surely improve the Japanese consumers' welfare.

Both true revisionists and true reformers would not object to dismantling *Dai-ten Ho,* or at least to implement, on the part of MITI, the law without favoring small stores. If what revisionist claim is correct, constructing a large retail store would not affect consumers' behavior, which prefers frequent visits to neighborhood stores. Reformers think that the *Dai-ten Ho* causes some distortion in the retail market. Although the retail sales per establishment is increasing, the pace of catching up to the United States and Germany is too slow. Hence, the *Dai-ten Ho* should be significantly weakened, if not abolished.

This paper has, we hope, clarified with ample quantitative evidence, one particular aspect, namely efficiency, of the distribution system in Japan. It is our hope that this discussion stimulates further research in this field.

Postscript. After this paper was completed, there were notable changes with regard to the *Dai-ten Ho* (Large-scale Retail Store Law). In May 1990, MITI revised its ministry guidelines so that it would be possible for a store to open for business within a year and a half after the intent to do so is expressed to the MITI local office. Since previously it was common for opening to be delayed up to three years, this revision could result in a significant shortening of the process.

In May 1991, the Diet enacted a revision of the *Dai-ten Ho*. Under the revised law, *sho cho kyo* (a local committee to review applications) was abolished, with the *dai ten shin* (a national council on large stores) now responsible to examine applications, applying a common national standard. However, small stores are planning to pressure local business groups to establish an alternative to *sho cho kyo* (the alternative would be called *sho mon kyo*). Moreover, the revised law is not specific enough to predict whether significant change will take place. For example, *dai ten shin* (as of August 1991) does not specify standards for accepting or rejecting applications.

Hence, it remains to be seen whether the procedural change of May 1990 and the May 1991 revision of the law will in fact change the process in any meaningful way.

References

Achaval, D. D., ed. 1984. Special issue: Productivity in Retailing. *Journal of Retailing* 60, no. 3 (Fall).

Beckman, T. 1957. The Value Added Concept as a Measure of Output. *Advanced Management* 22:6–9.

Bucklin, L. 1978. *Productivity in Marketing.* Chicago: American Marketing Association.

Flath, David. 1988. Why Are There So Many Retail Stores in Japan? Working Paper no. 17. Center on Japanese Economy and Business, Columbia University.

———. 1989a. The Economic Rationality of the Japanese Distribution System. Working Paper no. 29. Center on Japanese Economy and Business. September.

———. 1989b. Vertical Restraints in Japan. *Japan and the World Economy.*

Flath, David, and Tatsuhiko Nariu. 1989. Returns Policy in the Japanese Marketing System. *Journal of the Japanese and International Economy* 3 (March): 49–63.

Ingene, C. A. 1982. Labor Productivity in Retailing. *Journal of Marketing* 46: 75–90.

Ito, Takatoshi, and Masayoshi Maruyama. 1989. Is the Japanese Distribution System Really Inefficient? Discussion Paper no. 215. Hitotsubashi University, Institute of Economic Research, December.

McCraw, Thomas K., and Patricia A. O'Brien. 1986. Production and Distribution: Competition Policy and Industry Structure. In *America versus Japan: A Comparative Study,* ed. Thomas K. McCraw, Chap. 3, pp. 77–116. Boston: Harvard Business School Press.

Maruyama, M., Y. Togawa, K. Sakai, N. Sakamoto, and M. Arakawa. 1989. Distribution System and Business Practices in Japan. Paper presented in the 7th EPA

International Symposium, Economic Research Institute, Economic Planning Agency, Tokyo.

Ministry of International Trade and Industry (MITI). 1988. *White Paper, 1988.* Tokyo: Ministry of Finance.

———. 1989. The Distribution System in Japan. Mimeographed, April.

Nihon Keizai Shinbunsha, ed. 1989. *Nichibei Masatsu* (U.S.-Japan conflicts). Tokyo: Nihon Keizai Shinbunsha.

Nishimura, Kiyohiko, and Hiroshi Tsubouchi. 1989. Commerce Margins in Japan. Discussion Paper 89-J-8. Faculty of Economics, University of Tokyo, August.

Rangan, V. K. 1989. Efficiency in the Distributive System. Paper presented at the 4th MITI/RI conference, MITI, Japan.

Ryūtsū Keizai Kenkyusho. 1988. *Ryūtsūgyō no Kokusai Hikaku ni Kansuru Chōsa Kenkyū* [Research for the international comparison of distribution industry].

Smith, A. D., and D. M. W. N. Hitchens. 1985. *Productivity in the Distributive Trades: A Comparison of Britain, America, and Germany.* Cambridge: Cambridge University Press.

Tajima, Y., and M. Miyashita. 1985. *Ryūtsū no Kokusai Hikaku* (International comparison of distribution). Tokyo: Yuhikaku.

Takeuchi, H., and L. P. Bucklin. 1977. Productivity in Retailing: Retail Structure and Public Policy. *Journal of Retailing* 53, no. 1: 35–46.

Telser, L. 1960. Why Should Manufacturers Want Fair Trade? *Journal of Law and Economics* 3: 86–105.

6   The Japanese Distribution System and Access to the Japanese Market

Motoshige Itoh

6.1   Introduction

There has been an increasing amount of criticism from both inside and outside Japan about the efficiency of the Japanese distribution system and the difficulty in obtaining access to the Japanese import market. According to this criticism, the Japanese distribution system is quite complicated, Japanese business practices are outdated, the system is inefficient, and it leads to trade barriers.

The following points are often made: (1) The Japanese distribution system has many small-scale firms, both wholesale and retail, and a multilayer structure that consists of many layers of wholesalers. (2) There seems to be a strong linkage among the domestic producers, wholesalers, and retailers. It is not easy for new entrants, foreign or domestic, to penetrate the market.

This paper concentrates on the economic mechanisms that underlie the Japanese distribution system and its business practices. In section 6.2, I present a rough overview of the system; in section 6.3, I discuss the theory of repeated and long-term transactions; in section 6.4, I analyze structural change in the Japanese distribution system using apparel distribution as a case study; and, in section 6.5, I consider the issue of access to the Japanese market.

6.2   The Basic Characteristics of the Japanese Distribution System

Table 6.1 compares some characteristics of the Japanese distribution system with those of Western countries. This table shows that Japan has a large number of shops, given its population, and a smaller number of workers in each shop than Western countries do.

Motoshige Itoh is associate professor of economics at the University of Tokyo.

175

Table 6.1   **Comparison of Distribution Markets among Major Countries**

	Countries				
	Japan (1985)	West Germany (1985:3)	United States (1982)	France (1986:1)	United Kingdom (1984)
Retailers:					
Shop density:					
No. of shops/ 1,000 km²	4,311	1,636	205	1,018	1,406
No. of shops/ population of 10,000	135	67	81	102	61
No. of workers per shop	3.9	5.8	7.5	3.9[a]	6.8
Wholesalers:					
Shop density:					
No. of shops/ 1,000 km²	1,093	505	40	290	
No. of shops/ population of 10,000	34	21	16	29	
No. of workers/ 1,000 retailers	85	309	196	285	
No. of workers per shop	9.7	7.0	12.6	9.9[a]	
W/R ratio	4.2	1.8[b]	1.9	1.6[a]	

Source: Ministry of International Trade and Industry (1988). Data: *Annuaire statistique de la France, Statistisches Jahrbuch, Retailing Business Monitor, Statistical Abstract of the United States, Census of Business,* and *Commercial Statistics of MITI.*
[a]1983.
[b]1984.

Table 6.2 shows the share of the market that retailers in various countries have. In Japan there are few large-scale retailers and many small-scale retailers, called "papa mama stores" (shops run solely by family members).

Another important characteristic of the Japanese distribution market is that goods go through many layers of wholesalers. To confirm the existence of a multilayer structure, one calculates the ratio of the amount of wholesale transactions to the amount of retail transactions (*W/R*). The higher the ratio is, the more wholesalers are involved in transactions. The last column of table 6.1 shows the *W/R* ratio for various countries: it is distinctively high for Japan.

Although there are some difficulties with using *W/R* as an index of multilayer structure,[1] other methods confirm this characteristic of the Japanese distribution system (see Tamura 1988).

1. For example, the ratio covers transactions in both consumption goods and intermediate goods. Since Japan imports many materials and intermediate goods and exports final goods, the ratio has a tendency to be high for Japan.

Of course, this does not imply that the entire distribution system is multilayered. For some goods, the distribution channel is very simple. For example, the distribution channel for bread is much more vertically integrated in Japan than in the United States. But there are more goods whose distribution markets have a multilayered structure in Japan than in other developed countries.

The dominance of the small-scale firms in Japan implies that the distribution system is decentralized and not highly integrated vertically. Wholesalers play an important role in a decentralized distribution system. Therefore, the distribution system is multilayered. Conversely, multilayering and the role played by wholesalers make it easy for small retail firms to enter the market, since they can use the wholesalers' services.

Various factors explain the dominance of small-scale firms in the Japanese distribution system. Governmental regulation protects small-scale firms, for example. They receive preferential tax treatment and a "Large Store Act" regulates the establishment of new stores by big retailers. Okuno-Fujiwara (in this volume) discusses how the act retards the establishment of new large stores.

However, neither the size of firms in the distribution system nor the number of wholesalers involved in transactions implies inefficiency. Small or medium-scale firms do not dominate only the distribution market; they also dominate the manufacturing sector and are usually said to be the source of competitiveness for the Japanese economy. The subcontracting system in the motor vehicle industry is a typical example.

Table 6.2   **Size Distribution of Retailers in Major Countries**

	Year	Japan (%)	France (%)	United Kingdom (%)	United States (%)
Share of large-scale retailers	1976	24.9		56.7	
(share in terms of the amount	1977		30.0	57.8	51.4
of sales)	1978			59.0	
	1979	27.9	31.1		
The share of the number of small-scale retailers (share in terms of the number of shops)		61.1 (1979)	63.7 (1980)		43.0 (1977)
The share of the number of very small-scale retailers (shops run by family member alone; share in terms of the number of shops)		56.4 (1979)	41.5 (1980)		

Source: Tamura (1988).

One of the essential characteristics of the Japanese system, both in manufacturing and distribution, is the network of large and small firms that cooperate. It is a decentralized system, characterized by what is called Japanese-style business relations. This is in contrast to an integrated system, where complicated exchanges are conducted within large firms and transactions between firms are at arm's length. This issue is discussed in greater detail in section 6.3.

Table 6.3 compares the distribution margin for consumption goods between Japan and the United States (this table is based on the results in Nishimura and Tsubouchi 1989). This table shows that the margin is not much different between the two countries. The distribution margin includes not only value added of the distribution sector but also intermediate inputs of the sector. If the Japanese distribution system were inefficient, we would expect the distribution margin to be much higher in Japan than in the United States.

6.3 Transactions in a Decentralized Distribution System

For a decentralized distribution system to function properly, there must be communication and cooperation among firms in the distribution market. There are a variety of externalities among firms in distribution markets. This is quite different from a pure market exchange. In a pure market exchange, the quality of the products is known to both the seller and the buyer, and simple market transactions are possible. The only relevant variable for transactions in this pure market exchange is the price of the commodity. Commodities exchange in this type of system are said to be "standardized."

However, commodities exchanged between retailers and customers are often "unstandardized." For example, with complicated home electrical appliances, the consumer's utility depends to a great extent on the level of service that the retailer provides. These services include quick and appropriate repair and maintenance and the provision of appropriate information. These services may be provided by firms that specialize in repair; if that is the case, then retailers deal only with the commodity, and it is quite standardized. But in Japan in the past, most repairs and other services are provided by retailers.

Table 6.3   The Distribution Margins in Japan and the United States (%)

	Japan			United States, 1977
	1975	1980	1985	
The distribution margin of consumption goods	. . . (30.9)	36.8 (33.9)	38.6 (35.1)	35.7

Source: Nishimura and Tsubouchi (1989).

Note: The figures in parentheses are the ones before correction was made by the authors.

Consumers expected many things of retailers, and the relationship between seller and buyer was not simply a pure market transaction.

In the case of home electrical appliances, manufacturers adopted a marketing strategy of establishing a network of retailers to sell their products. The largest manufacturer in this industry, Matsushita (known as Panasonic in foreign countries), is reported to have about 27,000 retailers all around the country specializing in Matsushita products. Other manufacturers adopted a similar strategy.

This strategy is basically what economists called "vertical restraints." Electric appliances were very expensive in the 1960s when the market was expanding rapidly. For example, the price of an ordinary color TV set in the 1960s was about 10 times as high as the starting monthly salary of a college graduate. Thus, consumers expected many services of retailers. As the literature on vertical restraint makes clear (see, e.g., Williamson 1983; Tirole 1988), manufacturers may or may not enhance consumer welfare, depending on the nature of the market and other elements. Thus, we cannot conclude that vertical restraint by Japanese manufacturers enhanced welfare. However, it did become a barrier to entry.

The distribution channel for home electrical appliances has changed to a great extent in recent years, though. Products have become much cheaper, and quality is more reliable. So discounters have emerged specializing in no particular brand. This new distribution channel is also more profitable for manufacturers.

The relationship between manufacturers and wholesalers, and between wholesalers and retailers, is even farther from a pure market. Many retailers depend heavily on wholesalers for collection of information about market trends and the availability of products. They also look to wholesalers for financial services, quick and individualized delivery, and assumption of the risk for unsold stock. In that sense, retailers do not buy a standardized product from wholesalers. A similar argument can be made for the relation between manufacturers and wholesalers.

One example illustrates how this type of coordinated transaction in the Japanese distribution system can provide good service for consumers. In the distribution market for books, retailers can order any amount of books from the wholesalers, and wholesalers can order any amount of books from the publishers. All unsold books are returned to the publishers (this business practice is called *henpinsei* in Japan).[2] Thus, publishers assume all of the risk for unsold books.

Publishers usually print thousands, or tens of thousands, of volumes at a time for technical reasons. Without *henpinsei*—that is, if retailers and wholesalers assumed the risk for unsold books—the publisher would have to store

2. There are some exceptional cases in which the retailers must commit themselves to purchasing books from the publishers.

most of the books in its warehouse and wait for order from wholesalers. With
henpinsei, on the other hand, the bookstores' shelves store unsold books.
Without *henpinsei,* consumers would not have direct access to as many books
(they would have to order from catalogues).

Because of *henpinsei,* wholesalers can provide quick delivery service of
any books ordered from retailers. It usually takes, at most, a week for any
books ordered in a bookstore to be delivered. There are few wholesalers and
many publishers. Therefore, the wholesalers are in a better position to respond to the orders from the retailers.

Transactions in intermediate goods are even more complicated. For automobile parts, for example, there is a subcontracting system between parts
producers and assemblers. In order to provide assembling firms with the necessary products, the parts makers probably have to make specific investments
that cannot easily be applied to other uses (see, e.g., Klein, Crawford, and
Alchian 1978; Hart and Holmstrom 1987; Grossman and Hart 1986). In addition, effective coordination of production between the assembling firm and
the parts makers is extremely important (one example is Toyota's just-in-time
system). Therefore, both sides must share information and coordination is not
simply a matter of adjusting production schedules; it also includes changing
the parts themselves, creating new products, and improving old ones.

It would be very difficult to carry out this type of transaction in a market
based on explicit contracts. As pointed out by Williamson (1975), and also
Hart and Holmstrom (1987), it would be nearly impossible to draw up and
agree on a contract that would cover any and all future contingencies. It would
be even more difficult to implement such a contract successfully. Klein et al.
(1978) present an interesting study of vertical integration illustrated by Fisher
bodies and General Motors. For many reasons (as stated in Itoh and Matsui
1987), transactions in Japan are based on implicit agreements.

Even a product like paper, which seems to be a typical standardized good,
has transaction relationships similar to those of automobile parts. Interviews
with paper production technicians and with managers in newspaper publish-
ing point to an important problem regarding the transaction relationships in
the Japanese distribution system and the issue of access to the Japanese
market.

For newspaper publishers, who are under great pressure to meet deadlines
as they try to get their newspaper printed, the cost of having paper tear in the
midst of printing is extremely high.[3] Therefore, it is important to obtain newsprint paper that is highly resistant to tearing and is appropriate to the presses
used by the publishers.

Newspaper publishers buy newsprint from a limited number of paper companies on a long-term basis. At fixed intervals, for example, once a month,

3. A person who works for a newspaper told me of his using taxi cabs in the middle of the night
to deliver newly printed newspapers after a delay in printing.

the publishers calculate the tear ratio and other figures for the paper purchased from each company. Even if the results do not immediately affect how much will be purchased in the next period, they do provide a basis for long-term plans. Thus, the evaluation of each paper company is based on long-term performance and not affected by short-term disturbances.

So called "face-to-face" competition may actually be more intense than anonymous market competition. According to a technician in a paper-producing company, a drop in the company's rating puts intense pressure on technicians and provides an important motivation for product improvement.

In spite of the fact that imported paper is much cheaper than domestic paper, and the fact that the cost of paper constitutes a considerable portion of the total cost of a newspaper, Japanese publishers are reluctant to use imported papers. Some publishers have now started using imported paper only for a limited purpose: for special editions, like the Sunday paper, which are not under the same time pressure. Still, imported paper represents less than 20 percent of the total amount of paper used.

6.4 A Structural Change in the Japanese Distribution System—the Case of Apparel

When the distribution market is dominated by small or medium-scale firms, the market will become decentralized. Three important factors explain the emergence of a decentralized distribution system:

1. *Downstream factors.* Each shop serviced a few customers because the population was spread all over the nation, and people did not drive far to shop. (See fig. 6.1 for the pace of motorization in Japan.) Thus, shops in small local communities tended to generalize rather than to specialize.

2. *Upstream factors.* The manufacturing sector was dominated by small or medium-scale forms, which had neither the ability nor the incentives to vertically integrate their distribution channels.

3. *Technological factors.* Telecommunication, computers, and transportation were not well developed.

These three factors have been changing gradually, and the Japanese distribution system is now changing structurally. Of the three factors, the first is probably the most important. In this section, I only consider the effect of changes in downstream factors. (Itoh and Matsushima 1989 deals with the other factors.)

Japan has experienced a rapid increase in the number of automobiles in the recent past (see fig. 6.1). There has also been a drastic shift in population to urban areas, especially to Tokyo, Osaka, and Nagoya.

In order to see how downstream factors affect the structure of the distribution system, let us consider the case of apparel. Table 6.4 illustrates the typical structure of an apparel distribution system in Japan. Traditionally, Japan had only type-1 distribution: retailers could not specialize in a limited number of

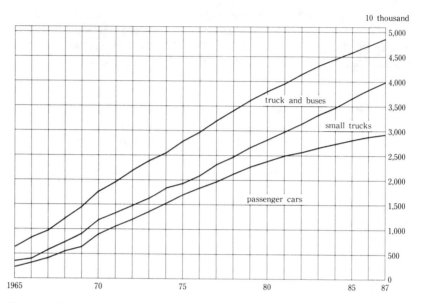

10 thousand

Fig. 6.1   The registration of motor vehicles in Japan

Table 6.4   Two Types of Distribution System of Apparel Products

	Type 1	Type 2
Retailers	Department stores, local small shops	Nationwide chain stores (specialized chain stores and general merchandisers)
The way goods are sold	A wide variety of goods	Specialized (or standardized)
Location	Traditional local shopping areas or near railway station	Suburban shopping centers, roadside, or railway station building
The role of wholesalers	Active	Minor
Transaction relation	Repeated and long-term relation (so-called Japanese-style business relation)	Simple market transaction

products, because the population was spread out and people did not drive far to shop. Type-2 distribution emerged only after the number of cars increased and the population moved into urban areas, allowing retailers to specialize in a limited number of products.

Type-1 retailers include department stores and small-scale retailers in local shopping areas. They depend heavily on wholesalers. The wholesalers (who often manufacture as well) play an active role in sales of apparel, particularly in the department stores. They also do pricing and arrange commodities. In one sense, the department stores only provide a location and clerks (some of whom are provided by wholesalers and manufacturers) to the wholesalers; the wholesalers sell their products. This system uses *henpinsei* (the practice whereby unsold goods are returned to wholesalers) and the *rebate system* (basically a nonlinear price system under which incentives are given to the retailers with high sales). In this sense, transaction relationships between retailers and wholesalers (and manufacturers) are far from simple market transactions. They involve implicit contracts and tacit negotiations.

This system has its own rationale. A wholesaler, transacting with retailers in various regions, can enjoy scale economies for such activities as information collection and dead stock risk management. For small-scale local shops, it would be impossible to cover the risk of dead stock, and to collect information about market trends and the availability of products. Fashion trends in apparel change quite frequently and rapidly. Even for department stores that sell a large variety of goods at a limited location, it is far better to use the resources of wholesalers. For example, it was reported in *Nikkei Ryutu* (which means distribution) *Newspaper* that the return rate (unsold rate) of female apparel in the department stores was more than 35 percent in 1988. Wholesalers, often much more specialized in certain limited kinds of commodities than retailers, have a comparative advantage for such activities.

Type-2 retailers include nationwide chain stores (which specialize in particular types of apparel), and large-scale nationwide supermarket chains (which carry general merchandise). The Idol chain, for example, specializes in children's apparel and has about 200 shops all around the country. Each shop is very small, only about 70 to 150 square meters. Thus, the chain can only specialize in limited types of commodities. For such specialized shops to be viable, there must be good transportation and a concentration of people within a metropolitan area. Because Idol sells the same types of products all over the country, the volume for each item is very large. Manufacturers supply Idol with customized products, according to its specifications. Wholesalers sometimes are involved in the distribution of Idol's products, but their role is much more limited than in the type-1 example. Unsold products are not returned to manufacturers or wholesalers.

Large-scale nationwide supermarket chains also use this distribution system. These supermarkets have more than a hundred branches all around the country and can enjoy economies of scale. They sell only limited varieties of commodities, and far fewer items than the department stores sell. Thus, it is easier for the supermarkets to cover the risk of dead stocks and to collect information about products. Supermarkets need not depend heavily on wholesalers, and the relationship between supermarkets and wholesalers (and manufacturers) basically is a simple market one. Exchange is conducted on the basis of explicit contracts.

Both systems are reasonable, and it is not clear which is the more efficient.

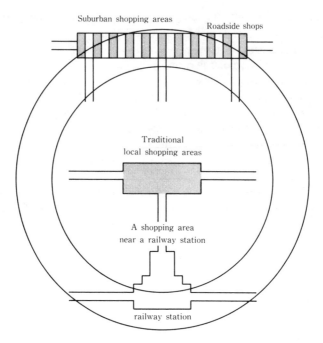

Fig. 6.2   The geographical structure of shopping areas in a typical local city

That depends on many factors, including the types of goods being sold. The type-2 system might be more efficient for standardized goods, whose sales are quite stable and predictable. But this does not imply that the traditional type-1 distribution channel will disappear.

Figure 6.2 is a shopping map of a typical local city. There are three shopping zones: the traditional shopping zone (the oldest one); the shopping zone around railway stations, which started about 60–70 years ago (department stores are the core of this zone); and the suburban shopping zone (which has large shopping centers and roadside shops). Consumers expect to find different kinds of shops and services in each shopping zone, and they use the zones accordingly.

6.5   Access to the Japanese Market

Japanese transaction relationships and the related distribution system are barriers to new entrants, not only foreign but also domestic. The existence of long-term transaction relationships implies that any new entrants will have difficulty doing business with incumbent wholesalers or retailers, even if the new entrants' products are cheaper than the competition's. Vernon's (1966) product cycle theory—in which the trade and production pattern of commod-

ities differs considerably depending on which stage the commodities are in—
provides an important insight to the Japanese problem.

Consider the case of dishwashers, for example. In their early stages, dishwashers were far from being standardized. The size of the market for the product was still small, the product itself left much room for improvement, and
there was considerable uncertainty about the future state of the product.

The development process for dishwashers involved trial and error; there
was a lot of interaction between the producers and the market (wholesalers,
retailers, and consumers). Factories, far from being large-scale and modern,
were more like laboratories. Also, the location of the factories was quite important because the producers had to be close to the consumers to find out
what they wanted. Thus, it was natural that dishwashers first appeared in the
United States, where there was a strong potential demand for them. The price
of the product in that early stage was only one important factor for the producers.

In their later stages, dishwashers became much more standardized. The
market for the product grew, and there was little room for improvement in it.
At that point, production cost was the most important element for the producers. They took advantage of scale economies, built large, modern factories,
and located them without regard to distance to the market. In fact, if labor
cost was very important, the factory would probably be located in a foreign
country.

For certain types of goods, this product cycle story can illustrate structural
change in the distribution channel. Home electrical appliances, discussed in
section 6.3, are a good example. A large number of home electrical appliances are now standardized, and their distribution channel has changed
greatly. As a result, it is now easy for foreign products to penetrate the Japanese market.

Apparel does not have a product cycle like home electrical appliances. But
apparel products can be classified into two types; type 2 is much more standardized than type 1. Figure 6.3 illustrates the production route of a toddler's
trousers sold in the Idol chain.

The reason why this one product goes through so many Asian countries is
that each country has a different pattern of comparative advantage. The wage
level is much lower in Vietnam than in Thailand and Hong Kong, but there
are some stages in the production process of the good that cannot be handled
in Vietnam or Thailand. It takes two to three months for this production process to be completed, and the Idol chain takes on all the risk of unsold products. Therefore, it is vital for the success of the system that the product be
sold in large quantities. In this market, it is quite easy for foreign products to
penetrate.

However, it is easier for foreign products to penetrate a type-1 market if
they are from a well-established brand. In the type-1 distribution channel,
there is a strong linkage between retailers and manufacturers (and wholesal-

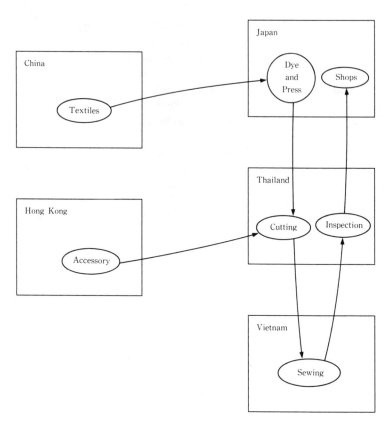

Fig. 6.3   The production route for toddlers' trousers

ers) that serves as a barrier to new entry. Efficiency of allocation and new entry are in conflict here.

References

Grossman, S., and O. Hart. 1986. The Costs and Benefits of Ownership: A Theory of Lateral and Vertical Integration. *Journal of Political Economy* 94:691–719.
Hart, O., and B. Holmstrom. 1987. The Theory of Contracts. In *Advances in Economic Theory, Fifth World Congress,* ed. T. F. Bewley. Cambridge: Cambridge University Press.
Itoh, M., and A. Matsui. 1987. Organizational Transactions: One Aspect of Japanese-Style Business Relations. Paper presented in the Hitotsubashi-Stanford Conference on Perspectives for Corporate Behavior, Kawana, Japan.
Itoh, M., and S. Matsushima. 1989. Nihon no Ryutu: Sono Kozo to Henka (Japanese distribution system: Its structural change). *Business Review,* Hitotsubashi University.

Klein, B., R. G. Crawford, and A. A. Alchian. 1978. Vertical Integration, Appropriable Rents, and the Competitive Contracting Process. *Journal of Law and Economics* 21:297–326.

Ministry of International Trade and Industry. 1988. *White Paper on International Trade and Industry*. Tokyo: MITI.

Nishimura, K., and H. Tsubouchi. 1989. Nihon no Shogyo Margin (The distribution margin of Japan). Discussion paper, Faculty of Economics, University of Tokyo.

Tamura, M. 1988. *Nihon-gata Ryutu Sisutemu (The Japanese-style distribution system)* Tokyo: Chikura-Shobo.

Tirole, J. 1988. *The Theory of Industrial Organization*. Cambridge, Mass.: MIT Press.

Vernon, R. 1966. International Investment and International Trade in the Product Cycle. *Quarterly Journal of Economics* 80 (May): 190–207.

Williamson, O. E. 1975. *Market and Hierarchies: Analysis and Antitrust Implications*. New York: Free Press.

———. 1983. Credible Commitments: Using Hostages to Support Exchange. *American Economic Review* 73:519–40.

Comment   David Flath

There are three different concepts of inefficiency implicit in references to the "inefficient" Japanese distribution system. One is regulatory distortion: the large-scale store law cartelizes department stores and protects small stores. A second is disguised unemployment: the distribution sector is economically backward, intractably governed by tradition rather than economic calculation. And a third is monopoly distortion: manufacturers and wholesalers restrict the price and nonprice competition of downstream distributors, which results in contrived scarcities.

The usual evidence that the Japanese distribution system is inefficient is not really evidence at all. The usual evidence is (*a*) the ubiquity of small stores; (*b*) the complexity of wholesale distribution channels; (*c*) the wide practice of exclusive dealing, resale price maintenance, liberal acceptance of returns, and customer restrictions, little impeded by Japan's weakly enforced antimonopoly laws. One may accept each of these characterizations of the Japanese distribution system as true and still logically maintain the absence of inefficiency in any of the three senses listed before. This is the essence of arguments that might be labeled the "revisionist" view.

Ito and Maruyama present new evidence to the effect that value-added per worker, gross margin, and retailer and wholesaler operating expenses relative to sales and profits relative to sales are all lower in Japan than in the United States or Germany. Their reporting profit and expense ratios by kind of business is probably a bit of overkill, especially for the wholesale sector because they make no adjustment for double counting in wholesale sales. The "gross margin," defined as percentage difference between final price and producer

David Flath is an associate professor of economics at North Carolina State University.

price, is not subject to this bias. They find that this gross margin is in aggregate less in Japan than in the United States or Germany, and they cite other estimates in the literature that reach a similar conclusion. On this evidence Ito and Maruyama argue that inefficiency of the Japanese distribution system is not the cause of seeming differences in consumer prices between Japan and elsewhere. I think they are correct. But this is a much weaker claim than one that states inefficiencies either do not exist or that they lack economic significance. For instance, the disguised-unemployment sort of inefficiency would manifest itself as overemployment of resources in the distribution sector so that services such as next-door delivery are provided to consumers at prices less than the true economic cost. This is annoyingly consistent with the evidence that Ito and Maruyama present. And Ito and Maruyama themselves assert as "plausible" that the large-scale store law and the vertical restraints do result in inefficiencies. They interpret their own evidence as showing that any economic rents resulting from regulatory distortions and contrived scarcities are merely not shared by the distribution sector.

I am left still curious about the actual significance of the large-scale store law and the alleged peculiarites of Japanese manufacturers' management of distribution channels. In the second paper, Motoshige Itoh goes some ways toward evaluating the latter. By relating his discussion of the allegedly peculiar marketing practices of Japanese manufacturers to the broader literature on the economics of vertical restraints, Itoh makes an important point: practices like resale price maintenance, customer assignment, exclusive dealing stipulations, and tie-in sales are not unique to Japan. It is probably true that the antimonopoly laws of Japan (as actually enforced!) permit wider application of vertical restraints than is the case in the United States. Penalties for violating the laws are rather small, and the powers of Japan's Fair Trade Commission to gather evidence and initiate action are weak. But it is far from clear that allowing vertical restraints is more harmful to consumers than attempting to ban them. There is a substantial body of scholarship associated with the University of Chicago and with the University of California, Los Angeles, arguing that America's antitrust laws have added to the costs of marketing products and have not corrected monopoly distortions. In this view, the relatively permissive antitrust policy of Japan, and the correspondingly wide application of vertical restraints there, can be a hidden advantage that contributes to the low distribution margins documented by Ito and Maruyama.

Itoh makes the added point that even vertical arrangements that efficiently resolve problems in the marketing of products can nevertheless impede entry. But the reason entry is made less profitable and is impeded is that the arrangements lead incumbents to expand output, which lowers prices. Efficient vertical contracts, although they may indeed deter imports, cannot logically explain why identical products have higher prices in Japan than elsewhere.

My final comments concern the large-scale store law, the law which requires approval of the national government for opening a store in Japan with floor space in excess of a set amount. This law has been mentioned in several of the papers presented in this volume. In prefectures of Japan with fewer department stores (on which the law has had the most impact) there are rather more of other kinds of stores.[1] The elasticity of number of other stores with respect to variation in the number of department stores ranges from essentially zero in the case of drug stores to -10% to -20% in the case of food, liquor, and apparel. There are about five times more department stores per person in the United States than in Japan, which is certainly a reflection of the law's effects on numbers of department stores. But according to the estimates just mentioned, this cannot fully account for Japan's superabundance of other stores, including food stores. That is, although the law clearly does protect small shop owners, there must be indigenous factors that favor a ubiquity of small stores. Having a proliferation of stores makes household shopping rather more convenient and enables economies on household storage space and travel time but also adds to the costs of the retail sector. High household storage costs and the lack of motorization mentioned by Ito favor the rationality of a distribution system with many small stores. But then shop owners, because of their numbers, become a powerful political force, and legislation is passed that exaggerates the natural tendency toward fragmentation and decentralization of the distribution sector. Similar forces are operative in the United States, but in an opposite direction. Indigenous factors in the United States, including motorization, have long favored larger stores. And, not coincidentally, here in the United States, laws including local zoning, which separates commercial and residential activity, have furthered the domination of large stores over smaller ones. The large-scale store law of Japan distorts the distribution system of Japan and is a source of economic inefficiencies. But the law itself is a reflection of the distribution system.

1. David Flath, "Why Are There so Many Retail Stores in Japan?" *Japan and the World Economy* 2 (1990): 365–86.

7   The Japanese Financial System and the Cost of Capital

David M. Meerschwam

This paper considers the role of "corporate finance" in contributing to Japan's economic performance. I highlight the role of the financial system while the "cost of capital" (typically expressed as a weighted average cost of capital [WACC]) is played down. The main reason for this is that, at least during the high growth phase of the Japanese economy (1945–74), a rationed capital allocation system was used in Japan in which the price mechanism played only a subordinated role. Not surprisingly, in such an environment models of capital budgeting do not conform to those that would obtain in a price-driven market. And while this does not mean that standard models such as discounted cash flow (DCF) analysis are obsolete, the appropriate inputs to a DCF model would be more difficult to ascertain.

With a focus on the institutional organization this paper shows how the Japanese financial system may have dealt effectively with problems currently associated in the finance literature with agency problems and information asymmetries. In this sense the institutional structure in which "corporate finance" took place may have given Japanese firms (with access to funds in the rationed system) a competitive advantage relative to their foreign competitors operating in institutional environments less well organized to deal with these issues.

In this paper I also show how, partly as a result of its own success and partly due to external forces, the distinctiveness of the institutional system would be eroded—in Japan the price system would start to play a more important role. In this sense, the emerging Japanese financial system allows for a much more

David M. Meerschwam wrote this paper while an assistant professor at the Graduate School of Business Administration, Harvard University.

The author is grateful to Carliss Baldwin, M. Colyer Crum, Jeffrey Frankel, James Hodder, Paul Krugman, Andre Perold, and Jeremy Stein for helpful comments and suggestions.

meaningful comparison between the cost of capital of Japanese and foreign firms, even though this is happening precisely at a time when, due to an increase in capital mobility, it is more difficult to explain how the underlying interest rates for corporations in the various countries would differ.

Still, several corporate executives and business publications have taken the role of corporate finance in Japan to be *a*, if not *the*, major factor in understanding the "competitive decline" of the United States and the ascendancy of Japan. For example, in March 1989, Ken Olsen, president of Digital Equipment Corporation, told the New England Council of the American Electronics Association that, in contrast to small increases in the cost of energy or in taxes, the cost of capital was a major culprit in causing U.S. firms to lose international competitiveness: "With a 10, 11, 12, percent interest on capital, you just can't compete."[1] Olsen was not alone in attributing many of U.S. corporations' problems in competing for international market share to the cost of capital, nor did he point to a new phenomenon. A 1985 *Harvard Business Review* article had been titled "Capital Markets and Competitive Decline" (see Richard Ellsworth 1985), while a study by the Chase Manhattan Bank in 1980, had warned that for the semiconductor industry: "The lower cost of capital of the Japanese companies provides them with the advantage that their required return on investments are lower than those of the U.S. semiconductor companies" (Chase Manhattan Bank 1980, pp. 1–10; quoted in Abegglen and Stalk 1985).

It seems that finance has become a favorite "whipping boy," to explain Japan's impressive performance (especially in comparison to the remarkable loss of international assets observed in the United States). Apart from obvious misconceptions (such as Olsen's apparent confusion between nominal, and inflation and exchange rate adjusted interest rates), it is surprising that so many executives in U.S. industry take capital market effects to be so important. While there is little doubt that finance and the cost of capital play a role, it is not obvious how important these costs are in comparison to, for example, labor productivity, SGA expense control, and product quality. Perhaps it is easier to blame faceless capital markets for competitive decline than other issues more directly under the control of managers.

Still, there is little doubt that finance has played an important role in Japan's transformation from a war-exhausted, resource-poor country to an international economic superpower. Those who focus on finance in this transformation often paint a breathtakingly simple picture of the Japanese financial system: the authorities, after isolating the domestic financial markets from the international capital markets, kept interest rates low and allowed financial intermediaries to steer funds to preferred sectors of the economy so that the corporations, unimpaired by bothersome shareholders with short term-

---

1. Reported in *Electronic News* (March 20, 1989).

horizons, were free to enter into long-term strategies to gain market share. As in most appealingly simplistic explanations, this is nothing but a *caricature*— it contains some truths, but surely does not capture the complexity and trade-offs that underlay the Japanese financial environment.

To evaluate the importance of "finance" in contributing to Japan's success, especially in cross-national comparison, one should consider the role of the financial system, the method of capital budgeting, and the "cost of capital." Of course, apart from these "firm-specific" issues, the overall availability of financial resources (irrespective of the distribution mechanism) plays a role. With a surplus of national savings, the national income identity dictates a current account surplus, which can be translated to the firm level as showing "competitive" advantage in order to generate a trade surplus.[2] Given a certain amount of national savings, the institutional arrangements in the financial system provide a link between the micro- and macrolevels.

Many authors have pointed out that in cross-national perspective the Japanese savings rate was high, and papers such as Feldstein and Horioka (1980), and a veritable cottage industry of related investigations, have explored the link between national savings rates and national investment. For Japan both were high in comparison to the United States (See table 7.1). Given these macrophenomena it is usually the cost of capital that provides the link to the micro (firm) level, which leads to a natural focus on the interest rates.

I argue though, that at least for the high growth phase of the Japanese economy (1954–74), the very structure of the Japanese financial system makes measures of the (weighted average) cost of capital not very useful as indicators of the relative abundance of financial capital to industries or as the determinants of industry structure and "international competitiveness." What really mattered was that a financial system was created that allowed for guided capital rationing. While some may call this a form of "national capital budgeting," perhaps in line with the popular notion of a "Japan Inc.," this would be an oversimplification: it is increasingly understood today, not only in finance but also in other aspects of industrial policy, that a subtle set of dependencies, power relationships, and informal understandings was in operation rather than a system reliant on simple directives.

In this paper, I concentrate, therefore, first on the development of the financial system that operated in Japan until the mid-1970s. Focusing on institutional considerations, the preference for bank financing (and high leverage) is explained, while the role of the rationed capital market is explored. Next, the impetus for change is presented as a sudden and dramatic reversal in the flow of funds in the domestic economy toward the government. I conclude with a few remarks about the current cost of capital debate, as the Japanese financial system is moving toward a more price-driven capital market. This last issue—

---

2. For simplicity, the service account is ignored here or at least assumed to be less than totally offsetting the capital account.

Table 7.1   U.S. and Japanese National Savings

| | United States | | | | Japan | | | |
| | Net Savings as % of Net Investments | All as % of GDP | | | Net Savings as % of Net Investments | All as % of GDP | | |
		Net Savings	Net Investment	Current Account		Net Savings	Net Investment	Current Account
1960	114.6	9.18	8.00	.62	101.4	22.12	21.81	.60
1965	110.2	11.34	10.29	1.07	97.4	18.17	18.65	1.11
1970	106.9	7.84	7.33	.39	104.4	26.89	25.75	1.01
1975	125.4	5.96	4.75	1.36	97.5	19.45	19.95	−.10
1980	105.5	5.93	5.67	.44	99.2	18.32	19.45	−.03
1981	102.8	6.43	6.26	.31	99.4	17.88	17.98	.49
1982	98.9	2.68	2.71	−.03	102.1	17.03	16.68	.70
1983	65.8	2.22	3.37	−1.00	109.7	16.07	14.64	1.81
1984	62.9	4.38	6.97	−2.44	116.5	17.05	14.63	2.84
1985	53.1	3.15	4.95	−2.93	120.7	17.96	14.88	3.69
1986	42.7	2.47	5.79	−3.44	126.4	18.46	14.60	4.33

Source: OECD National Accounts, 1988, Paris, pp. 32–35.

Note: Net savings = gross savings minus consumption of fixed capital; net investment = gross capital formation minus consumption of fixed capital. Due to "statistical discrepancies," net savings minus net investment may deviate from current account.

the financial product's price and the interest rate question—is taken up in great detail by Frankel (in this volume).

7.1   The Traditional Financial System

Japan's traditional financial system, here taken as the system that prevailed between 1945 and 1975, has, like so many other aspects of modern Japan, roots that go back to the Meiji Restoration of 1868. Many descriptions can be found, such as Presnell (1975), Bronte (1982), Prindl (1981), Crum and Meerschwam (1986) and Wallich and Wallich (1976). They all confirm some basic characteristics of the system. When a rudimentary banking system was set up and the Bank of Japan attained a monopoly on the issuance of notes in 1882, Minister of Finance Count Matsukata argued for the establishment of specialized financial institutions. These institutions were to play an important role in attaining the objectives of Japan's new rulers: "a strong army and rich country." With the government actively supporting the financial institutions and direct involvement in targeted industrialization efforts, a second set of financial institutions would rise to prominence whose power derived from their central place in industrial groupings (*zaibatsu*).

In this sense three characteristics of the system were put in place early on: close relationships between the authorities and the financial institutions, segmented financial product markets, and powerful banks at the center of networks of corporations. These three attributes of the system operated not always according to plan, but in essence provided the foundation for a financial system that would come to full bloom in the postwar years.

When the war ended, Japan's financial system was one part of the country's institutional framework that the Occupation powers reviewed. It was decided to remove the specialized financial institutions, to dissolve the powerful banks at the centers of the old business groups, and to stimulate a more active equity market as large corporations were sold to the public. Furthermore, in conformity with the U.S. financial system, Occupation planners imposed further segmentation between the commercial and the investment banking business.

The transformation of the system lasted only as long as the Occupation was in force. Soon after it ended, Japan's financial system started to resemble the old one again; specialized financial institutions, a heavy preference for indirect (i.e., bank intermediated) versus direct (i.e., corporate bonds and equity) financing, steering and guidance by central authorities, and suppression of the price mechanism in financial transactions. Central to all this was the development of a wide, deep, and sophisticated network of informally directed relationships, to which I return below. This system would operate for almost three decades.

In Japan, financial institutions faced an environment that segmented the product market according to maturity and purpose of finance. For example, long-term credit banks were the only institutions allowed to raise long-term funds and did not engage much in maturity transformation. City banks, the successors to the old banks that had stood at the center of the industrial groupings, again started to play a role as both repositories of deposits and active suppliers of bank finance to the rapidly growing industrial corporations. Specialized institutions dealt with foreign-exchange-related transactions, others with agricultural enterprises or fisheries, and yet others with forestry. Trust banks and various forms of mutual institutions looked after their dedicated markets, while regional banks functioned in particular geographic areas, often as gatherers of funds for the cash-hungry city banks, which in turn lent to the industrial sector. Special financial institutions for small business were in existence, while yet a whole other set of institutions operated in the securities industry (see table 7.2). Of course, segmentation by product market was also seen in other countries such as the United States. However, a comparison of the two systems in Crum and Meerschwam (1986) shows Japan's system more tightly controlled than that in the United States.

The highly segmented Japanese system operated under price controls. Both cooperative agreements in setting lending rates as well as official policies through a "temporary interest rate adjustment law" (instituted in 1947 but still partially in effect today) were observed, while several institutions, such as the Postal Savings System and other (semi-)official intermediaries allowed the

Table 7.2   Selected Japanese Financial Institutions (1988)

1. **The Bank of Japan**

2. **Banks**
   City banks
   Regional banks
   Trust banks
   Long-term credit banks

3. **Foreign banks**

4. **Financial institutions for small businesses**
   Mutual loan companies
   Credit cooperatives
   Urban credit associations
   Commercial and industrial cooperatives
   Labor credit associations

5. **Financial institutions for agriculture, forestry, and fisheries**
   Cooperative bank for agriculture and forestry
   Prefectural agricultural associations
   Fishery cooperative associations
   Fishery credit cooperatives

6. **Securities finance institutions**
   Securities finance companies
   Securities companies

7. **Insurance companies**

8. **Government financial institutions**
   Peoples Finance Corporation
   Housing Loan Corporation
   Export-Import Bank
   Japan Development Bank
   Agriculture, Forestry, and Fisheries Finance Corporation
   Small Business Finance Corporation
   Hokkaido and Tohoku Development Corporation
   Environmental Sanitation Business Finance Corporation

9. **Government**
   Trust Fund Bureau
   Postal Savings System
   Postal Life Insurance

Source: Economic Statistics Annual, 1988, Research and Statistics Department, Bank of Japan, pp. 1–6.

government to influence the prices of funds in the economy.[3] But the system cannot be fully appreciated without considering the informal, unwritten, traditions and customs that were an essential feature and caused dependencies, trade-offs, and negotiations.

Several examples point to these dependencies. Take the "over-loan" prob-

3. In spite of the many price regulations some price freedoms did exist. For example, a call (interbank) market was observed. Similarly, many observers point to the system of "compensating

lem (see, e.g., Wallich and Wallich 1976, pp. 284–90). During the high growth phase of the Japanese economy, the authorities decided to keep the regulated interest rates low, apparently in order to stimulate investments (but, in reality, to create a rationed capital market). And while banks were not able to aggressively compete for funds, due to the interest rate restrictions, savings seemed to have remained high, partly due to the elaborate Postal Savings System and partly due to cultural and historical norms.[4] With low, regulated rates, banks were faced with many more lending opportunities than they could satisfy, even after allowing for the funds gathered through the interbank market from the regional banks. It was the Bank of Japan that supplied the city banks with funds to make up for their overlending at rates that did not reflect "market conditions." And while the absolute amount of these loans was never very large, the banks' dependence on the central bank for marginal funding made them much more receptive to following the wishes of the authorities (see table 7.3).

These wishes were expressed during frequent reviews of bank balance sheet growth and composition. But there were further avenues to enforce the communications and dependencies. A system of "parachuting" executives from a higher organization in the financial hierarchy to a lower one was standard. Thus, bureaucrats from the most prestigious Ministry of Finance and Bank of Japan often ended their careers as executives at the financial institutions. The institutions themselves often "parachuted" their (older) executives to related corporations and subsidiaries.

Dependencies were also seen in other financial interactions. The funding of the public sector, a relatively unimportant demand on the total funds generated (initially due to the Occupation-imposed Dodge-line of balanced budgets), was not the outcome of a price-competitive auction. Instead, a well-instituted system of "forced" absorption of the issues by financial firms existed at prices set by the authorities (see, e.g., Feldman 1986, p. 51). Such a system is not totally unique. In the United Kingdom, the discount houses were, in effect, "forced to cover the tender" after price consultation with the Bank of England (Revell 1973, pp. 223–27). In Japan, without an active secondary market, the financial institutions typically held on to issues for one year, after which the Bank of Japan mostly monetized them, clearing the balance sheets of the institutions for the next round of the forced tender.

Even in the market for direct finance (corporate bonds and equities), methods were devised to enhance relationships. Some observers suggest that the method of equity issue itself enhanced relationships by favoring long-term

---

balances" (observed in many other countries as well), which allowed effective rates to differ from the officially quoted ones. See Bronte (1982, p. 17). Still, there is widespread agreement that in effect few price freedoms existed and that a highly regulated system operated.

4. Many authors have tried to explain the apparently high Japanese savings rate. See, e.g., Hayashi (1986) and Frankel (in this volume).

Table 7.3   **Overloans and the City Banks: City Bank Data (in Trillions of Yen)**

	Total Deposits	Loans from Bank of Japan	Call Money	Total Liabilities
1955	2.4	.03	.07	2.9
1960	5.6	.4	.2	6.9
1965	12.5	1.1	.9	16.3
1970	24.3	2.1	2.0	32.6
1975	52.9	1.5	2.4	71.7
1980	85.4	1.8	4.5	110.4
1985	125.6	3.5	6.8	191.4

Source: Economic Statistics Annual, various issues, Research and Statistics Department, Bank of Japan.

shareholders. In Japan, until the early 1970s, new equity issues were made at par rather than at the much higher market prices of the equity. Existing shareholders typically had "rights" to purchase the new shares at the par rate. This, according to some, favored long-term relationships, supposedly since shareholders held on to their shares in expectation of future rights issues, again priced below the market rate. In this interpretation equity financing was "expensive to the corporation," since the issues were sold "cheap."

However, this is *incorrect*. Rights issues are not expensive "to the corporation," and a "good deal to the shareholders" since the two are interchangeable. Because a par issue with rights to existing shareholders can take place at any price this is most easily seen if one considers the par issue at a par price of zero. In this case a stock split takes place, and for other than signaling reasons associated with a possible dividend increase, no shareholder wealth effect is observed.[5]

With respect to this issue, Wallich and Wallich (1976), while still arguing that rights issues are "expensive to the corporation" and will inspire long-term shareholders, suggest a "juxtaposition" which, they argue, allows for the relationships in equity financing through the long-term shareholders:

> to believe that the shareholder is enriched by rights, stock dividends, and splits, a different interpretation is required—one in which the corporation is an entity with a life of its own and the stockholder is a kind of subordinated creditor. This interpretation is not irrational so long as it places the corporation and the old stockholders in juxtaposition with the new stockholders from whom the funds are obtained. To view old stockholders in that way raises the fundamental question of what, if anything, the corporation maximizes and on whose behalf. (p. 301)

5. In fact, finance models that rely on information asymmetries between managers and investors actually show how the effective increase in the dividends may be viewed as a positive signal about the future cash flows of the firm, therefore increasing the market valuation of the firm. See Asquith and Mullins (1986) and Miller and Rock (1985).

The above rationale for the relationships in the equity market relies, therefore, on the failure of full identification of the shareholder and the corporation. Aoki (1984), as outlined below in the context of Japanese leverage, shows how, in a model with special shareholder groups, such as banks, it is indeed not possible to apply the simple shareholder-wealth/share-price maximization paradigm. However, even without having to rely on the "long-term" holdings of the individual retail investor, a simpler way to find indications of relationships in equity finance is to look at the importance of the crossequity holdings between major corporations. Bank of Japan data suggest that such equity holdings (excluding financial institutions) increased between 1966 and 1974 from 18.6% to 27.1% (after which period the share stabilized). These equity holdings were traditionally extremely stable and reflected much of the prewar *zaibatsu* structure.

The corporate bond market used another method to deal with informational problems that afflict the securities markets. Only fully secured bond issues were acceptable, while an inactive market placed a large portion of the relatively few issues in the hands of financial institutions (see table 7.4). It can be no surprise that in this system there was no role for "rating agencies." Their mission and business purpose is precisely to convey information between lenders and borrowers in the absence of a relationship between the two; in Japan this was of little concern. The relationships facilitated information sharing, while fully secured bonds reduced the risks even further and excluded potential newcomers, who lacked assets. The absence of a commercial paper market, or a CD market (where transactions occur purely on a price-driven basis) fits naturally within the system that relied so heavily on relationships.

In short, in Japan during the high growth phase of the economy, a financial system operated that segmented the financial product market and that restricted price competition both through regulation as well as through the lack of financing alternatives. With the markets for public securities restricted through traditions, a high growth rate naturally drove the corporations to the banks, for both long-term (long-term credit banks) and short-term (city banks) financing (see table 7.5). There, access to funds was facilitated through long-established relationships. The many restrictions that were used to close the domestic market from foreign influences are well known and will not be presented here—they closed any escape route for those companies outside the relationship system. In combination, all of this gave the authorities influence to steer the system through a rationed capital market that favored established corporations to rely more heavily on "cheap" indirect debt financing and thus high leverage.

7.2 Direct versus Indirect Finance

The Japanese financial system favored indirect (bank) financing over direct (securities) financing. This would therefore not only lead to high leverage, but

Table 7.4   Industrial Bonds and the Banking Sector: Bond and Bank Asset Data (100 Million Yen)

	Industrial		A + B Industrial Bonds (C)	Industrial Bonds at Banks (D)	Total Bank Assets (E)	D as % of E (F)	D as % of C (G)	D as % of A (H)
	Nonconvertible Bonds (A)	Convertible Bonds (B)						
1955	2,273	...	2,273	1,695	51,028	3.3	74.6	74.6
1960	6,927	...	6,927	4,555	129,480	3.5	65.8	65.8
1965	17,493	...	17,493	9,969	313,249	3.2	57.0	57.0
1970	26,983	1,043	28,026	15,870	631,661	2.5	56.6	58.8
1975	55,153	11,323	66,476	21,154	1,444,280	1.5	31.8	38.4
1980	89,635	11,986	101,621	19,834	2,308,461	.9	19.5	22.1
1985	96,435	44,261	140,696	19,958	3,762,367	.5	14.2	20.7
1986	96,700	66,188	162,888	22,022	4,215,506	.5	13.5	22.8
1987	99,187	98,327	197,514	22,721	4,755,789	.5	11.5	22.9
1988[a]	106,300	138,098	244,398	24,399	5,265,417	.5	10.0	23.0

Source: Economic Statistics Annual, 1988, Research and Statistics Department, Bank of Japan, pp. 44–45, 203–4.

Note: The Bank of Japan does not supply exactly matching figures and several rows rely on the author's calculations.

[a]Several of the 1988 figures are estimates.

Table 7.5   **Financing of Nonfinancial Corporation: Direct and Indirect Financing**

	Direct Financing as % of Total	Indirect Financing as % of Total	External Financing as % of Total	Indirect Financing as % of External	Internal Financing as % of Total
1961–64	14.0	44.6	58.6	76.1	32.1
1965–69	7.2	43.7	50.9	85.9	38.0
1970–74	6.1	47.1	53.2	88.5	32.9
1975–79	8.2	37.9	46.1	82.2	46.3
1980–82	6.5	38.0	44.5	85.4	45.6
1982–85	7.9	36.8	44.7	82.3	48.5

Source: Tamura (1987), p. 3

Note: Direct financing = equity and bond issues; indirect financing = long- and short-term borrowing; external financing = direct + indirect financing; internal financing = retained earnings + depreciation.

to a heavy reliance on bank debt (see table 7.6, "Borrowed Funds"). While stock exchanges were established in 1878 in both Tokyo and Osaka, the role that the equity and fixed income market were to play in Japan would be highly restrictive. It was only for a brief period, between the two world wars, that the markets for direct finance provided funds roughly equal in magnitude to those generated through internal funds and loans (see Japan Securities Research Institute 1986). In 1937 all three sources of funds accounted for approximately ¥2 billion. After the Second World War, however, the role of the securities market as a supplier of funds would be vastly surpassed by the banking sector, despite early attempts of the Occupation powers to dissolve the old industrial groupings by selling their shares to the public.[6]

The preference for bank financing can be explained in various ways. As far as the bond markets were concerned, the fully secured nature of the securities and inactive secondary trading made it, in effect, an underdeveloped market (see, e.g., Presnell 1975, pp. 427–30). For the relative unimportance of the equity market, Monroe (1973) returns to the par issue method and suggests that Japanese investors were focused on dividend yield, while he implicitly seems to assume that Japanese firms consider dividend yield the relevant cost of equity indicator. With par issue, and a dividend traditionally maintained as percentage of the par price, the stock price reduction after the issue in effect raises the overall dividend yield. Hodder (1985), in a similar vein, notes that the dividend yield on stocks was greater than the cost of bank borrowing, and thus reliance on bank debt could be expected. Note that such arguments have

---

6. A Securities Coordination Liquidation Committee oversaw the Securities Democratization Movement. However, this only concerned a transformation of ownership rather than the raising of new funds.

Table 7.6   Sources of Funds (% of Funds Raised by Nonfinancial Corporation)

	Internal		External			
	Retained Earnings	Depreciation	Equity	Bond	Borrowed Funds	Other
1961–64	7.9	24.2	12.1	1.9	44.5	9.4
1965–69	15.3	22.7	5.2	2.0	43.7	11.1
1970–74	13.3	19.6	4.5	1.6	47.2	13.8
1975–78	10.7	35.6	4.6	3.6	37.9	7.7
1979–82	13.4	32.2	4.4	2.1	38.0	10.0
1983–85	10.8	37.7	4.6	3.3	36.8	6.8

Source: Tamura (1987), p. 3.
Note: This table is directly copied from the Fair Fact Series.

to consider the dividend yield as the relevant cost of equity measure. And indeed, anecdotal evidence suggests that Japanese executives may have viewed dividends in such a way. Still, some doubt can be cast on the "par issue–dividend yield" argument: table 7.7 shows that, even when the system changed in the early 1970s from par issue to market issue, there was no appreciable effect on the relative funding importance. Between 1965 and 1969 equity financing accounted for 10.2% of external funding; between 1970 and 1974 for only 8.4%.

While Hodder's argument would lead to a straightforward relative price story, other reasons for the relatively high leverage ratio's may have to be considered too. Aoki's (1984) model shows that it may be in the interest of the corporation to "overleverage" if significant share ownership rests with a bank that also supplies borrowed funds to the corporation. Another, simpler explanation would be in conformity with Modigliani-Miller; in a system with low bankruptcy probability (see below) for the established players, the expected costs of financial distress was low—thus debt financing was preferred for those with *access in the rationed system.* In the absence of a well-developed bond market, this meant bank borrowing.

Still, the reliance of the Japanese major firms on bank financing cannot only be a function of relatively favorable bank interest rates due to price controls and cartels in the banking sector; no government can regulate the rates down for all potential demanders of funds. Instead, the price regulations allowed the "preferred" corporations access to the bank loans. Note that such a distribution mechanism itself may explain in part why Japanese firms built higher leverage than most American counterparts (see Table 7.7). Remember that the relationship between the Bank of Japan and the city banks was strong. This meant that implicitly approval was granted of the balance sheet structure of the banks. In turn, banks may have reasonably expected that the likelihood of serious problems with a loan portfolio, which reflected the Bank of Japan's approval, would be less, thus allowing for higher leverage of their clients.

And indeed, institutional features of the Japanese system helped to "socialize" some of the risks and costs associated with high leverage and financial distress. For example, an "anti-recession cartel law" operated, which reduced cash-flow concerns. Similarly, the strong relationships inside the industrial groupings assured assistance to the weakest from the strongest (see, e.g., Abegglen and Stalk 1985, pp. 166–67). Finally, the role of the main bank was to help in the reorganization of a client during times of financial distress. All of the above facilitated information sharing. Hoshi, Kashyap, and Scharfstein's (1988) recent empirical investigation of the role of information sharing through relationships between established corporations and their banks confirmed this. They showed that the investment behavior of those firms

Table 7.7   **Leverage of U.S. and Japanese Manufacturing Industry: Equity as a Percentage of Total Liabilities plus Equity**

Year	United States	Japan	United States/ Japan
1960	65.9	32.3	2.0
1961	64.8	30.6	2.1
1962	61.1	30.9	2.0
1963	61.0	29.6	2.1
1964	60.8	28.1	2.2
1965	59.7	26.9	2.2
1966	56.4	26.3	2.1
1967	58.5	25.5	2.3
1968	54.8	23.8	2.3
1969	54.6	23.0	2.4
1970	53.8	22.1	2.4
1971	53.4	20.7	2.6
1972	52.3	20.4	2.6
1973	49.0	20.3	2.4
1974	53.1	19.9	2.7
1975	52.5	18.5	2.8
1976	53.4	18.4	2.9
1977	52.4	19.3	2.7
1978	51.8	20.4	2.5
1979	50.2	20.6	2.4
1980	49.5	21.8	2.3
1981	48.9	22.7	2.2
1982	48.5	24.1	2.0
1983	49.1	26.3	1.9
1984	47.7	27.6	1.7
1985	45.1	29.6	1.5
1986	44.0	31.5	1.4
1987	42.8	33.1	1.3

Sources: Economic Statistics Annual, various issues, Research and Statistics Department, Bank of Japan; and U.S. Federal Trade Commission, *Quarterly Financial Report for Manufacturing, Mining and Trade Corporations.*

with access to the group banks differed indeed from those without such access.

Applying models of imperfect information (and corporate incentive schemes) the role of indirect finance attains high significance. The Japanese financial system, where, due to severe product market segmentation and price regulation, relationships flourished, seems to have been able to deal with many of the information problems in an effective way. Here the role of the financial institutions is important and reflects insights such as those offered by Bernanke (1983) in the context of the Depression in the United States.

In this line of reasoning the traditional Japanese financial system was distinct in its method of "capital rationing." The system allowed the authorities "guidance maximization," and those with access to the funds indeed faced "below-market rates." But the system relied not only on providing favored corporations with access, it also had to ensure that those excluded could not mount a credible threat against the system, for example, by accessing well-developed, price-driven, public securities markets.

An emphasis on growth, starting with the Meiji Restoration, and consultation between various bureaucracies helped the system to produce outcomes that were favorable to all established players. While this is not the place to reevaluate the role of organizations like MITI,[7] there can be no doubt that in cross-national comparison the Japanese policies reflected a production- rather than consumption-growth bias. With rapid growth, the financial system rewarded the established players. Those with access in the rationed model benefited from preferential prices, the intermediaries were able to attain their growth objectives as their client showed an appetite for funds, and the authorities maximized their guidance. The "losers" in this environment were those with no established relationships—the outsiders to the system. However, precisely because they had no established relationships they were unable to break the system as it produced Japan's high growth rates. Thus, high leverage became feasible as long as the system operated with rewards for all who held power.

The high leverage record of the Japanese firms was not only a result of the availability of bank finance to the preferred players; the high growth rates themselves skewed the financing structure this way, due to an absence of equity financing. In looking at leverage in Japan, I first assume that sales growth is the corporate objective (as will be seen, this is not necessarily inconsistent with standard notions of shareholder value maximization). Here I do not try to show formally why such an objective may have been followed, but anecdotal and empirical evidence suggests that sales growth and market share played a major role for Japanese firms. Abegglen and Stalk (1985) quote a survey study contrasting corporate objectives in Japan and the United States. In conformity with popular perception, the number one goal for Japanese cor-

---

7. The classic reference is Chalmers Johnson (1982).

porations was Market Share (4.8 on a 1–10 scale of ranking by importance) with Return on Investment (RoI) following in second place (4.1). For U.S. firms, RoI dominated with 8.2 while Market Share followed in distant third place with 2.4.

Given the exposition so far, the emphasis on growth and market share may have been fully "rational" in the context of the system described. With an interaction of national goal development and guidance power by the authorities and banks, the firms eager to attain the preferential funds had to forge a consistency between their own goals and those of the authorities; here a "market-share goal" leading to funds access may be synonymous with (corporate) wealth maximization. McCraw and O'Brien (1986) present an account of how, in the steel industry during the high growth phase of the 1960s, growth and efficiency achievements were in effect rewarded with license to increase capacity.

If indeed market share and growth objectives are taken seriously, then high leverage is a natural outcome; rapid sales growth typically leads to asset growth. With the equity base of a company growing at the rate of retained earnings, any sales growth in excess of the growth of the equity base will lead to higher leverage. Only with repeated equity issues can the leverage be contained, an avenue unpopular in Japan, as discussed before. Thus, given a particular corporate return on assets and a fixed dividend pay-out ratio, the more highly levered firm can grow its sales more rapidly since it has a higher return on equity.[8] While the financial risk of the typical shareholder increases in this scenario, it was already been shown how the Japanese system "socialized" some of these risks.

In this interpretation the high leverage would be most advantageous for the members of the large industrial groupings with the best growth opportunities and the relatively low risk of financial distress. They would also be the least likely firms to find themselves to be capital (borrowing) constrained. Such a system would provide many incentives for the various players to "play along." If indeed the growth would be established, the established players coopted into the system would benefit. But here a problem of interpretation arises: for the successful high growers, unsuccessful "low" growers had to be found if we assume, for simplicity, that market size was exogenously determined. While external markets might provide an opportunity to gain market share at the cost of foreign firms, the internal markets would, in effect, only allow for zero-sum games. It is, in this light, not surprising that Japanese internal market dynamics were often described as "viciously" competitive. For the overall

---

8. This is a result of the "sustainable growth" concept, which shows the relationship between sales growth (g), Return on Equity (RoE), and the dividend payout ratio (p): To sustain a particular capital structure, in the absence of equity issues, sales growth cannot exceed the growth rate of the equity base: $g = \text{RoE} \times (1-p)$. Applying the Dupont decomposition of RoE, it follows that $g = [\text{RoS} \times S/A \times A/E] \times (1-p)$, where RoS is the return on sales, S/A represents the asset intensity of the firm, and A/E (the ratio of assets to equity) can be thought of as the leverage.

success of the country though, external growth markets had to be found to earn in the international markets the resources required for the domestic developments.

In this interpretation, the role of bank finance is essential. It provided the authorities the means to influence the distribution of capital along lines consistent with favored sectors of the economy, while internal competition would guarantee efficiency. Here, the role of the internal investment decisions of the firms plays a different role, and there is no reason to believe that anything like "discounted cash flow" models would be extensively used. And indeed there is no evidence that this method of capital budgeting was prevalent in Japan. Several authors have looked at the method of investment decisions in Japan. Hodder (1985) concludes that, in quantitative analysis, NPV or DCF models play at best a very subordinated role. Gultekin and Taga (1987) produce survey results from 1986 that show that only 11% of 87 major corporations in Japan consider DCF evaluations, 18% IRR, 20% ARR, while 41% employ pay-back techniques. Hodder (1986) provides an excellent evaluation of investment decision-making practices in the United States and Japan. And while he concludes that there is evidence that managers use the concept of time value of money in their decisions, there is no evidence to support the "simple" application of NPV or DCF models. In short, not only is it not clear how important the cost of capital was as an internationally competitive weapon; the whole method of investment decision making should be seen in light of a fundamentally different institutional environment.

This brings back the question of the difference between reliance on direct and indirect financing. With direct financing, the performance of the corporation is directly judged by arm's length investors. And while we do not suggest that such relationships always force "short-term" profit maximization at the cost of long-term profits, Stein (1989) showed in a theoretical model under information asymmetries how long-term profit considerations, especially in markets where long-term market-share power may be built, may be compromised due to a short-term investor horizon. Thus, perhaps somewhat surprisingly, a perfectly decentralized and disintermediated market for direct finance may not generate a first-best outcome; informational and commitment problems may be more efficiently solved in an indirect, intermediated, bank market with strong relationships. In the international economics literature, papers such as Krugman (1988) on "strategic trade policy" essentially refer to similar phenomena.

What this does point to is that the Japanese financial system, by allowing a complex form of rationed capital allocation within the context of steering and guidance by authorities (without a rigid capital allocation plan), provided the beneficiaries of the preferential funds to embark on growth strategies without having to rely, to a large extent, on impersonal capital markets. Here the real importance seems to rest more in the method of financing (direct vs. indirect) than in the high leverage per se.

The implication of the above is not to suggest that the cost of capital played no role in explaining the success of various Japanese firms in attaining world market share. It does, however, point to three caveats. One applies to the individual firm level. Here I suggest that, for those with the access to the preferential funds, the actual cost of capital advantage seems unambiguously low relative to those *inside* Japan without such access. Compared to firms *outside* Japan, taking into account the relatively closed nature of the Japanese financial market until the 1970s, many different evaluations can be found, and they are discussed in greater detail by Frankel (in this volume).

The second caveat applies to the importance of the cost of capital calculation. If many of the prices charged for funds by the intermediaries reflected the relationships with the firms, then there is little reason to believe that, given the possibly different corporate objectives, the cost of capital had a major influence on investment decisions as would be expected from standard models such as DCF. Again, the results from Hoshi et al. (1988) provide evidence.

Third, one should consider the importance of the cost of capital on the overall national performance of Japan (especially in the cross-national perspective). As noted, it seems that a rationed capital market was created; here there should be no a priori presumption that, even if standard models of investment analysis are used, the economywide cost of capital was low. Instead, the argument should revert back to overall saving behavior and the national income identity. What could be argued, though, is that if the relationship system was effective in dealing with capital market imperfections due to information problems in financial transaction (see, e.g., Myers and Majluf 1984), then the financial system, rather than the cost of capital per se, may have contributed to the extraordinary performance of Japan.

Still, even here the relative importance of the financial system has to be judged compared to the impact of the saving behavior, the proverbial work attitude of the Japanese, the methods of conflict resolution, the "reverse engineering abilities," and so on. More important, I show next how the "traditional" relationship system in finance is being eroded as internal and external pressures force a transition toward a system more reliant on impersonal prices, thus making the Japanese system less distinct.

7.3 From Relationships to Transactions

The relationship system described above functioned well. It assisted Japan in rapid rebuilding, high growth, low inflation, and low unemployment—the country seemed to have been doing everything right. Yet change was to come to the system. Many observers have, during the 1980s, described the "liberalization" of the Japanese financial markets, but I suggest that the impetus for change occurred much earlier: it was in the wake of the oil shock that many of the carefully designed dependencies of the system started to break down. Later, with pressures exercised from abroad to "open up" Japan's financial system, further change occurred (see, e.g., Frankel 1984), in a system that had already started to let prices play a more active role due to domestic pressures.

It was Japan's response to the oil shock of 1974 that changed the financial system. With a dramatic reversal of the growth rates from almost 10% in 1973 to −1% in 1974, the Japanese authorities embarked on a Keynesian countercyclical expansion; they allowed for a large budget deficit to be generated. At the same time that domestic growth collapsed and a major international recession occurred, Japan's corporations saw their fund needs evaporate. With high depreciation charges and low investment appetite, cash flows burgeoned and the loan dependency was reduced (see table 7.6). This meant a basic reversal in the national flow of funds; the government became the net large absorber of funds, replacing the corporate sector (see table 7.8).

Table 7.8   Government Financing Need

	Japan's Central Government's General Account (100 million Yen)		
Year	Government Revenue (A)	Government Securities and Borrowing (B)	B as % of A (C)
1965	37,730	1,972	5.23
1966	45,521	6,655	14.62
1967	52,994	7,093	13.38
1968	60,598	4,620	7.62
1969	71,092	4,126	5.80
1970	84,591	3,471	4.10
1971	99,708	11,871	11.91
1972	127,938	19,499	15.24
1973	167,619	17,662	10.54
1974	203,791	21,599	10.60
1975	214,734	52,805	24.58
1976	250,260	71,981	28.71
1977	294,336	95,612	32.48
1978	349,072	106,739	30.58
1979	397,792	134,719	33.87
1980	440,406	141,702	32.18
1981	474,433	128,998	27.19
1982	480,012	140,447	29.26
1983	516,529	134,863	26.11
1984	521,833	127,813	24.49
1985	539,925	123,079	22.80
1986	564,891	112,549	19.92
1987	582,141	105,390	18.10
1988	566,997	88,410	15.59

Source: Economic Statistics Annual, 1988, Research and Statistics Department, Bank of Japan, p. 227.

Table 7.9   **Bank Profitability**[a]

	Compound Growth Rates of Bank Profits and Assets	
	Assets (%)	Profits (%)
1960–65	19.7	9.0
1965–70	14.8	23.5
1970–75	17.4	3.4
1975–80	9.7	3.8
1980–85	9.5	13.0
1985–87	12.3	24.9

Source: Economic Statistics Annual, 1988, Research and Statistics Department, Bank of Japan, p. 104.
Note: Profits are reported on first half–last half basis until 1980; after 1980, fiscal years are used.
[a]Banks included are city banks and regional banks.

For the financial intermediaries, the world changed almost overnight. Now they had to absorb ever-larger public securities issues while the normally profitable lending opportunities to corporations shrank. The government, unwilling to allow for a competitive tender, instead focused on keeping its financing costs low. As a result, the (forced) bond subscription became a serious concern for the banks (see tables 7.9 and 7.10). Profitability at the city banks, the central players in this game, was compromised at the time that the power relationship between them and the authorities had changed—now the authorities had to ask for funding and no longer the overloaned banks.

The outcome of the changed relationship was that the banks asked for, and attained, new interest rate freedoms (see, e.g., Feldman 1986, pp. 50–56 and Bronte 1982, p. 21). At first only few interest rates of particular products were affected, but an unmistakable step was taken away from the strictly controlled price system. Similarly, new freedoms were granted in an incipient secondary market where the institutions could "unload" some of their holdings, as the Bank of Japan was no longer willing to repurchase the issue.

A second set of events furthered the transition toward more price-oriented financial transactions. With the breakdown of the international financial system after the Smithsonian agreement, new exchange-rate freedoms were observed. And while the Japanese financial authorities continued to try to isolate their domestic markets from foreign pressures, balance of payments pressures allowed for "leakages" to develop in this sector of the market as well, first in response to the current account deficit related to the oil shock, later in response to the current account surplus. For example, in 1975 Matsushita became the first Japanese corporation allowed to issue a dollar-denominated convertible debenture; in 1977 Euro-yen bonds were allowed (albeit only for nonresident issuers). Add to this that in the 1980s Japan's current account surplus started to show an embarrassment of riches with concomitant pres-

Table 7.10   Government Bond Holdings by City Banks and All Banks as % of
                 Total Assets

	All Banks	City Banks
1965	.1	.1
1970	.9	.9
1973	1.4	1.1
1974	1.0	1.0
1975	2.3	2.2
1976	4.4	4.3
1977	5.9	5.7
1978	7.8	7.5
1979	7.4	6.6
1980	6.6	5.2
1981	6.3	4.6
1982	5.8	4.0
1983	5.6	4.0
1984	5.0	3.5
1985	4.3	3.0
1986	4.4	3.3
1987	4.6	3.4
1988	5.0	3.7

Source: *Economic Statistics Annual*, 1988, Research and Statistics Department, Bank of Japan,
pp. 44–52.

sures for further liberalization, and the host of events that took place between 1977 and 1989 can only be seen as steps in a transition away from a relationship system toward a system that is increasingly driven by price transactions.

The increased reliance and popularity of the price-driven instruments has another reason as well. In financial transactions, "learning" by the market participants takes place. In this context the changes in the corporate finance structure of many U.S. firms, which have "discovered" the highly leveraged buy-out and merger transactions, are nothing but the acceptance of a new orthodoxy, or, as some skeptics may argue, nothing but the actions of newer participants who have forgotten some of the lessons of financial prudence, driven home to many older participants by memories of the 1930s. Such learning in Japan is seen in the eager experimentation with many of the highly price-sensitive products developed in foreign markets, where Japanese individuals and firms increasingly place their capital account deficit. The development of interest rate swaps and stock index futures are but two examples.

The impact of these changes can be profound. Take, for example, the new interest rate swap. Before, specialized financial institutions divided the financial product market by maturity of finance. In particular, only long-term credit banks could issue long-term debentures, while city banks could only fund on a short-term basis, while neither of the two types of institutions engaged in much maturity transformation—the introduction of a swap market in effect renders such funding segmentation obsolete. Similarly, the introduction of a CD market with true interest freedoms has changed the funding behavior of the banks, while the introduction of a CP market has allowed corporations new funding opportunities and new investment outlets.

The changes that have occurred on the banking side of the financial system can only be interpreted as a move toward greater reliance on the price mechanism, a mitigation of the specialized financing functions of the various institutions, and a move toward greater convergence with the financial systems operative in other major financial centers, such as the United States and the United Kingdom. But the movement toward a less distinctive system was not only seen in bank finance. Change occurred in securities transactions as well.

While rights issues were popular in Japan, it was from the early 1970s that increasingly issues at market were to take place. After the first such market-priced issue had taken place in 1969 for a musical instrument maker, Nihon Gakki, this method of raising funds became more fashionable over time, and while the oil-shock's impact on funds needs slowed the growth of such market issues for some time, they would eventually come to dominate. In issuing at market, rather than at par, Japanese firms faced an interesting effect on their dividend policies. Typically, dividends had been set as a percentage of the par price of the shares; with the new issues at market, the corporations at first kept their dividend policies unchanged, thus vastly reducing the effective dividend pay-out ratio. A self-regulatory order of the securities industries changed this practice, and through a rule of "the Distribution of Profits" in effect set minimum dividend pay-out ratios.

The bond market also showed change. Traditionally, only fully secured debentures could be issued, since in 1905 a Secured Bond Trust Law had been enacted. The fully secured bonds did not only, in effect, enhance the relationship between the issuer and investor—traditionally, to a large extent, financial institutions—but such full collateralization also excluded many nonestablished players from the market. An example can be found in the financing moves of a company like Ito-Yokado, a nontraditional firm, started in the wake of the Second World War to become Japan's second largest supermarket chain. Without traditional relationships it was capital constrained in an industry that was, in Japan, capital intensive. With few assets (such as properties) that could be subsequently used as collateral for bond issues, Ito Yokado was constrained by the full collateral requirement and had to explore new ways of financing its operations. The company became one of the financial entrepreneurs eagerly embracing (and often trying to further) financial innovation that reduced the dominance of relationships from which they were excluded. Thus, Ito Yokado used, for example, innovative lease financing to attain asset use.

Other innovations in the bond markets took place as well. In 1979, a subsidiary of Sears Roebuck was the first issuer of an unsecured yen-denominated debenture. A year later Matsushita Electronics was the second company to use the debenture format. While at first very rigid standards were employed in granting permission to issue such unsecured bonds, standards were relaxed, actually following the looser standards that had been approved for the earlier Euroyen unsecured bonds. Similarly, issuing standards for convertible bonds were relaxed as well. It can be hardly a surprise that, in this new environment, rating agencies have appeared that resemble their Western counterparts.

In the money market, change has equally been observed. Call money interest rates have been liberalized, RePos have found more price flexibility, the introduction of a CP market was noted, and the price sensitivity of CDs enlarged. In short, it is much more difficult than before to highlight the distinctive nature of the Japanese financial markets. This does not mean to suggest that the Japanese market is identical in structure to the market of, say, the United States. What is observed, though, is that the market is relying more on prices in distributing funds than it did before, while at the same time the interactions with foreign markets have increased as foreign financial institutions have entered the Tokyo market looking for opportunities to introduce new techniques and products and as Japanese financial firms have entered foreign markets.

7.4   The Impact of Change

While it is impossible to present a complete list of the changes that have taken place in the Japanese financial system, especially as much change is still ongoing, the impact of the changes can be speculated upon. I suggested, in the description of the high growth phase of the Japanese economy, that the overall system design seemed to have fit very well with an industrial targeting policy, and that a combination of reliance on indirect finance, relative isolation from the securities market as far as corporate control is concerned, and close cooperation between the banks, authorities, and corporations helped along a remarkable performance.

In this interpretation, finance did provide Japan with a competitive advantage in its quest for world market share, but through a complex system rather than through simply keeping the cost of capital low. In the emerging environment other questions have to be raised, if indeed a move toward a price-competitive system in the allocation of capital is taking place. As the traditional "rationed-bank-finance" system is superceded, new techniques for investment decisions, capital allocation, and capital funding have to be found.

Such new techniques have to be developed at times when new pressures face the various corporations. For example, the impact of the newly established rating agencies has to be considered. Will they start to apply leverage targets in rating the publicly issued securities, and, if so, will the traditionally higher leverage of Japanese firms start to show costs associated with the attained ratings? Note that in the absence of the full collateralization, leverage considerations should play a more important role, as it opens the markets for new, nontraditional borrowers.

But there are other considerations that should be taken into account as well. The financial system changed at a time when, and in this interpretation *because*, the high growth phase of the economic development of Japan came to a screeching halt. The success of the system had been in large measure defined as (as well as relied on) creating the high growth rates, this allowed all established players the rewards needed to assure their conformity with the system, while it facilitated the exclusion of the "outsiders." As the growth stopped, the financial structure of the corporations would change. Now, less asset growth had to be financed while retained earnings would augment the equity component of the capital structure. With more reliance on retained earnings, leverage was to come down, an outcome consistent with the lower growth opportunities from a risk perspective. Furthermore, as I already pointed out, the advantages of leverage are great when high growth strategies are being pursued. Note that, in traditional corporate finance, given a particular return on assets (RoA), the higher RoE associated with higher leverage does not necessarily translate to higher shareholder value, since the required return on capital (or the cost of equity capital) would typically rise with higher financial risk at the corporate level.[9] Depending on one's beliefs about the efficiency of the markets and the "value" of tax shields, in effect the debate is simply about the optimal capital structure. Assuming, for simplicity, no changes in the relationship between the market and book value of a corporation, the higher return requirement on equity, as leverage increases, can equally be seen in lower P/E ratios.

While many caveats should be made in considering Japanese P/E ratios—many investigations have stumbled on complex accounting issues and the values of "hidden assets"—in the low growth phase of the economy P/Es have indeed decreased, even though the surge in the stock market since 1984 has shown, for more recent periods, high ratios. At the time that these P/E ratios declined (1976–84), leverage declined as well.

Within a traditional corporate finance evaluation such a P/E decline is unusual; with lower financial risk the P/E ratio would normally be expected to rise. However, given the interpretation provided so far, the lower leverage of the Japanese corporations (between 1974 and 1984) cannot necessarily be identified with lower financial risk—the overall financial system changed away from the strongest relationships. Since these relationships provided implicit guarantees, the changes that have occurred may have, in effect, caused the financial risks of the corporations to increase despite their attempts to unlever. Of course, this argument cannot explain the remarkable increase in P/E ratios that has taken place since the early 1980s and is discussed by Frankel (in this volume).

9. This follows from: $RoE = RoA \times A/E$.

In short, it seems that it was not only the financial system that lost some of its distinctiveness, but the financial structure observed in the corporations moved away from the characteristic very high leverage to lower ratios. Completely in conformity with this trend, the reliance on indirect financing declined, while direct financing became a more important source of funds. While between 1970 and 1974 corporations raised 33% of their funds internally (13% through retained earning and 20% through depreciation charges), borrowings accounted for 47%, with the equity market supplying 5% and the fixed income market 2% of all required funds. Between 1983 and 1985, this picture changed. Now 49% was raised through internal funds (11% through retained earnings and 38% through depreciation charges) and only 37% through borrowings, with the equity market still only supplying 4.6% of funds, but the bond market now accountable for 3.3% (see table 7.6).

Concentrating on nonfinancial corporations listed on the first section of the Tokyo Stock Exchange (TSE), the numbers are even more dramatic, as internal funds doubled to supply 71% of funds needs, up from 35% during the period 1970–74. Borrowings, on the other hand declined from 41% between 1970–74 to 6% for 1983–85. Note that this "magnification" effect for the listed companies on the TSE should be no surprise; the larger, well established corporations had been the primary beneficiaries of the relationship system.

It is difficult to avoid the conclusion that, as the financial system changed, the corporations' financing techniques also seem to have lost some of their unique characteristics. Of course, a question of causality may be raised; did the system change because the corporations had become unhappy with their capital structure or did the change in the system force corporations to change their capital raising procedures and their financial structure? Here the interpretation is that neither of the two suggestions is correct but that instead the two should be seen as outcomes of the same driving forces for change. Thus I do not suggest that the financial structure during the traditional phase was the result of the particular financial environment; the two interacted in complex ways with each other, one reinforcing the other.

Take, for example, the city banks. Without the rapid growth of the established firms, their loan demand would have been less. Without the loan demand, the banks would not have been required to be marginally funded by the Bank of Japan. Without the last dependence, the method of "window guidance" would have been less effective. At the same time, without the loan demand, the financial institutions would have found it more difficult to accept the forced-subscription method for the public government issues, which in turn would have forced more interest-rate freedoms. Many similar dependencies could be found.

If the above is correct, it is remarkable to note that, as Japan moved away from the traditional system, its overall performance has remained exceptional. Current account accumulation replaced high growth as the new enviable trait of the country. It seems that the hypothesis about the influence of the financial system on Japan's performance cannot be correct for the traditional phase if, during the emergence of the new system, an equally successful performance is observed. On the one hand it should be emphasized that the changes toward a system more reliant on the price mechanism has not totally abrogated the old relationship system. On the other hand, a speculation may be made about the role the system is currently playing in achieving a different kind of success from what has been observed before.

As the primary role of the system was to ensure a particular allocation of capital during the traditional phase, in the newly emerging system more standard forms of competition for capital *within* Japan have occurred. Here relationships and a position of acceptance play less of a role. At the same time it is now the overall national saving behavior that reflects the most distinguishing feature of the Japanese economy. To put it differently: with high national savings and trading partners such as the United States, with negative national savings, the performance of the Japanese economy fits very simply within any standard, open macroeconomic framework. In contrast, during the traditional phase, growth was stimulated through a guided rationing system that may have been able to deal with certain information problems effectively.

This is the reason to suggest that careful measures of the cost of capital may provide, at best, marginal insights for the developments during that period. If, however, a financial system is currently observed that conforms more to standard notions and if, at the same time, the Japanese corporations face more standard financial trade-offs and are perhaps more driven to apply choice models in investment decisions that explicitly recognize a price-competitive capital market, then it is more likely that, in international competition, business decisions may today indeed be differentially affected for Japanese versus U.S. corporations, by cost of capital considerations.

Take, again, the impact of rating agencies on Japanese bond issuers. They will enforce, through their rating standards, new methods of firm evaluation. Similarly, with many corporations' equity investments currently residing in the so-called Tokkin funds, different pressures for stock performance can be expected. If, allowing for these developments, more traditional U.S. corporate objectives will be assimilated into Japanese business practice, models such as DCF analysis are bound to play a larger role. Again, I do not suggest that the Japanese corporate decision-making process will be identical to the one in the United States, but the direction of change will be such that a less rather than a more distinct structure will be seen.

7.5   The Cost of Capital

Since another contribution (Frankel, in this volume) deals explicitly with the cost of capital issues, I will only present the highlights of the controversy in relation to what has been argued before. With evidence being almost continuously produced (revised and refined), the investigation into a possible cost of capital advantage for Japanese firms has proven to be a growth industry. Contributions such as Hatsopoulos (1983), Hatsopoulos, Krugman and Summers (1988), Baldwin (1986), Ando and Auerbach (1985) and (1987), Friend and Tokutsu (1987), Hodder (1988) and Luehrman and Kester (1988) have all looked at (aspects of) the cost of capital to explain differences in corporate performance between the United States and Japan. Not surprisingly, given the vastly different institutional environments in the two countries, the papers either had to try to account for specific national conventions (e.g., hidden reserves, pension fund liabilities, etc.) or to ignore them. A third avenue of pursuit rested on looking at a "stripped down" version of the controversy— ignoring the cost of capital for firms, but instead looking at one determining factor, such as the risk-free interest rate.

The ultimate purpose of these investigations, in contrast to macroeconomic explorations into the national saving behavior, was to explain corporate performance and investment decisions, and, mostly implicitly, the significant gain of world market share by Japanese firms, often at the cost of U.S. firms. Still, the investigation into possible different WACCs for Japan and the United States, has shown contradictory results after increasingly careful estimation, even for the same authors (cf. Ando and Auerbach 1985 and Ando and Auerbach 1987). But even recent studies are able to generate very different conclusions. Baldwin (1986) concludes that the cost of capital differences on a risk-adjusted basis are minor, while Ando and Auerbach (1987), in contrast, find significant cost advantages for Japanese firms. Hodder (1988) provides a synthesis between the two results, relying heavily on information problems and monitoring costs.

Attempting to avoid the company specific problems in measuring the WACC, Luehrman and Kester (1989) focus instead on a central input of the WACC and concentrate on a real risk-free return comparison between the United States and Japan. They find that real returns are not equalized between the two countries, but that the deviations do not systematically favor Japan. Such differences in the real returns are consistent with findings by authors such as Frankel and Froot (1987) if one considers long-run, sustained deviations from purchasing power. The latter finding, however, suggests that the yen-dollar relationship has been characterized by a long-term appreciation of the yen, thus leading to suggest that the real return, even in the absence of barriers to capital mobility, should have remained favorable to Japan.

Since I argue that the institutional framework has been central in considering corporate finance in Japan, rather than a simple measure of the cost of capital (such as the WACC), it is more important to consider the cost of capital controversy with an eye toward the future. Two important trends have to be acknowledged; one is that the relationship system in Japan is receding—it may mean that many of the information-related problems, so effectively dealt with in the older system, will start to play a more traditional role. The other is that increasingly international capital market integration is taking place and that thus the access of corporations from one country to another country's capital market is facilitated.[10]

However, even if one were to assume that the cost of capital was identical to Japanese and U.S. firms, that companies in both countries employed identical investment-decision models, that tax structures were similar, and that for all companies the same pressures from shareholders and debt holders obtained, it is clear that the U.S. "competitiveness" problem could still not be solved through the corporate cost of capital "equalization." Instead, the underlying reasons for the loss of U.S. world market share has to be acknowledged as a lack of national savings in the United States.

While some, such as Scott (1984), have argued about a possible loss of U.S. "competitiveness" early on, it is only more recently that the concept has captured popular attention. Clearly the large current account imbalances have aided in the recognition of the problem. Still, these very current account imbalances indicate that the cause of the problem cannot lie in the cost of capital difference; it has to rely on a national savings argument.

Thus, much of the debate about the cost of capital may be about the internal distribution of growth of corporations within the confines of the national savings behavior. In this respect, it is not surprising that a group of prominent U.S. economists asked their colleagues recently to petition for a sales tax to generate national savings; in contrast to individual executives who may concentrate on their cost of capital, for this group of professional economists it is the aggregate performance of U.S. industry that stands central. Similarly, it should be clear that, for Japan, a requirement of national dissaving becomes imperative, given its large (and sustained) current account surplus. To achieve such adjustments in the national saving rates will require policy initiative, as it seems clear that during the last half-decade automatic adjustment has been elusive at best. In particular, emphasis can be put on the U.S. government's saving behavior as a major influence on the national saving rate as shown by Summers and Carroll (1987).

7.6 Conclusions

This paper argues that both the financial system and the cost of capital matter in explaining the relatively extraordinary performance of Japan—not as the sole determinants but as important inputs. It is shown that Japan's distinct national financial system displayed characteristics that were established in a relatively short period of time after the Meiji Restoration (1868) and fully developed in a period of two decades (1954–74). The central feature of the

---

10. While international capital mobility may have increased, several authors have shown that due to a failure of purchasing power parity in the short term, this does not mean that real interest rate equalization takes place (see Frankel's contribution to this volume).

"relationship" system was that it allowed for guided capital rationing. It achieved this outcome through financial product market segmentation, price regulation, and hierarchical organization. Within the context of standard economic models, the system was organized in such a way as to deal effectively with many problems currently associated with terms such as asymmetric information, agency problems, and incentive compatibility.

A complex, rich, institutionally varied system undoubtedly helped Japan to focus on its growth strategy, reflecting a national consensus of objective and an inability of those excluded from access to preferential capital to seriously challenge the system. In Japan, indirect finance came to dominate and allowed for capital structures significantly different from what was observed in the United States. At the same time, there seems to have been built into the system an ability for corporations to avoid earnings performance pressure; access to financial capital was not the result of profit targets but instead was vested in the relationships with the suppliers of finance. Obviously investment decision making did not conform with simple models that stress share-price maximization through discounted cash flow. In this sense it is misguided to expect indicators such as the weighted average cost of capital to shed significant light on the relative performance of Japanese firms as compared to their U.S. counterparts.

It was argued that the Japanese financial system underwent significant change during the 1970s. Not, as is commonly suggested because of external pressures to liberalize the financial service sector, but simply because the aftermath of the oil shock broke some of the dependencies and carefully created balances that had allowed the Japanese relationship to flourish. Again, the importance of institutional factors is enormous. With a less important relationship system, the Japanese financial market started to more closely resemble that of the United States. With new institutional factors, such as a less heavy reliance on bank financing, which had incorporated many information-sharing advantages, and new corporate organization forms (such as the Tokkin funds), new pressures may come to bear on the Japanese firm. Not surprisingly, rating agencies have now surfaced in Japan. In this new environment, shareholder pressures may grow, and one may speculate that more traditional models such as DCF may gain in currency—now, cost of capital differences may start to play a more transparent role, but they will have to be related to either institutional differences that allow for differences in capital structure or to failures of international capital mobility.

As a result it may be surprising that Japan has been able to continue to perform enviably, even though it is now the international asset accumulation rather than the growth performance that commands the center of attention. Here, I argue, it is most useful to revert back to the basic national income identity: it is the national saving behavior of the Japanese economy rather than individual corporations cost of capital advantages that deserve attention.

References

Abegglen, J. C., and G. S. Stalk, Jr., 1985. *Kaisha, The Japanese Corporation*. New York: Basic Books.

Ando, A., and A. J. Auerbach. 1985. The Corporate Cost of Capital in Japan and the U.S.: A Comparison. Working Paper no. 1762. National Bureau of Economic Research, Cambridge, Mass., October.

———. 1987. The Cost of Capital in the U.S. and Japan: A Comparison. Working Paper no. 2286. National Bureau of Economic Research, Cambridge, Mass., June.

Aoki, M. 1984. Shareholders' Non-unanimity on Investment Financing: Banks vs. Individual Investors. In *The Economic Analysis of the Japanese Firm*, ed. M. Aoki. New York: North Holland-Elsevier.

Asquith, P., and D. W. Mullins. 1986. Equity Issues and Offering Dilution. *Journal of Financial Economics* 15:61–89.

Baldwin, C. Y. 1986. The Capital Factor: Competing for Capital in a Global Environment. In *Competition in Global Industries*, ed. M. E. Porter. Boston: Harvard Business School Press.

Bank of Japan. Various issues. *Economics Statistics Annual, Research and Statistics Department*.

Bernanke, B. 1983. Non-monetary Effects of the Financial Crisis in the Propagation of the Great Depression. *American Economic Review* 73:257–76.

Bronte, S. 1982. *Japanese Finance: Markets and Institutions*. London: Euromoney Publications.

Chase Manhattan Bank. 1980. Chase Financial Policy. Report prepared for the U.S. Semiconductor Industry Association. New York, June.

Crum, C., and D. M. Meerschwam. 1986. From Relationship to Price Banking: The Loss of Regulatory Control. In *America versus Japan*, ed. T. K. McCraw. Cambridge, Mass.: Harvard Business School Press.

Ellsworth, R. R. 1985. Capital Markets and Competitive Decline. *Harvard Business Review* (September-October), pp. 171–83.

Feldman, R. A. 1986. *Japanese Financial Markets, Deficits, Dilemmas, and Deregulation*. Cambridge, Mass.: MIT Press.

Feldstein, M., and C. Horioka. 1980. Domestic Saving and International Capital Flows. *Economic Journal* 90:314–29.

Frankel, J. 1984. The Yen Dollar Agreement: Liberalizing Japanese Capital Markets. Policy Analyses in International Economics, no. 9. Institute for International Economics, Washington, D.C.

Frankel, J., and K. Froot. 1987. Short-term and Long-term Expectations of the Yen/Dollar Exchange Rates: Evidence from Survey Data. *Journal of the Japanese and International Economies* 1:249–74.

Friend, I., and I. Tokutsu. 1987. The Cost to Capital to Corporations in Japan and the U.S. *Journal of Banking and Finance* 11:313–27.

Gultekin, N. B., and T. Taga. 1987. Financial Management in Japanese Corporations. Manuscript. Wharton School, University of Pennsylvania.

Hatsopoulos, G. 1983. High Cost of Capital: Handicap of American Industry. Study for the American Business Conference and Thermo Electron Corp.

Hatsopoulos, G., P. R. Krugman, and L. Summers. 1988. U.S. Competitiveness: Beyond the Trade Deficit. *Science* (July), pp. 299–307.

Hayashi, T. 1986. Why Is Japan's Saving Rate so Apparently High? In *NBER Macroeconomics Annual 1986*, ed. Stanley Fischer, 1:147–234. Cambridge, Mass.: MIT Press.

Hodder, J. 1985. Investment and Financial Decision Making in Japanese Firms: A Comparison with U.S. Practices. Manuscript. Stanford University.
———. 1986. Evaluation of Manufacturing Investments: A Comparison of U.S. and Japanese Practices. *Financial Management* 15, no. 1:17–23.
———. 1988. Capital Structure and the Cost of Capital in the U.S. and Japan. Manuscript. Stanford University.
Hoshi, T. A. Kashyap, and D. Scharfstein. 1988. Corporate Structure, Liquidity and Investment: Evidence from Japanese Panel Data. Working Paper no. 2071-88. Sloan School of Management, MIT, Cambridge, Mass.
Japan Securities Research Institute 1986. *Securities Market in Japan.* Tokyo.
Johnson, C. 1982. *MITI and the Japanese Miracle: The Growth of Industrial Policy, 1925–1975.* Palo Alto, Calif.: Stanford University Press.
Krugman, P. R. 1988. Introduction: New Thinking about Trade Policy. In *Strategic Trade Policy and the New International Economics.* ed. P. R. Krugman. Cambridge, Mass.: MIT Press.
Luehrman, T., and W. C. Kester. 1989. Real Interest Rates and the Cost of Capital: A Comparison of the United States and Japan. *Japan and the World Economy* 1:1–23.
McCraw, T. K., and P. O'Brien. 1986. Production and Distribution: Competition Policy and Industry Structure. In *America versus Japan,* ed. T. K. McCraw, pp. 77–116. Cambridge, Mass.: Harvard Business School Press.
Miller, M., and K. Rock. 1985. Dividend Policy under Asymmetric Information. *Journal of Finance* 40:1031–51.
Monroe, W. F. 1973. *Japan: Financial Markets and the World Economy.* New York: Praeger Publishers.
Myers, S. C., and N. S. Majluf. 1984. Corporate Financing and Investment Decisions When Firms Have Information That Investors Do not Have. *Journal of Financial Economics* 13:187–221.
Presnell, L. S., ed. 1975. *Money and Banking in Japan.* New York: Macmillan Press.
Prindl, A. R. 1981. *Japanese Finance, A Guide to Banking in Japan.* New York: Wiley.
Revell, J. 1973. *The British Financial System.* London: Macmillan.
Scott, B. R. 1984. National Strategy for Stronger U.S. Competitiveness. *Harvard Business Review* (March-April), pp. 77–91.
Stein, J. 1989. Efficient Capital Markets, Inefficient Firms: A Model of Myopic Corporate Behavior. *Quarterly Journal of Economics* 104:655–59.
Summers, L., and C. Carroll. 1987. Why Is U.S. National Saving so Low? *Brookings Papers on Economic Activity,* no. 2: 607–35.
Tamura, Tatsuro. 1987. Changes in Corporate Fund Raising and Management, pt. 2. *FAIR Fact Series: Japan's Finance Markets,* vol. 29.
U.S. Federal Trade Commission. *Quarterly Financial Report for Manufacturing, Mining and Trade Corporations.* Washington, D.C.: Government Printing Office.
Wallich, H. C., and M. I. Wallich. 1976. Banking and Finance. In *Asia's New Giant, How the Japanese Economy Works,* ed. H. Patrick and H. Rosovsky. Washington, D.C.: Brookings.

Comment   Koichi Hamada

Meerschwam discusses various historical, institutional, and policy-related factors that could have affected the cost of capital in Japan or that could have made the concept of the cost of capital itself less relevant in Japan than in Western countries. The topics covered are rather extensive so that the paper serves as a good introduction to this issue as well as an informative background paper on the quantitative study of the cost of capital by Frankel. The attempt to relate the issue to the incentive mechanism under asymmetric information is a very useful one. As an economist, I wish this paper were written in such a way as to enable the reader to see transparently what kind of theoretical model is behind various arguments contained in it. In any case, this paper let me reconsider several institutional features of the Japanese financial market. I will discuss some of these issues that came to my mind while I was reading this extensive work.

As the author argues, the Japanese financial system was a highly regulated system during the 1950s and 1960s. Already in the 1960s, the market mechanism became quite dominant. The author emphasizes the year 1974 as the turning point that marks the period when the high growth of the Japanese economy was halted and the resulting accumulation of government debt changed the structure of the flow of funds. The process of deregulation or liberalization had already started, however, during the late 1960s. One factor to which the author does not pay sufficient attention is the ceiling of nominal interest rate, like the Regulation Q in the United States. Large depositors were given implicit interest by various side payments; for example, the gift of furniture or tickets to an excursion trip. But the small depositors could only get such trifles as tissue paper, and even the amount of that was once limited by coalition talks among banks. This low cost of supply of funds to commercial banks must have been a factor to reduce the cost of capital to the insiders that had access to commercial lending from large *keiretsu* banks. Also, the existence of the very high interest rate (often more than 100 percent per annum) indicates that the outsiders had to be satisfied with the very high cost of capital. Certainly, the existence of a segmented financial market was a factor that makes the calculation, as well as the interpretation, of the cost of capital difficult. I cannot agree with the author to the extent that the discounted cash flow or the cost of capital was irrelevant, but I agree in that we should at least get an explicit account of the segmentation of the market.

It makes sense to argue that the traditional segmented system gave an advantage to insiders in terms of incentives to invest. Face-to-face customer relationships might have been a better way to cope with asymmetric information than the impersonal, standardized channel of funds through marketable

Koichi Hamada is a professor of economics at the Economic Growth Center, Yale University, and a research associate of the National Bureau of Economic Research securities. The questions remain, however. Why did this system develop in Japan and not, for example, in the United States? And why has it been replaced by the market system in the present Japan? The entry barrier to the insiders should have been very high. Then, these collusive activities might have been quite expensive from the standpoint of depositors and small customers of commercial banks.

Finally, let me discuss the author's concluding remark that not the cost of capital but the amount of savings is the crucial problem to understanding the relative decline of productivity growth in the United States. First of all, as the author admits in the introduction, such factors as labor productivity and quality control are important as well. Second, I do not think that the amount of savings and the cost of capital are alternative concepts. The cost of capital can be measured by the abscissa of the intersection of the demand and the supply curve of funds. If the supply curve shifts to the right, then the realized price of the funds will tend to be lower. If the world capital market is fully integrated, the cost of capital among countries will be equated by the flow of funds from high-saving countries to low-saving ones. If there exist impediments to international capital flows, as Feldstein and Horioka argue, then the high-saving countries will normally enjoy the lower cost of capital unless investment opportunities among countries are drastically different.

Comment   Robert Alan Feldman

David Meerschwam's paper contributes to our knowledge of Japanese financial markets by emphasizing two major themes, the role of the financial system as a risk bearer and the importance of the insider-outsider phenomenon. Rather than nitpick at arguments in the paper, I would like to offer some reflections that it stimulated.

The Financial System as Risk Sharer

The financial industry exists to transform assets, to disburse risk, and to provide a menu of combinations of return and insurance. In examining the evolution of a financial system, it is important to ask what types of asset transformation were carried out, whom this transformation benefited, how risks were disbursed, what combinations of return and risk were provided, and who were the providers and beneficiaries of the implicit or explicit insurance. The precise mix of risks faced by both firms and intermediaries is a critical determinant of financial structure. The types of contracts and risk-sharing formulas

Robert Alan Feldman is vice president and senior economist at Salomon Brothers, Inc.

that are optimal for any system naturally reflect this structure of risks, which may change over time.

The high growth period in Japan was one of relatively great risks external to firms, the variability of growth being the key risk. However, international conditions, for example, external demand and oil and commodity prices, were stable. Risks internal to the firm were also mixed. The high educational level of the work force relative to the stage of development meant that labor shortages could be overcome; the ability to follow practices in other countries and improve on them was a source of growth without excessive R&D burdens. But management mistakes were inevitable in an economy changing so rapidly. For banks, credit risk was high but system risk low, especially with government policy playing so large a role in ensuring the safety of intermediaries.

With the end of the high-growth period, however, the mix if risk characteristics changed for both firms and intermediaries. The variability of the cycle has been much lower. But international conditions have been far more variable, with major oil shocks in both directions, exchange rate fluctuations, and changing growth patterns in the rest of the world. For banks, credit risk remains important, but the greater integration of world financial markets has increased system risk substantially. And event risk has raised the correlation of returns on assets held by intermediaries.

In light of this new mix of risks, it seems inevitable that the Japanese financial system would change its mode of operation. An economy with good long-term prospects but high short-term variability naturally lends itself to long-term banking relationships that preserve access to credit in lower growth periods in return for the banks' implicitly taking a piece of the action through equity positions. But with less variability and more worry about longer-term performance, it seems logical for firms to stop paying insurance premia for credit access in downswings and for banks to shift to shorter-term horizons in asset choice. Greater event risk would also tend to weaken long-term relationships, since, because of its international nature, the losers and the gainers from shocks cannot be brought into the same insurance pool.

The Insider-Outsider Problem

Many of the papers at this conference, including Meerschwam's, have touched on the insider-outsider problem. Even for Japanese firms, it can be difficult to penetrate established long-term relationships, and so it is important to understand the nature of such relationships. I think that *The Evolution of Cooperation,* by Robert Axelrod, has much to contribute to this understanding.[1]

Axelrod asserts that life is not a bowl of cherries but rather an iterated prisoner's dilemma game of unknown length. He then shows that, under reason-

---

1. Robert Axelrod, *The Evolution of Cooperation* (New York: Basic Books, 1984).

able payoff matricies, the optimal strategy is tit for tat, that is, to cooperate on the first move and then respond as your opponent acted on the previous move. He also shows that a colony of "tit for tat-ers" can, if sufficiently large, invade a world of mean-strategy opponents and not only prosper but grow. This model may hold the key to understanding insider-outsider (i.e., *keiretsu*) behavior in Japan. Even though members of a cooperating group tend to have lower average scores than some clever but mean opponents, they still thrive in the long run. This result suggests that one way for foreigners to crack the Japanese market is to become members of the insider groups. Such membership is particularly important in an age when information exchange is a key element in value creation.

8   Japanese Finance in the 1980s: A Survey

Jeffrey A. Frankel

8.1 Introduction

The structure of Japanese financial markets and the behavior of observed financial prices have raised a number of important interrelated questions in the minds of American observers, among others. The first set, of particular concern to American businessmen, pertain to:

1. *The cost of capital to Japanese firms.* Is it lower than the cost of capital to U.S. and other firms, providing an explanation for the higher rate of investment in Japan? And if so, why? What are the implications, if any, for the trade balance? The cost of capital is usually represented as a weighted average of the cost of borrowing (measured, e.g., by the real interest rate) and the cost of equity financing (inferred, e.g., from the ratio of required corporate earnings to the price of equity). A major theme of Meerschwam (in this volume), and for the conclusion of this paper as well, is that this standard way of viewing the cost-of-capital question is incomplete. But, for the moment, it does serve to introduce the next two Japanese financial prices whose behavior has raised puzzles.

2. *The Japanese interest rate.* Is it lower than that in the United States and other industrialized countries, in real terms? If so, why?

3. *Japanese equity prices.* Why are they so high relative, for example, to earnings? Alternatively, why did they rise so much in the 1980s? One of a number of possible contributing explanations for high price/earnings ratios is number 2 above, a low interest rate (used to discount expected future earnings

Jeffrey Frankel is professor of economics at the University of California at Berkeley and a research associate of the National Bureau of Economic Research.

The author gratefully acknowledges advice and suggestions from David Meerschwam and comments on earlier drafts also from Robert Dekle, Ken Froot, Michael Kinsley, Paul Krugman, Hiro Lee, Yuzuru Ozeki, Ulrike Schaede, Hiroshi Shibuya, and Shinji Takagi. A disclaimer that the survey is not exhaustive applies, particularly with respect to writings that appear only in Japanese.

or dividends into current equity prices). Another is a high expected real growth rate in the economy (raising expected future earnings relative to observed current earnings). Because corporations hold land, yet another of the contributing factors to high equity prices is high Japanese land prices.

4. *Japanese land prices.*   Why are they so high relative, for example, to rents? Alternatively, why did they rise so much in the 1980s? The two contributing explanations given for high equity prices apply equally here: a low interest rate (used to discount expected future rents into current land prices) and a high expected economic growth rate (raising expected future rents relative to observed current rents). A final question that, the paper shall argue, may be intrinsically tied to the question of low Japanese interest rates, relates to the exchange rate.

5. *The foreign exchange value of the yen.*   Why is it so high, in real terms? Alternatively, why has it increased so much over time? What are the implications?

No single paper can hope to answer all these questions. Much is written on the subject of Japanese financial markets every year. The institutional details, as well as the market prices themselves, change rapidly, by virtue of domestic financial deregulation and innovation, international financial liberalization, and tax reform. A goal of this paper is to survey the issues, including a variety of recent contributions (many of them unpublished) to the study of one or another of the financial market prices enumerated above, in brief enough form that one can see how the different questions fit together. The survey does not purport to be exhaustive of the literature, however.

There is a fundamental thread that winds through the issues, and it is worth spelling it out here. This paper subscribes to the common view that a low real interest rate and a high expected growth rate are two major factors explaining high price/earnings ratios in the stock market and high price/rental ratios in the land market in Japan. One respect in which the paper deviates from conventional views is in arguing that the Japanese real interest rate may have remained low in the 1980s despite high integration into international financial markets. Even so, a major apparent puzzle that remains is to explain why price/earnings and price/rental ratios were not just as high (or even higher) in the 1960s and 1970s, when Japanese real interest rates were just as low (or even lower) and Japanese growth rates were just as high (or—until 1973— even higher). The difficulty, in other words, is to explain why price/earnings and price/rental ratios increased so much in the 1980s.

The proposed answer is that, in previous decades and especially prior to 1973, institutional aspects of the Japanese financial system, such as those discussed in Meerschwam (in this volume), rendered the observed interest rate in large part irrelevant for the pricing of assets such as equities and land. This answer implies that anyone able to borrow from a bank or government agency at artificially low interest rates for the purpose of acquiring land or corporate equity, could have made "excess" profits; but not just anyone was able to do so. Such sources of funds were not available to the man in the street, or even to the corporation in the street. To those favored corporations that did have access to such funds, such as members of the industrial groupings known as *keiretsu,* the number of profitable investment projects typically exceeded the supply of funds available.

The international financial liberalization that has taken place in Japan over the last 10 years has been important for many reasons, not least because it forced the pace of domestic financial liberalization. But it is possible that the primary effect of the structural changes in the 1970s was *not* to bring the level of "the" cost of funds in Japan up to the level of the world real interest rate as is conventionally suggested.[1] *Rather, the primary effect was to bring the cost of capital facing a typical unaffiliated Japanese firm or institutional investor down toward the cost of capital facing a favored* keiretsu *firm.* This process included both the accumulation of a vast pool of savings—particularly in the hands of institutional investors—and the development of active bond and equity markets in which these funds could be invested. The increase in the pool of funds available for arbitrage purposes helps to explain the price increases in equity and land markets in the 1980s.

The paper begins with the issue of access to cheap borrowing, then shifts to a consideration of the equity markets (including such issues as dividend-payout rates, P/E ratios, and corporate taxation), considers domestic and international determinants of the real interest rate, and concludes with a discussion of internal financing. Measurement and accounting problems occur from the beginning and will be discussed as we proceed. But, throughout, the paper attempts to concentrate on those trends in financial prices that are so strong that one cannot easily attribute them entirely to measurement problems.

8.2   The Standard Weighted-Average Measure of the Cost of Capital

The claim that the cost of capital is lower in Japan, perhaps giving Japanese firms an "unfair" advantage, arose with some American businessmen in the early 1980s. The original statements (Semiconductor Industry Association 1980; Hatsopoulos 1983), while highly influential, are considered by some to have been somewhat simplistic. Later versions are more persuasive (e.g., Hatsopoulos and Brooks 1986, 1989 and, esp., Hatsopoulos, Krugman, and Summers 1988). A traditional measure of the cost of capital is a weighted average of the cost of borrowing and the cost of equity:

$$(1) \qquad\qquad r_c = w\, r_d + (1 - w)\, r_e,$$

1. For example, by Balassa and Noland (1988, p. 113). As of May 1990, one year after the first draft of this paper was written, the cost of capital does appear to be approximately as high in Japan as in the United States, as the result of increases in interest rates and an accompanying decline in the Japanese stock market.

where r_d is the cost of debt, r_e is the cost of equity, and w is the relative weight of debt in total financing. Under this definition, the claim can be broken down into some combination of the following three possibilities: (*a*) the cost of borrowing is lower in Japan, (*b*) the cost of equity is lower in Japan, or (*c*) the weight on debt financing (versus equity financing) is higher in Japan. All three statements contain some truth.[2]

8.2.1   Real Interest Rates

Nominal interest rates in Japan have been below those in the United States during most of the postwar period, and continuously since 1977. Japanese inflation has also been relatively low since 1977, and it is of course the real interest rate, not the nominal rate, that matters for investment. But calculations using 10-year government bond yields suggest that Japanese real interest rates were below U.S. real rates virtually continuously from 1967 to 1988 (see fig. 8.1).[3]

Bernheim and Shoven (1986) estimate that the Japanese real interest rate, on average, lay below the U.S. real rate during the period 1971–82, although the difference was quite small for the long-term rates, which presumably are the ones that matter for investment: 0.23, 0.30, or 0.93, depending whether expected inflation is estimated by, respectively, the inflation rate over the preceding year, the average ex post rate, or a simple ARIMA model.[4]

In the period 1982–84, the U.S. long-term real interest rate rose substantially above that in Japan and other G-7 countries.[5] This differential is widely considered to have been the result of a U.S. fiscal expansion (which was accommodated neither by monetary policy nor by private saving in the United States), counterpoised to fiscal contraction in Japan and some major European countries.[6] Bernheim and Shoven (1986) put the U.S.-Japan long-term real interest differential, on average for the period 1983–85, at 2.02.

2. The three-way breakdown has been calculated by Friend and Tokutsu (1987), among others.
3. The charts are borrowed from an uncirculated paper by Lawler, Loopesko, and Dudey (1988). Fig. 8.1 above may understate the Japanese real interest rate in the 1970s, both because the actual inflation rates that are used overstate expected inflation rates and because the government bond rates that are used were too low to be willingly absorbed by private investors.
4. Lawler, Loopesko, and Dudey (1988, p. 26) show real interest rates on Japanese one-year government bonds that have been below U.S. yields during virtually the entire 1965–88 period. Friend and Tokutsu (1987) find that the real cost of debt, weighted between short term and long term, was .80 percentage points lower in Japan than the United States on average over the period 1962–84 (1.70 lower over the period 1970–84).
5. The increase in the U.S. real interest differential from 1981 to mid-1984 is often credited with much of the explanation for the contemporaneous appreciation of the dollar. The differential vis-à-vis the real interest rate in Japan was no larger than that vis-à-vis Germany and some other countries. But then the movement of the dollar against the yen was actually less than against the mark and other major European currencies (contrary to a widespread impression) and peaked in 1982 rather than February 1985.
6. One of the many possible references on the capital inflow that resulted from the shift in the U.S. monetary/fiscal mix in the 1980s is Frankel (1988a). References on the forces behind the inflow from Japan in particular are given in Frankel (1988b).

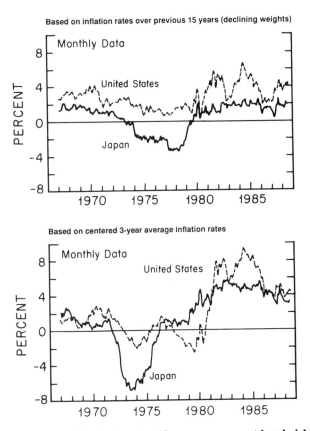

Fig. 8.1   Long-term real interest rates, 10-year government bond yields
Source: Lawler, Loopesko, and Dudey (1988).

The U.S.-Japan real interest differential has been smaller in the years since 1985 than it was in the first half of the 1980s.[7] This differential, even if small, was still present, however, in mid-1989 (anywhere from one-half percent to 3 percent, depending on the measure). I estimated the 10-year real interest differential to have been 0.8 percent as of the end of August, 1989.[8] (We post-

7. This was .58 since 1985 according to French and Poterba (1989, p. 40) (average of first quarters of 1986, 1987 and 1988); they use long-term government bond yields minus the previous year's inflation rate.

8. On 23 August 1989 the nominal interest differential between the United States and Japan was 3.3 percent for 10-year government bond yields, 3.5 percent for one-year Eurocurrency rates, and 5.6 percent for bank prime lending rates. A survey of forecasters conducted by Alan Teck on that day put the difference in expected inflation rates at 2.5 percent for the 10-year horizon (4.75 percent in the United States vs. 2.25 percent in Japan) and 2.6 percent for the one-year horizon. (*Currency Forecasters' Digest*, White Plains, N.Y., September 1989.) The CPI inflation differential was 3.3 percent in 1988 and 2.0 percent in the first five months of 1989 (IMF data). As noted earlier, some further narrowing of the real interest differential took place in early 1990.

pone, until sec. 8.4, the question of how such a differential can have persisted despite the apparent international integration of financial markets.)

The standard "capitalization" formula for the equity price/earnings ratio and the price/rental ratio is

$$(2) \qquad \frac{1}{r - g},$$

where r is the real interest rate used to discount expected future earnings or rents to the present, and g is the expected growth rate of earnings or rents, as the case may be. ("Earnings" should really be defined as net profits after new investment, for the formula to be correct; see n. 18 below.)[9] Sometimes the best we can do to get an idea of the expected growth rate of earnings or rents is to assume that they are equal to the expected growth rate of the economy. If $r - g$ were a number like .02 in the world economy at large (which admittedly may be too low), then the Japanese interest rate would only have to be lower by .01—or the growth rate higher by .01, for that matter—to explain a doubling of the price/earnings ratio.[10]

Nevertheless, because the real interest differential is thought to be small, with the exception of the early 1980s, those who argue that the cost of capital is low in Japan and that this has presented a problem for the competitiveness of U.S. industry ever since 1973 (e.g., Hatsopoulos, Krugman, and Summers 1988) tend not to emphasize the real interest rate. They choose, rather, to emphasize the cost of equity financing and the relative weight of debt versus equity in corporate financing. (We will return to the role of the real interest rate later, however.)

8.2.2 Leverage (Debt/Equity Ratios)

In the past, Japanese corporations have had a much higher ratio of debt to equity than U.S. corporations, that is, they have been much more highly leveraged. (In terms of eq. [1] earlier, the debt/equity ratio is $w/(1 - w)$.) In the period 1970–72, for example, debt/equity ratios in Japan were four times as high as in the United States. This commonly observed characteristic of the Japanese system is one major reason why calculations often show a lower overall cost of capital in Japan than in the United States; equity financing is known to be more expensive than debt financing in any market, presumably

9. The formula also works for firms' dividend/price ratio, again with the growth rate properly defined.

10. A similar point is made by French and Poterba (1989, p. 19). However, they conclude that, while a lower real rate of interest in Japan might be able to explain the high level of Japanese stock prices *on average* during their sample period (the 1970s and 1980s), it cannot explain the *increase* during the last three years, 1986–88.

because portfolio investors demand a higher expected return on equity to compensate them for higher risk.[11]

How have Japanese firms been able to rely so heavily on debt? As a number of authors have pointed out, a particular debt/equity ratio that would be very risky for a U.S. firm may have been less risky for a Japanese firm. There are several reasons for this. (1) Much of the borrowing, particularly for members of a *keiretsu,* was from the firm's main bank. A main bank would not cut off lending in time of financial difficulty; to the contrary it would do all it could to see the company through (e.g., Abegglen and Stock 1985; Crum and Meerschwam 1987; Meerschwam, in this volume). (2) Until recently, all loans had to be collaterized. This certainly reduced the risk from the viewpoint of the bank, which in turn helps explain the reduced danger, from the viewpoint of the corporation, that bank lending (as well as the ability to sell bonds) would dry up in time of difficulty. (3) It has been suggested that such government policies as allowing the formation of cartels in event of recession reduced the risk of financial difficulty or bankruptcy.[12] (4) It has also been suggested that the practice of paying workers a substantial fraction of their compensation in the form of twice-yearly bonuses that vary with the success of the company acts as a sort of profit-sharing mechanism and again reduces the risk of bankruptcy.[13]

In any case, it is important to note that the seemingly robust regularity that "Japanese firms are highly leveraged" now appears to be a thing of the past. The debt/equity ratio fell throughout most of the 1970s and 1980s, and has by one measure fallen *below* the level in the United States, as shown in the last two columns of table 8.1 (from French and Poterba 1989).[14] This reversal is due only in small part to the increase in corporate leverage in the 1980s that generated so much alarm in the United States, partly because of its association with "junk bonds." The reversal is due primarily to the decline in Japan, which is in turn due, at least in an arithmetic sense, to the soaring value of Japanese equities and to decreased reliance on the main bank system as well as to the

11. The apparent conclusion that a firm can lower its cost of capital by increasing the weight on debt would only hold if the cost of equity could be assumed to be independent (whereas it might in fact be expected to rise as the firm's levered beta rises).

12. On the so-called recession cartels, see Yamamura (1982) and Meerschwam (in this volume).

13. Other reasons have been given as well why a given corporate balance sheet that might spell excessive risk in the United States would not be as worrisome in Japan. For example, Abegglen and Stalk (1985, p. 165) argue in this connection that a typical Japanese firm does not consolidate the financial assets held by its subsidiaries into its own balance sheet—where a corresponding U.S. firm might do so—and carries land and securities on its books at original cost. (But the fact that much of Japanese equity is held by other firms, so that the total amount of equity in Japan is not as large as appears on the books, seems like a reason why Japanese debt/equity ratios might be understated.) Some of these accounting questions are discussed under the heading of price/earnings ratios below.

14. This occurred in 1986. The debt/equity ratio actually fell to half the U.S. level in an estimate for 1988 (according to French and Poterba 1989, p. 8 and table 4).

Table 8.1   **Price-Earnings Ratios (P/E), Dividend-Price Ratios (Div/P, in %), and Debt-Equity Ratios (D/Eq), Japan and the United States, 1970–88**

Year	P/E		Div/P		D/Eq	
	Japan	United States	Japan	United States	Japan	United States
1970	9.0	18.6	3.9	3.3	1.63	.54
1971	13.5	18.7	3.9	2.9	2.13	.50
1972	23.3	19.3	2.4	2.5	2.23	.48
1973	13.9	12.3	2.1	3.4	1.38	.69
1974	16.5	7.9	2.7	5.0	1.44	1.04
1975	25.2	11.8	2.5	3.8	2.13	.78
1976	22.0	11.2	2.1	3.7	1.88	.72
1977	19.3	9.1	2.0	5.0	1.82	.85
1978	21.5	8.2	1.7	5.2	1.62	.91
1979	16.6	7.5	1.8	5.3	1.78	.82
1980	17.9	9.6	1.6	4.4	1.59	.64
1981	24.9	8.2	1.5	5.3	1.64	.76
1982	23.7	11.9	1.4	4.6	1.44	.70
1983	29.4	12.6	1.2	3.7	1.03	.62
1984	26.3	10.4	1.2	4.1	.93	.74
1985	29.4	15.4	1.2	3.4	.71	.66
1986	58.6	18.7	.8	3.0	.45	.65
1987	50.4	14.1	.8	3.2	.43	.71
1988	54.3	12.9	.6	3.0	.36[a]	.71[a]

Sources: From French and Poterba (1989), who give original sources for the ratios. Entries reflect values on last trading day of each year. The debt-equity ratio is defined as the book value of debt divided by the market value of equity.

[a]French and Poterba's estimates.

reduced need for external financing of any sort after 1973. Each of these factors will be discussed below.

8.3   Equity Capital

8.3.1   The Rate of Return on Equity: Stock Prices and Dividends

The third of the standard components of the overall cost of capital is the cost of equity financing, r_e in the standard equation. It is the most ambiguous of the components to measure. One approach has been to use the realized market rate of return on equity, that is, the dividend/price ratio plus the rate of increase of equity prices. Baldwin (1986) and Ando and Auerbach (1985) computed the overall return to debt plus equity in what are intended to be improvements on the Hatsopoulos (1983) approach of omitting equity altogether on the Japanese side of the calculation. They both found little evidence of a difference between Japan and the United States.[15] Ando and Auerbach (1985) found that the market rate of return to equity was in fact much *higher* in Japan (13.6% for the median of their sample of firms, vs. 2.2% for the U.S. firms). Subsequently, on a much larger sample of firms but with a similar methodology and time period, Ando and Auerbach (1988) found that the overall rate of return on capital was substantially lower in Japan than in the United States after all.[16]

Stockholders' realized rate of return on equity is, in any case, a very noisy indicator of their ex ante expectations, however. Friend and Tokutsu (1987, p. 317) pointed out that, while realized market rates of return on equity have been higher in Japan (over the period 1962–84) than in the United States, a reverse answer results if the dividend/price ratio is added to the rate of growth of dividends per share, rather than to the rate of growth of prices. Furthermore, looking at the problem from the viewpoint of the market investor rather than the firm might give the wrong answer if the stockholders' return to capital, measured over a finite sample, differs from what managers perceive as their required rate of return. Hatsopoulos and Brooks (1989) and Hodder (1988b, 1991) dissent from the Baldwin and Ando-Auerbach approaches on these grounds.[17]

In the absence of a speculative bubble, stock prices can be thought of either as the present discounted value of expected future dividends or the present discounted value of expected future earnings (as a proxy for cash flow,[18] which is more correct, as explained in n. 21 below). In both the United States and Japan the dividend payout rate (Div/E) is substantially less than 1, which suggests that the expected rate of growth of dividends is greater than the expected rate of growth of earnings (properly averaged over the perhaps distant future). Many rapidly growing companies pay no dividends at all, for example, preferring to reinvest all earnings into highly profitable projects. I consider the subject of dividends first and then turn to earnings in the next subsection.

There has been no upward trend in Japanese dividends per share over the last 20 years.[19] This makes it especially difficult to explain the high level of

15. Baldwin (1986) computes a risk-return frontier for each country and finds little difference between the two; i.e., the level of expected return for any given level of risk is similar. Ando and Auerbach (1985) is based on a fairly small sample of firms (for the period 1966–81). In addition to their calculation of the average rates of return, they also look at earnings/price ratios, discussed below.

16. They found that the before-tax returns were 6.5 percent in Japan, 12.3 percent in the United States. After-tax returns were 2.5 percent vs. 5.6 percent. The time period was 1967–83.

17. We save until later the argument that firms may have access to some funds that are cheaper than the expected rate of return on capital (that internal financing is cheaper than *both* the cost of debt and the cost of equity).

18. Free cash flow is defined as profit after tax minus changes in working capital minus other capital spending plus depreciation.

19. Minimum dividend-payout rates were established in the early 1970s (Meerschwam, in this volume).

Japanese stock prices, if one follows the common approach of choosing the present-discounted-value-of-future-dividends formula and estimating expected dividends from actual realized dividends. On the other hand, the observed high level of prices relative to dividends would be perfectly understandable if the increase in dividends were thought still to lie in the future. If dividends are treated as expected to grow at a constant rate gd from now on, then the current dividend/price ratio should equal $r_e - gd$, where r_e is the required rate of return on equity capital (which may be higher than the real interest rate because of a risk premium). As of 1988, the dividend price ratio was only .006 in Japan, as compared to .030 in the United States (third and fourth columns of table 8.1). If r_e is assumed to be the same in the two countries, then the current levels of stock prices make sense if and only if the dividends are expected to grow at a rate 2.4 percent faster in Japan than in the United States.

Why should Japanese dividends grow rapidly in the future, given that they have not done so in the past? We have no good theory of how shareholders wish to receive the return on their equity investment, that is, in the form of dividends or capital gains, or of how managers choose to pay dividends. In a sufficiently abstract (Modigliani-Miller) world the payout rate is indeterminate. On the one hand, tax considerations point to postponing the payment of dividends. On the other hand, the hypothesis that managers sometimes use funds for purposes other than maximizing shareholder welfare points to shareholders insisting on early payment of dividends. But dividends do get paid, and one hypothesis is that some shareholders like to receive quarterly checks for liquidity reasons. They could instead sell some stock to generate cash, but there are transactions costs to doing so. The ratio of retirees to working-age people is close to a minimum in Japan now, and will soon begin to rise until, by 2020, it will be the highest of the major industrialized countries. It is entirely plausible that wealthy Japanese retirees in the future will wish to receive high dividend payments on their holdings. Thus it is not entirely implausible that the expected future growth rate of dividends in Japan should be almost as high as the rate of return on capital, or that it should be 2.4 percent higher than the growth rate in the United States, notwithstanding the dividend record of the past 20 years.

An alternative approach is to look at the amount of *earnings* the firm is required to generate per unit of equity, that is, the inverse of the price/earnings ratio. If one is trying to determine whether the Japanese stock market may be overvalued, looking at earnings or cash flow has the advantage that they may be tied more directly to the productive capacity of the economy, as compared to dividends.[20]

---

20. Lawler, Loopesko, and Dudey (1988, p. 25) point out that the Japanese rate of growth of earnings per share need not be correlated with the rate of growth of the Japanese economy. On the other hand, dividends would appear to be one step further removed than are earnings, via the (difficult to determine) procedure whereby firms set their payout rates.

8.3.2   Price-Earnings Ratios

The price/earnings ratio (like the price/dividend ratio) has been observed to be higher in Japan than in the United States ever since the early 1970s. Because this difference could be explained by a lower discount rate in Japan, it is often the basis of arguments that the cost of equity capital is lower in Japan. But the difference could also have other explanations, such as a higher expected growth rate in Japan. If a high growth rate were the complete explanation, one would not want to attribute the high P/E ratios to a low discount rate. More broadly, one would not want to attribute the superior performance of Japanese industry necessarily to a low cost of capital. The paper now turns to the subject of the high and increasing P/E ratios in Japan, an important question in its own right.

Some, such as Ando and Auerbach, have looked at the P/E ratio because they are interested in the cost-of-capital question, and they consider P/E to be inversely related to the required rate of return r_e. Others, such as French and Poterba (1989) and Lawler, Loopesko, and Dudey (1988) are interested in the P/E ratio for its own sake. As shown in the first two columns of table 8.1, the reported P/E ratio for Japanese firms has been higher than the P/E ratio in the United States ever since 1972, and reached 58.6, three times as high as the U.S. level, in 1986. In the stock market crash of October 1987, the decline in Japan was smaller and shorter-lived, with the result that, by the end of 1988, Japan's reported P/E was more than four times that in the United States or the rest of the world (see fig. 8.2.)

Such an apparent discrepancy would be difficult to explain. If earnings are expected to grow at rate ge, then the earnings/price ratio should equal $r_e - ge$. The end-1988 differential between reported earnings/price ratios in the United States and Japan was .06[= .078 − .018]. The real growth rate of the Japanese economy averaged 1.56 percent faster than the U.S. economy over 1980–88; there is no particular reason to expect the real growth rate of the economy to increase in the future, or to expect the growth rate of earnings or cash flow to be higher than the growth rate of GNP. Thus the rate of return on capital r_e would have to be more than 4 percentage points lower than in the United States to explain the difference in reported P/E ratios. Such a finding would support the cost-of-capital-advantage school, but seems too large to be plausible.[21]

French and Poterba (1989), Ando and Auerbach (1985, 1988), and Lawler, Loopesko, and Dudey (1988), all emphasize the importance of correcting earnings for a number of measurement problems. Ando and Auerbach (1985) focus on three distortions related to inflation: depreciation accounting, inven-

---

21. As mentioned above, a more correct calculation would use free cash flow, which subtracts off investment, in place of earnings. More of earnings go to net investment in Japan than in the United States, in line with its higher growth rate. The implication is that the true equity cost of capital r_e is even lower in Japan than would appear from our attempt to apply the capitalization formula to the P/E ratio.

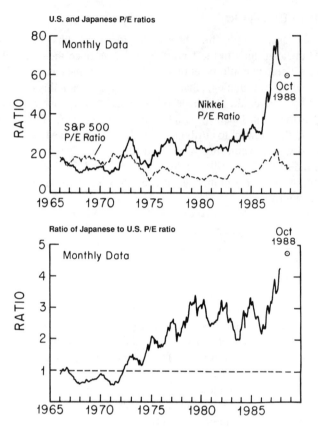

Fig. 8.2   Price/earnings ratios
Source: Lawler, Loopesko, and Dudey (1988).

tory accounting, and accounting for nominal liabilities. They find that correcting for these distortions increases estimated earnings, and therefore reduces the P/E ratio, for virtually all the Japanese firms in their sample, while it has no systematic effect for the U.S. firms.[22] The principal apparent source of the effect is that the Japanese firms rely more on debt than equity (see above), so the fact that inflation reduces the real value of their outstanding liabilities is more important for them.[23] If this is indeed the source of the effect, then the fact that the debt/equity ratio in Japan appears to have fallen

22. When Ando and Auerbach (1988) apply a corresponding correction for their measure of total return to capital, on the other hand, they find that the median rate for Japan falls more than that for the United States.
23. Apparently the fact that the inflation rate is lower in Japan has less of an effect than the higher debt/equity ratio.

below that in the United States in 1986 (and that inflation fell in both countries in the 1980s), suggests that the inflation accounting may no longer be as important for the P/E comparison.

French and Poterba (1989) have some other corrections to make to reported earnings and, therefore, P/E ratios. First is the point that earnings reported by U.S. corporations include the profits of subsidiaries, while those reported by Japanese firms do not (only actual dividends received from subsidiaries), so their earnings look smaller. A calculation to convert P/E ratios to what they would be if there were no cross-holding of corporate equity (which requires adjusting both earnings by removing intercorporate dividends and share prices) reduces the Japanese P/E ratio. In 1988 the adjustment is big enough to reduce it from 54.3 to 36.3.

Second, reported Japanese earnings also look smaller because they deduct (both on the firms' tax returns and on their financial statements) generous allowances for special reserves for such possible future contingencies as product returns, repairs, and retirement benefits. But this effect is relatively small.

Third, Japanese firms often take greater depreciation allowances, which, like the previous two factors, works to reduce reported earnings. (Unlike U.S. firms, when a Japanese firm claims a high depreciation allowance for tax purposes, it must do the same on its income statement.) French and Poterba (1989) consider two alternate ways of correcting for the difference in depreciation accounting (see table 8.2).

The effect of all three corrections together is to reduce the 1988 P/E ratio from 54.3 to either 23.2 or 32.1, depending on which depreciation correction is used. Lawler et al. (1988, p. 24) make their own adjustments for depreciation and consolidation of earnings, which produce a very similar result (see figs. 8.3 and 8.4). The analogous downward adjustment in U.S. P/E ratios is much smaller. Overall, these accounting differences in earnings explain about half of the difference between Japanese and U.S. ratios.[24] This still leaves Japanese equities about twice as high as U.S. equities. Or, if our interest is in the cost-of-capital question rather than in the is-Japan's-market-too-high question, the correction still leaves Japanese earnings/price ratios at about half U.S. levels.

Once we get the corrected Japanese earnings/price ratio up to the neighborhood of .04, it becomes slightly easier to explain the differential vis-à-vis the United States (which is at .09 when similarly adjusted by French and Poterba). If, for example, the expected rate of growth of earnings ge in Japan were 2.5 percent faster than in the U.S. and the required rate of return were 2.5 percent lower, that would explain the differential. But if it is true that the

---

24. When Aron (1989) converts the Japanese P/E ratio to U.S. accounting practices, and adjusts for cross-holding, he lowers it from a reported 49.6 in 1989 to 19.1 (compared to 13.5 in the United States).

Table 8.2   **Adjusted P/E Ratios, Japan, 1975–88**

Year	Unadjusted P/E	Cross-Holding Factor	Cross-Holding Interim P/E	Reserves Factor	Depreciation Adjustment Method 1 Factor	Method 1 P/E	Method 2 Factor	Method 2 P/E
1975	25.2	.784	19.8	.98	.599	11.5	.905	17.2
1976	22.0	.824	18.1	.97	.655	11.6	.920	16.1
1977	19.3	.797	15.4	.97	.684	10.2	.926	13.7
1978	21.5	.792	17.0	.97	.704	11.7	.931	15.3
1979	16.6	.778	12.9	.97	.717	9.0	.935	11.7
1980	17.9	.770	13.8	.97	.755	10.1	.947	12.6
1981	24.9	.764	19.0	.97	.702	13.0	.932	17.1
1982	23.7	.769	18.2	.97	.700	12.4	.931	16.3
1983	29.4	.795	23.4	.97	692	15.8	.936	21.1
1984	26.3	.734	19.3	.97	.711	13.3	.943	17.5
1985	29.4	.694	20.4	.97	.668	13.3	.924	18.2
1986	58.6	.695	40.7	.98	.624	24.8	.908	35.7
1987	50.4	.665	33.5	.97	.660	21.5	.920	29.8
1988	54.3	.669	36.3	.97[a]	.660[a]	23.2	.920[a]	32.1

Source: French and Poterba (1989). Their calculations are described in the text. The unadjusted P/E ratio corresponds to the NRI 350 index.
[a]Values for 1988 estimated using 1987 data.

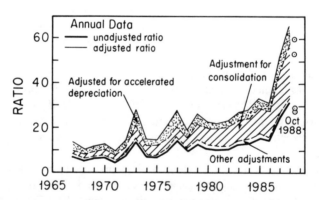

Fig. 8.3   Adjustments to price/earnings ratio
Source: Lawler, Loopesko, and Dudey (1988).

required rate of return is lower by, say 2.5 percentage points, what might be the source of this difference?

We consider in turn three possibilities: more favorable tax treatment, a lower real interest rate, and internal financing that is cheaper than the market interest rate. In the end, the paper will favor the third explanation, especially

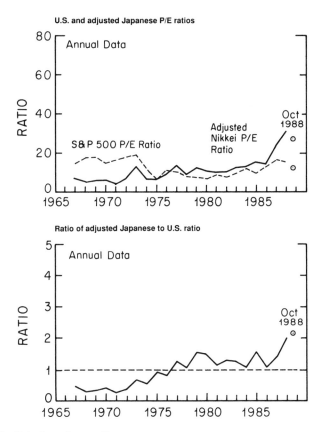

U.S. and adjusted Japanese P/E ratios

Ratio of adjusted Japanese to U.S. ratio

Fig. 8.4 Price/earnings ratios
Source: French and Poterba (1989).

for the period before liberalization, together with the second explanation, especially for the period since liberalization.[25]

8.3.3 Corporate Taxation

Corporate taxation is one of the respects in which the effective cost of capital facing the firm can differ from the observed rate of return on investment:

---

25. There is a fourth possibility, that the "equity premium" (defined as the expected rate of return on equity minus the interest rate) is smaller for Japan, which would in theory require that the Japanese stock market be less risky than the American stock market. Ueda (1990, pp. 362–64) argues that the risk premium in the Japanese stock market declined sharply between 1982 and 1988, but can find little evidence of a corresponding decline in riskiness. Lawler, Loopesko, and Dudey (1988, pp. 26–27) conclude that uncertainty in the two stock markets was roughly similar in the late 1980s (despite some possible differences in the past), whether estimated from the standard deviations of monthly changes or expected volatilities implicit in stock index options. (Baldwin 1986 and the appendix to Ando and Auerbach 1988 find no sign that the expected rate of return on Japanese securities is lower, even for a given amount of risk.)

it is of course the *after*-tax cost of capital that should matter for investment decisions. It would presumably be more convenient for any American businessman who wished to claim that Japanese industry had an "unfair advantage" in the form of a low cost of capital, if the source of the advantage were more favorable tax treatment by the Japanese government. In the past, the corporate income tax rate in Japan has been much *higher* than in the United States, especially after the more favorable U.S. tax treatment of business adopted in 1981, or even than in other countries such as the United Kingdom, which cut its corporate tax rate in 1984 (Hale 1987, p. 1). In 1985, the Japanese government raised 5.9 percent of its tax revenue from corporations, as compared to only 2.1 percent in the United States (Shoven 1989; see also Noguchi 1985). This has made it difficult to claim a tax advantage for Japanese industry.[26]

Indeed, when Ando and Auerbach (1985) computed after-tax earnings/ price ratios and after-tax return-to-capital rates, they found that "it is Japanese, not American, firms that are taxed more heavily on their real incomes" (p. 25). They registered two possible qualifications. First, one would prefer to look at the marginal effective tax rates that are relevant to the firm's decision whether to invest, rather than the average tax rate; but they noted that such measures were unavailable for Japan. Second, their calculations apply to the unlevered firm, but a corporation derives tax advantages from borrowing since interest payments are tax deductible, and one might expect these advantages to be larger for Japanese firms (both because they have had higher debt/equity ratios until recently and because the corporate tax rate that they are deducting against is higher). But Ando and Auerbach compute an upper bound on this tax advantage, and claim that it is very small. Thus they feel able to "rule out" the claim that the corporate tax system gives Japanese firms a cost-of-capital advantage (p. 37). Noguchi (1985), taking into account the advantages of borrowing, also concludes that the tax burden is higher on Japanese, not U.S., corporations.

Other authors have ascribed more importance to the tax advantages of borrowing in Japan. Hatsopoulos and Brooks (1989), for example, emphasize that the definition of tax-deductible borrowing is more permissive in the Japanese tax code than in the American.

Bernheim and Shoven (1986) dispute the prevailing approach in public finance of presupposing that the (pretax) real interest rate must be constant across countries, in light of the observed failure of this condition. They first compute the after-tax cost of capital under the 1980 tax codes, using the actual interest rates and inflation rates that held on average for the 1970s (which entails assuming a U.S.-Japan real interest differential of 1.5 percent). They

---

26. The paper treats separately the possibility that favorable treatment of *saving* in the Japanese tax system has been one of the causes of high household saving in Japan. This effect, if it existed, would operate via a low real interest rate.

find a smaller tax wedge on capital in Japan than in the United States, with the result that the after-tax cost of capital in Japan is negative.[27] They attributed this result to the greater importance of interest payments (tax deductible, on a nominal basis) in Japan.

Bernheim and Shoven then repeat the computations for 1985 tax codes, using the actual interest and inflation rates for the early 1980s. Despite the adoption of accelerated depreciation allowances in the U.S. tax code in 1981, the estimated U.S. cost of capital rises substantially in the 1980s as a result, particularly, of the much higher real interest rate (5.0 percent, as compared to 2.0 percent in the 1970s).[28] The real interest rate was higher in Japan as well, but there remains a substantial difference in the after-tax costs of capital in 1985 (5.48 for the U.S. vs. 2.76 for Japan).

The central message of Bernheim and Shoven was that variation in real interest rates tends to dwarf variation in corporate tax laws as determinants of the cost of capital. They include in this message the changes in the 1986 tax reform (including the removal of the investment tax credit that had been increased in 1981), which was under debate at the time that they were writing. Fukao (1988, pp. 339–41) finds a larger tax wedge (less negative) for Japan than the United States during the period 1981–84 but also finds that the combination of the 1986 U.S. tax reform and lower inflation rates brought the post-1986 tax wedge in the United States very close to that in Japan.

In December 1988, the Japanese Diet approved a tax reform that had been long sought by the ruling Liberal Democratic party. The reform, among other things, cut the Japanese corporate tax rate from 42 percent to 37.5 percent (with the full cut not effective until 1990).[29] This leaves the tax rate only slightly higher than the current rates in the United States (34 percent) or the United Kingdom (35 percent).[30] Shoven (1989) updates his calculations of the effective tax rates on corporate investment. He finds that the effective tax rate on investments in Japan is up sharply to 32 percent in 1988 (as compared to 5 percent in 1980). Part of the reason is the tax reform: in Shoven's calculations (unlike Ando and Auerbach 1985), the high *average* corporate tax rate in Japan worked to reduce the effective *marginal* tax rate on new investment, because it increased the value to the corporation of borrowing to finance the

27. Consistent with the findings of Shoven and Tachibanaki (1988).

28. Bernheim and Shoven artificially boost the U.S. real interest rate for the 1970s up a bit, because it was in fact observed to be negative, which would "wreak havoc" with the methodology that they adopt to evaluate tax systems.

29. The tax rate on undistributed profits during the period 1984–87 was 43.3 percent (Homma, Maeda, and Hashimoto 1986, p. 14; Homma 1987, p. 21). However, it had been lower in the 1950s and 1960s, ranging from 35 percent to 40 percent (Homma et al. 1984, p. 124, table 2.39; Shoven and Tachibanaki 1988, table 3.6).

30. When state and local taxes on corporations are added in, the Japanese rate is about 50 percent and the U.S. rate about 40 percent. These numbers are taken from Shoven (1989). One of several motives for the Japanese tax reform is that the Ministry of Finance fears that, in the absence of international harmonization of corporate tax rates, business would increasingly be able to find ways to arbitrage across tax jurisdictions.

investment and then deducting the interest payments from its taxable income. He thus estimates that the reduction in the average corporate tax rate in itself raised the effective tax rate 9 percentage points.

The major reason for the increase in the marginal effective tax rate on investment is not the tax reform, however, but rather the sharp decline in expected inflation relative to the 1970s. This decline is estimated to have raised the effective tax rate by 23 percentage points. The fall in the inflation rate in Japan (from 9 percent in the 1970s to 1 percent) means that the favorable distortion caused by the tax deductibility of nominal interest payments is reduced. This leaves the effective Japanese tax rate still somewhat below the U.S. rate, which was at 41 percent in 1988 (up from 29 percent before the Tax Reform Act of 1986).

It is possible that the moderate tax advantage that remains in Shoven's numbers does not adequately take into account the downward trend in the Japanese reliance on debt,[31] and that by now little is left of the Japanese tax advantage. Ando and Auerbach (1985, 1988) dismissed the importance, in this context, of taxes altogether.[32] Bernheim and Shoven (1986, p. 3) concluded that "under prevailing tax systems, differences in the cost of capital between countries are largely attributable to differences in domestic credit market conditions, rather than to taxes." Since the time that these two papers were written, the difference in tax treatment between the two countries has, if anything, narrowed. (At the same time that the U.S. tax reform of 1986 rolled back investment incentives for U.S. firms, the Japanese tax reforms that took effect in April of 1988 and April of 1989 raised the tax rate on Japanese saving in a number of ways.)[33] If the public finance experts think that taxes are of, at best, second-order importance in comparing the cost of capital between the United States and Japan—or that the difference has, if anything, gone *against* Japanese corporations—why should international economists disagree?

8.3.4   Total Stock Market Capitalization and the Late-1980s Run-up

The empirical fact that dominates the study of Japan's stock market is the tremendous run-up in prices since 1970, especially in the 1980s. We have

31. Recall the figures from French and Poterba (1989) that by 1988 the debt/equity ratio in Japan had fallen below that in the United States. Noguchi (1985, pp. 9, 18) lists the fall in the debt/equity ratio as one of several reason why the tax burden on Japanese investment increased in the late 1970s and early 1980s (though, like Ando and Auerbach, Noguchi thinks that the Japanese burden has been higher than the U.S. burden all along). The most important of the reasons (as with Shoven 1989) is the fall in the inflation rate.

32. Takenaka (1986) concludes that the impact of the investment tax credit on Japanese investment is negligible.

33. The previously existing prosaving bias in the Japanese tax system, compared to the American system, constituted part of the difference in "tax wedges" computed by Bernheim and Shoven (1986). It is discussed below under the topic of determinants of the real interest rate in Japan. Iwata and Yoshida (1987) calculated that the abolition of the prosaving bias in the then-proposed reforms would increase the total tax wedge in Japan (and thereby narrow the differential in the corporate cost of capital vis-à-vis the United States), despite the accompanying reductions in Japanese corporate taxes. (They, unlike Shoven, find that the latter work to reduce the after-tax cost of capital in Japan.)

already discussed the level of stock prices when they are compared to dividends and when they are compared to earnings. The same trend is evident when comparing total capitalization (price times number of shares) in Japan to capitalization in the United States.

Total stock market capitalization in Japan had, by 1989, surpassed the United States: 44 percent of the world versus 29 percent, in the conventional statistics.[34] But market values need to be adjusted for the double counting that results from intercorporate share ownership. Nearly two-thirds of corporate equity in Japan is held by other corporations. When French and Poterba (1989) adjust the Japanese market for cross-holdings, they find that it is still smaller than the United States: 33 percent of the world capitalization versus 36 percent for the United States. When McDonald (1989) adjusted for cross-holdings (or *mochiai* in Japanese) he found, as of early 1989, that the Japanese market was indeed larger than the U.S. market: 39 percent versus 33 percent. But the ranking again reversed with the fall of Japanese stock prices in early 1990. In any case, the growth of the Japanese market in the 1980s is astounding by any measure (a 68-fold increase over 1970).

French and Poterba observe that the magnitude of the 1986–88 run-up in the stock market is equally impressive when measured relative to GNP. Their computed ratio of adjusted equity to GNP fluctuated between .14 and .33 during the period 1970–85 and then rose sharply to .68 by 1988. (Meanwhile, the U.S. ratio, though more than twice as high as the Japanese ratio in the early 1970s, was only .49 in 1988.)

The only ratio where French and Poterba do not find potentially explosive behavior is the ratio of equity prices to the replacement cost of capital, that is, Tobin's Q. They do find that the Q ratio in Japan increased about 35 percent from 1973 to 1987, to .67 or .77, depending on the method of calculating net equity outstanding. But the U.S. ratio, at .71, is in about the same range. The fact that the replacement cost of capital in Japan has increased almost as much as stock market prices is tentatively attributed by French and Poterba to the fact that land prices have almost doubled since 1983 and the fact that companies hold a lot of land.[35] They thus tentatively conclude that the puzzle as to why equity prices rose so much in the 1980s may be the same as the puzzle why land prices rose so much in the 1980s. (See comparison of stock prices and land prices in major cities in fig. 8.5.)[36]

34. Hale (1989) opines that the dramatic reversal of the rankings of U.S. and Japanese capitalization over the course of the 1980s represents the financial market's negative judgment on Reaganomics as compared to policy-making by bureaucrats in the Japanese Ministry of Finance. But when Murphy (1989) observes the same reversal, he worries that Japan's policymakers are not ready to accept the responsibility of greater weight in the world.

35. Japanese companies usually carry land on their books, not at current market price, but at the price of acquisition (which, in the case of land held since the nineteenth century, is essentially zero).

36. Ueda (1990, p. 357) finds that the market value of corporate shares after 1983 surpassed the reported value of corporate assets including land. But the final version of the paper does not rule out the possibility that land prices explain the rise in stock prices, in light of claims that official land prices are greatly understated.

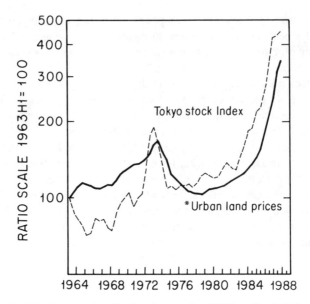

Fig. 8.5   Real Japanese urban land prices and real Tokyo Stock Index
Source: Lawler, Loopesko, and Dudey (1988).
Note: Both series deflated by an index of consumer prices.
*Index of urban land prices, six largest cities, commercial area.

8.3.5   Land Prices

The soaring price of land in Japan is a major phenomenon in its own right. In 1986 the price of land in Tokyo (for residential use) was 150 times the price in New York, 16 times the price in London, 35 times in Paris, and 11 times in Munich (Iwata and Yoshida 1988, p. 509). The unit cost of land for the country overall was about 40 times as high as in the U.S.[37] Thus the value of all the land in Japan is several times as great as the value of all the land in the (much larger) United States.[38] A favorite "factoid," which is apparently true, is that the grounds of the Imperial Palace in Tokyo, when evaluated at the land prices of the adjoining Otemachi area, is worth more than all the land in the State of California (see, e.g., Boone and Sachs 1989; Boone 1989b).

The price of land, analogously to the price of equity, should equal the present discounted value of future rents (in the absence of a speculative bubble). If rents are expected to grow at rate *gr*, then the price/rental ratio should be given by

---

37. Ito (1989). In 1987, the average price of usable land in Japan was 90 times that in the United States, according to Boone (1989a).

38. In 1984, the value of land in Japan was 3.17 times GNP, while in the United States it was only .80 times GNP (Sachs and Boone 1988).

$$P_{land}/\text{rent} = \frac{1}{r - gr}.$$

Thus the same possible explanations arise for high land prices as arise for high equity prices: a low discount rate r or a high growth rate gr. Noguchi (1987, as described by Ito 1989) observes that the price/rental ratio is much higher in Tokyo than in other major world cities,[39] and concludes that about half of the Japanese land price is a speculative bubble, that the demand for land is based on a self-confirming expectation of future capital gains. But Ito (1989) disagrees, arguing that Noguchi omits the possibility that expectations of rising land prices could be correctly based on fundamentals, because the relative price of land will increase in a growing economy where the supply of land is fixed by geographical and other factors.[40]

In terms of the above equation, gr could be high. Ito shows in an overlapping generations model, in which land is a substitutable factor of production, that if land is in fixed supply, its relative price will increase at a rate essentially given by the real growth rate of the economy. Boone and Sachs (1989) argue similarly. Boone (1989b) concludes that one can explain the difference between Japanese and U.S. land values by fundamentals if Japanese GNP is expected to grow at roughly 2 percent a year faster than U.S. GNP.

The institutional factors that are listed in note 40 above are often cited as causes of the high cost of land in Japan. They are one component of the Structural Impediments Initiative (SII) launched by the U.S. government in 1989, on the theory that the high cost of land is in turn a cause of low consumption and low imports in Japan. But in the absence of macroeconomic differences like interest rates and expectations, these institutional factors could not in themselves explain the high price of land. In the first place, Boone (1989a) studies data across regions of Japan and finds that factors such as excess concentration in the Tokyo region, agricultural protection, and tax policies cannot explain differences in land costs. In the second place, even if these institutional factors could explain the high cost of land in Japan overall, they cannot serve as an explanation for the high price/rental *ratio*. As Boone (1989a, p. 14) notes, they would predict that, not only land prices in Tokyo, but *rents* as well, should far exceed those in other world capitals, which is not the case.

The expected-growth argument favored by both Boone and Ito tells us why land price/rental ratios in Japan are currently high. But it does not tell us why they should have *increased* so much over the last 18 years. In the theory, with

39. It is about five times higher than London. Boone (1989a, p. 47) estimates that the price of land in Tokyo is 150 times that in New York, despite little difference in rental rates on apartments and buildings.

40. There are a number of special institutional features that affect the Japanese land market, such as building height restrictions and sunshine laws, special protection for rice paddies, and a level of taxation of capital gains at the time of sale that is much greater than annual property taxes (on the last point, see K. Takagi 1989). Some of these features can be viewed as contributing to the inelasticity of the supply of land.

growth in the economy, the price and rent should each rise proportionately. Instead, while land and housing prices have skyrocketed, the rental rate has remained approximately constant in real terms (see the last four lines of table 8.3). The price/rental ratio for housing increased by 67 percent between 1970 and 1987.[41]

8.3.6 Speculative Bubbles

There is always the possibility of a speculative bubble in the 1980s, to explain the price of land, the price of equity, or both. It is sometimes argued that special institutional features of the Japanese stock market, such as the dominance of trading by the big four security firms and administrative guidance by the Ministry of Finance,[42] keep prices artificially high. It has been argued, for example, that such features might explain why the Japanese market "was not allowed" to fall as far in the crash of October 1987 as were other countries' markets (Lawler, Loopesko, and Dudey 1988, pp. 31–33; Murphy 1989). Hardouvelis and Peristiani (1989, p. 19) find that "margin requirements in Japan have proved to be an effective tool of controlling wild gyrations in stock prices." But financial economists have not yet been able to construct good models of what gets speculative bubbles started or what causes them to collapse. We do not even have much idea whether bubbles are more or less likely in perfectly competitive "efficient" markets than in markets where trading is characterized by turnover taxes, larger transactions costs, oligopolistic market makers, and government intervention (all characteristics that are sometimes attributed to Japanese stock markets).[43]

It is possible that some short-term movements in financial markets represent speculative bubbles. But before we do anything so radical as attributing the longer-term movement in Japan's equity and land prices to a speculative bubble, we return to the possibility of a low discount rate in Japan.

8.4   Determinants of the Real Interest Rate

If one thinks of the real interest rate as equilibrating the various sources and uses of funds, then a low real interest rate would be explained by some com-

41. The price of land alone went up even more than the price of housing over this same period. The price/rental ratio for land increased by 14 percent between 1975 and 1986 (27 percent in the three big cities). The source is Iwata and Yoshida (1988, p. 510). Ito's (1989) theory may, however, give us a reason why land price/rental ratios in Japan should be higher than in the United States, even aside from any difference in real growth rates of the economies. Ito shows that if the supply of available land increases at the growth rate of the economy, then the relative price of land will be constant. In terms of the equation, if the supply of land is more elastic in the United States than in Japan, then gr will be lower, and, therefore, P_{land}/rent will be lower in the United States.

42. The Ministry of Finance began to look after the stability of the Japanese stock market after a crash in 1965. S. Takagi (1989) discusses the history and institutional features of the market.

43. Aggarwal, Rao, and Hiraki (1990) have found evidence in the Tokyo Stock Exchange that stocks with low P/E ratios have higher returns than stocks with high P/E ratios (as others have found in the United States.) Seasonal anomalies have also been found.

Table 8.3   **Increases in Prices of Nontraded Services in Tokyo**

Category	Ratio of 1987/ 1972 Prices
Electric light	1.72
Gas	2.39
Water	5.83
Mail	4.10
Phone	1.00
Telegram	2.22
Freight	3.46
Rail	3.89
Tramcar	7.00
Bus	5.33
Newspaper	3.15
Receiving fee	2.24
Cinema	2.14
Bathing	5.93
Hairdressing	4.04
Cleaning	2.49
Lodging	2.40
House price	3.40
House rental	2.29
Tokyo CPI (prewar base)	2.47
National CPI	2.45

Source: Economic Statistics Annual, Bank of Japan (March 1988), pp. 329–30, except for "house price" and "house rental," which are from Iwata and Yoshida (1988), p. 510.

bination of four factors: a high corporate saving rate net of investment, a high public saving rate, a high household saving rate, or a high availability of savings from abroad. Each factor probably has played a role at one time or another in Japan.

We know that the government was a source of cheap capital for many firms in the 1950s and 1960s, but that it went sharply into deficit and became a big *user* of funds after 1973. The Ministry of Finance took pains to cut the government budget deficit in the early 1980s, but the deficit has nevertheless been relatively high throughout the post-1973 period and thus cannot explain a low real interest rate during this period.[44] The corporate sector was in deficit in the postwar period until the first oil shock. We know that the corporate deficit has been sharply lower since then,[45] as the result of a fall-off in the previously

44. It is easy enough to explain the real interest differential and international capital flows vis-à-vis the United States in the early 1980s by the U.S. fiscal expansion.
45. Indeed, Balassa and Noland (1988, p. 84) report that the Japanese corporate sector was in surplus in the years 1974–77, although others show only a declining deficit (where both financial and nonfinancial corporations are included; Lincoln 1988, table 3-2, pp. 76–77).

high level of investment (which helps explain the extension of the period of cheap capital well past 1973). But the high Japanese private saving rate is the factor most often cited as applying throughout the period.

8.4.1   Household Saving Rate

The Japanese household saving rate, at 23.0 percent of disposable income averaged over 1970–86, is among the highest among the industrialized countries. Other figures for comparison are the United States at 11.5 percent, the United Kingdom at 10.4 percent, and France at 17.7 percent (Blades 1988, p. 18). The question of why the saving rate is so high in Japan is another major topic in itself. We briefly run through some of the arguments that have been suggested.[46]

Hayashi (1986) claims that much of the apparent differential in personal saving rates between Japan and the United States can be explained by four accounting differences. But even after adjustment, a substantial differential remains.[47]

At least six reasons for the high Japanese saving rate have been given, by Hayashi, Horioka, and others.

1. *A high growth rate.* The older dissaving generation are always outweighed by the younger saving generation.[48]

2. *Demographics.* Currently, Japan has one of the longest life expectancies and smallest ratio of aged to working-age population (15 percent, vs. 20 percent in the United States and 23 percent over all the OECD countries).[49] Horioka (1986) has estimated that the age ratio can explain a difference in saving rates of 11.5 percent.

An additional possible explanation for the high saving rate in Japan—not one of the six explanations that appear on standard lists—is that it is the most nonnuclear country of the G-5. Slemrod (1988) points out that a higher perceived threat of nuclear annihilation should reduce people's saving rate by reducing their expected horizons, and he offers supporting evidence from a cross-section of 20 countries. Survey results show that Americans report a

46. Horioka (1990) offers the most up-to-date and comprehensive of a number of surveys.

47. According to Blades (1988, pp. 18–19), adjusting for consumer durables in 1986 raises the U.S. household gross saving ratio from 11.5 percent to 22.1 percent, while only raising the Japanese ratio from 21.2 percent to 25.8 percent. When the saving ratios are averaged over 1970–86, adjusting raises the U.S. ratio to 23.6 percent and the Japanese ratio to 26.1 percent. See also Balassa and Noland (1988, pp. 80–96). Takayama et al. (1988) go so far as to say, on the basis of several accounting corrections, that the Japanese saving rate is not high at all.

48. As in the life-cycle hypothesis of Franco Modigliani.

49. Over the next 30 years, Japan will go from having the highest ratio of working age population to elderly out of the G-5 countries (5.9 in 1985) to the lowest (2.3 in 2020; see Shoven 1989). A simulation by Auerbach et al. (1989, p. 117), based on the rapid aging of the Japanese population, predicts that the national saving rate in Japan will decline from 22 percent (close to Germany's) to a minimum of 1 percent, over the period 1990 to 2028 (falling below the U.S. national saving rate in the year 2020).

higher perceived likelihood of world war than do the Japanese, and, indeed, Americans report the highest of all 20 countries.[50]

3. *An underdeveloped social security system.* There are conflicting effects on the saving rate,[51] and Horioka argues that they approximately cancel out.

4. *The bonus system of employee compensation.* The lump-sum payments at the end of each half-year might act as forced saving. This would require a sort of "calendar illusion." But Ishikawa and Ueda (1984) find that the bonus system does indeed have an effect on saving (though they estimate it to be at most three percentage points).

5. *The high price of land and housing.* Even before recent price increases (1985–87), housing prices in Japan were almost twice as high as those in the United States. They are 2.5 to 2.7 times higher if differences in floor space are taken into account (Horioka 1988, p. 218). As a result, housing constitutes 65 percent of saving in Japan as compared to 31 percent in the United States (Frankel 1988b, n. 33).

By itself, the saving implications of expensive housing are not as clear as often asserted.[52] But a positive effect on saving does follow from the unavailability of consumer credit; Hayashi, Ito, and Slemrod (1988) report that the Japanese have to accumulate up to 40 percent of the purchase price as a down payment.[53] Also, mortgage interest is not tax deductible as it is in the United States. The Japanese appear to have a greater cultural bias against personal indebtedness than do Americans; rather than using credit cards to postpone payment for purchases, for example, the Japanese are fond of magnetic cards that allow them to *prepay* and then deduct purchases as they are made.[54]

---

50. Not taken into account is any tendency for the Japanese to rate their odds of nuclear annihilation, conditional on world war breaking out, as lower than Americans.

51. On the one hand low Social Security benefits encourage workers to save more, but on the other it encourages them to retire early.

52. Sachs and Boone (1988) construct a model to answer the question of what would happen to saving if land prices fell, in response, for example, to the sorts of measures often urged on Japan by Americans: the ending of prohibitions on rice imports and the liberalization of land-use restrictions. Their model predicts that saving would *rise* rather than fall, due to the fall in wealth. Similarly, Shibuya (1988) estimates that the wealth effect would nearly eliminate any positive effects of land prices on saving; and Yoshikawa and Ohtake (1989) show that the estimated positive effect of higher land prices on saving by future home buyers may be more than offset by estimated reductions in saving on the part of those who abandon plans ever to buy a home.

53. Horioka (1988, p. 219) reports that Japanese families *plan* down-payment ratios of 45 to 55 percent, but that *actual* down payments are as low as 20 percent. He argues (p. 229) that an increase in the availability of mortgage credit would not increase total saving, but would only result in a combination of lower prepurchase saving (to make the down payment) and higher postpurchase saving (to pay off the loan).

54. Arguing against the idea that Japanese are culturally predisposed to save more is the fact that the high saving rates are only a phenomenon of the postwar era (as pointed out by Hale 1987, p. 26 and Balassa and Noland 1988, p. 81). Also sometimes listed as reasons for high saving rates in Japan are obstacles to consumption such as the inefficient retailing system, the lack of space in living quarters for consumer durables, and the lack of leisure time in the work schedule (see, e.g., Balassa and Noland 1988, p. 94). But economic theory is dubious as to the implications for the

Balassa and Noland (1988, p. 92) argue that a special combination of high housing prices and the strategic bequest motive on the part of the elderly are the best explanation of high saving.[55] Horioka (1985, 1988) reports that, while opinion surveys in the United States report old age as the most important motive for saving, surveys in Japan place saving to buy a house as more important (together with education and marriage). Horioka (1986) estimates that high land prices explain a difference in saving rates of 5.0 percent.[56]

6. *Tax incentives*. In the past, the tax system has deliberately increased the after-tax return to households in a number of ways. The Japanese could escape paying taxes on much of their savings by taking advantage of such exemptions as deposits in the *maruyu* system and the Postal Savings System. A family of four could legally hold $455,000 in tax-free assets.[57] The 1987 tax reform, effective April 1988, abolished the tax-exempt savings accounts. But it did retain two prosaving features of the tax system. First, when a saver does pay tax on interest earnings or dividends, they are taxed separately from his income and at a rate lower than the top marginal rate. Second, although the December 1988 tax reform, effective April 1989, instated the taxation of capital gains on sales of securities (which were previously not taxed), the tax rate is still below that of the United States (especially since the 1986 U.S. tax reform) and other major countries. The saver gets his option of 1 percent of the value of the transaction or 20 percent of the capital gain (Ministry of Finance 1988; Shoven 1989).

Although one of the reasons behind the Japanese tax reform was foreign pressure (*gaiatsu*) to make the Japanese system less prosaving and therefore more like the U.S. system, the effect of this decrease in the after-tax return on the supply of saving and therefore on the real interest rate is not clear. In theory, the substitution effect and income effect go in opposite directions. Saxonhouse (1982) believes that the Japanese are, in fact, target savers: because their goal is to save enough to buy a home, a decrease in the after-tax rate of return means that they now need to save *more*, not less, to achieve the same goal. In empirical studies, a positive effect of the after-tax return on the saving rate has been difficult to find. (For Japan, see Makin 1985 and Hayashi 1986. Iwata, Suzuki, and Yoshida 1988, p. 129–31, however, break down the tax

---

saving rate of institutional impediments that apply to future consumption as much as to current consumption. Wealth is only of use to the household to the extent that it is consumed sooner or later.

55. Dekle (1989b) also focuses on the behavior of the Japanese elderly, finding that they are not dissaving as they should. Dekle (1989a) shows that the reason could be a combination of a strong bequest motive and a constraint against borrowing on home equity.

56. Hale (1987, p. 27) believes that "any set of structural reforms which reduce the price of housing while increasing the tax incentive to own it could have a more dramatic effect on savings and consumption than many policies seemingly targeted on savings behavior itself."

57. The figure is from Shoven (1989). Furthermore, many households held more tax-free accounts than the number to which they were legally entitled; the total number of accounts in the Postal Savings System was said to be twice the population.

rate and other variables by income class and do find evidence of an effect in this way.) A simulation analysis in Hayashi et al. (1988) concluded that the Japanese saving rate would go down by a few percentage points if Japan were to abolish the *maruyu*, but this was not a statistical test.[58]

8.4.2 International Capital Mobility

Even if a tax reform or a land-use reform were to reduce the Japanese level of household saving toward that in Western countries, there is a serious further question as to whether such a change would lower the Japanese real interest rate or the cost of capital to firms. If capital is perfectly mobile internationally, it is argued, then a decline in national saving should not put any upward pressure on the rate of return within Japan but rather should be entirely offset by increased borrowing from abroad (and decreased lending abroad) at an unchanged rate of return.[59]

Feldstein and Horioka (1980) initiated what has proven to be a long-lasting debate by observing that changes in countries' rates of national saving in fact had large effects on their rates of investment and interpreting the finding as evidence of low capital mobility. The paper was subjected to many econometric attacks, but the basic results seemed to hold up.[60]

It is possible to test the international equalization of rates of return more directly. Many studies have documented the failure of real interest rates to be equalized across countries,[61] seeming to confirm the Feldstein-Horioka results. We saw in section 8.1 that the Japanese real interest rate was below the U.S. rate throughout the 1980s. But the Japanese government announced the removal of controls on international capital movements in 1979–80, and further liberalization measures in 1983–84, partly in response to pressure from the U.S. Treasury.[62] It is often argued that, if capital markets are open, international arbitrage should eliminate real interest differentials. Is it possible that the announced Japanese liberalization has failed to be genuine or complete?

A number of studies have shown, using data on *covered* interest differen-

58. So far, there has apparently been no sign of a significant decrease in the household saving rate in Japan since the April 1988 abolishment of the *maruyu*. (It should be noted that the latest tax reform also instituted a sales tax—indeed this was its politically most controversial feature—which could in theory have either a positive or negative effect on the saving/consumption decision, depending particularly on whether households believe that the government will raise the sales tax rate in the future.)

59. However it is fairly clear that such a decrease in saving *would* reduce the Japanese current account surplus—and all the more so if capital is highly mobile—which is what many Americans want.

60. The "saving-retention" coefficient finally began to decline in the 1980s, however, according to the latest studies: Feldstein and Bacchetta (1989) and Frankel (1991). The latter paper contains 65 references on the subject (many of them demonstrations that one can have a high correlation between saving and investment despite perfect capital mobility).

61. See, e.g., Mishkin (1984). Glick (1987) applies to Japan and other Pacific countries in particular.

62. The story of the U.S. Treasury campaign for the liberalization of Japanese financial markets, which began in October 1983, is told in Frankel (1984).

tials, that the 1979–80 and 1983–84 liberalizations did indeed have the effects advertized (Otani and Tiwari 1981; Otani 1983; Frankel 1984, 1988b, 1991; Eken 1984; Ito 1986). By now covered interest parity holds as well for Japan (vis-à-vis the Eurodollar market) as it does for such major countries as Canada, Germany, and the United Kingdom: the differential between the dollar interest rate and the interest rate on domestic currency is equal to the discount on the dollar in the forward exchange market. This finding suggests that Japan is highly integrated into world financial markets with respect to the movement of capital across national boundaries.

The finding still leaves open the possibility of differences associated with the *currency* in which an asset is denominated, as opposed to the *political* jurisdiction, in which it is issued. For example, investors' expectations that the dollar may in the future depreciate against the yen in nominal terms almost certainly explain why the yen interest rate was less than the dollar interest rate in the 1980s.[63] Similarly, expectations that the dollar may depreciate against the yen in *real* terms may explain why the yen *real* interest rate was less than the dollar *real* interest rate. In that case, the Feldstein-Horioka view is correct—real interest rates are not necessarily equalized internationally, and changes in saving (even if truly exogenous) need not be offset by borrowing from abroad and thus may be heavily reflected as changes in investment—and yet the explanation may be the imperfect international integration of goods markets that allows failures of purchasing power parity, rather than imperfect international integration of financial markets. If there is no way of arbitraging directly among countries' goods or among their plant and equipment, and if plant and equipment are imperfect substitutes for bonds *within* each country, then perfect international arbitrage among countries' bonds is not sufficient to equalize real rates of return among countries' plant and equipment.

8.4.3   Long-Term Real Appreciation of the Yen

It might be argued that real interest differentials and expectations of real depreciation exist only because of short-run factors such as sticky goods prices, and that they must vanish in the long run.[64] How then could the Japanese real interest rate have remained below the U.S. real interest rate for 30 years? One possible answer is that capital controls prevented equalization in

63. The interest differential could in theory be explained by either of two terms (after the possibility of a covered interest differential, or political premium, has been eliminated), both of them associated with the currency: expected depreciation or an exchange risk premium. The possible exchange risk premium between the dollar and yen is examined by Fukao and Okuba (1984), Fukao (1987), Frankel and Froot (1987), Ito (1988), and Frankel (1988b).

64. The real appreciation of the dollar against the yen and European currencies beginning in 1981 was widely considered an example of Dornbusch "overshooting" caused by shifts in monetary or fiscal policy: the real exchange rate change would disappear over time as U.S. traded-goods prices adjusted downward in response to excess supply and Japanese traded-goods prices adjusted upward in response to excess demand.

the 1960s and 1970s,[65] that the differential after liberalization in the early 1980s was a transitory phenomenon, and that henceforth the differential will be zero.

But an alternative possibility is that investors have expected the yen to appreciate in real terms throughout the last 30 years. Let us decompose the real interest differential, $r - r*$, by adding and subtracting the expected rate of appreciation of the yen, $appr^e$:

$$r - r* = (i - infl) - (i* - infl*),$$
$$= (i - i* - appr^e) + (appr^e - infl + infl*),$$

where i and $i*$ are the Japanese and U.S. nominal interest rates, respectively, and $infl$ and $infl*$ are the Japanese and U.S. expected inflation rates, respectively. We see that, even if the expected rate of returns on domestic and foreign bonds are equalized when expressed in a common currency, that is, $i - i* - appr^e = 0$, there will still be a nonzero *real* interest differential if there is a nonzero expected future real appreciation of the yen ($appr^e - infl + infl*$). Expected real changes in the exchange rate would be ruled out if purchasing power parity held, but it is well known by now that purchasing power parity in fact fails to hold.

One reason to believe that there has indeed been such an expectation is that survey data show that market participants in the 1980s indeed expected a rapid appreciation of the yen against the dollar (Frankel and Froot 1987; Ito 1990; Froot and Ito 1989). A second reason to believe this is that the yen in fact appreciated steadily against the dollar in real terms over the postwar period. During the fixed exchange rate era, 1950–73, the yen appreciated against the dollar at an average logarithmic rate of 3.66 percent per year in real terms (using the two countries consumer Price Indexes [CPIs] to deflate). During the floating rate era, 1973–89, the real appreciation of the yen continued at an average rate of 3.46 percent per year. Even if one believes that the yen overshot its equilibrium somewhat as of 1989—and many economists were saying that, to the contrary, the yen had not appreciated enough to be consistent with long-term fundamentals—the basic point about the trend in the real exchange rate would be little affected. With such a strong trend in the real exchange rate over the preceding 40 years, it is easy to believe that investors have long since come to incorporate into their long-term expectations a real appreciation of the yen of 3 percent per year. Thus it is easy to believe that, even if international arbitrage in the 1980s drove the U.S.-Japan interest differential to

65. One problem with identifying capital controls as the source of the U.S.-Japan real interest differential throughout the 1970s is that during the period 1976–78, when the covered interest differential was the largest in absolute magnitude, the nominal interest in Tokyo was *above* the yen interest rate in the London Euromarket, demonstrating that controls were acting to discourage capital inflow, not outflow, at least at the short-term end of the spectrum.

equality with expected appreciation of the yen, that this could have left a real interest differential as large as 3 percent.

How could the yen appreciate steadily against the dollar in real terms over such a long period? Many consider the tendency for purchasing power parity to hold at least in the long run to be virtually the most fundamental and traditional principle of international monetary economics. The observed trend also violates, to the extent that it is statistically significant, the currently popular hypothesis that the real exchange rate follows a random walk.

A number of explanations have been attempted for the long-term trend in the real yen, including a relatively low elasticity of imports with respect to income in Japan (Krugman 1989) and a relatively rapid rate of productivity growth in Japanese manufacturing (Marston 1987). A natural explanation is the classical observed pattern, most often attributed to Balassa (1964), that a rapidly growing country tends (1) to experience an increase in the price of its nontraded goods relative to its internationally traded goods (because of higher productivity growth in the traded-goods sector or else because nontraded goods are superior goods in consumption), and therefore (2) to exhibit an apparent real appreciation of its currency when the deflation is done using CPIs, which include a large share of nontradable goods within them.

Let us look at the real exchange rate defined in terms of consumer price indices:

$$(3) \qquad E_{real} = E\,[CPI^* / CPI].$$

We will represent the CPI in each country as a weighted average of nontraded goods and traded goods (in Cobb-Douglas form). We use a and a^* to represent the weights of nontraded goods in the domestic and foreign country's price indices, respectively:

$$(4) \qquad E_{real} = E[P_n^{*a*}\,P_t^{*(1-a*)}/P_n^a\,P_t^{(1-a)}]$$
$$= [(P_n^*/P_t^*)^{a*}/(P_n/P_t)^a][EP_t^*/P_t].$$

If the "law of one price" *does* hold for traded goods, then $P_t = EP_t^*$, and the last bracketed term in (4) drops out:

$$(5) \qquad E_{real} = [(P_n^*/P_t^*)^{a*}/(P_n/P_t)^a].$$

Equation (5) tells us that the real exchange rate will change if the *relative* price of nontraded goods changes in either the foreign country or the domestic country, even though purchasing power parity may hold perfectly well for the tradable share.

This description sounds like it was specially designed for Japan, where tradable goods consist primarily of manufactured, agricultural, and mineral products, and nontradables include housing, golf-club memberships, and other services. The model in Ito (1989) shows that if the supply of land is inelastic in Japan and elastic in the United States, the yen will appear to appreciate in real terms as the economies grow (where the price of housing services is included in the relevant CPI).

Testing the hypothesis of a change in the relative price of nontraded goods, however, is more difficult than it might seem. Most sectors are at least partly traded in character. Table 8.3 singles out 17 specific services that are fairly clearly *not* traded and shows the relative change in their prices in Tokyo over the period 1972–87. Ten of the services, including particularly the forms of urban transportation, went up in price more than the general CPI, and seven less.[66] This provides some support for the hypothesis, though less than one might have expected.

There is an alternative way to view the decomposition of the economy into traded and nontraded. Virtually all sectors use at least some amount of internationally traded goods as intermediate inputs in production (e.g., energy). At the same time, virtually all sectors involve at least some domestic value added before the product in question is sold to the consumer, even if it is only shipping, marketing, and retailing. Indeed, the amount of resources devoted to the distribution system is notoriously high in Japan. It is possible that each sector has experienced an increase in the price of nontraded value added and inputs relative to its traded value added and inputs. Such a trend would explain a real appreciation of the yen calculated with CPIs, or even more disaggregated industry prices, even if the law of one price held perfectly for the traded component. This hypothesis may show up in the increasing ratio of the CPI to producer price indices or unit labor costs in Japan. It is also relevant to the recent literature on pricing markups for Japanese imports and exports.[67] In any case, the hypothesis bears further investigation.

Regardless of whether the relative price of nontraded goods does in fact prove to be the correct explanation of the real appreciation of the yen, it is undeniable that a strong sustained trend of real appreciation has taken place, with the implication that a real interest differential of 2 or even 3 percent is perfectly consistent with highly integrated financial markets.

I have argued that, even if Japanese corporations are now no more highly levered than American corporations, and even if international arbitrage now equates the Japanese and foreign nominal interest rates (when expressed in a common currency), that the Japanese real interest rate could still lie below the foreign rate. A real interest differential in the 1980s—whatever its source—could in turn help explain high average price/earnings ratios in the Japanese stock market, high price/rental ratios in the Japanese land market, and a lower

66. The source is the Bank of Japan. If the price of housing and the rental rate are added to the list, then the number increasing faster than the CPI is 11 out of 19. The answers are the same regardless whether the Tokyo CPI is used (Management and Coordination Agency, a prewar base) or a national CPI (IFS).

67. On pricing-to-market by Japanese firms, see Branson and Marston (1989), Froot (1988), Marston (1990), and Ohno (1989).

cost of capital to some Japanese firms.[68] But the argument about the low real interest rate might seem to apply to the past in Japan as much as, or more than, to the 1980s. Similarly, the argument that the expected rate of real economic growth in Japan is high applies to the past as much as, or more than, it does to the present. How can one explain that price/earnings ratios and price/rental ratios were not also high in the past, that is, that they rose sharply in the 1980s?

8.5   Internal Corporate Financing and Relationship Banking, Versus the Market System

The standard formula for the price/earnings ratio and the price/rental ratio, $1/(r - g)$, assumes r, the real interest rate (or a required rate of return equal to the real interest rate marked up by a risk premium), is relevant for discounting expected future returns. This assumption is appropriate for economies where corporate finance is oriented around a unified central market, that is, a common pool of funds into which most savers deposit and from which most investors draw off.[69] This description applies to the United States, and it applies increasingly to Japan today. But it did not apply very well to Japan in the 1970s, and still less so in the 1960s, as Meerschwam (in this volume) explains at greater length.

The existence of lending by government agencies to favored firms in favored industries at subsidized rates, and the artificial "repression" of other interest rates through regulation and administrative guidance, have always been major ways that Japanese corporations have been thought to have an "unfair" cost-of-capital advantage in the past.[70] Equally familiar is the claim that large corporations or *keiretsu* take profits from one activity and cross-subsidize investment in another. But it has seldom been clear why Japanese industry should want to do this.[71]

68. One must note, however, that if "the" real interest rate was lower in Japan than the United States only because of an expected rate of real appreciation of the yen in terms of a basket of goods that includes nontraded goods, it can only explain high equity prices or a low cost of capital *within the nontraded goods sector* or for the average across the entire economy. It cannot explain a low cost of capital for Japanese firms producing *traded* goods, which are the ones from whom American businessmen fear competition.

69. Note that this does not preclude some firms having projects with rates of return greater than the market rate or internal funding sources at costs less than the market rate; it requires only that the market rate be the marginal cost of funds for most firms.

70. Of 12 government financial institutions—which as recently as 1980 supplied 17 percent of funds for investment in plant and equipment—the Japan Development Bank and the Small Business Finance Corporation were particularly notable in channeling subsidized investment funds to selected industries (Lee 1988, pp. 25–36). The more general low-interest rate policy of the government before 1973 was explicit (e.g., Tamura 1987).

71. See Abegglen and Stalk (1985), Gerlach (1987) and Hodder and Tschoegl (1985). If the investment is expected to be profitable in the long run, then it should take place in a market-oriented financial system such as the United States, with the investment funded by borrowing in the market if necessary, as readily as under the Japanese system.

Recent theoretical developments have helped us understand better how the cost of internal finance can be less than the cost of external finance.[72] One route is asymmetric information, between the firm's managers and the typical stockholder or bond holder in the market, regarding the rate of return on an investment; another route is incentive or "agency" problems. "Internal finance" in the United States would be the corporation's financing of an investment out of retained earnings (or out of depreciation charges), as opposed to financing at market rates by borrowing from a bank or issuing securities.

Retained earnings are also important in Japan, important in particular to understanding why the cost of capital remained low in the 1970s. Ever since the Japanese economic growth rate fell off with the oil shock of 1973, the number of profitable investment projects has fallen short of the supply of funds available. (In the national savings identity, the offset to the increase in the saving-investment balance of the corporate sector was primarily a large increase in the government budget deficit in the 1970s, followed by a large increase in the current account surplus in the 1980s.) In other words, since 1973, firms have been able to finance investments out of retained earnings to a much greater extent than previously. Retained earnings appear to be a cheaper source of financing than issuing corporate debt or equity, because they get around problems of incomplete information or incentive incompatibility.

It can be argued that in Japan "internal finance" de facto includes as well borrowing by a firm from its main bank under a long-term relationship. The reasoning is that the main bank, like a large shareholder (which, in fact, it often is) can keep close tabs on what goes on inside the firm, thus largely obviating information and incentive problems.[73] Hodder (1988b) concludes that the advantages of "lender monitoring" are key, and that they may explain why studies like Ando and Auerbach (1988) find that the cost of capital is lower in Japan than in the United States.[74]

Empirical evidence in support of the proposition that internal and main-bank finance are cheaper than external or market finance is offered by some recent microeconomic studies of the determinants of firm investment. It has

72. For example, Bernanke and Gertler (1989) in the macroeconomic literature, and Myers and Majluf (1984) and Jensen and Meckling (1976) in the finance literature. The first two focus on information costs, the last on incentive problems.

73. For example, Crum and Meerschwam (1986), Hamada and Horiuchi (1987), Hodder (1988a, 1988b), and Hoshi, Kashyap, and Scharfstein (1990a, 1990b). Japanese financial institutions (including not just banks, but also life insurance companies and other institutional investors), unlike their U.S. counterparts, are allowed to take large debt *and* equity positions in the same firm; Prowse (1989) argues that this difference constitutes in itself a way that the Japanese system is better able to circumvent agency problems.

74. His argument is that the advantages of lender monitoring may show up in part as low reported earnings/price ratios because banks receive payments for their services in the form of "compensating balances" and transactions fees, which come out of reported corporate earnings, rather than in the form of interest payments. On the general point that the apparent cost of borrowing is understated in Japan by the requirement of compensating balances, see, e.g., Bronte (1982, p. 17).

long been true that variables such as cash flow did a better job econometrically of explaining business fixed investment than theoretically preferable variables such as the real interest rate and Tobin's Q (at least when each factor was considered on its own; e.g., Jorgenson 1971; Meyer and Kuh 1957). The new theories of information and incentive problems, however, now provide the desired rigorous theoretical basis for including cash flow. Fazzari, Hubbard, and Petersen (1988) have estimated regression equations for investment on a cross-section of U.S. firms. They distinguish firms that pay low dividends, which they assume are liquidity constrained, from others. They show that cash flow is a more important determinant of investment in the former group, which they interpret as evidence in favor of the internal-finance hypothesis. (Tobin's Q, the ratio of the market price of equity to replacement cost, is also included as an explanatory variable, to capture expectations of the return on investment.) One can interpret such findings as analogous to the Feldstein-Horioka result: just as a high correlation of national saving and investment across countries suggests that there may exist some barriers that separate individual countries from the worldwide capital market, so does high correlation of corporate saving and investment across firms suggest that there may exist barriers that separate individual firms from the nationwide capital market.

Hoshi, Kashyap, and Scharfstein (1990a) apply a similar methodology to Japan, where the segregation of firms can be more persuasively accomplished. They break down a sample into two groups. One consists of 121 "affiliated" firms, those with ties to large banks (typically a main bank) that are part of its keiretsu. The other consists of 25 "independent" firms, without close links to any particular bank. They find that among the independent firms, cash flow positively affects investment (and Tobin's Q does not), while among the affiliated firms cash flow has no significant effect.[75] The conclusion is that the first group faces a barrier between the cost of financing investment out of retained earnings and the cost of borrowing, like American firms do, while the latter can borrow from their affiliated banks as easily as financing out of retained earnings. The authors conclude that one possible implication is that "the institutional arrangements in Japan may offer Japanese firms an important competitive advantage" (p. 24).

The hypothesis that internal and indirect finance (especially from the main bank) is cheaper than direct or market finance can thus support the claim that the true cost of capital to Japanese corporations (at least those that are members of *keiretsu*) has been low in the past. But established banking relationships have begun to break down in Japan and the market has begun to take their place, as corporations begin to use banks less and bond markets more, a

75. Hayashi and Inoue (1989) find that Q is significantly related to firm growth, and that much, though not all, of the power of cash flow to explain investment in a cross-section of Japanese firms disappears when correcting for the endogeneity of cash flow. They do not segregate affiliated and nonaffiliated firms.

process that accelerated in the 1980s as the result of international liberalization as well as domestic deregulation.[76] The share of bank lending in total external financing fell from 84 percent in 1971–75, to 57 percent in 1981–85, as many firms found they could borrow more easily or more cheaply on the open market. But if the relevant interest rate was higher in the 1980s than it was in the past, this raises some difficult questions.[77] The first question, which we now consider, is how one explains the fact that price/earnings and price/ rental ratios were lower in previous decades than today. (The second, why firms would voluntarily abandon advantageous banking arrangements, is addressed subsequently.)

We must ask who would have had the opportunity to arbitrage between the low "cost of capital" and the high expected future return to holding land or equities. For those who had the opportunity to buy land, plant and equipment, or equity, the *opportunity cost* of funds was high, a number more like the observed rate of return on equity or the growth rate of the economy than like the observed interest rate or the still lower cost of internal finance.[78] The individual small investor did not have such opportunities; he was given little alternative to depositing his savings in a low-interest-rate account.[79] The same was, to a certain extent, true of institutional investors such as pension funds and insurance companies, and in any case the pool of available savings in such institutions was far smaller than in the 1980s. A corporation that was favored with access to cheap loans from the government or from its main bank was not generally free to use those funds to "speculate" in land or in the shares of other corporations. Nor was it allowed for the firm to buy back its own shares, when it should have had plenty of profitable new projects to invest in (Hatsopoulos and Brooks 1989, p. 12). Thus the arbitrage between the interest rate and real assets that we take for granted in a market-oriented system was not entirely relevant in the earlier period.

As noted, firms have begun to rely less on banks for their financing and more on marketplace borrowing, due in large part to deregulation and internationalization. The most important liberalizations include: the removal of

76. Crum and Meerschwam (1986) and Meerschwam (in this volume), e.g., discuss the decline of "relationship banking" and its replacement by the market.

77. Despite the diminished importance of subsidized government lending and the main-bank system, the era of cheaper capital through internal finance was prolonged past 1973 in Japan by the greater availability of retained earnings when the number of profitable investment projects that needed to be financed diminished. The share of funds coming from internal finance narrowly defined (retained earnings and depreciation charges), as opposed to external finance (securities-issues and borrowings), rose from 32.9 percent in the period 1970–74 to 46.3 percent in the period 1975–78, and stayed in that neighborhood subsequently (1979–85; the source is Tamura 1987, p. 3). It is the changes of the 1980s that need explaining.

78. When markets in government bonds and other instruments did begin to develop, especially in the 1970s, the observed interest rate was presumably somewhere between the low cost of internal and subsidized finance and the high rate of return to physical investment.

79. As noted in Meerschwam (in this volume), only preexisting shareholders received advantageous new-share subscription rights.

ceilings on interest rates after 1978 (in response to growing reluctance on the part of banks to absorb growing quantities of government debt at artificially low interest rates), the switch to a presumption that firms were allowed to sell bonds to foreign residents (as part of the Foreign Exchange Law reform) in 1980, the legalization of warrant bonds in 1981, the legalization of noncollateralized bonds for sufficiently safe corporations beginning in 1983, and the liberalization of issues of Euroyen bonds as part of the yen/dollar negotiations between the Ministry of Finance and the U.S. Treasury in 1984. More recent measures taken pursuant to the Yen/Dollar Agreement include: establishment of new short-term financial markets (in yen-denominated banker's acceptances, June 1985,[80] short-term bonds, November 1986, and commercial paper, November 1987), further liberalization regarding the Euromarket (such as allowing foreign companies to lead-manage Eurobond issues in December 1986, and introducing rating systems for Eurobonds in 1987), establishment of an offshore market in Japan (December 1986), the admission of major American securities companies to the Tokyo Stock Exchange (approximately 22 by the end of 1987), and inclusion of foreign firms in the syndicate through which the Japanese government sells its bonds and in the trust business (nine banks authorized after October 1985). In addition, the Ministry of Finance liberalized restrictions on what share of their portfolios Japanese insurance companies and trust banks could hold in the form of foreign securities (in 1986 and 1987).[81]

Note that even for those steps that represent domestic innovation or deregulation as opposed to international liberalization, foreigners have been an important driving force. There has been both direct political pressure on the Japanese government from foreign governments and competitive pressures on Japanese financial institutions from the activities of foreign rivals.

In a follow-up paper, Hoshi, Kashyap, and Scharfstein (1990b) address the gradual weakening of the links between banks and affiliated firms that has been taking place in Japan. Choosing 1983 as the first year in which the effects of deregulation were fully felt, they begin with their sample of firms that had close banking ties during the period 1977–82, and divide it into a subsample that shifted emphasis thereafter from bank borrowing to direct market finance and a subsample who continued to rely primarily on their banks; they find that the former group developed a strong sensitivity of investment to cash flow after 1983, while the latter group did not. This constitutes further evidence that bank borrowing in Japan obviates some of the usual costs of external financing.

80. Volume in the yen-denominated Bankers' Acceptances market soon began to decline, however, in favor of other instruments, and it died out completely in November 1989 (*Nihon Keizai Shimbun*, 14 December 1989).

81. Shinkai (1988), Hoshi, Kashyap, and Scharfstein (1990b), Crum and Meerschwam (1986), Feldman (1986), Frankel (1984), Sakakibara and Kondoh (1984), Suzuki (1987), and Ido (1989), among many other sources.

Some have surmised that, if public policy and the main-bank system have kept the cost of capital artificially low in Japan in the past, the deregulation and internationalization of Japanese financial markets must now have eliminated that advantage. Even if we could be confident that the Japanese cost of capital has been raised in this manner, that would still leave open the question of whether or not the traditional system produced a greater level of economic efficiency for the economy overall. On the one hand, any way of obviating information or incentive problems must represent a gain. On the other hand, the exclusion of certain firms and certain industries from the privileges of cheaper financing is only beneficial if there exists some decision-making mechanism superior to the market to decide who is worthy of inclusion and who is not—a questionable proposition.

It is also possible that the previous system of denying Japanese savers, banks, and taxpayers an opportunity to earn an equilibrium rate of return on their savings, even if inefficient in the economists' sense that it failed to maximize intertemporal welfare, nevertheless produced an (artificially) high level of investment. Such a proposition would be consistent with the legendary Japanese corporate emphasis on maximizing market share at the short-run expense of current profits (e.g., Abegglen and Stalk 1985; Crum and Meerschwam 1986; Meerschwam, in this volume). An alternative line of argument, adopted by Hatsopoulos, Krugman, and Summers (1988), is that the U.S. market system gives rise to an inefficiently *low* level of investment because of excessive concern with short-term profits and capital gains, at the expense of longer-term investment opportunities.[82] Perhaps the United States has recently been working to "drag the Japanese down to its level."

In any case, a puzzle remains. If the effective cost of capital under the traditional system is less than the market interest rate under the new system, why are Japanese firms voluntarily giving up their advantageous main-banking relationships for the difficulties of the marketplace? Hodder (1988b) concludes that, if firms are leaving their main-bank relationships, it must be because it is advantageous to do so, although he also concludes that it must have been advantageous for them to enter into these relationships in the first place.

Hoshi, Kashyap, and Scharfstein (1990b) suggest a possible explanation to the paradox: there are hidden costs to the system of bank monitoring, and a cheaper way of overcoming the information and incentive obstacles to borrowing—which is available only to older, well-established, successful firms—is to take advantage of the firm's reputation by issuing highly rated bonds.[83] The alternative possibility is that the change is not desirable from the

---

82. McKinnon (1989) argues that excessively short investment horizons in the United States (in contrast to Japan) are attributable to high interest rates, which are in turn attributable to the risk of dollar depreciation against the yen under the floating exchange rate system. Stein (1989) offers a theory with more rigorous foundations.

83. It is noteworthy that agencies to rate the creditworthiness of corporations (the analogues of Moody's or Standard and Poor's) did not develop in Japan until recently.

viewpoint of the well-established firms. Unfortunately for this hypothesis, there is little evidence that banks and other financial institutions are supplying less credit to their domestic clients (or offering less-favorable terms) and instead taking advantage of the higher interest rates in the United States by lending abroad. Still, it may not be possible for trust and long-term relationships to survive in an environment where newcomers deal only in explicit contracts.

Even under this theory, which agrees that the typical *keiretsu* firm may face a higher cost of capital now than in the past, the deregulation and internationalization of Japanese financial markets over the last 10 years is advantageous to one group of firms: those that never had access to preferential financing from main banks or government agencies in the past. While small firms lack the reputation necessary to borrow abroad even today, there are many large and medium-sized firms that were never members of *keiretsu* or favored by the government and had little means of financing expansion before the advent of free financial markets. For this group, internationalization has probably lowered the cost of capital, whether they now finance themselves by issuing bonds in the Euromarket or in newly liberalized domestic markets.[84]

8.6 Conclusions

The overall conclusions that emerge from the literature may be summarized as follows. (1) The cost of capital was lower in Japan than in the United States in the 1970s and 1980s. (2) One aspect of this difference was lower real interest rates. (3) Low real interest rates and high expected growth rates can go far toward explaining the high *levels* of equity and land prices (relative to earnings and rents, respectively) but not the great *increases* of the 1980s. (4) The high Japanese saving rate was responsible for the low real interest rates; Japanese tax policy plays no clear role. (5) Financial liberalization narrowed cost-of-capital differences in the 1980s; now Japanese saving goes to finance investment abroad almost as easily as at home.

Further conclusions of this paper that are perhaps novel are as follows. (6) It is possible for the real interest rate in Japan to be below that in the United States, despite international arbitrage. (7) The main relevant effect of the internationalization in Japan may have been to accelerate the process whereby corporate finance becomes market oriented, so that (8) affiliated firms are losing the special privilege of borrowing at a cheaper rate, while (9) unaffiliated firms are now able to borrow more cheaply than before, at the going interest rate. Finally, (10) the increased availability of funds that can be used for asset-market arbitrage allowed the great run-up in equity prices and land prices in the 1980s.

---

84. Many Japanese corporations now borrow in the Euromarkets in, e.g., Luxembourg. Often convertible and warrant issues are ultimately acquired by *Japanese* residents. In this way internationalization facilitates an end run around domestic Japanese rigidities, and makes Japanese finance more market oriented, even when neither the borrower nor the lender is foreign.

References

Abegglen, James, and George Stalk, Jr. 1985. *Kaisha, The Japanese Corporation.* New York: Basic Books.

Aggarwal, Raj, Ramesh Rao, and Takato Hiraki. 1990. Regularities in Tokyo Stock Exchange Security Returns: P/E, Size, and Seasonal Influences. *Journal of Financial Research* 13, (Fall): 249–63.

Ando, Albert, and Alan Auerbach. 1985. The Corporate Cost of Capital in the U.S. and Japan: A Comparison. NBER Working Paper no. 1762, October.

———. 1988. The Cost of Capital in the U.S. and Japan: A Comparison. *Journal of the Japanese and International Economies,* 2:134–58.

Aron, Paul. 1989. Japanese P/E Multiplies: The Tradition Continues. *Japanese Research Report* no. 35. Daiwa Securities America, Inc., October 23.

Auerbach, A., L. Kotlikoff, R. Hagemann, and G. Nicoletti. 1989. The Economic Dynamics of an Aging Population: The Case of Four OECD Countries. *OECD Economic Studies* no. 12 (Spring): 97–130.

Balassa, Bela. 1964. The Purchasing Power Parity Doctrine: A Reappraisal. *Journal of Political Economy* 72:584–96.

Balassa, Bela, and Marcus Noland. 1988. *Japan in the World Economy.* Washington, D.C.: Institute for International Economics.

Baldwin, Carliss. 1986. The Capital Factor: Competing for Capital in a Global Environment. In *Competition in Global Industries,* ed. Michael Porter, 185–223. Boston: Harvard Business School Press.

Bernanke, Ben, and Mark Gertler. 1989. Agency Costs, Net Worth and Business Fluctuations. *American Economic Review* 79:14–31.

Bernheim, B. Douglas, and John Shoven. 1986. Taxation and the Cost of Capital: An International Comparison. In *The Consumption Tax: A Better Alternative?,* ed. C. E. Walker and M. A. Bloomfield, pp. 61–85. Cambridge, Mass.: Ballinger.

Blades, Derek. 1988. Household Saving Ratios for Japan and Other OECD Countries. In *Global Role of the Japanese Economy With Affluent Savings and Accumulated Wealth.* Papers and proceedings of the Fifth EPA International Symposium. Tokyo, October 13–14.

Boone, Peter. 1989a. Perspectives on the High Price of Japanese Land. EPA Discussion Paper no. 45. Economic Planing Association, Tokyo.

———. 1989b. High Land Values in Japan: Is the Archipelago Worth Eleven Trillion Dollars? Manuscript. Harvard University, November.

Boone, Peter, and Jeffrey Sachs. 1989. Is Tokyo Worth Four Trillion Dollars? An Explanation for High Japanese Land Prices. Manuscript. Harvard University.

Branson, William, and Richard Marston. 1989. Price and Output Adjustment in Japanese Manufacturing. NBER Working Paper no. 2878. Cambridge, Mass., March.

Bronte, Stephen. 1982. *Japanese Finance: Markets and Institutions.* London: Euromoney Publications.

Crum, M. Colyer, and David Meerschwam. 1986. From Relationship to Price Banking: The Loss of Regulatory Control. In *America vs. Japan,* ed. T. McCraw. Boston: Harvard Business School Press.

Dekle, Robert. 1989a. A Simulation Model of Saving, Residential Choice, and Bequests of the Japanese Elderly. *Economic Letters* 29:129–33.

———. 1989b. Saving, Bequests, and Living Arrangements of the Japanese Elderly. *Journal of the Japanese and International Economies* 4, no. 3 (September).

Eken, Sena. 1984. Integration of Domestic and International Financial Markets: The Japanese Experience. *International Monetary Fund, Staff Papers* 31:499–548.

Fazzari, Steven, R. Glenn Hubbard, and Bruce Petersen. 1988. Investment and Finance Reconsidered. *Brookings Papers on Economic Activity,* no. 1: 141–96.

Feldman, Robert. 1986. *Japanese Financial Markets: Deficits, Dilemmas, and Dereg-ulation.* Cambridge, Mass.: MIT Press.
Feldstein, M., and P. Bacchetta. 1991. National Savings and International Investment. In *National Saving and Economic Performance,* ed. B. D. Bernheim and J. Shoven. Chicago: University of Chicago Press.
Feldstein, M., and C. Horioka. 1980. Domestic Saving and International Capital Flows. *Economic Journal* 90:314–29.
Frankel, Jeffrey. 1984. The Yen/Dollar Agreement: Liberalizing Japanese Capital Markets. *Policy Analyses in International Economics,* no. 9. Washington, D.C.: Institute for International Economics.
———. 1988a. International Capital Flows and Domestic Economic Policies. In *The United States in the World Economy,* ed. Martin Feldstein. Chicago: University of Chicago Press.
———. 1988b. U.S. Borrowing From Japan. KSG Working Paper 174D, Harvard University (in *Structural Change in the American Financial System,* ed. G. Luciani; excerpts [trans. into Japanese] also appear in *Kinyu Journal,* July 1988 and February 1989).
———. 1991. Quantifying International Capital Mobility in the 1980s. In *National Saving and Economic Performance,* ed. B. D. Bernheim and J. Shoven. Chicago: University of Chicago Press.
Frankel, J., and K. Froot. 1987. Short-term and Long-term Expectations of the Yen/Dollar Exchange Rates: Evidence from Survey Data. *Journal of the Japanese and International Economies* 1:249–74.
French, Kenneth, and James Poterba. 1989. Are Japanese Stock Prices Too High? CRSP Seminar on the Analysis of Security Prices, University of Chicago, April; rev., NBER, August.
Friend, Irwin, and Ichiro Tokutsu. 1987. The Cost of Capital to Corporations in Japan and the U.S.A. *Journal of Banking and Finance* 11:313–27.
Froot, Kenneth. 1988. Adjustment of the U.S. and Japanese External Imbalances. In *Global and Domestic Policy Implications of Correcting External Imbalances.* Papers and Proceedings of the Fourth EPA International Symposium, March 15–17. Tokyo: Economic Planning Agency, pp. 287–303.
Froot, Kenneth, and Takatoshi Ito, 1989. On the Consistency of Short-Run and Long-Run Exchange Rate Expectations. *Journal of International Money and Finance* 8, no. 4: 487–510.
Fukao, Mitsuhiro. 1987. A Risk Premium Model of the Yen-Dollar and DM-Dollar Exchange Rates. *OECD Economic Studies* 9 (Autumn): 79–104.
———. 1988. Balance of Payments Imbalances and Long-Term Capital Movements: Review and Prospects. In *Correcting External Imbalances,* ed. Masaru Yoshitomi. Tokyo: Economic Planning Agency.
Fukao, Mitsuhiro, and T. Okubo. 1984. International Linkage of Interest Rates: The Case of Japan and the United States. *International Economic Review* 25 (February).
Gerlach, Michael. 1987. Alliances and the Social Organization of Japanese Business. Ph.D. diss., Yale University.
Glick, Reuven. 1987. Interest Rate Linkages in the Pacific Basin. *Economic Review* 3:31–42.
Hale, David. 1987. Tax Reform in the U.S. and Japan: The Movement towards International Tax Convergence. Paper presented to the U.S.-Japan Consultative Group on International Monetary Affairs. San Diego, February.
———. 1989. The Japanese Ministry of Finance and Dollar Diplomacy during the Late 1980s: or, How the University of Tokyo Law School Saved the United States from the University of Chicago Economics Department. Manuscript. Kemper Financial Services, Inc., July.

Hamada, Koichi, and Akiyoshi Horiuchi. 1987. The Political Economy of the Financial Market. In *The Political Economy of Japan: Vol. 1, The Domestic Transformation,* ed. Kozo Yamamura and Yasukichi Yasuba, pp. 223–60. Stanford, Calif.: Stanford University Press.

Hardouvelis, Gikas, and Steven Peristiani. 1989. Do Margin Requirements Matter? Evidence from the Japanese Stock Market. Working paper. Federal Reserve Bank of New York, October.

Hatsopoulos, George. 1983. High Cost of Capital: Handicap of American Industry. Study sponsored by the American Business Conference and Thermo Electron Corporation, April.

Hatsopoulos, George, and Stephen Brooks. 1986. The Gap in the Cost of Capital: Causes, Effects, and Remedies. In *Technology and Economic Policy,* ed. Ralph Landau and Dale Jorgenson, pp. 221–80. Cambridge, Mass.: Ballinger.

———. 1989. The Cost of Capital in the United States and Japan. In *Technology and Capital Formation,* ed. D. Jorgenson and R. Landau. Cambridge, Mass.: MIT Press.

Hatsopoulos, George, Paul Krugman, and Larry Summers. 1988. U.S. Competitiveness: Beyond the Trade Deficit. *Science,* July 15, pp. 299–307.

Hayashi, Fumio. 1986. Why Is Japan's Saving Rate So Apparently High? *NBER Macroeconomics Annual 1986* 1:147–234. Cambridge, Mass.: MIT Press.

Hayashi, Fumio, and Tohru Inoue. 1989. The Relationship of Firm Growth and Q with Multiple Capital Goods: Theory and Evidence From Panel Data on Japanese Firms. Institute for Empirical Macroeconomics Discussion Paper no. 13. Federal Reserve Bank of Minneapolis, May.

Hayashi, Fumio, Takatoshi Ito, and Joel Slemrod. 1988. Housing Finance Imperfections, Taxation, and Private Savings: A Comparative Analysis of the U.S. and Japan. *Journal of the Japanese and International Economies* 2, no. 3 (September).

Hodder, James. 1988a. Corporate Capital Structure in the United States and Japan: Financial Intermediation and Implication of Financial Deregulation. In *Government Policy towards Industry in the USA and Japan,* ed. J. Shoven, chap. 9, pp. 241–63. Cambridge: Cambridge University Press.

———. 1988b. Capital Structure and Cost of Capital in the U.S. and Japan. Manuscript. Stanford University, July.

———. 1991. Is the Cost of Capital Lower in Japan? *Journal of the Japanese and International Economies* 5, no. 1 (March): 86–100.

Hodder, James, and A. Tschoegl. 1985. Some Aspects of Japanese Corporate Finance. *Journal of Financial and Quantitative Analysis* 20:173–90.

Homma, Masaki. 1987. An Overview of Tax Reform in the U.S. and Japan. Paper presented to the U.S.-Japan Consultative Group on International Monetary Affairs. San Diego, February.

Homma, M., N. Atoda, F. Hayashi, and K. Hata. 1984. *Setsubi Toshi to Kigyo Zeisei* (Investment and corporate tax structure). Economic Planning Agency: Tokyo.

Homma, M., T. Maeda, and K. Hashimoto. 1986. The Japanese Tax System. *Brookings Discussion Papers in Economics.* June

Horioka, Charles. 1985. Household Saving in Japan: The Importance of Target Saving for Education and Housing. *Kyoto University Economic Review* 55, no. 1 (April): 41–78.

———. 1986. Why Is Japan's Private Savings Rate so High? *Finance and Development* 23 (December): 22–25.

———. 1988. Saving for Housing Purchase in Japan. In *Global Role of the Japanese Economy with Affluent Savings and Accumulated Wealth.* Papers and proceedings of the Fifth EPA International Symposium. Tokyo, October 13–14.

———. 1990. Why Is Japan's Household Saving Rate So High? A Literature Survey. *Journal of the Japanese and International Economies* 4, no. 1 (March): 49–92.

Hoshi, Takeo, Anil Kashyap, and David Scharfstein. 1990a. Corporate Structure, Liquidity, and Investment: Evidence from Japanese Panel Data. *Quarterly Journal of Economics*.
———. 1990b. Bank Monitoring and Investment: Evidence from the Changing Structure of Japanese Corporate Banking Relationships. In *Asymmetric Information, Corporate Finance, and Investment*, ed. R. Glenn Hubbard. Chicago: University of Chicago Press.
Ido, Kiyoto. 1989. Internationalization and Implementation of the New Foreign Exchange Control Law. *FAIR Fact Series: Japan's Financial Markets*, vol. 19.
Ishikawa, Tsuneo, and Kazuo Ueda. 1984. The Bonus Payment System and Japanese Personal Savings. In *The Economic Analysis of the Japanese Firm*, ed. M. Aoki. Amsterdam: Elsevier Science Publishers.
Ito, Takatoshi. 1986. Capital Controls and Covered Interest Parity. *Economic Studies Quarterly* 37:223–41.
———. 1988. Use of (Time-Domain) Vector Autoregressions to Test Uncovered Interest Parity. *Review of Economics and Statistics* 70:296–305.
———. 1989. Japan's Structural Adjustment: The Land/Housing Problem and External Balance. Manuscript, International Monetary Fund. Rev. February, NBER Summer Institute.
———. 1990. Foreign Exchange Rate Expectations: Micro Survey Data. *American Economic Review* 80, no. 3 (June): 434–49.
Iwata, Kazumasa, Ikuo Suzuki, and Atsushi Yoshida. 1988. Capital Costs of Housing Investment in Japan. Discussion Paper no. 44. Economic Planning Agency, Tokyo, December.
Iwata, Kazumasa, and Atsushi Yoshida. 1988. Housing, Land and Taxation System in Japan. In *Global and Domestic Policy Implications of Correcting External Imbalances*. Papers and proceedings of the Fourth EPA International Symposium. Tokyo: Economic Planning Agency.
———. 1987. Capital Cost of Business Investment in Japan and the United States under Tax Reform. In *Technology and Capital Formation*, ed. D. Jorgenson and R. Landau. Cambridge, Mass.: MIT Press.
Jensen, M., and W. Meckling. 1976. Theory of the Firm: Managerial Behavior, Agency Costs and Ownership Structure. *Journal of Financial Economics* 3:305–60.
Jorgenson, Dale. 1971. Econometric Studies of Investment Behavior: A Review. *Journal of Economic Literature* 9:1111–47.
Krugman, Paul. 1989. Differences in Income Elasticities and Trends in Real Exchange Rates. *European Economic Review* 33, no. 5 (May): 1031–47.
Lawler, Patrick, Bonnie Loopesko, and Marc Dudey. 1988. An Analysis of Some Aspects of the Japanese Stock Market. November 10 (this paper is not to circulate or be quoted without permission of authors).
Lee, Hiro. 1988. Imperfect Competition, Industrial Policy, and Japanese International Competitiveness. Ph.D. diss., University of California, Berkeley, September.
Lincoln, Edward. 1988. *Japan: Facing Economic Maturity*. Washington, D.C.: Brookings.
McDonald, Jack. 1989. The *Mochiai* Effect: Japanese Corporate Cross-Holdings. *Journal of Portfolio Management* 16, no. 1 (Fall): 90–95.
McKinnon, Ronald, and David Robinson. 1989. Dollar Devaluation, Interest Rate Volatility, and the Duration of Investment. CEPR Conference on Economic Growth and the Commercialization of New Technologies. Stanford, Calif., September 11–12.
Makin, John. 1985. Saving Rates in Japan and the United States: The Roles of Tax Policy and Other Factors. Paper prepared for Savings Forum, Philadelphia, May.
Marston, Richard. 1987. Real Exchange Rates and Productivity Growth in the United

States and Japan. *Real-Financial Linkages in Open Economies,* ed. S. Arndt. Cambridge, Mass.: MIT Press.

———. 1990. Pricing to Market in Japanese Manufacturing. *Journal of International Economics* 29 (November): 217–36.

Meyer, John, and Ed Kuh. 1957. *The Investment Decision.* Cambridge, Mass.: Harvard University Press.

Ministry of Finance. 1988. Main Points of Tax Reform. Tokyo, December 24.

Mishkin, Frederic. 1984. Are Real Interest Rates Equal across Countries? An Empirical Investigation of International Parity Conditions. *Journal of Finance* 39:1345–58.

Murphy, R. Taggart. 1989. Power without Purpose: The Crisis of Japan's Global Financial Dominance. *Harvard Business Review* (March-April), pp. 71–83.

Myers, Stewart, and N. Majluf. 1984. Corporate Financing and Investment Decisions When Firms Have Information That Investors Do Not Have. *Journal of Financial Economics,* 187–221.

Noguchi, Yukio. 1985. Tax Structure and Saving-Investment Balance. Paper presented to the U.S.-Japan Consultative Group on International Monetary Affairs. Hakone, March.

———. 1987. Land Price Swollen by Bubbles (in Japanese). *Toyo Keizai* 77 (November): 38–45.

Ohno, Kenichi. 1989. Export Pricing Behavior of Manufacturing: A U.S.-Japan Comparison. *International Monetary Fund Staff Papers* 36, no. 3 (September): 550–79.

Otani, Ichiro. 1983. Exchange Rate Instability and Capital Controls: The Japanese Experience, 1978–81. In *Exchange Rate and Trade Instability: Causes, Consequences and Remedies,* ed. D. Bigman and T. Taya. Cambridge, Mass.: Ballinger.

Otani, Ichiro, and Siddath Tiwari. 1981. Capital Controls, and Interest Rate Parity: The Japanese Experience, 1978–81. *International Monetary Fund Staff Papers* 28, no. 4 (December): 793–815.

Prowse, Stephen David. 1989. Firm Financial Behavior in the U.S. and Japan: The Role of Agency Relationships. NBER Summer Institute, August 11.

Sachs, Jeffrey and Peter Boone. 1988. Japanese Structural Adjustment and the Balance of Payments. *Journal of the Japanese and International Economies* 2, no. 3.

Sakakibara, Eisuke, and Akira Kondoh. 1984. *Study on the Internationalization of Tokyo's Money Markets.* Center for International Finance Study Series no. 1. Tokyo, June.

Saxonhouse, Gary. 1982. Japanese Saving Behavior: A Household Balance Sheet Approach. Manuscript. University of Michigan, November.

Semiconductor Industry Association. 1980. U.S. and Japanese Semiconductor Industries: A Financial Comparison. Report prepared by Chase Financial Policy, June.

Shibuya, Hiroshi. 1988. Japan's Household Savings: A Life-Cycle Model with Implicit Annuity Contract and Rational Expectations. Manuscript. International Monetary Fund, February.

Shinkai, Yoichi. 1988. The Internationalization of Finance in Japan. In *The Political Economy of Japan:* volume 2, *The Changing International Context,* ed. T. Inoguchi and D. I. Okimoto. Stanford, Calif.: Stanford University Press.

Shoven, John. 1989. The Japanese Tax Reform and the Effective Rate of Tax on Japanese Corporate Investments. In *Tax Policy and the Economy,* ed. L. Summers. Cambridge, Mass.: MIT Press.

Shoven, John, and Toshiaki Tachibanaki. 1988. The Taxation of Income from Capital in Japan. In *Government Policy towards Industry in the United States and Japan,* ed. J. Shoven. Cambridge: Cambridge University Press.

Slemrod, Joel. 1988. Fear of Nuclear War and Intercountry Differences in the Rate of Saving. NBER Working Paper no. 2801. Cambridge, Mass., December.

Stein, Jeremy. 1989. Efficient Capital Markets, Inefficient Firms: A Model of Myopic Corporate Behavior. *Quarterly Journal of Economics* 104:655–69.

Suzuki, Yoshio. 1987. *The Japanese Financial System.* Oxford: Clarendon Press.

Takagi, Keizo. 1989. The Rise in Land Prices in Japan: The Determination Mechanism and the Effect of the Taxation System. *Monetary and Economic Studies* 7, no. 2 (August).

Takagi, Shinji. 1989. The Japanese Equity Market: Past and Present. *Journal of Banking and Finance* 13 (March): 537–70.

Takayama, Noriyuki, et al. 1988. Household Asset Holdings and the Saving Rate in Japan. In *The Global Role of the Japanese Economy with Affluent Savings and Accumulated Wealth.* Papers and proceedings of the Fifth EPA International Symposium. Tokyo, October 13–14.

Takenaka, Heizo. 1986. Economic Incentives for Industrial Investment: Japanese Experience. Institute for Fiscal and Monetary Policy, Ministry of Finance, Japan, February.

Tamura, Tatsuro. 1987. Changes in Corporate Fund Raising and Management, pt. 2. *FAIR Fact Series: Japan's Financial Markets,* vol. 29.

Ueda, Kazuo. 1990. Are Japanese Stock Prices too High? *Journal of the Japanese and International Economies* 3, no. 4 (December): 351–70.

Yamamura, Kozo. 1982. Success that Soured: Administrative Guidance and Cartels in Japan. In *Policy and Trade Issues of the Japanese Economy,* ed. K. Yamamura, pp. 77–112. Seattle: University of Washington Press.

Yoshikawa, Hiroshi, and Fumio Ohtake. 1989. An Analysis of Female Labor Supply, Housing Demand and the Saving Rate in Japan. *European Economic Review* 33, no. 5: 997–1023.

Comment   Robert Dekle

Jeffrey Frankel's main aim in the paper is to try to explain the high Japanese stock and land prices by the fundamentals valuation equation. Ruling out speculative bubbles, the price-rental or price-earnings ratios will be high when the expected rate of economic growth is high or the real interest rate is low. The puzzle, as stated by the author, is this: Why have the price-rental ratios risen so rapidly in the 1980s compared to the 1960s when today the expectations of future economic growth are so much lower and the observed real interest rate is probably higher? The paper proposes an innovative answer. In the past, capital in Japan was rationed by the banking system, and only the large blue chip firms could raise funds at the low real interest rate. The use of these funds, however, was strictly monitored by the banks, and the firms could not use these funds to freely engage in large-scale purchases of land and equities. Hence, in the 1960s and early 1970s, there was imperfect arbitrage between the low cost of capital and the high expected future returns to holding land or equities. The deregulation of Japanese financial markets in the late

Robert Dekle is an assistant professor of economics and international relations at Boston University.

1970s and 1980s enabled smaller firms and individuals to take advantage of this arbitrage opportunity, and the result was the bidding up of asset prices.

The argument, unfortunately, is not entirely convincing. First, the effective cost of capital for the highly leveraged large companies in the 1960s was not as low as the author alleges. It is well known that many Japanese banks during this period demanded "compensating balances" from the consumer firms, adding to the firms' cost of borrowing, the spread between the deposit rate, and the return from productive investment. Yoshio Suzuki estimates that the effective loan rates to large firms in the 1964–73 period were between 8 and 12 percent, which were well above the regulated interest rates of 3–4 percent.

Second, it is unclear whether the demand for funds by small and medium-sized enterprises actually exceeded the supply of funds. During the late 1960s, the local banks, which primarily lend to small and medium-sized enterprises, had more deposits than the demand for loans. The surplus was channeled through the Japanese "call money" market to the large city banks, which lend mostly to the large firms.[1] If they so desired, the small and medium-sized sector should have been able to borrow and purchase land and equities.

Third, it is somewhat misleading to argue that the Japanese government until recently regulated speculation in the asset markets. The stock market crash in 1964–65 was exacerbated by securities companies using their market power to prop up prices.[2] The surge in land prices between 1972–73 was largely caused by companies purchasing land nationwide in anticipation of Premier Tanaka's massive regional public works projects.

Consequently, it appears that even before the recent financial deregulation, investors were able to and did take full advantage of arbitrage opportunities between the real rate of interest and the expected return on land and stocks.

What then are the causes for the recent rise in the land price-rental and equity-price earnings ratios? The paper reads as if company earnings and land rents are driven by the same mechanism. For an office-space leasing company, rents and earnings may move identically, but for firms producing goods that are intensive in physical capital, land rents and earnings are likely to diverge. Corporate profits in Japan have drastically fallen as a share of GNP in the period between 1970 and 1985, and one reason for the fall is the decline in the marginal product of physical capital. As an economy grows and accumulates capital, it may be possible to observe corporate profits falling, and the returns to the fixed factor, land, rising. For example, falling returns to physical capital and rising returns to land may be observed in a three-factor (land, labor, capital) Cobb-Douglas production function.

If corporate profits have fallen, why have Japanese stock prices risen? There

---

1. The call market essentially corresponds in function to the federal funds market in the United States.
2. As a consequence of the crash, Yamaichi Securities was almost driven to bankruptcy.

are two popular hypotheses. The first is called the "restructuring hypothesis" and explains the high cross-section correlation between stock and land prices. Take the example of Ishikawajima Harima Heavy Industries, a shipbuilder with high stock prices but with depressed corporate profits. Ishikawajima Harima owns much land in Tokyo Bay, an area expected to receive large government public works funding over the next decade. There is to be a landfill and major office buildings and retail complexes, and apartments are to be constructed. In the future, if Ishikawajima is able to use its land efficiently, say, by converting its shipbuilding factories to retail outlets, then the firm's profits should soar. The present high price for Ishikawajima's stock partly reflects the expectation that the firm, by restructuring, will be able to use its assets efficiently and raise its future profits.

Cross-section econometric studies have shown that firms with high price-earnings ratios generally own expensive land. The "restructuring" hypothesis does not, however, explain why land prices have doubled over the last three years. The second hypothesis relies on imperfect international capital mobility and excess Japanese liquidity to explain both high land and equity prices. From the fall of 1986 until now, the growth in the Japanese money supply has been much higher than in the previous half-decade. It has been said that the Bank of Japan had embarked on a loose monetary policy to prop up the dollar. Exchange rate risk has limited the flow of Japanese funds abroad and, given the artificially low rate of return on Japanese bank deposits, funds have flowed into real estate and stocks, bidding up the price of these assets.

9 Industrial Policy in Japan: A Political Economy View

Masahiro Okuno-Fujiwara

9.1 Introduction

In this paper, I argue first that, contrary to perceptions outside of Japan, Japanese industrial policy per se does not play a critical role either in strategically restructuring the Japanese economy or in forming government-industry cartels to promote Japanese exports. If contemporary industrial policy is important, it is because of its role in coordinating the planning and managerial decisions of individual firms and in helping in the dissemination of information.

In the first half of this paper, I try to support this view by providing a brief historical account of Japanese industrial policy. To be more precise, I argue that postwar Japanese industrial policy was transformed toward the end of the 1960s. Until then, its major aim was to promote several key industries in order to take advantage of the benefits of international trade. Policies tended to involve direct regulation requiring government involvement, such as licensing and granting the authority to allocate foreign exchange.

Since then, the trend has changed, and the main focus of policy seems to be correcting market failures, including promoting private research and development (R&D) efforts and assisting in the structural adjustment of the economy. Policies also have become *soft measures,* such as assisting in the relocation of workers (or factories) from depressed areas (or industries) to growing ones, and promoting research associations to help private firms engage in cooperative R&D efforts.

Nonetheless, access to the Japanese market seems to be heavily restricted.

Masahiro Okuno-Fujiwara is a professor of economics at the University of Tokyo.

The author is grateful to Laura Tyson, Marcus Noland, and other participants of the NBER conference for helpful comments and criticism. He has also benefited from useful comments provided by C. Tsukuda, K. Yokobori, and other participants of a Ministry of International Trade and Industry seminar.

There is also an export downpour: that is, Japanese firms pour down their exports to foreign markets over very short periods, harming the domestic producers. This paper argues that these problems originate not from the strategic nature of industrial policy but from the way policy decisions generally are made and put into practice in Japan. In this sense, the problem is far broader than industrial policy per se.

To put it succinctly, policy decisions in Japan reflect the interests of insiders (usually only producers—consumers are excluded). Moreover, decisions are not made on some abstract philosophical basis, nor are they made according to clearly spelled-out rules. Instead, they are made on a practical basis by negotiation among insiders; the policies that are most easily implemented, and that cause the least political conflict, tend to be adopted.

The paper is organized as follows: section 9.2 defines the concept of industrial policy and briefly surveys recent theoretical contribution on industrial policy. In section 9.3, a very brief historical account of Japanese industrial policy is presented. Sections 9.4 and 9.5 describe major contemporary industrial policies in Japan: R&D assistance and dealings with trade conflicts. In section 9.6, the system of Japanese policy-making from the viewpoint of political economy theory is summarized. Section 9.7 briefly discusses the Large Stores Law to support our view on how Japanese policies are practiced. Section 9.8 concludes the paper.

9.2 Industrial Policy: Its Scope and Limits

In economics, industrial policy is a relatively new concept that lacks a well-accepted definition. In this paper, I use the following definition: Industrial policy is any "policy that attempts to achieve the economic and noneconomic goals of a country by intervening in resource allocation across industries or sectors, or in the (industrial) organization of an industry or sector" (Itoh et al. 1991).[1] This definition emphasizes microeconomic aspects of the economy and focuses on inter- and/or intraindustry resource allocation. An alternative definition, often assumed to be implicit in Japan, is that of Kaizuka (1973, p. 163): "With little sarcasm, I would define industrial policy to be the policy that MITI implements." I shall follow this definition when I give historical accounts of Japanese industrial policy.

For the purpose of this paper, it is useful to classify industrial policies into two basic subcategories: *strategic policies* and *corrective policies.* Strategic policies promote certain industries (sectors) for the benefit of domestic welfare; corrective policies improve economic efficiency by correcting market failures. However, these two types of policies are not mutually exclusive.

---

1. For other related definitions, see Komiya, Okuno, and Suzumura (1988) and Suzumura and Okuno-Fujiwara (1987).

9.2.1   Strategic Policies

Recent theoretical contributions have identified two cases where strategic policies may be effective: where there are externalities and where monopoly rents may be shifted.

First, some form of externality may create economies of scale on a national level and nonconvexity in the economy. The traditional infant industry argument, which emphasizes external dynamic economies, is an example of this approach.[2] Alternatively, if Marshallian externality exists so that, as an industry's total output increases, the industry's average cost declines and its productivity improves, there may be multiple equilibria: one where the industry produces no output because average cost is too high compared with the demand price, and the other where positive production takes place using (industry-level) economies of scale. Moreover, these equilibria often are Pareto ranked. Hence, if an economy is trapped in a Pareto-inferior equilibrium, policy intervention to reallocate interindustry resources may shift the economy to a Pareto-superior equilibrium (see, e.g., Okuno-Fujiwara 1988).

Questions still remain as to how Marshallian externality (or national-level economies of scale) evolves. Ethier (1982) and Okuno-Fujiwara (1988) showed that Marshallian externality indeed may occur if several industries are interrelated and if monopolistic or oligopolistic competition prevails in a critical part of this nexus, for example with parts suppliers for an industry that has the potential to draw a large portion of laborers. The latter, further identified coordination failure among monopolistic firms may be the cause of this phenomenon. In other words, if these firms' expectations about the future course of the economy change (from one rational expectation to another rational expectation), a Pareto-superior equilibrium may be achieved. Thus, policies to coordinate firms' incentive or to change future expectations of economic agents may be effective in moving the economy away from the Pareto-inferior equilibrium.[3]

If one believes in this explanation, one of its inescapable conclusions is that the industrial structure of an economy may not be determined by tastes and resource endowments alone, as is the case with the Heckscher-Ohlin model. Instead, industrial structure may be determined by historical accidents and policy interventions. This implies that free trade may not be the best system, as an economy or the world may be trapped in an inferior equilibrium. Some sort of coordinated policy intervention or managed trade may be desirable.[4] This type of strategic policy may be justified because it could improve the

2. For details of the infant industry protection argument, see Itoh et al. (1989), chap. 4; and Corden (1974).
3. For the explicit treatment of expectation in a dynamic model with multiple rational expectation equilibrium paths, see Matsuyama (1989).
4. For the detail of this argument, see Okuno-Fujiwara (1988) and Itoh et al. (1989), chaps. 5–6.

welfare of the country, and even of the world, by substantially reducing the price of the industry's product. Moreover, the benefit of such a policy may be relatively large if the nexus of industries that become competitive draws a big share of resources.

Critics of this approach emphasize that this type of strategic policy is justified on the grounds of externality. Externalities being difficult to identify and measure in practice, they argue that application of this approach is severely limited.

A second line of explanation for strategic policies relies on the strategic behaviors in international oligopolistic rivalry. Originated by Brander and Spencer (1981, 1983), it suggests that providing a subsidy to domestic firms may benefit the country if these firms face oligopolistic competition with foreign rivals. The underlying logic is that the subsidy makes domestic firms' behavior more aggressive and, more important, that this change in the firms' attitude becomes *credible* to their rivals because the subsidy changes the firms' own incentives. The resulting expansion in the firms' production occurs at the cost of foreign rivals, shifting monopoly rent from foreign firms to domestic firms. It also affects the consumer surplus in the market in which rivals compete, as more aggressive behavior may cause the price of the product to fall.

Although this explanation drew more attention than the first approach, there are limitations to the argument. First and most seriously, as far as rent shifting between foreign and domestic firms, this policy is of the "Beggar-thy-Neighbor" type: the country obtains benefits at the cost of foreign countries. This policy is likely to draw retaliation from other countries, and the chain of retaliations might destroy world trade. Second, its main argument relies on rent shifting in one industry, which may be too small to justify policy intervention. Moreover, the argument depends upon the existence of entry barriers, for otherwise monopoly rent would dissipate.[5]

To sum up, strategic policies should not be denounced outright. Some may benefit not only the home country but also the foreign countries. On the other hand, certain strategic policies benefit the home country at the cost of the foreign countries. The difference is that, in the former, the policies help to reduce the social production cost (that is, the sum of production costs incurred by private firms and the cost of government support) while, in the latter, policies help to reduce private cost without changing the social production cost.

9.2.2 Corrective Policies

Two branches of corrective policies are relevant in the following discussions: policies to promote private R&D and policies to assist structural adjustments. R&D is one of the prime examples of economic activities that are

---

5. For more extensive review of this theory, see, e.g., Brander (1986) and Grossman (1986).

prone to market failures. Fruits of R&D cannot be appropriated to investors, and they spill over easily to other firms, so it is often claimed that there is a socially insufficient incentive for R&D without government support. To correct this, subsidizing private R&D and providing incentives in other forms have become popular in developed countries.

Theoretically speaking, however, other aspects of R&D may make private efforts socially excessive. If the results of R&D can be patented, for example, then pursuing economic rents accruable to resulting innovations may induce socially excessive competition.[6] Even if there is uncertainty in the outcome, R&D creates negative externalities, as it may reduce the probability that other firms can secure the same outcome. As the externalities affect an industry's firms indiscriminately, R&D again may become socially excessive (see Loury 1979; Lee and Wilde 1980). Whether public support is justified or not, therefore, should depend upon the relative magnitude of these two effects and can only be determined empirically. Nonetheless, policymakers in many countries seem to take it as a foregone conclusion that government support is required in this area, and Japan is no exception.[7]

Another policy—which may be classified as corrective—that has been utilized extensively in Japan is that of assisting industries that are harmed by changes in external environments, such as a rise in oil price or an unexpected change in exchange rates. These are called structural adjustment policies. When a change in external environments occurs and a country's comparative advantage changes, resources must move from one (declining) industry to another (growing) industry. Many resources are industry specific, however, and cannot move within a short period. If there is an additional market failure, such as wage rigidity, resources trapped in declining industries may suffer from unemployment, and inefficient resource allocation will result. Policy assistance is called for.[8]

The first-best policy for structural adjustment is eliminating the market failure that causes unemployment (e.g., wage rigidity in the earlier example). If the first-best policy is not available, several possibilities remain.[9] As declining industry suffers from deteriorated export opportunities, or from increased competition from foreign imports, trade restriction provides relief. However, protection provides incentives for resources to stay within the declining industry, which is the opposite of what structural adjustment intends. To provide the correct incentives and to assist adjustment, it is critical that trade restric-

6. For the detail of this argument, see Barzel (1968).

7. For survey of theories of R&D incentives see, e.g., Itoh et al. (1989), Scherer (1980), Tirole (1989) and Kamien and Schwartz (1982).

8. Existence of industry-specific resources makes resource owners in the declining industries suffer from lower return, but this alone does not justify policy interventions. For, as long as there are no market failures, this is the unavoidable cost to the economy. See, e.g., Mussa (1982).

9. For details on this, see, e.g., Itoh and Negishi (1987) and Itoh et al. (1989).

tion (and other help for declining industries) is provided only temporarily. The time limit must be made explicit and credible.

If unemployment results because of external shocks, another possibility is to provide wage subsidies. Although this, like trade restriction, is effective for improving employment, it shields consumers from the changes in relative prices (terms of trade) that are caused by external shocks and, hence, is inferior to trade restriction.

Cartelization is another often-used policy measure. Declining industry is encouraged to form a cartel to limit the level of production or the extent of capacity utilization. By this, domestic price may be kept high and damage may be eliminated. However, allowing cartelization may enhance collusive behavior, which harms consumers' welfare. Forcing the exporting country to form a (voluntary) export cartel and to restrict the amount of exports works the same as obstructing competition.

Helping growing industries to absorb new equipment is called *positive adjustment policy* (PAP). The policies listed above to help declining industries maintain their employment are called *negative adjustment policy* (NAP). PAP is often thought to be superior to NAP. However, the issue is subtle. Even without PAP, economic incentives exist to direct resources from declining to growing industries. But is facilitating this resource movement beneficial to the country? If there is no additional market failure, it may be best not to intervene in the market mechanism, as was shown by Mussa (1982). Moreover, as Neary (1982) and others have shown, it might be better to slow the movement of resources. For example, suppose wages are rigid and capital is industry specific in the short run. If the declining industry is relatively more labor intensive than the growing industry, then accelerating the movement of labor from the former to the latter may increase unemployment, as the growing industry cannot absorb enough workers in the short run.

9.3 A Brief History of Industrial Policy in Japan

Though some time has passed since foreign interests in Japanese industrial policy evolved, some myths about the policy still seem to exist. There are strong opinions abroad that the policy is one of the main elements of the "Japan, Inc"; that is, a nexus of private corporations and the Japanese government that effectively controls the Japanese economy through conspiratorial cartels and regulations. Some also believe that the policy is designed to protect domestic industries from foreign competition through the use of overt and covert measures. In this section, I try to argue that these beliefs are not well founded from a historical viewpoint.

Chronologically, industrial policy in postwar Japan may be divided into three different time periods: 1945–60, 1960–73, and 1973 to the present. In this section, we shall provide brief historical account of each period.

9.3.1   1945–60[10]

This is the period when Japan tried to reconstruct its economy after devastating defeat. The 1946 production index was one-fifth of the prewar peak, and one-quarter of the national wealth had been lost during the war. In addition, international trade was severely restricted by the allied force. In order to sustain its economy and provide food for a large population, which included 7.6 million discharged soldiers, the government continued wartime regulation and control. This is typified by the so-called Priority Production System (PPS) of 1946–48. Designed by a Marxist economist, H. Arisawa, the PPS was intended to start reconstruction by concentrating domestic resources into two critical industries: steel and coal. The only available natural resource at the time was coal. But there was a bottleneck in increasing coal production: a lack of steel. With the PPS, the entire coal production effort was thrown into the steel industry. The entire steel production was then cast in coal production. By repeating this process, it was hoped that both steel and coal production would increase and would eventually make other industries revive. To help PPS, materials, workers, and funds were ordered to be concentrated in these two industries.

Direct governmental regulation of the economy typified by the PPS continued until late 1950s, but there was less emphasis on direct control toward the end. There were three factors that made government take this position. First, although the Korean War boom boosted reconstruction, the Japanese economy did not recover from defeat until mid-1950s. Some form of government intervention was necessary, for international trade was still restricted, and large disguised unemployment existed in agricultural sector.

Second, the government had many levers with which to adopt direct regulatory measures. The Temporary Commodities Demand and Supply Adjustment Law of 1946 gave the government extensive power to intervene in private economic activities. Under this law, the government could ration any commodity (for consumption and production), or prohibit or restrict usage of and production or shipment of any commodity whose supply was limited. This law lost its effect in 1952, but many powers with which to regulate the private sector remained with the government until the late 1950s or early 1960s. Access to foreign exchange was essential for firms that need foreign resources to construct new plants and to obtain technology licenses from technologically advanced foreign firms. But foreign exchange and foreign capital were controlled and rationed. The Enterprise Rationalization Promotion Law of 1952 provided special depreciation allowances and tariff exemption to key industries.

Third, after the *zaibatsu* (the family-held groups of companies that domi-

10. For more details, see Kosai (1986, 1988).

nated the prewar economy) were dissolved by the occupation force, the government's influence increased. Heavily influenced by the experience of wartime control, bureaucrats of this period seemed to have come to believe in governmental control and direct regulation of the economy.

To sum, industrial policy in this period aimed at directly regulating and controlling economic activities of the private sector. The philosophy behind such a policy stance reflected the training that bureaucrats received in the wartime, controlled economy. Toward the end of this period, the Japanese economy started to take off. Some believe that industrial policy was responsible for the relatively quick reconstruction and take-off. However, strong entrepreneurial spirits existed in the private sector, despite the bureaucratic attempts to contain them. Many economists believe these spirits were the major factor of the Japanese economy's performance in this period (see Kosai 1986, 1988).

9.3.2   1960–73[11]

This is the famous "rapid growth" period of the Japanese economy. It is also considered the heyday of Japanese industrial policy. Between 1960 and 1970, Japan enjoyed an average growth rate of 11.6% in real terms. Industrial structure transformed dramatically from agriculture to manufacturing and from light industries (such as textiles) to heavy industries (such as steel, petrochemicals, and automobiles). This transformation was accelerated by the explosion of exports in heavy industry products.

In 1960, the government announced the Plan for Trade and Foreign Exchange Liberalization. Until then, many imports were restricted by the system of licenses and foreign exchange quotas. With the liberalization, however, the ratio of imports with the automatic approval system increased from 49% in 1960 to 92% in 1963 and eventually to 97% in 1967. In 1964, Japan became an Article 8 country of the IMF and obtained membership in the Organization for Economic Cooperation and Development (OECD).

Despite these developments, industrial policy in this period was characterized by an emphasis on strategic policies. The Ministry of International Trade and Industry (MITI) tried to promote several key industries by trade protection, tax advantages, and subsidies in various forms. Industries were selected, at least officially, according to three main criteria: productivity growth, income elasticity, and employment relatedness. Industries that appeared to (1) promise high productivity growth, (2) be characterized by large income elasticity of demand so that an increase in demand could be expected with the growth of the world economy, and (3) have many related industries whose growth would promote employment were assisted with various policy measures.

MITI bureaucrats also attempted to control the level of private capacity investment. They believed that, in industries characterized by scale economies,

11. For more details, see Kosai (1986) and Tsuruta (1988a).

competition would create excessively many small firms with excessively large total capacity within the industry. The resulting "excessive competition" was believed, in turn, to jeopardize Japanese competitiveness in the world. In order to secure "orderly" competition, each firm was advised to specialize in production of certain goods so that they would not compete with each other. Public assistance was provided to renovate production facilities in order to take advantage of scale economies. Mergers were also encouraged to reduce excessive competition.

Partly in order to facilitate these measures and partly in order to meet the effects of trade and foreign capital liberalizations, MITI proposed the Law on Extraordinary Measures for the Promotion of Specified Manufacturing Industries in 1962. This law was to integrate and strengthen existing laws so that MITI would have wide-ranging effective power to apply direct regulatory measures. Moreover, the law proposed a new government-business relationship, called *kan-min kyocho hoshiki*. Based on public committees consisting of bureaucrats, business leaders, and academic experts, the proposed new relationship was expected to rechannel the principal determinant of resource allocation away from the market mechanism and into the artificial coordination of government and business sector. However, it met with strong opposition from the private sector, notably from the financial sector, and it was never enacted. This typified the new trend that, though government tried to keep its hand in managing the economy as in the previous period, the private sector started to resist public intervention in favor of free market mechanism.

Moreover, although many industries such as automobiles, electric appliances, and steel have succeeded in dramatically increasing their exports, this success should not be ascribed solely to government assistance. With trade and foreign capital liberalization, the government lost much of the leverage it needed in order to intervene in the private sector. Perhaps the most effective step in promoting exports in this period was the government's announcement of the liberalization schedule of various products. With this announcement each industry, knowing that foreign competitors would soon start their business in its domestic market, endeavored to improve its productivity, or the quality of its products, and renovate its facilities. Moreover, the government delayed trade liberalization of certain key industries as long as foreign pressures allowed, a move which provided sufficient time for these industries to take necessary actions. Many industries were thus ready for competition with foreign rivals not only in the domestic market but also in markets abroad by the time the actual liberalization took place.[12]

To sum up, this period may be characterized by the use of strategic policies. The mechanism behind strategic policy in this period seems to be close to the externality-based explanation of the previous section. It is doubtful, however, that in designing their policy MITI bureaucrats were conscious of such a

12. For theoretical analysis behind these facts, see Matsuyama and Itoh (1985).

mechanism. Their criteria for industry selection may have been simply cos-
metic.[13] In fact, Komiya (1988) suggests, "I believe that the government promoted exactly those industries that most Japanese felt the country had to
have."

This period was also characterized by the strain between the government
and the private sector. The government attempted to intervene in the market
mechanism by applying direct regulation, but private corporations resisted all
such attempts. The attempt to restructure the Japanese automobile industry in
this period is another well-known example of this strain. In 1961, MITI announced a plan to reduce the number of automobile producers to, at most
three, one each for mass-production of cars, specialty cars, and minicars. This
proposal again met strong opposition and ten Japanese automobile manufacturers still remain today, nine of which produce mass-production cars.

Toward the end of this period, MITI officials reluctantly gave up the idea of
direct regulation and shifted their policy emphasis from "hard" measures to
"soft" measures. Namely, their main policy goals changed to helping coordination among private firms, suggesting desirable directions for the Japanese
economy, and providing public assistance and/or incentives so that private
firms will follow the suggested course. Prime examples of this kind include
the announcement of various MITI "visions" and "plans," which suggest a
consistent and desirable course that the Japanese economy might take in the
next five or ten years. These visions and plans were drafted in governmental
committees by members from various sectors of the economy. Some observers
believe that these plans may have worked as a coordination device as well as
functioning as a means of informational exchange among private firms (see
Komiya 1975; Okuno-Fujiwara 1988).

9.3.3   1971 to the Present

This is the period when Japanese economy repeatedly suffered from external as well as internal drastic structural changes. In 1971, President Nixon
announced the suspension of the dollar's convertibility to gold and the imposition of an import surcharge. With this announcement, the fixed exchange
system of the postwar period ended. Between 1973 and 1974, the price of oil
quadrupled by OPEC's initiative. With the mismanagement of domestic monetary policy, the inflation rate jumped to 30%, and the rate of the nominal
wage increase to 50%. In 1974, the unemployment rate doubled and the country's real growth rate recorded the first negative number in the postwar era.
Because of yen appreciation and increases in the price of oil, many (heavy)
industries, which are very dependent on imported oil and export possibilities,
started to have structural problems.

Shortly after the recovery from the first oil shock, there was steep yen ap-

13. In fact, MITI tried to promote almost all major industries, such as shipbuilding, steel,
automobile, oil refinery, aircraft, airplane engines, petrochemical, etc.

preciation between 1977–78; the second oil shock hit the Japanese economy in 1979–80. The problems of troubled industries got aggravated and their needs for further public help were voiced loudly. With the level of accumulated public debts quickly becoming unbearably high, however, macro-oriented fiscal assistance was abandoned and microbased industrial adjustment policies were employed. After the recovery from this crisis, the yen remained relatively cheap until the Plaza agreement of 1985. The agreement, however, induced another sharp rise in the yen, but its effect was relatively mild, contrary to the expectation of many Japanese.

In spite of these developments, Japanese trade as well as current accounts have recorded increasingly large surpluses, except for the two oil shock subperiods. Strong foreign criticisms were cast, first on the chronic trade surplus, then on the Japanese government's policy attitudes, and finally on the behavior of Japanese firms and the Japanese people in general. Meeting with these "trade conflicts" as well as "economic conflicts" became one of the most important objectives of industrial policy in this period. In section 9.5, I shall come back to a more detailed account of these conflicts.

Another trend of industrial policy existed in this period: decreasing emphasis on strategic policies. Partly because the Japanese economy had already grown sufficiently and few industries needed assistance for promotion, and partly because foreign criticisms against industrial targeting became too fervent to be ignored, the MITI tried to shift its policy emphasis from strategic policies to corrective policies. The MITI's position in international trade has gradually changed to support free trade. With continuous reduction of tariff rates, Japan became one of the countries whose overall tariff rate is lowest in the world (see Komiya and Itoh 1988). With visible trade barriers removed, the MITI's stance became, at least publicly, that of a protector and promoter of the free trade system in the world.

To sum up, there were three main objectives of industrial policy in this period: providing adjustment assistance to troubled industries suffering from the aforementioned structural changes, meeting with foreign criticisms and demands concerning Japan and trading problems, and encouraging R&D in the private sector. Assistance for R&D may be viewed to reflect the shift of the MITI's emphasis on corrective policies. Among policies that are of a corrective nature, however, R&D assistance seems to be most fitted to MITI, as it may work as strategic policy as well. Although the amount is negligible in nominal terms, various forms of policies to assist private R&D were attempted in this period. I shall discuss these policies somewhat extensively in the next section.

Adjustment assistance for domestic industries took several forms: assisting workers to relocate and to train themselves for new jobs, providing assistance for depressed areas, and so on. However, the major policy tools were the following two: the establishment of joint credit funds to purchase scrapped facilities with bank-loan guarantees (this was done to handle the disposition of excessive facilities), and allowing a capacity-reduction cartel in designated industries. According to Sekiguchi and Horiuchi (1988) the first tool was apparently not too attractive for firms, as firms did not have much use for the guarantees. They are also doubtful about the effectiveness of allowing cartel formation, as there is no significant difference in the level of capacity reduction between designated and undesignated industries. Nonetheless, one cannot deny the possibility of undesignated industries tacitly colluding to form cartels. As Lawrence (1989) points out, Japanese adjustment assistance policies in general were not very transparent.

9.4 Industrial Policy for Private R&D

One of the focuses of Japanese industrial policy in the 1980s has been to assist private R&D efforts. Japanese R&D expenditure has been dominated by the private sector. For example, in 1987, more than 9 trillion yen (2.57% of GNP) was spent on R&D activities, of which only 19.9% was funded by the government. This ratio is substantially low when compared with other major developed countries (see table 9.1). Moreover, this ratio of government-funded R&D to total R&D expenditure has been steadily declining (except for the last few years). One might note, however, that this low ratio partially stems from the fact that in Japan the amount of defense-related government expenditure is negligible.

In the postwar era, two types of technology-related policies have been used to assist private firms: assistance for technology imports and assistance for R&D by domestic firms. Until the 1960s, the former policy played an impor-

Table 9.1

Country	Year	R&D Expenditure as % of GNP[a]	Government Funds		
			As % of Total R&D[a]	Without Defense-related R&D	As % of Total Private R&D[a]
Japan	1983	2.29	22.2		2.9[b]
	1987	2.57	19.9	19.3	1.7
United States	1987	2.65	48.2	26.8	35.1
West Germany	1987	2.81	37.7	34.4	15.3
United Kingdom	1986	2.29	38.5	17.2	25.0
France	1986	2.29	43.7	28.9	22.8[c]

[a]See *Indicators of Science and Technology,* 1989, Science and Technology Agency, Tokyo.
[b]See *Movements of Major Indicators of Research and Development in Japan,* 1985, Agency of Industrial and Science Technology, Tokyo.
[c]1987 data.

tant role for Japanese firms trying to catch up with the international level; these firms had been left behind technologically due to the closure of the economy during the war. Today, technology import is still an important factor in some industries, such as the semiconductor industry and other high-tech industries. However, in general, the policy emphasis has shifted to promoting domestic R&D.

As is indicated in table 9.1, the amount of direct and indirect subsidies provided to promote domestic R&D in Japan is relatively small even among the most industrialized countries. This reflects in part MITI's current stance of not engaging in the "hard" policy measures and also reflects the small role played by the Japanese defense budget. However, government support, though small, has been concentrated in the areas that would help commercial production. MITI has been consciously aiming "at promoting commercialy optimal technology," and this is in sharp contrast to the American policy whose major contractor (the Defense Department) "tends to emphasize the design of new and better components and systems rather than process refinement" (Okimoto, Sugano, and Weinstein 1984, pp. 182–83). To facilitate private efforts to improve production technology and cost-reduction know-how, MITI tried several devices to promote private R&D efforts by furnishing coordination incentives. Perhaps the best publicized such device is the organization of *technology research associations* (TRA).

The TRA is an association of several (from two to more than 50) private firms that is organized to conduct joint R&D effort with the help of government assistance, usually in the form of a subsidy. The idea of the TRA was imported from United Kingdom in 1961. Unlike the British research associations, however, the Japanese TRA is organized as needed to solve specific technological challenges (rather than organized as one group within each industry) and organized as a temporary organization, deemed to be dissolved after the designated period (rather than organized as a permanent entity) (see Wakasugi 1986).

The Technology Research Association for Very Large Scale Integrated Circuits (VLSI) is perhaps the best-known and most successful Japanese TRA.[14] This TRA was organized with five Japanese computer producers (Fujitsu, Hitachi, Mitsubishi Electric, NEC, and Toshiba) for the period of 1976–79 with the aim of developing high-density high-speed semiconductors. These would be used for new domestically produced computers being developed to challenge the next-generation IBM mainframe computer (the future system). During this period, MITI provided a subsidy of ¥29 billion (about $116 million at the concurrent exchange rate). With the fund provided by the member firms, the total budget for this project amounted to about ¥70 billion, which

14. See Okimoto, Sugano, and Weinstein (1984) for the details of this project and a background comparison of the semiconductor industry in Japan and the United States.

was about the half of the total R&D expenditure of the semiconductor industry.[15]

This TRA is considered to be successful because it produced more than 1,000 patent applications, some of which are thought to be world-leading technology. Many members of the TRA thought that, with the results of this TRA, the Japanese semiconductor industry caught up with IBM in the integrated-circuit (IC) production technology. Indeed, executives of IBM visited this TRA site several times during and after the operation (Sakakibara 1981). Although the VLSI project is considered to have been successful, not all the TRAs produced similar results. For example, Wakasugi (1986) computed research funds spent for each patent application. While the private-sector average during 1973–82 as ¥1.6 million, six chosen TRAs only scored ¥4.7 to ¥65.7 million.

Moreover, the mechanism of the TRA is not very well understood. Unless member firms have complementary roles, such as parts supplier versus assembler, their interests normally conflict with each other. In the case of VLSI, for example, all members were competitors in the commercial computer market, and so their interests were at best mixed; obtaining better technology is a plus, but the rival's acquisition of the same technology is a minus. Moreover, assuming that the results of their efforts would belong to all member firms, providing no effort should have been the dominant strategy as long as the effort level of the firm could not be observed by other members.

The case of VLSI is relatively unique in some respects, however. First, in the computer industry at the period, IBM was the clear leader, and the member companies could not have survived had they not made the technological breakthroughs that the TRA aimed at. In this sense, their interests were similar and cooperation incentives existed. Second, this project was a rare example in this period (and even today) in that it had its own research facility. Instead of bringing back the problem to each company, member firms sent research workers to the facility where the research was done jointly. This created competition among research workers as their results were observable by the fellow researchers. Third, the amount of the subsidy was relatively large. In fact, according to Wakasugi (1986) again, the average ratio of government subsidy to total R&D expenditure for the semiconductor industry was about 22% in 1976–79, while it was only 2.9% in the 1980–82 after the project ended. Fourth, the target of the project was not to develop a computer or an IC itself, the market in which member firms were harshly competing with each other, but mainly to develop new methods to produce better ICs. The interests of member firms, then, were not in deep conflict.

Nonetheless, the example of VLSI also illustrates the problem of R&D or industrial policy in Japan in general. First, as already explained, there is no clear logic as to why and how the TRA would work. A large amount of public

15. Estimated by Wakasugi (1986).

funds was poured into this industry, despite the fact that many experts were uncertain about the idea. Second, some may criticize it as a disguised strategic policy.[16] Indeed, as we have seen, a relatively large amount was given to this industry, which is only a limited group of domestic firms. Although, MITI now attempts to open TRA memberships to foreign firms, many chosen research topics are in high-tech areas, which seem to reflect the policymaker's inclination to promote these types of industries. Moreover, outsiders could not have access to the results of the TRA for VLSI. Only after negotiations between the U.S. and Japanese governments, were all patents, held either solely by the government or jointly by the government and the member firms, made public and freely accessible to outsiders.

Third and most important, it is not clear why and how the five member firms were chosen. Clearly, becoming a member provides benefits either in terms of public funding or the resulting technological advancement. Compared with both domestic and foreign outsiders, member firms enjoyed these benefits during the project period; they also held a more advantageous position created by the elevation of their technological level after the project. However, there were many domestic semiconductor producers who ended not participating in the project. Even one major computer producer Oki Electric, who had a joint venture with an American maker, was excluded from the TRA.[17] In sum, the VLSI project seems to be another example of a government policy that favors industry's insiders.

9.5 Trade Negotiations

Postwar trade between Japan and the United States has been riddled with numerous trade and economic disputes. Starting with the textile problem of 1960s, the number of disputed items has been constantly increasing, and the nature of the problems has been changing and becoming more and more complicated. Roughly speaking, the disputed area has shifted from "excessive Japanese exports" such as export downpour to the United States to "barriers to American exports into Japan," and from problems about "Japanese commodity exports" to "other activities of Japanese firms," such as dealings with intellectual properties, direct investments to the United States, and collusive behaviors of Japanese firms. In this section, we shall focus on those problems that are caused by Japanese commodity exports, especially in semiconductor industry.

Past trade disputes between Japan and the United States may be classified into two distinct groups. The first group is made up of those disputes that were

---

16. However, employing policy itself should not be denounced outright as I discussed in sec. 9.2.

17. Strictly speaking, however, the members are chosen on the grounds of voluntary application. I could not prove whether or not there was any government intervention in the choice of member firms.

processed in a legitimate manner according to the American legal system. The second is those brought up and solved politically with bilateral negotiations.

If an American industry believes that Japanese exports have injured the industry because of unanticipated developments, it can file a petition to the U.S. International Trade Commission (USITC) to restrict Japanese imports (this is based on the safeguard clause). Similarly, if it believes that Japanese products are being sold by unfair trade practices, such as dumping, it can file a petition to the Department of Commerce (DOC) and USITC (based on the antidumping and countervailing duty clause). The USITC (and/or DOC) will investigate the case and determine whether the industry is indeed injured and whether the injury is caused by unfair trade practices on the part of the Japanese. If the answer is yes, a discriminatory tariff may be imposed on the import from Japan. If the Japanese industry believes that the ruling does not reflect the true situation, it can in turn petition to the General Agreement on Tariffs and Trade (GATT). According to the current rule, GATT encourages reconciliation, but, if that fails, disputants can call together a panel of third-party representatives whose ruling may become "binding" if approved by the GATT council.

A large number of disputes have been solved through this legitimate process. For example, between May 1986 and March 1989, the USITC gave final rulings on 23 items, 13 of which were ruled as caused by dumping and other Japanese unfair practices, 9 were found not guilty, and the ruling for the last item was mixed.[18] One may note, however, that despite all these petitions filed by American firms and all these guilty rulings given by the USITC (and DOC), neither the Japanese firms nor the Japanese government ever formally protested these rulings by petitioning GATT.

A significant number of disputes, however, took a different course. Either before or after they file a petition alleging Japanese dumping, many American industries, such as those producing steel, automobiles, machinery, and semiconductors, have applied political pressures to the U.S. administration as well as to Congress in order to obtain protection from Japanese imports. The typical consequence is that the Japanese industries, with the support of the Japanese government, voluntarily restrain their exports to the U.S. market.[19] From the U.S. perspective, the reason for the choice of voluntary restraint is clear. Unlike imposing protective duties, which is explicitly prohibited by GATT, asking the Japanese government to help create voluntary export cartels does not infringe on GATT clauses, though it is clearly contrary to the GATT philosophy.

The semiconductor industry provides a major example of this type of case. Let me briefly outline the history of this dispute.[20] The integrated circuit (IC)

---

18. MITI, *White Paper on International Trade*, various issues.
19. For an explicit account of these experiences, see, e.g., Destler and Sato (1982).
20. For a more detailed account, see Okimoto, Sugano, and Weinstein (1984) and Pugel (1987).

was invented and first marketed by U.S. firms in the early 1960s. Helped by industrial policy, however, Japanese firms started to capture a significant share of the U.S. IC market in the late 1970s. The Japanese share in the U.S. market increased rapidly in the early 1980s with little penetration into the Japanese market by U.S. competitors. This alarmed the U.S. firms, which started lobbying in the Congress. In February 1985, market-oriented, sector-selective (MOSS) talks between the Japanese and U.S. governments started for all electronics industries, including semiconductors. In June of the same year, the U.S. Semiconductor Industry Association (SIA) filed a petition with the U.S. government alleging that the Japanese semiconductor industry (according to the petition) denies U.S. firms access to the Japanese market and helps dump products in the U.S. market, thus violating Article 301 of the Trade Act of 1974. This was followed by dumping petitions from individual American producers on 64K DRAMs (dynamic access random memory) and EPROMs (erasable-programmable read-only memory). In December 1985, the U.S. government itself filed a dumping suit against Japanese producers of 256K DRAMs, an unusual step in the history of trade disputes.

In May 1986, the USITC issued a final ruling on 64K DRAMs, finding the Japanese producers guilty of dumping, anti-dumping duties started to be imposed. Two months later, the Japanese government, fearing the application of Article 301 that would have triggered retaliatory tariffs on IC as well as non-IC products, made an agreement with U.S. government. With this agreement, the Japanese government established a cost-price monitoring system on IC products so that Japanese firms will not export these products to the U.S. market at prices lower than their "fair market value" (FMV). The Japanese government also agreed to (1) monitor export price in general so that Japanese exports to the U.S. through third countries will not injure American competitors and (2) take proper actions to facilitate sales of American IC products in the Japanese market.

In April 1987, however, the U.S. government imposed a 100% retaliatory tariff on personal computers, electric machinery, and color TVs on the basis of the Japanese government's alleged violation of the agreement on items 1 and 2 above. On the other hand, the European Community (EC) filed a petition to GATT that item 1 was in violation of the GATT agreement. In March 1988, the GATT panel found item 1 in violation of GATT Article 11.

How should we assess these consequences of the IC trade conflict? There are two broad issues, one concerning the validity of the legal system and the other concerning U.S. demands and Japanese responses.

Let me start with the problem about issues concerning the American legal process with the particular focus on the IC case. First, the legal process in the American system states that protection in the form of a protective tariff is given if the practice under scrutiny is found to be injuring the American producer. Thus the American consumer's interest is not reflected in the legal process. Indeed, much past research has shown that voluntary export restraint

(VER) arrangements and other protective measures for the steel and automobile industries have seriously damaged the American consumers and users.[21] In figure 9.1, the movements of the world IC dollar prices (in logarithmic terms) is shown before and after the trade disputes. The secular downward trends typical of this industry until 1984 were clearly disrupted after 1986.

Second, the unfair trade practice that is most often cited in cases against Japanese products is "dumping." The antidumping law in the United States defines dumping as pricing below fair market value. Oftentimes, the sum of "constructed value" and a certain profit margin is used as the fair market value. Constructed value (excluding the profit margin) is the sum of direct production cost and indirect costs (which equals at least 10% of the direct production cost). This definition may particularly harm Japanese producers, as they tend to be producers of diverse products. For example, NEC, one of the major IC producers in Japan, also produces personal computers (PCs), telecommunication equipment, and other home electrical appliances. In short, many Japanese producers may be enjoying economies of scope due to the existence of large overhead costs. The normal accounting procedure of calculating the "fully distributed cost" may be quite artificial and cause unnecessary burden on producers who enjoy economies of scope.

Third, IC production has special technological properties. Its yield is known to improve as experience in production accumulates, and production cost diminishes as accumulated production increases. As is well known, the marginal cost of production with such a learning effect is the marginal cost of accumulated production when the learning effect ceases to exist.[22] That is, even if enough learning has not taken effect, and the current production cost is high, rational pricing behavior should take account of the long-run marginal cost that is the marginal production cost after sufficient learning will have occurred. Hence, the use of constructive value, which only reflects the current production cost and does not reflect the economically relevant production cost, is likely to impose a handicap on firms who expect to capture a large market share.

Finally, a major reason that the Japanese government accepted the agreement was the threat of Article 301. Procedurally speaking, there is good reason to believe that the article itself is in violation of GATT. Unlike escape clauses and antidumping laws, Article 301 does not have GATT approval, and its application is based only on the U.S. government's unilateral judgment.[23]

21. For example, Tarr (1987) estimated the costs of the steel agreement of 1985. According to his estimation, if terms of trade effect is not counted, costs to American consumers exceed $1 billion annually, and costs to the entire economy between $0.8 billion and $1 billion annually. These costs may be reduced by up to $73 million if the terms of trade effect is accounted for. Crandall (1984) estimated that the automobile export restraint between 1981–83 cost American consumers $4.5 billion annually. See Feenstra (1984) for the effect of quality and other general equilibrium effects in automobile case.
22. For theoretical analysis, see, e.g., Spence (1981).
23. This judgment is based on Matsuhita (1988).

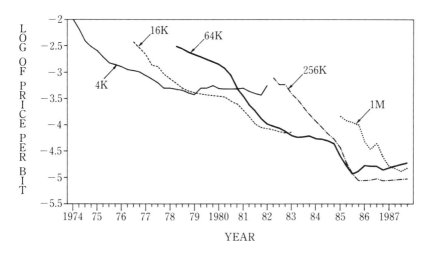

Fig. 9.1
Source: Dataquest.

Moreover, this article permits the U.S. government to impose retaliatory tariffs on products that are completely different from the product that allegedly is involved in unfair practices. It seems a dangerous tool in the international trade system in that it may trigger a retaliatory war.

All of these points make one wonder why the Japanese government accepted the IC agreement of 1986 or the other VER agreements in general. Indeed, many Japanese suggested their government bring the case to the GATT panel before the agreement was settled. The reason that the government did not take this action seems to be the familiar one; in spite of their public stance to promote free trade, they do not make policy decisions on a philosophical basis because doing so might induce strong objections from disputants. As long as no strong opposition exists, they tend to ignore the stated stance.[24] Instead, the government tends to make decisions on a pragmatic basis, which results in less confrontation among the disputants, especially when the resulting decision favors the domestic members of the dispute. Accordingly, they chose the solution that benefited Japanese producers as well as U.S. producers by forming the de facto government-supported producers' cartel.

This method of solving trade disputes has been popular in Japanese bureaucracy. It is practical and conforms to their experience. They can solve the disputes easily by this method as long as the dispute is nonrepetitive. However, this cartel solution creates rents to those industries (stockholders, managers, and workers) who eventually obtain cartel agreement. Thus, more and

24. Another example is the MITI's promotion of the Voluntary Export Restraint by Korean knit producers for export in Japan in 1989.

more U.S. industries start lobbying to obtain protection, sometimes on dubious grounds.

9.6 Japanese Policy-making

According to the theory of rent seeking (and the theory of economic regulation), political decision making suffers from the political bias. Democratic decision making is heavily influenced by political activities such as lobbying by pressure groups, which takes up private resources. Only those who expect to obtain more benefit from the activities than the associated political cost will engage in these activities. But policy decisions tend to mean more, in per capita terms, to the group of people who are directly affected by the policy (such as producers whose products are protected by a quota imposition), and mean less to the group whose benefits and losses are diluted by the group's large numbers (such as consumers in the case of trade protection). It follows that political decision making tends to favor those whose interests are directly connected to the policy decision itself (see, e.g., Downs 1957; Stigler 1971; Krueger 1974; Ordeshook 1986; and Peltzman 1989).

In view of this theory, many trade conflicts between Japan and the United States were induced by U.S. producers (and sometimes labor unions) who were seeking economic rents that would be realized by artificially raising the domestic price at the expense of American consumers and users. Despite the fact that aggregate loss incurred by consumers (and users) may exceed the gain accrued to the producers, the loss is diluted by the large number of losers. Since political decisions in the United States are strongly influenced by lobbying activity, these rent-seekers tend to influence heavily international negotiations, with results that are oftentimes against total U.S. interests.

On the other hand, according to this theory there seem to be at least three reasons why the tendency to favor insiders' interests exists in the decision-making policies of the Japanese government. First, for more than 30 years, the Liberal Democratic party (LDP) has controlled the Japanese Diet without any disruption. Moreover, the Japanese Diet system follows British parliamentary democracy, in which party decisions bind the voting behavior of all the party legislators, making the LDP decision practically the final Diet decision. This contributed to the economic growth of the country by providing continuous and consistent economic policies.

However, since there was no changeover of political power, it was practically impossible to demolish vested interests from whoever had obtained political rents. In other words, the current Japanese political system is an intricate nexus of vested interests, shared by political groups, major party politicians, and government bureaucrats. This system made the political cost of changing existing policies extremely high. Except on rare occasions (such as the recent tax revision), only those pressures applied by strong foreign governments seemed to be effective in making drastic policy changes.

Second, Japanese bureaucracy is divided into many independent ministries, and the policy research division of the LDP (the Policy Research Affairs Council, or PRAC) consists of committees parallel to each ministry so as to cover different industries, such as manufacturing, agriculture, finance, telecommunication, and so on. Each ministry is supposed to be responsible for overseeing "sound development" of the industry, so industry-specific interests tend to be reflected in the closed decision-making process within the bureaucracy and/or the major party. This renders industry-specific interests more politically effective and consumer interests less effective.

Moreover, the final political decision is made, as I explained above, within the level of the major party and its bureaucracy. Thus, if there is a conflict among several industry-specific interests, it tends to be solved by closed negotiations among ministries and legislators from various committees of the PRAC. In a sense, through this negotiation process, producers of different industries play a cooperative game in seeking a mutually efficient agreement. This seems to be in sharp contrast to the U.S. system, where these conflicts tend to be solved in the Congress through open discussion. There, Congressmen are not bound by the party vote, thus voting decisions may be made independent of party decisions. The U.S. system may be characterized as a noncooperative game in which each player pursues the outcome that is best suited for his or her industry.

Compared with the noncooperative process, the negotiation-based solution tends to favor the status quo. If some player finds the proposed agreement to be worse than the status quo, he or she can simply deny the proposal; that is, negotiation allows veto power. There are further contrasts between negotiation and the noncooperative decision-making process.

Following Bulow, Geanakoplos, and Klemperer (1985), let us call an action of a player (an endorsement of a policy by an industry, in our context) *aggressive* if the action (the policy) harms the other players (industries). It is straightforward that the negotiated outcome, which tends to be mutually efficient among the players, is less aggressive than the noncooperative outcome. Hence, if industries play a political game to achieve their desired outcome, cooperative games tend to choose less aggressive outcomes, while noncooperative games tend to select more aggressive ones.[25] This seems to be another reason why vested interests are apt to be preserved in Japanese policy decisions.

However, this does not necessarily imply that the cooperative outcome is worse than the noncooperative outcome. Clearly, the cooperative outcome is better than the noncooperative outcome for the negotiating parties. Moreover, if the more aggressive behavior of the negotiating party harms third par-

25. For example, Kiyono, Okuno-Fujiwara, and Ueda (1991) showed that, if the extent of trade protection is politically determined in a small country with two import-competing industries pursuing their industry-specific interests, the resulting protection level is higher in the noncooperative game than that which occurs when the possibility of negotiation is added.

ties, then the cooperative outcome Pareto dominates the noncooperative outcome.

Third, the Japanese as a people prefer agreements through compromise to direct confrontations. Government is no exception. Whenever there is a conflict, a solution is sought to satisfy all the disputants in a backdoor closed negotiation. This tendency, with the lack of an open and public decision-making process, makes the process of policy decision-making, as well as the implication of the chosen policy, opaque and less transparent. Consequently, costs to organize the opposition are high. All of these factors contribute to the fact that Japanese consumers as a group have little voice in politics.

9.7   The Case of the Large Stores Law

Perhaps the tendency in Japanese policy-making is best illustrated by the way the Law concerning the Adjustment of Retail Activities by Large-Scale Retail Stores (Large Stores Law) has been put into practice.[26] The stated purpose of this law is to control retail activities by large stores in order to (1) secure the business opportunities of local retailers and (2) provide sound development of the retail trade industry, and at the same time (3) avoid hampering consumers' benefit. The law is applied to establishing and extending buildings for retail business whose size exceeds 500 square meters. In principle, it allows large stores to start their business only with notifications to the MITI (in case the size of the enterprise exceeds 1,500 square meters, and to the prefectural governor otherwise) with the following restrictions.

It requires MITI to review each notification. If MITI finds sufficient reason to believe that the activity of the large store may damage local small retailers, MITI is allowed, after consulting with the (governmental) Large Stores Council, to advise the entrant to postpone opening and to reduce its business space. The Large Stores Council, in turn, must consult the opinion of the local Chamber of Commerce, which sets up the Council to Accommodate Commerce Activities (CRCA) in order to accommodate differences in local interests. The CRCAs are supposed to consist of owners of local commercial business, consumers, and neutral members.

The law explicitly restricts the review process as follows. Two notifications are required to be filed. An Article 3 notification must be filed first by the builder of the building, and large stores (or buildings, to be more precise) may not start their business until seven months following this notice. The Article 5 notification requires that retailers who intend to do business in this building to declare, among other things, the starting date of the business and the total shop space in the building. The review is made and advice must be given within four months from this notification. The discussion by the CRCA is also restricted to a three-week period. Hence, as long as notifications are filed

26. Much of what is written below depends upon Tsuruta (1988b).

properly, any store should be able to start its business seven months after the Article 3 notification.

However, a procedure that is completely different from the spirit of this law has been widely utilized. After the Article 3 notification is made to MITI, it has become a custom to obtain an advance opinion of the local Chamber of Commerce (before the Article 5 notification is allowed) and, for that purpose, to hold what is called the "prior CRCA" to accommodate interests of local retailers. This process, which is not written into the law, became authorized by MITI as a part of the formal process. Because the prior CRCA is only an informal institution, however, there is no time limit for handing its conclusion to MITI, nor are the names of its members disclosed. Consequently, many years are wasted until prior CRCA gives its opinion and until a large store can eventually open its building. For example, in one case it took five and a half years between the Article 3 and Article 5 notifications, which resulted in eight and a half years between the store's announcement and its actual opening. In another case, more than 10 years elapsed between the announcement of the store and the store's actual opening.[27]

MITI gave a directive (*gyosei shido*) in 1979 that the actual opening must be made within 13 months from the Article 3 notification. After this directive, however, prior explanation by the large store to local people, which was supposed to be made before the Article 3 notification, became a forum to obtain the agreement of local stores; this is the "prior prior CRCA." This again is an informal institution, and opponents can block any conclusion indefinitely. There are also many similar regulations laid down by local governments, some of which regulate practically all establishment and expansion of retail buildings.

Because of these procedures, not only are large stores prevented from opening their new establishments, but also overt and covert forms of pecuniary transfer are prevalent. In one case, in order to obtain consent from local stores, one-third of the building space in a new establishment was allocated to local retailers at a rate one-third the rental cost of the other spaces. In other cases, bribes are allegedly paid to members of prior CRCA in order to secure prompt and more advantageous rulings. Because members of prior CRCA are nonpublic officials, these acts are not necessarily illegal.

In spite of these procedures that impose large entry costs to new entrants, large domestic distributors did not voice their opposition to this system publicly until it became criticized openly by the U.S. government. Of course, part of the reason for such behavior is the political cost to the lobby that pursues the change. However, having such a system of entry cost may work to benefit those stores who intend to enter. For example, suppose this system creates an entry cost of $3 million, which is not necessary if the system is abolished.

27. The former is the case of JUSCO, which opened in Kamisato-cho in 1987, and the latter of NICHII in Honjo in 1989. Both are shopping malls with large supermarkets.

Suppose the market provides $5 million if there is only one large store, $2 million each if there are two such stores, $1 million each if there are three. The first large store that announces its intention to open can obtain $2 million after payment of the entry cost because there is no incentive for further entry. However, if the system is eliminated, three stores will enter and each can receive only $1 million.

The system of the Large Stores Law is a system for insiders, where not only local stores and large stores who have already entered, but also large stores whose entry is temporarily blockaded may benefit from the system. Consumers are the real losers, but there is no place where they can file their complaints.

9.8   Concluding Remarks

In this paper, I have given accounts of Japanese industrial policy both from the historical perspective as well as from the political economy perspective. Japanese industrial policy has increasingly put more emphasis on soft policy measures, such as coordinating private incentives and disseminating information. Although no formal analysis has been seriously attempted, this kind of policy measure might be contributing to the Japanese export (or investment) downpour. For, by the very nature of these measures, private firms are forced to coordinate their timing in increasing exports to a particular market and investment in a particular country. I believe serious theoretical as well as empirical analyses on these and other behaviors, which are typical in Japanese firms, needs to be carried out in the future.

On the other hand, policy decisions in Japan are formed by negotiation of insiders and *not* made on clearly spelled-out rules. Outsiders who are harmed by the decision have little opportunity to get compensation, as hardly any formal grievance process exists in Japan. This system seems to aggravate foreigners' feelings that Japanese society is not "fair." I believe, however, that it is not a question of fairness but the system of public decision making that is at the core of most conflicts between Japan and other countries.

I should also emphasize that foreign demands to Japan, especially U.S. demands, tend to reflect similar political biases. These demands often reflect industry-specific interests and may work against consumers' interests of the objecting country. In international relations, it is most important to understand each other and to rationally solve conflicts without becoming excessively emotional. The issue of Japanese industrial policies, and other issues currently brought into question, should be solved quickly before political pressures and national emotions from both Japan and the United States destroy economic relations that are beneficial for both countries.

References

Barzel, Y. 1968. Optimal Timing of Innovations. *Review of Economics and Statistics* 50:348–55.

Brander, J. A. 1986. Rationales for Strategic Trade and Industrial Policy. In *Strategic Trade Policy and the New International Economics,* ed. P. Krugman. Cambridge, Mass.: MIT Press.

Brander, J. A., and B. J. Spencer. 1981. Tariffs and the Extraction of Foreign Monopoly Rent under Potential Entry. *Canadian Journal of Economics* 14:371–89.

Bulow, J. I., J. D. Geanakoplos, and P. D. Klemperer. 1985. Multimarket Oligopoly: Strategic Substitutes and Complements. *Journal of Political Economy* 93:488–51.

Corden, M. W. 1974. *Trade Policy and Economic Welfare.* Oxford: Oxford University Press.

Crandall, R. W. 1984. Import Quotas and the Automobile Industry: The Costs of Protectionism. *Brookings Review.*

Destler, I. M., and H. Sato. 1982. *Coping with U.S.-Japanese Economic Conflicts.* Lexington, Mass.: Lexington Books.

Downs, A. 1957. *An Economic Theory of Democracy.* New York: Harper & Row.

Ethier, W. 1982. National and International Returns to Scale in the Modern Theory of International Trade. *American Economic Review* 72:388–405.

Feenstra, R. C. 1984. Voluntary Export Restraint in U.S. Autos, 1980–81: Quality, Employment, and Welfare Effects. In *The Structure and Evolution of Recent U.S. Trade Policy,* ed. R. E. Baldwin and A. O. Krueger. Chicago: University of Chicago Press.

Grossman, G. 1986. Strategic Export Protection: A Critique. In *Strategic Trade Policy and the New International Economics,* ed. P. Krugman. Cambridge, Mass.: MIT Press.

Itoh, M., K. Kiyono, M. Okuno-Fujiwara, and K. Suzumura, 1991. *Economic Analysis of Industrial Policy.* New York: Academic Press.

Itoh, M., and T. Negishi. 1987. Disequilibrium Trade Theories. In *Fundamentals of Pure and Applied Economics.* Chur, Switzerland: Harwood Academic Publishers.

Kaizuka, K. 1973. *Contemporary Problems of Economic Policy* (in Japanese). Tokyo: University of Tokyo Press.

Kamien, M. I., and N. L. Schwartz. 1982. *Market Structure and Innovation.* Cambridge: Cambridge University Press.

Kiyono, K., M. Okuno-Fujiwara, and K. Ueda. 1991. Industry-Specific Interests and Trade Protection: A Game Theoretic Analysis. *Economic Studies Quarterly,* forthcoming.

Komiya, R. 1988. Introduction, to *Industrial Policy of Japan,* ed. R. Komiya et al. New York: Academic Press.

Komiya, R., and M. Itoh. 1988. Japan's International Trade and Trade Policy, 1955–84. In *The Political Economy of Japan: Vol. 2, The Changing International Context,* ed. T. Inoguchi and D. I. Okimoto. Stanford, Calif.: Stanford University Press.

Komiya, R., M. Okuno, and K. Suzumura, eds. 1988. *Industrial Policy in Japan.* New York: Academic Press.

Kosai, Y. 1986. *The Era of High-Speed Growth.* Tokyo: University of Tokyo Press.

———. 1988. The Reconstruction Period. In *Industrial Policy in Japan,* ed. R. Komiya et al. New York: Academic Press.

Krueger, A. O. 1974. The Political Economy of the Rent-Seeking Society. *American Economic Review* 92:291–303.

Lawrence, R. Z. 1989. A Depressed View of Policies for Depressed Industries. In

Trade and Investment Relations among the United States, Canada, and Japan, ed. R. M. Stern. Chicago: University of Chicago Press.

Lee, T., and L. Wilde. 1980. Market Structure and Innovation: A Reformulation. *Quarterly Journal of Economics* 94:429–36.

Loury, G. C. 1979. Market Structure and Innovation. *Quarterly Journal of Economics* 93:395–410.

Matsuhita, M. 1988. *International Economic Law: Regulation of International Trade and Investment* (in Japanese). Tokyo: Yuhi-Kaku.

Matsuyama, K. 1989. Increasing Returns, Industrialization and Indeterminacy of Equilibrium. Mimeographed. Northwestern University, Evanston, Ill.

Matsuyama, K., and M. Itoh. 1985. Protection Policy in a Dynamic Oligopoly Market. Discussion Paper Series, Faculty of Economics, University of Tokyo.

Mussa, M. 1982. Government Policy and the Adjustment Process. In *Import Competition and Response,* ed. J. Bhagwati. Chicago: University of Chicago Press.

Neary, P. 1982. Intersectoral Capital Mobility, Wage Sickness, and the Case of Adjustment Assistance. In *Import Competition and Response,* ed. J. Bhagwati. Chicago: University of Chicago Press.

Okimoto, D. I., T. Sugano, and F. B. Weinstein, eds. 1984. *Competitive Edge: The Semiconductor Industry in the U.S. and Japan.* Stanford, Calif.: Stanford University Press.

Okuno-Fujiwara, M. 1988. Interdependence of Industries, Coordination Failure and Strategic Promotion of an Industry. *Journal of International Economics* 25:25–43.

Ordeshook, P. C. 1986. *Game Theory and Political Theory.* Cambridge: Cambridge University Press.

Peltzman, S. 1989. The Economic Theory of Regulation after a Decade of Deregulation. *Brookings Papers on Economic Activity: Microeconomics,* pp. 1–59.

Pugel, T. A. 1987. Limits of Trade Policy toward High-Technology Industries: The Case of Semiconductors. In *Trade Friction and Economic Policy,* ed. R. Sato and P. Wachtel. Cambridge: Cambridge University Press.

Sakakibara, K. 1981. Organization and Innovation: Case Study of VLSI Technology Research Association (in Japanese). *Hitotsubashi Ronso* 86:160–75.

Scherer, F. M. 1980. *Industrial Market Structure and Economic Performance.* Chicago: Rand McNally.

Sekiguchi, S., and T. Horiuchi. 1988. Trade and Adjustment Assistance. In *Industrial Policy of Japan,* ed. R. Komiya et al. New York: Academic Press.

Spence, M. 1981. The Learning Curve and Competition. *Bell Journal of Economics and Management Science* 12:49–70.

Stigler, G. J. 1971. The Theory of Economic Regulation. *Bell Journal of Economics and Management Science* 2:3–21.

Suzumura, K., and M. Okuno-Fujiwara. 1987. Industry Policy in Japan: Overview and Evaluation. In *Trade Friction and Economic Policy,* ed. R. Sato and P. Wachtel. Cambridge: Cambridge University Press.

Tarr, D. G. 1987. Costs and Benefits to the United States of the 1985 Steel Import Quota Program. In *Trade Friction and Economic Policy,* ed. R. Sato and P. Wachtel. Cambridge: Cambridge University Press.

Tirole, J. 1988. *The Theory of Industrial Organization.* Cambridge, Mass.: MIT Press.

Tsuruta, T. 1988b. The Rapid Growth Era. In *Industrial Policy of Japan,* ed. R. Komiya, et al. New York: Academic Press.

———. 1988a. How Should the Large Stores Law be Reformed in the Age of Internationalization (in Japanese). *Economist,* Dec. 13.

Wakasugi, R. 1986. *Economic Analysis of Technological Innovation and R&D* (in Japanese). Tokyo: Toyo Keizai Shimpo Sha.

Comment   Laura D'Andrea Tyson

There are three major propositions about Japanese industrial policy offered in the paper by Masahiro Okuno-Fujiwara: first, the objective of Japanese industrial policy has changed from what he calls a strategic objective of industrial restructuring or the targeting and promoting of key industries to something he calls a corrective objective of addressing market failures; second, the means of Japanese industrial policy have changed from so-called hard measures, such as preferential allocation of foreign exchange and capital and other direct control and subsidy measures, to soft measures, such as structural adjustment assistance and R&D support; and third, to understand Japanese industrial policy and the difficulties that outsiders have in breaking into the Japanese market, one must understand the "insider," cooperative-game nature of Japanese policy-making. I agree with the second two propositions but I strongly disagree with the first.

Okuno-Fujiwara characterizes strategic industrial policy as "industrial targeting"—choosing certain industries for promotion because of their special features, including their productivity growth, their growth potential, and their technological potential. In his opinion, this kind of industrial policy was characteristic of Japan through the early 1970s, but then gave way—in part in response to private-sector resistance to government intervention and private-sector support for the free market—to so-called corrective industrial policy.

In contrast to strategic industrial policy, corrective industrial policy responds to market failures, particularly failures that arise in the R&D process and failures in moving resources out of declining industries. According to Okuno-Fujiwara, the three main objectives of corrective industrial policy are to provide adjustment assistance to troubled industries, to encourage R&D in the private sector, and to address foreign criticisms of Japan's foreign trade behavior.

In my opinion, there has been no dramatic change in Japan's industrial policy objectives. Instead, I would argue, there has been continuity in two ways: continuity in the basic approach of targeting leading industries, activities, and even firms for promotion (although the forms of promotion have changed), and continuity in the objective of industrial policy—to encourage competitiveness in targeted industries because of the special economic benefits they are expected to generate for the entire economy.

True, as Okuno-Fujiwara argues, there has been more emphasis on adjustment, especially in the 1970s when higher energy costs made industrial restructuring critical. There has also been a change in the tools of industrial policy toward more reliance on cooperative R&D funding. But industrial policy objectives remain strategic.

Laura D'Andrea Tyson is a professor of economics and director of the Institute of International Studies at the University of California, Berkeley.

If the objectives were merely corrective, and if market forces were accorded the dominant role they are accorded in the United States, then corrective policy in high technology would be as neutral across industries as possible. Imagine the United States with a corrective industrial policy. What would it look like? The government would not directly choose which technologies, industries, or players benefited from these policies. The government's selective or targeting role would be limited to choices among technologies for defense purposes. There would be no targeting—no picking of winners and losers—for commercial purposes.

Now look at the case in Japan. Japanese high-technology R&D support is targeted selectively, by activity, by industry, and often by firm. And the goal of such support is commercial, not military. The idea driving Japan's programs is that government can and should play a role in picking high-tech winners and promoting them.

A partial list of current and recent R&D projects funded by MITI, either directly or through its Agency for Industrial Science and Technology (AIST), gives a flavor of the "selective" Japanese approach to "corrective" R&D support (see tables 9C.1 and 9C.2).

All of these projects, like the VLSI project and earlier projects that went before them, have several distinctive features. First, all of the projects focus on a so-called precompetitive or generic technology problem, the solution of which will benefit a large number of companies. The fact that the problem is a common one and that the solution will have benefits that cannot be appropriated by a single firm does not mean, however, that the project involved does not have an industry focus. The VLSI project was designed to solve technical problems for the semiconductor industry; the SIGMA project is designed to solve technical problems for the software industry. To say that R&D support is "generic" is not the same thing as saying it is neutral. Generic R&D support of the Japanese variety most assuredly picks industrial winners.

Second, the government provides direct funding as well as a variety of tax incentives to support its R&D projects. Third, the targeting of a particular technology by the government acts as a signaling device to the business community and encourages a bandwagon effect, as individual companies commit resources to compete with one another. And, fourth, the projects are cooperatively funded by business and government. The government acts to facilitate cooperation among individual firms, both directly by bringing together a selected group of them to design and implement projects, and indirectly by providing an antitrust environment conducive to such cooperation. Cooperation among individual companies encourages them to share technological information, to adopt common standards, and to create personal networks of scientists and engineers for future collaboration.

All of these features of Japanese industrial policy were ingredients of MITI's optoelectronics project, which began in 1979 and was extended through 1987. Fourteen companies, chosen by MITI, worked together to de-

Table 9C.1   **Ongoing AIST National Technology Projects**

Project	Purpose
Manganese nodule mining system, 1981–91, 20 billion yen	To develop a hydraulic mining system for harvesting large quantities of manganese nodules from the deep-ocean floor
High-speed computer, 1981–89, 23 billion yen	To develop high-speed computer systems for scientific applications
Automated sewing system, 1982–90, 10 billion yen	To develop an automated continuous sewing system for the textile industry
Advanced robot technology 1983–90, 20 billion yen	To develop advanced robot technology to replace humans in dangerous work
Observation system for the ERS-1, 1984–90, 23 billion yen	To develop, with the STA, an observation system for the earth resources satellite ERS-1
Water treatment system, 1985–90, 11.8 billion yen	To develop a bioreactor to process and purify waste water
Interoperable data base, 1985–91, 15 billion yen	To enable data bases with different operating systems to exchange information
Advanced material processing, 1986–93, 15 billion yen	To develop advanced material processing equipment, such as high-power excimer lasers and high-performance machine tools
Advanced high-power chemical products, 1988–96, 15 billion yen	To produce advanced chemical products such as dyes and insulating materials using marine-life resources

Source: AIST (total budget figures have been estimated), as cited in Steven K. Vogel, "Japanese High Technology, Politics, and Power," BRIE Research Paper no. 2, Berkeley Roundtable on the International Economy, University of California, Berkeley, March 1989.

velop optical measurement and control systems. About one-third of the total funding for the project was provided directly by MITI, with company funds making up the remainder. MITI orchestrated the organization of the project into smaller groups to work on complementary questions for specific opto-electronics devices. A special cooperative R&D laboratory was established by MITI and the business participants for the project.

The optoelectronics project is widely regarded both inside and outside of Japan as a success. Largely as a result of this project, within six years Japanese companies went from positions of inferiority to virtual domination in the optoelectronics area. Their success in this area bolstered their competitiveness in a wide range of commercial products, including video discs, optical fibers, laser beam printers, medical lasers, and fax machines. The same Japanese companies who cooperated in the joint R&D project on optoelectronics now

Table 9C.2   Other Major MITI Projects

Project	Purpose
Sunshine project 1974–	To develop coal liquefaction and gasification, solar power generation, and geothermal and hydrogen energy
Moonlight project 1978–	To develop energy conservation technology such as magnetohydrodynamic (MHD) power generators, high-efficiency gas turbines, chemical heat pumps
Basic technologies for future industries 1981–	To stimulate R&D for next-generation technology and to promote cooperation between companies, universities, and the government in research on new materials, biotechnology, and new devices
Fifth generation computer 1982–	To develop advanced computers that will use artificial intelligence to make them easier to run
SIGMA (software industrialized generator and maintenance aids) 1985–89	To develop an automated system for producing software

Source: AIST, as cited in Steven K. Vogel, "Japanese High Technology, Politics, and Power," BRIE Research Paper no. 2, Berkeley Roundtable on the International Economy, University of California, Berkeley, March 1989.

compete with one another for global leadership in these and other products embodying optoelectronic technology.

Not all cooperative R&D projects are as successful as the VLSI project or the optoelectronics project. There have been well-known difficulties in the fifth-generation computer project to develop artificial intelligence and in the SIGMA project to develop automated systems to produce software. But it would be premature to write off these projects as failures. Some of the machines developed under the fifth-generation project are now being successfully tested in Japan and abroad. And the VLSI project, which was terminated in response to U.S. pressure, was technically a failure since it did not perfect x-ray lithography. But the project is widely credited as a critical factor behind the success of Japanese companies in DRAMs. As these examples indicate, one needs to be careful about the definition of success and the time frame used in judging the success of cooperative R&D projects in Japan.

What are the consequences of Japan's continued commitment to a strategic industrial policy in several high-technology industries for its pattern of foreign trade? First, Japan's successful infant-industry promotion has been an important factor in its export successes in a variety of technology-intensive industries, particularly those in the electronics sector. Second, Japan's targeting has had a significant effect on the competitive strategies of both domestic and foreign companies. The Japanese companies favored by targeting have been encouraged to invest aggressively to dominate the Japanese market, while foreign competitors have been discouraged from undertaking the investment necessary to break into that market.

Third, the R&D programs that have become the backbone of industrial targeting have been yet another factor in the Japanese environment that encourages cooperation among Japanese firms to the disadvantage of outsiders. These programs have reinforced the patterns of specialization, distribution, cooperation, and trust that were fostered by the long period of formal protection and that are still encouraged by the *keiretsu* system. As a result of these patterns, Japanese companies continue to prefer to buy from one another rather than from an outsider, even when that outsider is a new Japanese entrant and especially when that outsider is a foreign company.

There is no doubt that overt trade and investment barriers to the Japanese market have been largely eliminated. But government R&D subsidies continue to target activities and industries for promotion, and these subsidies continue to advantage Japanese producers in both domestic and global competition. In addition, structural barriers continue to persist in a variety of forms, including standards, testing, and certification procedures, procurement and bidding practices, and the pattern of cooperative business relationships that Japan's strategic industrial policy continues to foster. To many foreign producers, especially those competing with Japanese companies in activities that have been accorded strategic significance by the Japanese government, the Japanese market, while formally open, is effectively closed.[1]

Comment   Edward M. Graham

Masahiro Okuno-Fujiwara gives us a succinct, balanced, and useful analysis of Japan's post–World War II industrial policy. Even so, this analysis is unlikely to please many Americans who have made a career of commenting upon Japan.

For example, there are those Americans who see Japan's success in international trade as the result of MITI "targeting" of specific industries and granting of subsidies to favored firms in these industries. These firms, it is claimed, then "dump" their output in international markets (e.g., the United States), sowing havoc among non-Japanese competitors (e.g., U.S. rival firms). In the extreme, it is alleged that U.S. rivals of the chosen Japanese firms are deliberately slated for annihilation by Japan's warlike government/industrial alli-

---

1. For more detail on the continued closure of the Japanese market see Laura D'Andrea Tyson and John Zysman, "Developmental Strategy and Production Innovation in Japan" in *Politics and Productivity: The Real Story of Why Japan Works*, ed. Chalmers Johnson, Laura D'Andrea Tyson, and John Zysman (Cambridge, Mass.: Ballinger Press, 1989).

Edward M. Graham is a senior research fellow at the Institute for International Economics.

ance. My depiction here may sound like a caricature, but having changed my residence to Washington, D.C., barely six months ago [1989], I hear depictions such as these frequently articulated, most recently by a person quite senior in the Executive Office of the President of the United States.

Okuno-Fujiwara's analysis suggests that the model implicit in this depiction better describes Japan before the first oil crisis than Japan of today. But even in the heyday of MITI activism, the model is somewhat simplistic; today, it just is not descriptive of what really goes on in Japan. Indeed, one of the major contributions Okuno-Fujiwara makes is to remind us that Japan's industrial policy has been anything but invariant during the past 40 or so years. Rather, it has evolved and undergone quite significant changes, so that generalizations about this policy that might have been valid in 1965 can be completely off the mark in 1991.

But, at the other extreme, there are Americans who assert that Japan's economic success is simply the result of good macroeconomic management combined with high rates of domestic savings and capital formation. Apart from differences that are readily explained via the Economics 101 textbook, they claim, Japan is really no different from any other advanced market-based economy.

Okuno-Fujiwara, although clearly more sympathetic to this view than to the former, disabuses the more extreme proponents of the "Japan is no different" school. Japan's political system is, he admits, stacked very heavily in favor of the interests of the established, large producers. To be sure, the same could probably be said of all of the large industrial democracies (and even more so of certain of the rapidly industrializing nations, e.g., Korea). But the degree to which producers' interests are favored by government policies over consumer interests is significantly greater in Japan than in the United States, Canada, or the nations of Western Europe.

Many readers doubtlessly will be disappointed by Okuno-Fujiwara's failure to attempt to assess the extent to which Japan's success as an economic power has been the result of deliberate industrial policy versus the extent to which other explanations are more powerful. My own feeling here is that the author is prudent in his unwillingness to take on this assessment. Japan's success is doubtlessly due to many interrelated factors, for example, high saving and investment rates (but why are these so much higher in Japan than in north America or Western Europe?), priority given to building an excellent education system (with the result that Japan easily has the most literate and numerate work force of all the advanced nations), cultural factors (leading to extraordinary ability of organizations to innovate and to adapt to changing circumstances?), effective macromanagement of the economy, low priority accorded to the military (but isn't Japan a "free rider" on the United States with respect to national defense?), intense rivalry among the major *keiretsu* groups, lifelong employment practices of major firms (enabling managers to take a "long-run" perspective on their functions?), and, yes, an industrial policy that without question is more activist than anything in the United States (although perhaps today not as activist as that of France).

Which of these factors explain Japan's success? I suspect that they all do to some degree, and I do not claim that my little list is exhaustive by any means. I further suspect that any effort to assign weights to any of these factors is doomed to failure. Any model to calculate such weights will likely be highly overspecified, and the explanatory variables highly collinear.

Alas, the implication of my remarks is that the debate between those who see Japan as "different" and those who see Japan as "no different" will never be resolved. This is unfortunate if for no other reason than that some of us would like to see extremists at either end of this debate silenced once and for all. But, given the unlikelihood that this will ever happen, the best we can hope for is analysis of the sort Okuno-Fujiwara gives us. This analysis is descriptive and historical, and he is wise not to attempt to use his considerable talents as a mathematician or econometrician in this domain. He cannot resolve our debate, but he can help ensure that our models of how Japan works, implicit and explicit, are consistent with the complex reality of that nation's economy.

10   U.S.-Japan Trade Negotiations: Paradigms Lost

Amelia Porges

10.1   The Political Setting

The NBER Conference on which this volume is based took place in a climate of increasing and changing interest in the U.S.-Japan economic relationship. Four years before, in the high-dollar days of 1985, the Senate had voted 92–0 to condemn Japan as an unfair trader, and the administration had been pushed into a new trade policy of aggressive bilateralism. A year before, Congress had passed by a veto-proof margin a massive trade bill, featuring "Super 301" provisions aimed at the U.S.-Japan trade relationship. In Japan, 1989 had brought the death of Emperor Hirohito, the Recruit bribery scandal, and three prime ministers in as many months. For both countries, the U.S. implementation of Super 301 and the debate over sales of the FSX fighter brought sharp debates on the nature of the U.S.-Japan trade and defense relationship. And 1989 was the year when revisionist views on the U.S.-Japan relationship became respectable and even mainstream in Washington, D.C. In Tokyo, revisionists emerged as well, urging a Japan that could "say no" to American demands.

Both Japan and the United States had operated since 1945 on the basis of a bilateral, special relationship. The terms of this relationship were formed in the American occupation of Japan: Japan would become the Switzerland of the Pacific, and America would be its protector and major export market. This

Amelia Porges was formerly associate general counsel, Office of the U.S. Trade Representative, and visiting fellow, 1988–89, at the Institute for International Economics, Washington, D.C.

The views expressed in this paper are personal and do not represent the position of USTR or the GATT Secretariat. The author gratefully acknowledges the support of the Council on Foreign Relations and the U.S. Trade Representative's Russell Long Fellowship. The author thanks the following individuals who offered helpful comments on this manuscript at various points: Thomas Bayard, C. Randall Henning, Paul Krugman, Joseph Massey, Marc Noland, David Walters, and especially David Schultz.

relationship was overwhelmingly important to each in its dealings with the other. Trade problems were dealt with inside the relationship by bilateral negotiation, and concerned primarily case-by-case appeals by Japan for access to the U.S. market for labor-intensive goods or by the United States for access to the Japanese market for U.S. products or investors. Both parties in the relationship had a strong interest in Japan's prosperity and political stability. Both in defense matters and in the sphere of trade relations, the United States intervened on Japan's behalf with third parties: for instance, U.S. commercial diplomacy was the key factor for Japan's entry into the GATT in 1955 and for its reentry into the world trading system.

The old paradigm of the special relationship was strained to the point of rupture by the economic events of the 1980s: the U.S. budget deficit, the recession of the early 1980s, the high dollar, and the ever-increasing bilateral trade deficit. Japanese competition, and U.S. appeals for trade relief, had moved from textiles to steel to semiconductors. In this climate, then, there were competing attempts to establish a new paradigm and new mechanisms for U.S.-Japan trade relations.

Economic and political revisionists have offered a critique of the Japanese political system, the Japanese economy, and Japan's relationship with the world. Their claim has been that Japan's political and social system makes this relationship different in nature from those with other U.S. trading partners and competitors. The political revisionists, Chalmers Johnson (1982), Clyde Prestowitz (1988), James Fallows (1989), and Karel van Wolferen (1989) present a picture of Japan as a neomercantilist society. Prestowitz critiques the way that the U.S. government deals with Japan trade issues. He and van Wolferen present a picture of Japanese society as totally oriented toward production, the source of national strength. Van Wolferen describes Japan as a vast and undemocratic "System" that exalts the producer at the expense of the consumer. Fallows simply says that Japan has different values: like Prestowitz, he argues that the United States has to find some new and different way to deal with Japanese trade. Meanwhile, economists such as Robert Z. Lawrence (ch. 1, in this volume) and Bela Balassa and Marcus Noland (1989), have pointed to the continuing low level of manufactured imports or intra-industry trade.

The economic critique was picked up by the CEO-level USTR Advisory Committee on Trade Policy and Negotiations in its February 1989 report on U.S.-Japan trade. Then the free-trade economist Jagdish Bhagwati was quoted (by Minard 1989) on the subject of Japan: "I think we are absolutely right in kicking the Japanese government a little. . . . Just as our government tells people to buy American, it would be a good idea to get the Japanese to buy foreign." And Rudiger Dornbusch of MIT—who in 1985 had testified that "an import surcharge is an awful idea" that would drive up the dollar (Dornbusch 1985)—came out for aggressive bilateralism and use of an import surcharge to force reduction in the U.S.-Japan trade deficit (Dornbusch 1989b). A report for Kodak by Dornbusch, Krugman, and Park (1989) rejected GATT in favor of aggressive market opening via bilateral deals.

In the year of *perestroika* and the fall of the Berlin Wall, 79% of respondents in a *Business Week* poll (1989) favored mandated targets for U.S. exports to Japan, 69% favored limiting imports from Japan, 61% favored raising tariffs on Japanese products, and 59% favored restricting technology outflow to Japan. A Washington Post–ABC News poll found that Americans now viewed Japan as the world's leading economic power, yet believed strongly that the U.S. government should do more to correct the perceived imbalance in the bilateral economic relationship. By May 1990, 75% of Americans in the same poll saw Japanese economic power as a greater threat to U.S. security than Soviet military power (Morin 1989, 1990).

Candidates for a new working paradigm have included bilateral balancing of trade, sectoral reciprocity, managed trade, Super 301, the Structural Impediments Initiative (SII) talks on basic imbalances, and the Uruguay Round of multilateral trade negotiations. This paper provides a legal and political perspective on trade talks between the United States and Japan, on the possible mechanisms for structuring negotiations, and on U.S. trade policy in the wake of the 1988 Omnibus Trade Bill. It suggests that the real challenge may come after the Final Act of the Uruguay Round is signed, as both countries turn to the issues they have not settled in the Round.

10.2 Negotiating with Japan: Background

The first step in evaluating the options for framing the trade relationship between the United States and Japan is to appreciate the setting and the two players. Negotiations themselves have usually (but not always) been conducted bilaterally, between governments, in the absence of their client industries. The world of GATT is significant as a framework for expectations in this bargaining, but many of the most sensitive issues are dealt with aside from, contrary to, or in evasion of GATT, as discussed below.

Crucial differences between the environment and the perceptions of the participants influence their behavior in negotiations. U.S. negotiators work for a government marked by congressional-executive conflict, a fluid, entrepreneurial political system in which fast decisions are possible, and in which there is antipathy to overt industrial policy as such. Japanese negotiators work for a government marked by stability, coincidence of interests (usually) between the Diet and the bureaucracy, a political system in which consensus is slow to emerge but solid, and a tradition of state involvement in the economy. Under current conditions sometimes these differences create synergy; sometimes they have created gridlock.

The U.S. negotiator works for the executive branch in a government with a strong executive constantly bargaining with a strong Congress. By giving foreign policy-making to the president and regulation of foreign commerce to Congress, the Constitution creates inherent conflict, which becomes one of the trade negotiator's central concerns. Various conflict-management devices have been tried over the years—such as the bargains involved in "fast-track" treatment for multilateral trade agreements. This conflict became sharper and sharper during the Reagan years, as interbranch struggle over arms control, the Contras, and other foreign policy issues intensified.

Separation of powers enables an executive branch negotiator to use pressure from Congress as an effective threat: either a threat of a known event (such as the threat that a quota on Japanese automobiles will be enacted by a veto-proof margin) or a threat of an uncertain but risky event (the threat of unspecified and drastic protectionist legislation). Among the many examples, a Danforth resolution condemning Japan, which passed the Senate 92–0 in March 1985, was immediately put to use by Commerce Undersecretary Olmer as leverage in telecommunications talks with the Japanese government; a Danforth bill in 1981 mandating a selective import quota on Japanese automobiles was the lever for Japanese agreement to the voluntary export restraint (VER) on automobiles.

Congress may determine not only the negotiator's threats but also his or her ability to make promises. For instance, "fast-track" treatment under the House and Senate Rules guarantees expedited, no-amendment treatment for the Uruguay Round results and for bilateral free trade agreements and, by extension, guarantees that a negotiator can deliver on implementation of deals made. The condition attached is that the trade committees in Congress be consulted regularly along the way and (implicitly) that their concerns be satisfied.

The U.S. negotiator works within a pluralistic trade policy system capable of making quick decisions and overriding minority views. Since the second Reagan administration, the focus for big-ticket decisions on trade has been the cabinet-level Economic Policy Council, now run on the Porter (1985) model of pluralism. One strength of this open system is the lack of barriers to new information and the large number of policy options that may be under consideration at any time. It has also been the stage for such stock Washington phenomena as lobbying by foreign interests, leaks, disinformation, and bureaucratic war by memorandum, as noted by Choate (1990, pp. 49–105) and Prestowitz (1988, 228).

The U.S. negotiator's environment has generally looked toward private parties to define the size and shape of the government's agenda of trade complaints, since industrial policy as such has been repeatedly rejected by the political process—from the failure of the National Industrial Recovery Act in the New Deal (Hawley 1966) through the early 1980s. Negotiators may know trade policy, but are seldom equipped to judge independently which microeconomic problems should be strategically important in the marketplace. Despite much rhetoric concerning "self-initiation" (initiation by government on its own motion) of cases under the unfair trade laws, self-initiation has happened almost always in response to industry requests; true volunteerism by the U.S. government has sometimes not been successful (Odell and Dibble 1988). Business stated on many occasions during the debate on the Omnibus Trade Bill of 1985–88 that it did not want wide-scale self-initiation of Section 301 cases. It follows therefore that a negotiator's success or failure is influenced not just by his or her own abilities, but also by the industry-client's ability to proactively define a set of workable goals.

The Japanese negotiator's job appears to be in some ways easier and in some ways more difficult. The negotiator starts with a parliamentary system in which one party has been in power for over 40 years and in which there is a high degree of coincidence of interests between Dietmen and the bureaucracy. Because legislation (generally drafted by the bureaucracy) gives the bureaucracy broad discretion in implementation, the bureaucracy has chips to trade with the Diet and the Diet has chips to trade with its constituencies.

To this picture, then, add the legal weakness of the state. Japanese administration is famous for the well-known tool of "administrative guidance": government by hints and persuasion and informal controls that fuzz the line between public and private spheres (Yamanouchi 1977; Samuels 1987). Haley (1986; 1987, p. 188) has pointed out that administrative guidance fills a gap left by the lack of other legal tools: Japanese ministries lack subpoena power, civil discovery powers, mandamus, or the other legal tools that U.S. bureaucrats can use to make private parties obey. From inability to order comes the need to induce compliance by less formal or visible means, such as by using discretionary statutes or other leverage such as licenses, permits or subsidies. The ministries' "turf-consciousness" creates paralyzing jurisdictional battles; the lack of means to settle interministry disputes may delay negotiating instructions or reduce them to the least common denominator.

Constitutionally, the prime minister and his cabinet are in charge of trade policy, but they are answerable to their party. Those who, like Johnson (1982, 1989), see Japan as a "capitalist developmental state" stress the leadership role played by an elite bureaucracy in composing industrial policy, formulating plans, writing legislation, and shepherding industry forward. A second view, from van Wolferen (1989), sees Japan as a grouping of overlapping and conflicting power centers, none of which has the power to make real change: in short, there is nobody to bargain with because nobody is in charge. The current Japanese consensus, represented by Muramatsu and Krauss (1987), Inoguchi (1987), and others, sees bureaucratic rule as a concept outdated by the rise of organized interest groups, within the Liberal Democratic Party (LDP), known as *zoku* or "tribes." This analysis of Japanese politics as "patterned pluralism" sees control as held by shifting alliances between the bureaucracy and *zoku* politicians.

The growth in power of *zoku* has been the major political development of the last 15 years. *Zoku* (such as the agriculture *zoku* or the construction *zoku*) are centered around LDP policy-making committees, and bind together those

Dietmen active in a policy area. They have become the major channel for policy-making and the route for climbing the ladder as an LDP politician. Pempel (1987) argues that the rise of *zoku* has been paralleled by changes in the relationship of government and business—as rising Japanese businesses escape from regulation and declining industries go to MITI for structural readjustment—and that these have in turn been paralleled by a decline in the power of the bureaucracy. Interministry disputes have increasingly gone to the LDP and the *zoku* for their resolution and not to mediation by senior ministries such as finance.

To the extent that *zoku* create a more efficient means of interest aggregation, they facilitate decision making for trade negotiations. At the same time they concentrate power in the hands of politicians most tied to domestic interests. In *zoku* and the Diet the most powerful groups are those least interested in trade liberalization: small business, agriculture, and construction. Farmers may be only 6% of the population, but through unequal apportionment of Diet districts, the strength of the farm vote is inflated to 18% of the whole, and it actually elects 25% of the Diet (*Economist* 1988). The system of allocating 2–6 Diet seats per medium-sized constituency makes Dietmen run against party colleagues and makes them vulnerable to negative-bullet voting by interest groups such as agricultural cooperatives. The opposite pull on the LDP has been its role in maintaining Japanese relations with the United States, Japan's largest market and its sponsor in the world trading system. The bilateral relationship is an important domestic political issue, and the LDP has a monopoly of the experience and political opportunities generated by dealing with it.

The result, according to Blaker's (1977) study of military negotiations, is a distinct "Japanese style of international negotiation . . . dominated by a philosophy of risk minimization and confrontation avoidance. Japanese policy-makers seem to prefer doing nothing when it is safe to do nothing and act only when the pressure of events forces them to act" (pp. 98–99). Japanese negotiators do not use the threats or histrionics that characterized classic Soviet bargaining behavior; they prefer deals worked out behind the scenes. The "Japanese game plan for bargaining victory" starts by probing the other side to set obtainable goals, then mobilizing resources to push and push again for them. Japanese offers are preceded by elaborate negotiations within the Japanese side apportioning the consequences. Positive demands tend to be modest, but since the opening position resulted from painful negotiations on the Japanese side, it is hard for the negotiator to budge. Japanese negotiators are "relentless and tenacious," relying on persistence and on arguing the rightness of their position. Concessions are late, are dribbled out bit by bit, and contingent on concessions by the other side; and the Japanese side keeps pushing (Blaker 1977, 100–1). The strategy described is one of Schelling-type precommitment both with respect to the opposition and with respect to the Japanese negotiator's own side. As Hiroya Sano, the Agriculture Ministry's lead negotiator on beef and citrus in 1984, puts it, "If you draw the other side's attention to your own freedom of action, you will be thought a clumsy negotiator and your mandate will be taken away" (1987, p. 14), noting that his best tactic in gaining U.S. acceptance of continued beef and citrus quotas in 1984 was to argue force majeure—that the Diet would veto liberalization.

The final key concept for understanding bilateral trade negotiating behavior is *gaiatsu*, a word translating literally as "outside pressure." A common Japanese view sees negotiations as a "*gaiatsu*-concession cycle" (Funabashi 1987, p. 6) of foreign pressure pulling unilateral concessions. The other side of the coin is the manipulation of *gaiatsu* by those in Japan who want to break gridlock, to accommodate important foreign relationships, or to serve their own purposes. Sometimes the really important stakes for the players inside Japan are not competition from foreigners, but the bureaucratic and political balance of power inside Japan. Johnson (1989) discusses the use by MITI (and its allied *zoku* politicians) of U.S. pressure in 1985 against plans by the Ministry of Posts and Telecommunications (MPT) (and its allied *zoku*) to regulate value-added telecommunications networks. MPT and its *zoku* wanted to regulate the software-telecommunications interface and capture the associated industry; MITI opposed MPT by deploying Dietmen from MITI's *zoku* and a study-group of proderegulation economists, and by mobilizing *gaiatsu* from the United States.

A phenomenon of the last few years, breaking former stereotypes, has been the increasing prominence of leading *zoku* Dietmen in trade negotiations and *zoku* groups as the place where the LDP leadership works out the political deals necessary for liberalization. This higher profile for the *zoku* has brought a bigger substantive role for specialized ministries such as Construction, MAFE, or MPT, breaking the Foreign Ministry's monopoly on negotiations. Tsutomu Hata, who was twice Minister of Agriculture, Forestry, and Fisheries and has held a range of LDP agriculture policy posts, was a key player in brokering the deals on the plywood tariff in 1985, cigarette imports in 1986, and beef and citrus in 1988. Ichiro Ozawa, prominent (like then–Prime Minister Takeshita) in the construction and telecommunications *zoku* and related to Takeshita by marriage, was sent as Takeshita's personal emissary to Washington to settle the construction issue in March 1988, and in spring 1989 was the LDP representative at talks settling the U.S.-Japan dispute over mobile telecommunications. The U.S. side showed its recognition of the importance of *zoku* politics when former Prime Minister Takeshita visited Washington in spring 1990; in a round of meetings, Cabinet officers discussed with Takeshita the commitments Japan might undertake in the Structural Impediments Initiative.

The prominence of political figures reflects a number of factors: the inevitable connection between market access issues and domestic Japanese politics; the power of *zoku* within their policy areas (and the bureaucracy's need for them as messengers for policy initiatives); the need of specialized *zoku* members for broader exposure in order to rise to high posts; the attractiveness of the political opportunities generated by brokering U.S.-Japan trade problems; and brokerage opportunities in mobilizing compensation for affected domestic interests. *Zoku* groups (such as the LDP Agricultural Products Liberalization Countermeasures Committee) are the place where antiliberalization Dietmen can publicly attest zeal, and the LDP leadership can quietly find out their real flexibility. Once a liberalization deal is made with a foreign government, the *zoku* can mobilize to obtain an impressive compensation package. After the beef and citrus deal of 1988, leaders in the beef and citrus caucuses, backed by the *zoku*, got subsidies raised to ¥106 billion for citrus and obtained a commitment that beef tariff receipts would be set aside for beef subsidies—an amount that may reach ¥100 billion per year or ¥22,000 per head per year for the entire beef and dairy herd (*Nihon Keizai Shimbun* 1988; *Mainichi Shimbun* 1988; Porges 1991).

10.3   How Can the United States Negotiate with Japan?

The next section describes the range of strategies and negotiating modes that have been used or proposed for trade negotiations between the United States and Japan, arranged from general to specific, from multilateral to bilateral, from less to more interventionist.

10.3.1   Macroeconomic Approaches

If the central trade problem between the United States and Japan is the trade imbalance, and that, in turn, is a function of savings-investment ratios, exchange rates, and economic growth, then macroeconomic approaches are the most appropriate. These have been tried: from the Carter Administration's 1978–79 "locomotives policy" of encouraging Japanese and German fiscal stimulation, to G-7 policy coordination, and the macroeconomic aspects of the SII. Yet this is not really a trade negotiation strategy and does not answer revisionist complaints that the Japanese market is closed.

10.3.2   Multilateral Negotiations under GATT

Multilateral rounds, such as the Uruguay Round of trade negotiations in GATT, offer the chance to solve problems that Section 301 or bilateral talks are unlikely to reach. One simple example is the tariff cut on an item for which the United States is not Japan's major supplier: Japan is only likely to make a binding tariff commitment on such an item in the context of a multilateral trade round where Japan can get credit for it. Because a round can produce a bigger package of gains, it can induce more liberalization and bigger domestic changes. Multilateral rounds can also serve as a negotiating forum for issues that a government believes to be too large and politically sensitive to be dealt with through unilateral action or even a bilateral deal—such as the Japanese internal support and border protection regime for rice.

The multilateral context also makes it possible for each participant to pool interests with other countries. In the Uruguay Round, Japan has found support from other countries for its positions (for instance) favoring agricultural import restrictions to protect food security, opposing certain antidumping practices of the United States and European Economic Community (EEC), and seeking discipline on trade-related investment measures (TRIMs). The United States has allied itself with the Cairns Group of agricultural exporting countries in seeking an end to Japan's ban on rice imports, has supported the antidumping practices opposed by Japan, but has taken positions similar to Japan's on TRIMs.

The changes made multilaterally in a successful Uruguay Round will affect the rules for bilateral relations as well. Antidumping offers an example: the antidumping rules on sales at "less than fair value" were a key part of U.S. leverage in negotiations for the 1986 U.S.-Japan semiconductor arrangement. Changes in the rules would therefore affect future such negotiations.

10.3.3   Bilateral Free-Trade Agreements

After a flurry of excitement in late 1988, during the issue vacuum after the trade bill, U.S. interest in a free-trade agreement (FTA) with Japan appears to have subsided. Critics, including Lawrence, Prestowitz, and Dornbusch/Krugman/Park, have pointed out that significant problems perceived by the U.S. side would not be touched by an FTA.

The strongest backers of the FTA concept were Japanese exporters, noted Stokes (1988, p. 3056). Japan's import-competing sectors were much less enthusiastic about an FTA which would, under GATT Article 24:6, be required to include "substantially all the trade," and which might lead to deregulation of financial services and an increased inflow of agricultural products. While there has been one FTA in GATT history that has excluded agriculture (the EFTA Convention), it is not clear that the U.S. Congress would agree to exclusion of such a large share of U.S. exports to Japan from the benefits of a U.S.-Japan FTA, or that the Diet could agree to an FTA that would include agriculture.

10.3.4   Structural Impediments Initiative

As described below, from July 1989 through mid-1990, the Japanese and U.S. governments engaged in discussions exploring the full range of structural impediments to trade and investment flows. These talks discussed practices of the governments and private businesses of both countries and are clearly only the start of a continuing bilateral process.

10.3.5   GATT Dispute Settlement

GATT Article 23 permits a GATT contracting party to seek redress for "nullification or impairment" of its GATT benefits in two contexts: either a violation by another contracting party of GATT rules or actions by another contracting party that are consistent with the rules but still nullify or impair a tariff concession.

To date, almost all GATT disputes under Article 23, including all U.S. cases against Japan, have focused on violation of GATT rules in the context of specific cases. The case is heard by a dispute settlement panel of neutral experts, whose panel report, if it finds a violation, recommends that the party in violation bring itself into compliance. The recommendation, if adopted, is legally binding and, if it is not complied with, the GATT contracting parties acting as a decision-making body may authorize retaliation. Because dispute settlement is a legal process in which panel decisions have some precedential effect, recourse to GATT dispute settlement in one case may have unforeseen results in others. A 1987 GATT dispute on a mere $100 million in Japanese agricultural import quotas triggered a finding that meant that Japan could no longer assert that its beef quota was consistent with its GATT obligations. This, in turn, was key to the 1988 liberalization of the beef and citrus quotas.

Still, a contracting party can only enforce the GATT rules as they are. For instance, the General Agreement requires that the products of contracting parties be accorded national treatment: treatment no less favorable than that accorded to like products of domestic origin. All the national treatment rule provides is a guarantee of nondiscrimination. If like products are given like treatment, GATT offers no recourse, even if the treatment is all equally bad. Furthermore, discrimination against foreign companies as such is a matter for bilateral treaties, not GATT. The remedies in GATT dispute settlement are also limited. GATT dispute settlement offers a means of getting another sovereign government to change its behavior and eliminate those measures that violate GATT rules—no mean feat. However, GATT offers no damage compensation for past acts.

GATT provides recourse not just in cases of rule violation but also when a government nullifies or impairs its tariff concessions through measures that are not explicitly prohibited by GATT norms (one classic example is nullification of a tariff binding by giving a subsidy to a competing domestic producer). A "nonviolation" challenge of this sort capturing the "U.S.-Japan trade problem" has been suggested in some quarters, including the Gephardt-Rostenkowski-Bentsen surcharge proposal (H.R. 3035). But aside from the strain such a case might put on the GATT, there are limits on what it could accomplish. First, GATT only addresses *government* measures, not private barriers, and is oriented toward specifics; a GATT action could not reach the range of measures discussed in SII. Furthermore, the remedies in "nonviolation" cases are limited. Since the measures complained of are already GATT consistent, the defendant need not change them. It need only provide compensation (in tariff cuts) for the concessions it has impaired. From 1983 to 1986, the EEC pursued initiation of a global case against Japan in the GATT but eventually switched to bringing complaints alleging violation of GATT norms in connection with specific products.

10.3.6   Problem Solving by Negotiation over Individual Cases

This has been the dominant mode of negotiation between Japan and the United States, whether in regularly scheduled encounters with set agendas or in specific negotiations such as those on agriculture or construction. The U.S. objective has usually been a unilateral market opening by the Japanese side. Issues get onto the U.S. agenda through contact by firms or industry associations with the U.S. Trade Representative (USTR), Commerce, Agriculture, and/or members of Congress. This bilateral negotiating format offers great flexibility and is not limited by the need to make a legal case. However, there are no deadlines built in.

Because remedies for unfair measures tend to be given a higher priority, complaining exporters may attempt to jump the queue, force U.S. government action, or improve their leverage by changing categories. They may point to evidence of Japanese unfairness or structure their complaints so as to fall under the unfair trade laws. This is not necessarily constructive for the bilateral relationship, as Prestowitz has repeatedly emphasized. It may not serve the exporter either, when it leads to management-by-law—emphasizing the aspects of a complaint that look the most unfair, rather than the aspects that address the core competitive problem.

10.3.7   Market Opening on a Systematic Industrywide Basis (MOSS)

At the January 1985 Reagan-Nakasone summit, both sides initiated a series of intensive market-oriented sector-selective (MOSS) talks on four sectors: telecommunications, electronics, forest products, and medical equipment and pharmaceuticals. The objective was for both sides to identify, and for Japan to unilaterally remove, all barriers to imports in those sectors. The talks consumed a major amount of attention and time for each government in 1985. The proposal for MOSS was itself a compromise between some on the U.S. side who urged the setting of import targets, and free trade "white hats" (Prestowitz 1988). The U.S. framed its goals by consulting U.S. firms active in the Japanese market. In 1986 another MOSS was initiated for transportation machinery (auto parts): these talks broke new ground by focusing on *keiretsu* and other private business practices and on U.S. firms' sales to Japanese-owned firms even in the United States.

A General Accounting Office (GAO) follow up (GAO 1988a, 1988b) found firms' reaction generally positive, though many still reported problems doing business in Japan. Though exports to Japan in the four original MOSS sectors rose 45% from 1985 to 1987 it was difficult to distinguish the effects of MOSS and the exchange rate. Prestowitz (1988, pp. 296–99) criticizes the entire enterprise as fundamentally misguided: the U.S. would never identify all the barriers in the Japanese regulatory state, much less get them peeled away; better to lay out specific goals and negotiate results.

In any event, a repetition of MOSS appears quite unlikely, because of the overwhelming expense and burden of the 1985 talks relative to their limited coverage. The baton has now passed from the micro-macro approach of MOSS to the macro-micro approach of SII.

10.3.8 Bilateral Negotiations under Section 301

Section 301 of the Trade Act of 1974 (19 U.S.C. 2411ff., as revised) provides a window for a private group to press the U.S. government to bargain on its behalf with a foreign government, under a deadline and with the threat of retaliation. Grievances of certain specific types can trigger the initiation of an "investigation" (the start of a negotiation): alleged violations of the GATT or other trade agreements or other foreign government acts, policies, or practices deemed "unjustifiable, unreasonable, or discriminatory" which burden or restrict U.S. commerce. The statute deems that certain specific types of foreign government action fit under one of these categories: for instance, industry targeting or denial of worker rights are each deemed to be unreasonable (and potentially punishable through trade retaliation). Over the years, successive revisions of Section 301 have oriented it more and more toward enforcement of U.S. rights, adding retaliation clout because of weaknesses perceived by Congress in international dispute settlement.

The USTR has complete discretion over whether or not to accept a Section 301 petition and initiate an investigation. Almost all petitioners consult with USTR before filing, so few petitions are filed and then rejected. USTR may also "self-initiate" an investigation, but, as noted above, true self-initiations have been rare. Once an investigation is started, Section 301, as revised in the 1988 Omnibus Trade Bill, requires the USTR to determine by a set timetable whether the act, policy, or practice complained of is unjustifiable, unreasonable, or discriminatory or violates or is inconsistent with a trade agreement. This determination is known as the "unfairness determination."

If the USTR's unfairness determination finds the act, policy or practice violates or is inconsistent with a trade agreement, or if USTR binds that it is unjustifiable and burdens or restricts U.S. commerce, then the law mandates retaliation (subject to presidential direction). If the act, policy, or practice is found to be unreasonable or discriminatory, then retaliation is discretionary. In practice, retaliation has been carried out by raising the tariff on specific products of the target country to a prohibitive level; in theory the USTR could impose quotas, reject further service-sector access licenses, or impose fees or restrictions on services. Significant exceptions are provided to the requirement to retaliate, but the statute makes their use transparent, and subjects it to close congressional supervision.

Congress has intended Section 301 not just as a remedy for existing unfair trade barriers but as a bargaining tactic in itself—to create leverage for Congress in its bargaining with the administration over the conduct of trade negotiations and for U.S. industry and the U.S. government in their dealings with foreign governments. The 1988 amendments announced a congressional mandate that certain types of behavior be subject to retaliation, by reducing the administration's discretion and creating a precommitment to retaliate. Schelling (1960, p. 24ff.) states that in a contest of precommitments, the gaming advantage goes to the first party that makes a commitment (such as mandatory retaliation) perceived as irrevocable by the other side; this advantage remains only as long as the commitment stays credible (p. 40).

In the Uruguay Round, a number of contracting parties have made clear their objections to bargaining conducted under threat and have demanded that, as a condition for agreement to new rules on intellectual property or dispute settlement, the use of unilateral enforcement measures such as Section 301 be foregone as well. Moreover, the scope for reciprocity and retaliation is being progressively eroded by the trend toward interpenetration of the U.S. and Japanese (and global) economies. Gilpin (1987) refers to this phenomenon as the *"nichibei* economy." Retaliation through tariff increases is ineffective when products can be resourced from another country or from U.S. production. Retaliation can create domestic political problems when the customer for a target product is a sensitive business or group or when the product is made abroad by U.S.-based multinationals. And retaliation against services is many times more difficult to implement; all Section 301 cases on services trade barriers have involved retaliation (or threats of retaliation) not against services but against products.

10.3.9 Super 301

The 1988 Omnibus Trade Bill instituted an additional mechanism for an aggressive trade policy, "Super 301," for the years 1989 and 1990 only. The basis for the Super 301 process as the National Trade Estimates (NTE) report on trade barriers, required to be published on 31 March 1988 and each April 30 thereafter. The NTE is an inventory of trade and investment barriers in every country, which is required to quantify the cost of barriers in terms of trade or investment forgone.

In the years 1989 and 1990, the USTR was required within 30 days after the appearance of the report NTE to identify a set of "United States trade liberalization priorities," including priority practices, priority countries, and the dollar cost of the practices in exports forgone. The choice of priority countries was to take into account both the number and pervasiveness of trade barriers and the export gains to be expected from full implementation of trade agreements to which each foreign country was a party. Within 21 days after the naming of priority countries and practices, USTR had to self-initiate Section 301 investigations against each practice: hence the name "Super 301." The Section 301 cases would operate just like standard Section 301 cases under the law as revised in 1988, with the exception that a greater degree of flexibility was provided for settling cases.

The 1989 Super 301 package led to six Section 301 investigations and the launching of the Structural Impediments Initiative with Japan, as described below. By 1990, attention had shifted to the Uruguay Round. After the release of the SII midterm report, and intense discussions that resolved the supercomputer and satellite issues, the administration went for the "zero option" and named no new practices or countries. The future of Super 301 remains to be seen. Congressional enthusiasm remains high for this mechanism of requiring the administration to take a militant approach on trade. Yet Super 301 gave rise to a strong reaction among U.S. trading partners, who have demanded a rollback of 301 as the quid pro quo for progress on dispute settlement in the Uruguay Round.

10.3.10   Managed Trade including VERs

Voluntary export restraints (VERs) in particular industries are a phenomenon of over 50 years' history, but recently economic writers such as Robert Kuttner (1989) have suggested the use of managed trade to achieve "systemwide reciprocity."

If the U.S. sought to achieve systemwide reciprocity through managing Japanese trade into the United States, there might be three routes to do so. All are unpromising. The first would be restriction of imports by the U.S. government by import quotas or import licensing. Aside from the welfare costs, such measures would be contrary to U.S. GATT obligations under almost any circumstances; even in the unlikely event that Japan waived (or refrained from claiming) its GATT rights, third countries could raise claims. The second path would be for the United States to obtain Japanese VERs for all bilateral trade. Such VERs would strengthen the Japanese bureaucracy and give the lion's share of quota rents to Japanese exporters; the VERs would also be open to challenge in the GATT. Finally, the parties to such a bilateral arrangement might ask the contracting parties to the GATT to authorize managed trade on the basis of a waiver; after all, the Multi-Fiber Arrangement has been legally provided for over the years, coexisting with GATT. There is, however, no reason to suppose that the GATT would cheerfully agree to such an arrangement, either now—when it would prejudge the outcome of Uruguay Round negotiations on textiles and grey-area measures—or at any time in the future.

The legal aspects of VERs deserve a fuller discussion. They have long been recognized to function as a rent-producing collaboration between the firms whose exports are restrained, their competitors in the importing country, and the governments, at the expense of the consumer. While the fiction is maintained that a VER is "voluntary," in fact it is often implemented by the exporting country as an alternative to import restrictions by the destination country; compliance by the exporting firms is then often compelled by the exporting country's government, in order to insulate the exporters from accusations of an antitrust conspiracy (Waller 1982). As seen in the history of textile trade, the exporting country has an incentive to seek expansion of the VER to cover competing suppliers elsewhere.

Much of the economic literature neglects the legal status of VERs or places them in the category of "grey-area measures" assumed to be quasi legal; see, for instance, Dornbusch, Krugman, and Park (1989, p. 33). This is incorrect. The dispute settlement panel that examined Japanese measures under the Japan-U.S. Semiconductor Arrangement concluded, in essence, that where a VER is enforced by government export restraint measures, or where a VER scheme could not exist without a government role, it is a quantitative restriction on trade contrary to the General Agreement (GATT 1988; Porges 1989). The major reason why VERs have so rarely been challenged in the GATT is that neither exporter nor importer has an incentive to complain. Challenge is nonetheless possible; the Semiconductor Arrangement measures were attacked by a third party, the EEC, whose interests had been affected by the Arrangement's provisions raising semiconductor prices in the European market. The wider a country's network of VERs expands, the more likely that VER effects on third parties would provoke such challenges.

The institutional aspect of VERs is also worth considering. Discretionary foreign exchange control legislation dating back to the Occupation has facilitated the making and enforcement of VERs by the Japanese bureaucracy (Haley 1986). In accounts of the 1981 U.S.-Japan automobile VER negotiations such as Amaya's (1982), MITI is depicted as persuading a reluctant auto industry to go along with little or no intervention from the political level, and the consensus view is that the auto VER only strengthened MITI in dealing with the Japanese auto industry. The conclusion would be that the broader the VER, the more that U.S. manufacturers are dependent on Japanese inputs, the more MITI's influence over the Japanese and U.S. economies could be expected to grow.

10.3.11   Managed Trade based on U.S. Export Expansion

The idea of a "voluntary import expansion" (VIE) has most often been linked to the U.S.-Japan Semiconductor Arrangement, but the concept is not unique to the high-technology sector. At various times since 1978, Japan, Korea, and Taiwan have tried to fix their trade figures through purchases of big-ticket items by the government or by state-owned enterprises: nuclear fuel, aircraft, turnkey plants, big construction projects, or gold for the mint. Since 1985, MITI has jawboned large companies to increase imports. Politically aware Japanese firms have expanded their U.S. sourcing of visible components, such as automobile seat leather. And the U.S. government has held concrete discussions on sourcing with Japanese automobile firms in the context of the auto parts MOSS mentioned above, in response to strong pressure by Rust Belt congressmen; USTR Carla Hills testified in April 1990 that "the United States and Japan will hold regular [government-industry] conferences to promote growth of strong business and sales relationships between American auto parts suppliers and Japanese auto manufacturers" (Hills 1990).

VIEs have been proposed most often as a solution to particular product-sector problems. Semiconductor-specific issues aside, VIEs have been proposed as an appropriate means of:

- *Affirmative action.* Breaking through a buyer's "taste for discrimination" against imports (Dornbusch, 1989a, p. 14) by forcing the buyer to get to know a new supplier and make the commitment to use a foreign component.
- *Market failure situations.* Abandoning fruitless arguments about "unfairness" in favor of frank discussions about sales and market share, in markets where government presence is strong (Prestowitz 1988).

However, picking sectors and negotiating VIE levels is not a scientific process. Even a VIE that looks neutral will have distributional implications for specific suppliers. Negotiations over the Japanese import quotas on citrus, for instance, have involved trade-offs between the interests of California dessert oranges, Florida juice oranges and juice, and grapefruit from Florida and Texas—each of which is a distinct product, marketed differently, with different interests and different political backing (Porges 191; Kusano 1983). The VIEs would seem most likely to be compatible with the U.S. political system in those sectors where government intervention is pervasive and accepted by the U.S. public—agriculture and defense, the only sectors with active government sales forces abroad (in the Agriculture and Defense Departments).

Talk of VIEs raises another subject, however: trade discrimination. In the EEC's GATT challenge to Japan's semiconductor measures, the EEC took up the VIE aspects of the Semiconductor Arrangement as well, asserting that its benefits were reserved for U.S. semiconductors in violation of the GATT's most-favored-nation clause, Article 1. The dispute settlement panel found no actual evidence of discrimination in that case, but VIEs that expand imports from only one country or one bloc would clearly be at odds with Article 1, the cornerstone of the GATT system. Such VIEs would discriminate in favor of the powerful to the detriment of smaller and developing countries. Those excluded could then legally attack such a preferential arrangement (GATT 1982). A trading regime based on VIEs would be quite different from the GATT regime: in a VIE system, small and weak countries would not share in the benefits of deals that would be made by the strong for the strong.

Moreover, if VIEs were to become a normal aspect of trade policy, like Food for Peace sales under P.L. 480 and the USDA's other agricultural sales programs, VIE priorities would be set on a political basis. Exporters could then be expected to respond by investing in lobbying, with the result that VIE rents would go not just to the (beleaguered) domestic industry but at least in part to its trade lawyers and lobbyists.

10.4 Trade Legislation, Super 301, and Onward

Japan and the "Japan trade problem" have been a recurring theme on Capitol Hill since the late 1970s. In 1985, when political pressure and the dollar hit twin peaks, concern with Japan was overwhelming. In the three years that followed, the Japan issue became cemented into law in the Omnibus Trade Bill of 1988, left to the new Bush administration to implement in spring 1989.

In a sense, the 1988 trade bill was one of the political costs of the high dollar of 1985. The business community, unable to persuade the administration of the need to take action to achieve a more favorable exchange rate, went to Capitol Hill instead. The result showed in the tactics of 1985—the Motorola and Gephardt Japan-trade-surcharge bills and the Danforth anti-Japan resolution, which was explicitly tied to the yen-dollar rate. Groups such as the Business Roundtable, supporters of the GATT process who had vocally opposed trade reciprocity two years before, began to urge Congress to revise the trade laws in favor of opening foreign markets through aggressive reciprocity.

Congress started with two approaches to dealing with Japan: fixing the aggregate figures (as in the initiatives of Congressmen Gephardt of Missouri) or case-by-case reciprocity tied to Section 301 (as proposed by Senator John Danforth, also of Missouri). Gephardt's key proposal, an amendment attached to the House trade bill in 1986 and 1987, would have had the U.S. government negotiate an agreement with an "excessive and unwarranted trade surplus country" to put its surplus on a 10% diet each year; otherwise, the United States would cut the surplus unilaterally through various means with import quotas as a backup. The proposal's major backers were organized labor and Chrysler and its suppliers, all of which saw automobile trade as an obvious place to begin surplus reduction. The Senate responded with its own alternative, adopted in the final trade bill: Super 301, a more-and-better version of the revised Section 301. For 1989 and 1990, the Super 301 provisions would require an aggressive program of Section 301 cases, picked to advance a trade strategy.

Japan also became an issue in another context: the Toshiba-Kongsberg trade sanctions legislation, punishing these companies for sales of advanced machine tools to the Soviet military. The Toshiba issue provoked a firestorm of anti-Japanese sentiment—members of Congress taking sledgehammers to Toshiba products for the network news and competing to pass trade sanctions. This, in turn, projected to the Japanese public as a rejection of the special relationship or perhaps of any relationship at all. The issue was inflammatory precisely because of its connection with national security. In the old paradigm of the U.S.-Japan relationship,the United States had tolerated Japanese economic success in its market because Japan was its junior partner against the common enemy, the Soviet Union. The allegations against Toshiba—that its subsidiary had violated CoCom export controls for profit—were a blow at that paradigm. Toshiba reacted with a life-or-death lobbying effort, and its customers joined in, underlying the growing dependence of U.S. high-technology companies on Japanese components. By Senator John Heinz's estimate, Toshiba and those associated with it spent $9 million on lobbying (Auerbach 1988; Dryden 1988). Toshiba and Kongsberg ended up subject to short-term sanctions on federal procurement, contracts, or imports of their products, but they benefited from significant loopholes.

The other "Japan issue" in the trade bill was the Exon-Florio proposal screening of foreign investment. Although the proposal was neutral, and the political battle against it was fought largely by European-based foreign investors, the issue had first arisen in the context of Fujitsu's attempt in late 1986 to acquire the semiconductor firm Fairchild Industries. At that time, U.S. law provided no means of blocking even a foreign takeover directly threatening national security, except if there were a presidential declaration of economic emergency. Once passed and implemented, Exon-Florio became the first investment-screening mechanism ever instituted in the United States.

The following spring, the trade world in Washington shifted its attention to the new administration and its trade strategy—with the implementation of Super 301 as the most closely watched indicator of that strategy.

The political mandate in the Omnibus Bill put trade—unusually—on the Cabinet agenda early in the new Bush administration. In long debates in the Economic Policy Council, some cabinet officers pushed for a long list of targets, and some pushed for none. Some pushed to cite Japan as a Super 301 country; Treasury and State pushed for a Structural Impediments Initiative as an alternative. The final White House strategy reflected both the administration debate and White House soundings that had indicated that Congress would not accept a decision not to cite Japan.

Ambassador Hills announced the package on 25 May 1989 at a press conference in the presence of 19 video cameras and hundreds of reporters. She listed as U.S. trade liberalization priorities first the Uruguay Round; then five priority trade liberalization practices were mentioned in general and with respect to a specific country and sector. Japan was named with respect to government procurement (for supercomputers and satellites) and technical standards (for imports of forest products); India was named with respect to services trade and investment restrictions, and Brazil, for import licensing. Three specific Section 301 investigations on Japan—on satellites, supercomputers, and forest products—were initiated 16 June 1989 together with those on India and Brazil.

On the same day, President Bush announced the Structural Impediments Initiative for Japan, separate from Super 301 and to be jointly led by USTR, State, and Treasury. The SII was launched in July 1989, and focused on problems identified by Japan and the United States in each other's economies. The U.S. side made 240 suggestions identifying Japanese savings and investment patterns, land use, the distribution system, exclusionary business practices, *keiretsu* relationships, and pricing mechanisms. The Japanese side made 80 suggestions in return identifying U.S. savings and investment patterns, corporate investment activities and supply capacity, corporate behaviour, government regulations, R&D, export promotion, and work force training and education. The groups met to explore this massive agenda; they took a joint survey of prices, which established (to nobody's surprise) that prices were higher in Japan for both foreign and domestic products. The working group bore down and produced its interim report on 5 April 1990, including a long list of commitments by both sides.

Meanwhile, the Japanese government kept a formal distance from Super 301 as such, maintaining the position that it would not discuss these issues in that context. Discussions eventually took place on the substance of the supercomputer, satellite, and forest products issues. The supercomputer and satellite issues were resolved with elaborate agreements providing in detail for opening of procurement. Both deals were essentially done by April 4. The forest products case was resolved later in April with an agreement on tariff cuts and changes in standards and building codes. On April 27, USTR Hills's second and final Super 301 package gave first and foremost place to finishing the Uruguay Round and did not name Japan.

The SII was a negotiation that went beyond national treatment—discussing not just the elimination of discriminatory rules, but the content of the rules themselves. Never before had there been a bilateral negotiation of this type. Some in Japan predicted that SII would make Japan more efficient. Other observers, including van Wolferen (1990), were less sanguine; in their view, although the Japanese government's promise to spend billions on public works was of obvious interest to contractors and politicians, it was less likely that the SII would disrupt the tight buying arrangements of *keiretsu* or loosen distribution channels.

10.5   Japan and the U.S. in the 1990s?

Viewed from Tokyo, 1989 was a year of political and social turmoil, and of upheaval of greater magnitude than ever experienced in the political lives of most Dietmen: the sheer scale of the Recruit scandal, the popular revolt against LDP incumbents, the "Madonna factor" and the revival of the Socialist Party, and the rapid passing of Prime Ministers Takeshita and Uno. Most interesting in the long run may be the extent of middle-class discontent with the quality of life, and resentment of the undeserving rich—real-estate millionaires, Recruit's politicians, and businesses that did not pass on the profits from yen revaluation to the consumer. It was as if there were a two-track Japan in which some owned real-estate and others never would be able to. Some Japanese, at least, connected this discontent with trade and the SII issues. The following spring, a poll in connection with the SII by Japan's leading business daily, the *Nihon Keizai Shimbun,* showed that nearly half of all Japanese at least basically agreed with the United States' demands that Japan review its economic structure and open its markets; three-quarters thought their government ought to try at least somewhat to listen to U.S. demands, and most cited the reason that such measures would be good for Japan and would improve the quality of daily life. Over sixty percent supported at least a partial opening of rice imports (Japan Economic Journal 1990).

Meanwhile, revisionism broke out in Japan as well. In the best-seller, *A*

Japan that Can Say No (1989), conservative politician Shintaro Ishihara and Sony CEO Akio Morita criticized the shortsightedness of American business, advocating that Japan learn to say no to American trade demands. Ishihara suggested that if, as the Soviet Union ceased to be the great common enemy, the United States decided that Japan was no longer needed as a partner, Japan could demonstrate how much U.S. defense hardware depended on Japanese technology, by selling semiconductors to the Soviet Union instead (p. 3–4).

Since 1989, trade policymakers in Washington and Tokyo have become increasingly preoccupied with the Uruguay Round. After closing of the Round, the first task will be the enactment of implementing legislation in each participating country. Both Japan and the United States will have to revise a long list of existing rules and devise domestic rules to implement agreements in areas such as services and intellectual property where trade policy has never gone before.

Recent Congresses have vigorously debated the more bilateral and interventionist options listed above for structuring trade bargaining. From a political perspective, the near-term benefits of brining maximum trade leverage to bear through retaliation may exceed the long-term costs to the multilateral trading system. Yet the globalization of manufacturing makes retaliation less effective as a tactic and trade remedies less effective as a strategy—as U.S. firms like Motorola increase their presence in Japan, for instance, and Japanese firms decrease their dependence on exports to the United States by investing there and elsewhere. In the Uruguay Round's new issue areas of services and intellectual property, there is hardly anything left of the traditional link between trade agreements and things grown or made within the national territory: they, like the corporations that will benefit from them, are borderless. Recession in the United States is only likely to increase the cleavage between globalized corporations manufacturing products and supplying services on a global basis, and those industries that remain localized in the United States. Even the revisionist van Wolferen has urged that the framework for trade with Japan be set by rules negotiated multilaterally.

Revisionism in U.S.-Japan relations has also affected, and will change, American trade relations with Korea, Taiwan, and other countries in Asia. The 1992 process in Europe is still another example of self-generated revision: the Community is redefining itself, and the rest of Europe (and the world) is being compelled to redefine its relationship with the Community. And the revision process in Eastern Europe and the Soviet Union is even broader. The direction that the United States and Japan take and the example they set in managing their relationship will have immediate effects on the interests of each in each of these other areas.

Will the 1990s be a decade of revision, then, leading to a new paradigm for the relationship between Japan and the United States? If this is only the beginning for revision, no one could now predict for sure when and where it would end or what the results might be—or whether it would come to rest in a new and better equilibrium for the United States and Japan, for the rest of the world, or for the multilateral trading system.

References

Advisory Committee for Trade Policy and Negotiations (ACTPN). 1989. *Analysis of the U.S.-Japan Trade Problem.* Report to Ambassador Carla Hills, February.

Amaya, Naohiro. 1982. What was the U.S.-Japan Car Problem? Interview with Professor Iida Tsuneo. *Journal of Japanese Trade and Industry* 1:22–27. See also Amaya Naohiro, "Rejecting Soap-Opera Nationalism," *Economic Eye* (Sept. 1981), pp. 20–26 (translation of "Sopu nashonarizumu o haisu," *Bungei Shunju* [July 1981]).

Auerbach, Stuart. 1988. Toshiba Corp.'s Costly Lobbying. *Washington Post,* October 13, p. C1.

Balassa, Bela, and Marcus Noland. 1989. *Japan in the World Economy.* Washington, D.C.: Institute for International Economics.

Blaker, Michael K. 1977. Probe, Push and Panic: The Japanese Tactical Style in International Negotiations. In *The Foreign Policy of Modern Japan,* ed. Robert Scalapino, pp. 55–102. Berkeley: University of California Press.

Business Week. 1989. Rethinking Japan: The New, Harder Line Toward Tokyo. August 7, pp. 44–53.

Choate, Pat. 1990. *Agents of Influence.* New York: Knopf.

Dornbusch, Rudiger. 1985. Testimony April 24, published in U.S. Senate Committee on Finance hearings, *Floating Exchange Rates' Impact on International Trading,* S. Hrg. 99–176, pp. 424–53.

———. 1989a. Is there a Case for Aggressive Bilateralism and How to Practice It? Paper for Brookings Institution Conference on Alternative Trade Strategies for the United States, Sept. 12.

———. 1989b. Getting Tough on Trade: Give Japan a Target and Say "Import!" *New York Times,* Sept. 24, p. 2 (business section).

Dornbusch, Rudiger, Paul Krugman, and Yung Chul Park. 1989. *Meeting World Challenges: Manufacturing in the 1990s.* Rochester, N.Y.: Eastman Kodak Co.

Dryden, Steven. 1988. The Battle of the Sumo Lobbyists. *Regardie's Magazine,* September.

Economist. 1988. Off with the mask. Dec. 17, p. 11.

Fallows, James. 1989. Containing Japan. *Atlantic,* May, pp. 40–54.

Funabashi, Yoichi. 1987. *Nichibei keizai masatsu* (Japan-U.S. economic friction). Tokyo: Iwanami Shinsho no. 376.

GATT. 1982. EEC—Imports of Beef from Canada. Panel Report L/5099, adopted 10 March 1981. In *Basic Instruments and Selected Documents, Twenty-eighth Supplement,* pp. 92–100.

———. 1988. Japan—Trade in Semi-conductors. Panel Report L/6309, adopted 4 May 1988. In *Basic Instruments and Selected Documents, Thirty-fifth Supplement* pp. 116–63.

General Accounting Office (GAO). 1988a. U.S.-Japan Trade: Evaluation of the Market-Oriented Sector-Selective Talks. U.S. General Accounting Office no. NSIAD-88-205. July 18.

Gilpin, Robert. 1987. *The Political Economy of International Relations.* Princeton: Princeton University Press.

Haley, John O. 1986. Administrative Guidance versus Formal Regulation: Resolving the Paradox of Industrial Policy. In *Law and Trade Issues of the Japanese Economy,* ed. Gary Saxonhouse and Kozo Kawamura. Seattle: University of Washington Press.

———. 1987. Governance by Negotiation: A Reappraisal of Bureaucratic Power in Japan. *Journal of Japanese Studies* 13(2):343–57.

Hawley, Ellis W. 1966. *The New Deal and the Problem of Monopoly: A Study in Economic Ambivalence.* Princeton: Princeton University Press.

Hills, Carla. 1990. Testimony before the Committee on Energy and Commerce, Subcommittee on Commerce and Competitiveness, U.S. House of Representatives, May 10.

Inoguchi, Takashi. 1987. *Zoku giin no kenkyu* (A study of *zoku* Dietmen).

Japan Economic Journal. 1990. Many Japanese Support U.S. Trade Stance. April 7, p. 6 (translation of article from *Nihon Keizai Shimbun* concerning poll taken March 16–19).

Johnson, Chalmers. 1982. *MITI and the Japanese Miracle: The Growth of Industrial Policy, 1925–75.* Stanford, Calif.: Stanford University Press.

———. 1989. MITI, MPT and the Telecom Wars: How Japan Makes Policy for High Technology. In *Politics and Productivity: How Japan's Development Strategy Works,* ed. Chalmers Johnson, Laura Tyson, and John Zysman, pp. 177–240. New York: Ballinger.

Kusano, Atsushi. 1983. *Nichibei Orenji Kosho* (Japan-U.S. Orange Negotiations). Tokyo: Nihon Keizai Shimbun.

Kuttner, Robert. 1989. *Managed Trade and Economic Sovereignty.* Washington, D.C.: Economic Policy Institute.

Mainichi Shimbun. 1988. August 26, p. 9.

Minard, Lawrence. 1989. "Pressure has its uses": A Chat with Jagdish Bhagwati. *Forbes,* June 12, pp. 96–98.

Morin, Richard. 1989. Americans Rate Japan No. 1 Economic Power. *Washington Post,* February 21.

Muramatsu, Michio, and Ellis Krauss. 1987. The Conservative Policy Line and the Development of Patterned Pluralism. In *The Political Economy of Japan.* Vol. 1, *The Domestic Transformation,* ed. Yamamura Kozo and Yasuba Yasukichi, pp. 516–54. Stanford, Calif.: Stanford University Press.

Nihon Keizai Shimbun. 1988. July 25, p. 3; August 26, p. 5.

Odell, John, and Anne Dibble. 1988. *Brazilian Informatics and the United States: Defending Infant Industry versus Opening Foreign Markets.* Pittsburgh: Graduate School of International Studies, University of Pittsburgh.

Pempel, T. J. 1987. The Unbundling of "Japan, Inc.": The Changing Dynamics of Japanese Policy Formation. In *The Trade Crisis: How Will Japan Respond?,* ed. Kenneth Pyle, 117–52. Seattle: University of Washington Press.

Porges, Amelia. 1989. Casenote: Japan Trade in Semi-conductors. *American Journal of International Law* 83, no. 2 (April): 388–94.

———. 1991. Agriculture: Law, Political Economy and the Last Beef and Citrus Deal. Manuscript.

Porter, Roger. 1985. *Presidential Decisionmaking.* Cambridge: Cambridge University Press.

Prestowitz, Jr., Clyde V. 1988. *Trading Places: How We Allowed Japan To Take the Lead.* New York: Basic Books.

Samuels, Richard J. 1987. *The Business of the Japanese State: Energy Markets in Comparative and Historical Perspective.* Ithaca, N.Y.: Cornell University Press.

Sano, Hiroya. 1987. Nichibei Nosanbutsu kosho no seijikeizaigaku (The political economy of Japan-U.S. agricultural negotiations). *Ekonomia* 95, December.

Schelling, Thomas. 1960. *The Strategy of Conflict*. Cambridge: Harvard University Press.

Stokes, Bruce. 1988. Eyes toward Asia. *National Journal* 21 (Dec. 3): 3052–57.

————. 1989. Off and Running. *National Journal* 22 (June 17): 1562–66.

van Wolferen, Karel. 1989. *The Enigma of Japanese Power*. New York: Knopf.

————. 1990. The Japan Problem Revisited. *Foreign Affairs* 69(4): 42–55.

Waller, Spencer Weber. 1982. Redefining the Foreign Compulsion Defense in U.S. Antitrust Law: The Japanese Auto Restraints and Beyond. *Law and Policy in International Business* 14(3): 747–818.

Yamanouchi, Kazuo. 1977. Gyōsei Shidō (Administrative guidance). Tokyo: Kōbundō.

Contributors

Alice H. Amsden
Graduate Faculty
Department of Economics
New School for Social Research
65 Fifth Avenue
New York, NY 10011

Daniel A. Citrin
Asian Department
International Monetary Fund
700 19th Street, NW
Washington, DC 20431

Robert Dekle
Department of Economics
Boston University
270 Bay State Road
Boston, MA 02215

Robert Alan Feldman
Salomon Brothers
SBAL Tokyo Economics Research
2–2 Otemachi 2-chome
Chlyoda-ku
Tokyo 100, Japan

David Flath
Department of Economics
North Carolina State University
Box 8110
Raleigh, NC 27695

Jeffrey A. Frankel
University of California at Berkeley
Department of Economics
787 Evans Hall
Berkeley, CA 94720

Edward M. Graham
Institute for International Economics
11 DuPont Circle, NW
Washington, DC 20036

Koichi Hamada
Economic Growth Center
Yale University
27 Hillhouse Avenue
New Haven, CT 06520

Takatoshi Ito
Institute of Economic Research
Hitotsubashi University
Kunitachi, 186 Tokyo, Japan

Motoshige Itoh
Faculty of Economics
University of Tokyo
7–3–1 Hongo, Bunkyo-ku
Tokyo 113, Japan

Paul Krugman
Department of Economics
Room E52–383
Massachusetts Institute of Technology
50 Memorial Drive
Cambridge, MA 02139

Robert Z. Lawrence
John F. Kennedy School of Government
Harvard University
79 Kennedy Street
Cambridge, MA 02138

Bonnie E. Loopesko
Research Department
Federal Research Bank of New York
33 Liberty Street
New York, NY 10045

Catherine L. Mann
International Finance Division
Mail Stop 23
Board of Governors of the Federal
    Reserve System
Washington, DC 20551

Richard C. Marston
Wharton School
2300 Steinberg-Dietrich Hall
University of Pennsylvania
Philadelphia, PA 19104

Masayoshi Maruyama
Department of Business Administration
Kobe University
Kobe 654, Japan

David M. Meerschwam
Graduate School of Business
    Administration
Harvard University
Boston, MA 02163

Marcus Noland
Department of Economics
University of Southern California
University Park
Los Angeles, CA 90089

Masahiro Okuno-Fujiwara
Faculty of Economics
University of Tokyo
7–3–1, Hongo, Bunkyo-ku
Tokyo 113, Japan

Won-Am Park
Korea Development Institute
P.O. Box 113, Chungryang
Seoul, Korea

Yung Chul Park
Department of Economics
Korea University
1, 5-Ga, Anam-Dong, Sungbuk-Gu
Seoul 136–701, Korea

Peter A. Petri
Department of Economics
Brandeis University
415 South Street
Waltham, MA 02254

Amelia Porges
Counsellor, Legal Affairs
GATT
Centre William Reppard
Rue de Lausanne 154
1202 Geneve 21
Switzerland

Gary R. Saxonhouse
Department of Economics
University of Michigan
Lorch Hall, Room 240
611 Tappan Street
Ann Arbor, MI 48109

Laura D'Andrea Tyson
Institute of International Studies
University of California
215 Moses Hall
Berkeley, CA 94720

Author Index

Subject Index

Advisory Committee for Trade Policy and Negotiations (ACTPN), 10
Agency for Industrial Science and Technology (AIST), 298
Agreements, interfirm, 108
Antitrust laws, Japan, 188
ASEAN (Association of South East Asian Nations): competition from, 96; economic development of, 112; exports of, 109–11

Balance of payments: East Asian NICs, 112; Japan, 53, 209–10
Banking system, Japan: decline of financing by, 218, 230–32, 258–60; financing practices of, 199–207, 209–11; historical, 194–95, 202, 221
Bank of Japan, 194, 197, 202, 209
Barriers to imports, Japan, 10, 12, 25, 30, 35, 39, 75
Bond market, Japan, 199, 201–2, 211–12, 215, 258, 260–61
Budget deficit, Japan, 247

Capital-intensive manufactures, Japan, 96–97, 100
Capital market, Japan: after-tax cost of, 239–43; components of cost of capital in, 227–32; costs of internal and external finance in, 257; rationing system and cost of capital in, 204–7, 218, 222, 225, 252–53, 268; weighted average cost of capital (WACC), 191, 216–17, 227–28.

See also Banking system, Japan; Relationships, Japanese business
Capital mobility, 251–52
Cartelization policy, 276
CD (certificate of deposit) market, Japan, 211–12
China, 112
Collusion, Japan. See Relationships, Japanese business
Commodity structure: East Asian NICs, 87, 90–92; Japanese trade, 62–78, 83–84
Comparative advantage: among Japan, EANICs, and ASEAN countries, 108–13; in Japanese distribution system, 185–86; in Japan's technology-intensive sectors, 77
Cost of capital. See Capital market, Japan
Council to Accommodate Commerce Activities (CRCA), 292–93
CP (commercial paper) market, Japan, 211–12, 260
CRCA. See Council to Accommodate Commerce Activities
Currency appreciation: effect of dollar, 137–39; effect of reality and expectation of yen, 253; effect of yen (*endaka*), 51–52, 57, 60–61, 77–78, 85–86, 280–81; effect on pricing behavior of yen, 133–36, 139. See also Exchange rate, real; Pass through; Pricing to market
Currency depreciation expectations, 252
Currency pass through. See Exchange rate, real; Exports; Pass through; Pricing to market

335